D1107673

THE FIRST CENTURY OF
AMERICAN LITERATURE

THE FIRST CENTURY
OF
AMERICAN LITERATURE

1770-1870

By

FRED LEWIS PATTEE

Author of "A History of American Literature since 1870,"
"The New American Literature," etc.

COOPER SQUARE PUBLISHERS, INC.
NEW YORK
1966

PREFACE

REJECTING from consideration John Neal's random sketches of American writers in *Blackwood's Magazine* of 1824, the first regular history of American letters was made by Samuel Lorenzo Knapp—his *Lectures on American Literature* (1829). Knapp was a Dartmouth man, class of 1804; Charles Francis Richardson, maker of the first systematic presentation of American literary history, was also a Dartmouth man, class of 1871. Beginning with *A Primer of American Literature* (1878), he finished his work with a two-volume *History of American Literature* (1886–1888).

Richardson was a pioneer scholar. Elected to the Winkley Chair of English at Dartmouth in 1883—a graceful way of saying that he was made the entire department of English in a college of four hundred students—one of his earliest acts was to add to the curriculum a three-hour course in American literature. The radical nature of this step it is hard today to realize. Hardly a college in the country had recognized the subject. Kate Sanborn, daughter of Richardson's eminent predecessor in the Winkley Chair, had in 1880 established at Smith College a lecture course in what she called "American Belle Lettres." Moses Coit Tyler in 1881 was offering at the University of Michigan that course disguised as American History, which afterwards was to be published as a literary history of the Colonial Period. A year later, in 1883, Professor J. C. Freeman of the University of Wisconsin was lecturing on the New England writers. Beyond these I can find in American colleges no courses, and among American publications no other works on the subject. Richardson's second volume I was fortunate enough to hear delivered in 1888 as a series of lectures. Then in 1896 came my own

v

first text-book history, and along with it Brander Matthews's little volume. Since that far day a veritable alcove of American literary history has been added to the college libraries of the land.

My own work in this field is finished with this volume. Projecting a series of three histories, I issued in 1915 *A History of American Literature since 1870;* in 1930 I added *The New American Literature.* To these, as a special study, belongs *The Development of the American Short Story* (1923). Not yet are these volumes gathered into a single edition. If ever they are so gathered, the general title will be *A Literary History of the American People,* the accent being upon the word "people."

My fundamental conception has been that American literature during its century and a half of existence has been an emanation from American life and American conditions. But I have begun in every case with the literary product rather than the historical background, my eye always upon the American *people.* As a result, I have been forced to study much material usually ignored by the literary historians. Much of my material, as for instance my chapter on the gift-books and annuals, has never been considered of enough importance to mention. I have watched for evolutions from peculiarly American conditions: the evolution of American humor, the American essay, the American newspaper, the American newspaper column, the American short story.

To all who have helped me in the work—librarians, colleagues, students in my classes—I render thanks. Especially would I thank Mr. James A. Anderson who has checked the manuscript from end to end for errors, verifying every date and most of the quotations. His help has been invaluable. The work on the manuscript of Mrs. Hannah Bonnet I cannot neglect to mention with commendation.

FRED LEWIS PATTEE

CONTENTS

vii

CONTENTS

PERIOD II

THE RISE OF ROMANTICISM

PERIOD III

THE MID-CENTURY RENAISSANCE

PERIOD I

THE CLOSING EIGHTEENTH CENTURY

THE LOSING FIGHT OF CLASSICISM

THE FIRST CENTURY OF AMERICAN LITERATURE

CHAPTER I

PRELIMINARY

I

THE HISTORY of North America from 1620 to the present, 1935, is a matter of 315 years. It splits into two halves, with the date 1776 near the center. On one side, a handful of straggling colonies; on the other, the United States Republic. In the century and a half before this famous year of independence a thin ribbon of settlements, a thousand miles long and perhaps a hundred miles wide, had been won with infinite toil from the primitive wilderness. As late as 1790, when was taken the first census of the newly organized Republic, the center of population was twenty-three miles east of Baltimore. Ten years later it was eighteen miles west of that city. Along this thin line there had arisen a half-dozen harbor towns that were in time to grow into dominating cities—Boston, New York, Philadelphia, Baltimore, Charleston, Savannah. On the near west, parallel with the entire shore-line and hemming in the settlements like the Great Wall of China, arose the formidable chain of the Appalachians—in the north the Alleghenies, in the center the Blue Ridge, in the south the Cumberlands and the Great Smokies, a chain unpenetrated by navigable east-and-west rivers and impervious to wagons save in a few ragged "gaps." Beyond was the vast continent of America, *terra incognita,* settled sparsely in the Southwest and in the Ohio River Valley, but claimed for the most part by France and Spain.

The effect of this mountain-chain upon early American history can hardly be exaggerated. As late as 1840 Emerson could remark that "Europe extends to the Alleghenies." The first settlements had been along the seacoast from Massachusetts to Georgia, and many of the colonial grants had had no limits fixed as to their westward extent, but this near-by wall had kept the English holdings narrow and at the same time had compelled them to be stretched out at such ridiculous length north and south that to Massachusetts on one end, Georgia on the other seemed as far away as England. "The difficulty of intercommunication, and the diversity of local interests, caused each State to regard the others as, in a great measure, foreign soil." [1]

Moreover, no two of the colonies were alike. They were not homogeneous in population: New York had been settled by the Dutch, Pennsylvania by Germans, Georgia by James Oglethorpe as a refuge for debtors. They clashed religiously: Puritans and come-outers in New England; Lutherans and German come-outers and Quakers in Pennsylvania; Romanists in Maryland and Delaware. Transportation between the sections was slow and uncertain, accomplished mostly in sailing vessels. When young Benjamin Franklin ran away from Boston, he was three days in reaching New York and a week more in reaching Philadelphia. To him the little Quaker city seemed like a foreign land. Its people were different, its manners, its money, even its bread. In short, the colonists during the whole Colonial period were a heterogeny, highly repellent particles, not a unit at all save as seen over three thousand

[1] Alexander Johnston, *History of American Politics* (1886).

miles of ocean by a muddling English king and a muddling
Parliament. That this rope of sand could be made to hold
together through a war of seven years was like expecting
the Indian tribes of the East and West to unite in a long-
sustained campaign against the invading whites. But for
a single element—a frontier individualism tested by a common danger—it would have been impossible.

One cannot dwell too long upon this element of colonial
provincialism; it affected even the literature of America
for generations. There was New England, for instance,
self-contained from the first, unshaken from its isolated
aloofness even by the establishment of the new government, not completely assimilated with the nation until
after the Civil War.

New England had not been colonized; it had been settled, it had been established deliberately as a *New* England,
created to eliminate the mistakes of the old land where the
people had been curbed in their independence. And they
had found a country that physically was in perfect harmony with Puritanism and independence. More like Scotland was it than like England—isolated on a corner of the
map, self-contained, mountainous, scanty of soil, scram-
bled in contour, the ruins of the great glacial period that
had swept over it like an avalanche. Geography individualistic, Puritanic. "The Almighty," said a witty Scotchman,
"practiced for a long time in making New England and
then made Scotland." The region of nonconformity, of
come-outers. Soon they could not abide even themselves;
from these come-outers came at length new swarms of
come-outers: Unitarians, Congregationalists, Christian
Scientists, Methodists, even Mormons, for Joseph Smith,
founder of the sect, was born at Sharon, Vermont. A history of American literature must look often at this isolated
northern province.

Four generations there had been in Colonial America
before the Revolution. One may illustrate with a single
family, the Mathers of Boston:

1. Richard 1596–1669
2. Increase 1639–1723
3. Cotton 1663–1728
4. Samuel 1706–1785

Ministers these Mathers were, and typical only of New England, but their dates are typical of the tenure of colonial families in America.

The first two generations had thought only of themselves; they were exiles in a vast wilderness, hewing out homes for themselves and their children amid hardships innumerable, unconscious of other colonies, unconscious largely that there was an overruling mother-country. They were of the First Colonial Period, which ended with the English revolution of 1688. Everywhere in the settlements this sixty-eight years of the first breaking of the wilderness had stamped its mark upon the settlers. Again, look at New England. Let Hawthorne be the interpreter:

[Life in the Puritan settlements] must have trudged onward with hardly anything to diversify and enliven it, while also its rigidity could not fail to cause miserable distortions of the moral nature. Such a life was sinister to the intellect and sinister to the heart; especially when one generation had bequeathed its religious gloom, and the counterfeit of its religious ardor, to the next. . . . The sons and grandchildren of the first settlers were a race of lower and narrower souls than their progenitors had been. The latter were stern, severe, intolerant, but not superstitious, not even fanatical; and endowed, if any men of that age were, with a far-seeing worldly sagacity. But it was impossible for the succeeding race to grow up, in heaven's freedom, beneath the discipline which their gloomy energy of character had established; nor, it may be, have we even yet thrown off all the unfavorable influences which, among many good ones, were bequeathed to us by our Puritan forefathers.[2]

During the eighty-eight years of what may be called the Second Colonial Period there had been forced upon the

[2] "Main Street," *The Snow Image and Other Tales.*

colonies more and more the idea of union. The revolution of 1688, which had placed William and Mary on the English throne, had been followed by a declaration of war against France, and this war, which was continued at intervals until the fall of Quebec at the end of the French and Indian War, was fought in part in the forests of the New World. For the colonists, war had followed war—Queen Anne's War, King George's War, and the final struggle with France. And from it all had been born the first idea of *Union*—union against France. In 1690 delegates from Massachusetts, Plymouth, Connecticut, and New York had met in New York to concert measures against the French, and this had been the beginning of many similar conventions. The tenacity of local ideas and aims, which had tended to keep the colonies apart, vanished before a common danger. Although the Union was at first only a frail affair, not involving all the colonies and having no reference to anything but temporary results, it was significant.

England had added greatly to her own strength by her wars with France and Spain, but she had unconsciously taught her colonies two great secrets—first, the strength of union, and second, the sturdy self-reliance which afterwards won for them their independence.

The eighty-eight years of the Second Colonial Period witnessed great changes in the life and spirit of the colonies. Old ideals were breaking down on every hand. The clergy began gradually to lose their supreme power in intellectual affairs. The laymen were turning their minds to their worldly surroundings and were fast losing the intense religious absorption of earlier days. Commerce was beginning to flourish; the cities of Boston, New York, and Philadelphia were growing into busy centers of trade; the shipping industry was increasing with vigor. The Colonial wars and the politics of the times, the struggles with charters and arbitrary governors, all had tended to turn the minds of the colonists from their souls to their bodies and their surroundings. Superstition was dying a natural death. In 1761 Dr. Boylston had successfully inoculated for small-pox in Boston, thus robbing this dread disease of much of its terror. The reaction against the witchcraft delusion, "that last spasm of expiring Puritanism," had done much to do away with religious fanaticism.

The newspaper, too, was an important agent in the intellectual emancipation of the colonies. The first attempt at journalism was made in 1690, when a little publication, more a pamphlet than a newspaper, was issued in Boston under the title *Public Occurrences both Foreign and Domestic*. This was intended to be issued monthly, but it was quickly suppressed by the General Court. The *Boston News-Letter* followed in 1704, and on December 21, 1719, came the *Boston Gazette,* printed, though not edited, by James Franklin, the brother of Benjamin Franklin. One day later came the first issue of the *American Weekly Mercury,* of Philadelphia. The *New England Courant,* famous for its connection with the early career of Benjamin Franklin, followed in 1721, a small sheet edited as well as printed by James Franklin. "I remember," says Benjamin in his *Autobiography*, "his being dissuaded by some of his friends from the undertaking, as not likely to succeed, one newspaper being, in their judgment, enough for America." Nevertheless, newspapers multiplied rapidly, until at the close of the period there were in all the colonies at least forty. There was even an attempt at magazine publication. In 1741 Franklin established in Philadelphia the *General Magazine and Historical Chronicle for All the British Provinces in America*. Although published only six months and containing little of literary value, it is of interest since it was the first attempt of the kind in America.

The population during all of the two Colonial periods had been everywhere prevailingly agrarian; on the whole this was a nation of farmers. Franklin, in 1766, before the English Parliament, testified that "the body of the people in the colonies" are "farmers, husbandmen, or planters." Their reading therefore was meager, confined to the almanac and, on Sundays, perhaps, to a few religious volumes.

The earliest generation had come to America, many of them, like Bradford and Winthrop and Nathaniel Ward and Richard Mather, in middle life. They were completely English; they had changed only their sky; they lived their lives out as exiles from home. Many of them like Captain John Smith and like Nathaniel Ward, who wrote the most readable prose work of the Colonial age in America, *The Simple Cobbler of Agawam* (1647), returned to England to spend their last years. *They* were Englishmen in America.

The fourth generation, after 1620, however, was far advanced in the evolution that soon was to render them a distinct people. They had been born in the land, and so had their fathers, many of them; three generations of them were *Americans*. Not at all did they think of themselves as exiles. They were becoming a new breed of men, born on the frontier and molded by frontier conditions. Even cities like Boston and New York still bristled with frontier conditions. Everywhere youth of sturdy stock, adventurous, pushing, daring, hard-working, independent. They were picked men and women, doubly picked. Only the virile, the courageous, the adventuresome had had the push to break from their age-old environment in Europe, to dare the perils of the Atlantic and the wilderness, and to work out for themselves homes and farms often against the very protest of Nature herself. And only the fit had survived. As a result, optimism, the forward look, restlessness, independence. On the frontier always freedom, democracy, self-reliance.

Thus along the whole thousand miles of Atlantic coast a generation impatient of control, schooled in come-outerism, outspoken, impetuous. Even in Massachusetts there was religious rebellion against the very fundamentals on which the colony had been founded. The solitudes of the frontier had taught freedom and self-determination. Autocracy is powerless on the frontier. A generation that could not be imposed upon. Franklin voiced it at the bar of the British House of Commons in 1766, the first real note of the new Americanism to penetrate the British consciousness. It was the uniting force that gathered them into armies and kept them for seven years a fighting force with victory as their reward. The American frontier taught Independence. There was no other uniting principle.

II

To look for literature from these frontier farmers on the long sprawl of the colonial coast-line is ridiculous. One may, by diligent research such as that done so thoroughly and definitively by Moses Coit Tyler a generation ago, gather a five-foot shelf of Colonial publications —reports to English proprietors like Captain John Smith's volume, exploited by literary historians as America's first real book; journals like Bradford's and Winthrop's, made with no literary intent; reprints in facsimile of such early hymnals as *The Bay Psalm Book,* a versification made in open defiance of all the Muses for the worship of God. And one may overleaf the four hundred and fifty polemic printings of Cotton Mather and the hundreds of barrels of bone-dry sermons poured out during two centuries of Sabbath days—one may read them all and find nothing worth saving. From time to time have been recovered and printed manuscripts which never have been published before, like the *Westover Manuscripts* of William Byrd of Virginia, first printed in 1841, in which appears "The History of the Dividing Line," a remarkable paper, the most important piece of prose written in the South before the Revolution. But most of the rescued writings have been without literary value. Many publications there have been of nonliterary journals, records of Indian captivity, some of them, like Mary Rowlandson's very popular, *The Sovereignty and Goodness of God* (1682), more than thirty editions of which were printed first and last.

Stories of Indian captivity were the best-sellers of their day. They are still valuable documents. Says W. B. Cairns, "The early accounts of captivity among the Indians are interesting for the pictures they give of pioneer hardships and the life of the savages; and they are important because in early New England they were almost the only form of writing that gratified the love for tales of adventure." [3] A popular journal of different variety was that of Sarah Kemble Knight (1666–1727), her travel experiences among the colonies, written with vivacity and humor.

Nonliterary and crude these materials for the most part, a primitive bouquet from a period almost wholly unliterary. Writings attempting literary distinction there possibly may have been, but they can hardly be accounted as American literature. Completely are they English productions. America was a group of English colonies, and whatever literature it produced was English literature. As Franklin testified before the House of Commons in 1766, "They consider themselves as a part of the British Empire and as having one common interest with it." Furthermore, the writings made in America during these one hundred and fifty English years had little influence in directing the literary current that was to grow more and more into a native stream in the years following the Revolution.

Therefore, defining literature in terms of beauty, and including in the definition nothing save "mere literature," before 1776 America produced nothing at all. Fiction along the whole thousand-mile line was under a ban: it was not till 1789 that the first novel appeared, a book quickly suppressed by the authorities. The drama, too, had been severely handled. As late as 1774 the Continental

---

[3] *Selections from Early American Writers* (1917), p. 190.

Congress had classed it with gambling and horse-racing and cock-fighting. Poetry was either rhymed dialectics like Anne Bradstreet's laborings or else jingling polemics like *The Day of Doom* of Michael Wigglesworth (1631–1705), a poem as grotesque in its theology and its metrics as its author's name. From the entire Puritan era, four generations, came not a single writing that is read today save by specializing students "under the birch."

A literature must have behind it an independent nation, a people with hope and vision and enthusiasm. And after 1776 such a nation began in the forests of the New World. A new voice there was among the nations, faint at first, yet from the first filled with a new spirit, a new hope. The study of *American* literature begins here. To grub among the printed rubbish of the settlement era may expose roots and influences, but it produced no writings for the anthology that contains only our own. Beginning with the vital year 1776 there was to grow that something new and strange which the world has been forced to recognize and admire.

CHAPTER II

THE REVOLUTION

I

THE STORY of the Revolution need not be told: every American is familiar with that desperate struggle. It was our Heroic Age. Compelled by force of circumstance, the colonists now turned to war and politics. The magnificent training, the self-control, the hardy endurance, and the self-reliance which a century and a half of frontier life, of struggle with the wilderness and savage men and beasts, had developed, stood them in good stead now. All of their energy and fortitude and will they threw into the contest with the army and navy of England, but it was a task to discourage even the stoutest heart.

Out of the furnace came the gold of our national character. It made our government and our literature possible. When the struggle was over, upon the ruins of the war arose the new nation, "conceived in Liberty, and dedicated" to a new ideal in the history of nations.

The American Republic was pitched from the first to the note of Liberty. Reverend Jno. Mayhew in the days of the Stamp Act agitation had preached to his congregation from I Cor. 3 : 17: "Where the Spirit of the Lord is, there is liberty"—according to Dr. C. A. Bartol, "the first peal on the trumpet of freedom in this western land, blown clear and loud enough to be heard over land and water far and wide." [1] Whatever economic basis the war may have

[1] M. C. Tyler, *The Literary History of the American Revolution* (1897), I, 122.

had, it is indisputable that the young men who were its
life-blood went into its armies with the crusader spirit and
fought for Liberty. An outpouring there was of fiery
oratory, all of it winged with deepest conviction, all of it
free from the slavery of studied models, all of it American in subject and theme and manner; but most of it
perished with its occasion. There was an eager outpouring
of propagandic pamphlets, of newspaper satires and argumentative essays, but for the most part it was mere
journalism. Fiery satires there were in abundance, and a
handful of ballads and elegies and patriotic songs, but
little that has survived to our own day. Wartimes never
increase a nation's literary wealth save as they create
materials to be used by poets and novelists in the leisure of
kindlier times when the battle-smoke has faded into romantic haze.

A few volumes have survived, however, to be classified
as literature. Some of the pieces in the three volumes of
Francis Hopkinson, America's first man of letters in
point of time, still are readable; Thomas Paine, the leading
propagandist of the storm-time, has lived most surprisingly into our own day; Franklin has become a world-
figure, destined, it would seem now, to go down the centuries as one of America's greatest men—not, however,
as a writer; Dickinson's one volume is still mentioned,
and the years have been kind to Trumbull and Freneau.
First of all there was Franklin.

II

Benjamin Franklin, more than any other American,
stands as a microcosm of the eighteenth century. His life
covered it almost exactly (1706–1790), was synonymous
with its ideals, its spirit, its values. Moreover, he stands
in Colonial and Revolutionary America as its typical
figure: its tendency toward prose, its interest in manners,
its practicality, its rationalism. Nothing romantic in

Franklin. His feet always were on the solid earth; he lived in this present world. The Puritan in early America was a pilgrim and a stranger, an exile. He sought a better country, but Franklin took the world as he found it, exulted in it, prospered in it, gave rules for living in it. One feels that he should have gone on living in it forever. His passing was illogical.

To treat Franklin as a literary man is like classifying Edison as a letter-writer. One may gather his "works" into a set, but the fact remains that only incidentally was Franklin an author, and seldom even then with anything like creative originality. So far as he wrote at all, he was a journalist: all his life he was connected with newspapers and publishing. His almanacs were journalistic productions. His "Richard Saunders—Philomath" introductions, his amusing arguments concerning the death of his rival almanac-maker, even his proverbs strung down through the weather predictions of his almanac were, as in later years he himself freely confessed, nothing original. From year to year he gave the people what the people wanted, what the people could understand and enjoy. "Father Abraham's Speech," which embodies all the proverbs in all the almanacs until 1757, is a mirror held up not so much to reflect Franklin as to reflect Franklin's century in America. He spoke in eighteenth-century American terms. When he wrote then, literature was to him a dressed-up matter even as it was to his contemporary, Dr. Johnson of London—nothing necessarily original, "nature to advantage dressed," worldliness in Sunday clothes. Franklin's proverbs are the wisdom of the ages retranslated, put into American terms by an eighteenth-century journalist. He had wit but not humor; he had style but not originality. S. L. Knapp, however, in his *Lectures on American Literature* (1829), found real poetry in the man:

Dr. Franklin would have no small claim to the reputation of a poet, had not his fame as a philosopher, politician, and prose

writer, thrown, as it were, into the shade, his occasional offering to the muses. If there is no rhaspody in his inspirations,
there is a sweet and beautiful flow of good sense and delicacy
of feeling. His love of Addison is discovered in his poetry as
in his prose.

Only once did Franklin forget his eighteenth-century
models and touch the spring of the spontaneous, laying
bare his soul. It was a happening purely accidental, unpremeditated, unliterary as he conceived of literature: his
Autobiography was created with no thought of a reading
public. Written primarily for his grandchildren, it was
poured out hastily in moments snatched from important
business. It is Franklin himself undressed for company,
at times all but naked. As a result, the book is a *man:* it
lives and breathes; it is a classic to be rated with the greatest of the world's autobiographies. And it lives simply
because for once Franklin forgot his art. What his grandson, William Temple Franklin, did for the artless thing in
1817, Franklin himself doubtless would have done had he
been called upon to put it into shape for publication. A passage in the first instalment is illuminating: "By my rambling digressions," he complained, "I perceive myself to
be grown old. I used to write more methodically. But one
does not dress for private company as for a private ball."
There is no better illustration of the nature of eighteenth-
century literary art than a comparison of Franklin's version with that of his grandson.[2] For good measure as to
the man's eighteenth-century style one might add Franklin's suggested revision of the King James Version of the
Bible.

More and more is it realized now that as a literary
figure in our national life Franklin must depend almost
wholly upon this single volume of which his own generation knew nothing. It was his *"carte de visite,"* as Walt

[2] See John Bigelow's edition of the *Autobiography,* 1868, and his
later editions in 1875, 1905, and 1910.

Whitman would have expressed it, to the generations of Americans to come. By sheer accident it had not been garbed by its author in eighteenth-century dress, but had been presented off-hand in the simplicity that is ageless. It is, therefore, Volume One in the book-list of the new America. Its naturalness, its evident genuineness, its atmosphere of nothing withheld, nothing glossed over, its lapses into colloquial diction, as, for instance, "Keimer star'd like a pig poison'd"—changed by its reviser, William Temple Franklin, to "Keimer appeared thunderstruck"—all mark it as a pioneer book. The peculiarly late date of its first publication, too, throws it into the new century.

Judged solely by the adventures attending its publication, it belongs to the curiosities of American literature. The first edition, a French translation issued in Paris in 1791, comprised only the first instalment. The second and the third editions, translations of this French translation, were issued in London in 1793. From one of these, it would seem, the Reverend Weems secured the text—grossly cut and garbled and added to—of his edition of 1815, perhaps the first edition of the *Autobiography* to be published in America. The fourth edition, with the addition of a part of the second instalment, was issued in France in 1798. In 1817 came the William Temple Franklin revised edition of the first three instalments. The fourth instalment appeared for the first time in a Paris edition in 1828. It was not until 1868, almost a century after he wrote the first instalment, that Franklin's *Autobiography* was given to the world entire as Franklin wrote it.

"Half peasant, half man of the world," ruled Woodrow Wilson. He might have remained wholly peasant, rules his latest biographer, Phillips Russell, but for his early reading in the current eighteenth-century writings. From this reading came his creation of the Philadelphia Public Library in

1731—"an attempt," says Russell, "to remove the peasant mind from himself and the American people." That he succeeded in this endeavor Franklin himself had no doubt:

Reading became fashionable; and our people having no public amusement to divert their attention from study, became better acquainted with books, and in a few years were observed by strangers to be better instructed and more intelligent than people of the same rank generally are in other countries.

III

The embodiment of Old Philadelphia, where for more than a century had been cultivated the graces and the Chesterfieldian arts more completely than elsewhere in the colonies, was not Benjamin Franklin, but Francis Hopkinson (1737–1791). One of the most versatile men was he in the America of his generation: a cultured gentleman of the old school, a poet, a statesman, a prose-writer with a light pen, a barrister of wealth and influence. Wise enough and courageous enough to avoid the fate of his Royalist friends and neighbors during the Revolution, he had sided with the patriots and, once at least, had done damage to the enemy—not with his sword, however, but with his pen.

His complete works in three volumes, issued the year after his death, reveal him as a literary man of distinction; in the department of "mere literature" more distinctive even than Franklin. Undoubtedly he was the first literary artist produced by America.

His writings fall into three classifications, first, literary propaganda, issued during the Revolution, like his rollicking ballad, "The Battle of the Kegs," so much quoted by the war generation in America, and his prose satires upon the times, like "A Pretty Story" and "The New Roof." His works also reveal humor apart from satire and propaganda. His essay describing the spring-cleaning mania peculiar to colonial—and noncolonial—"females"

at certain seasons of the year alone would rank its author
as a pioneer among the American humorists. It is autochthonic, done with attention upon American actuality
rather than upon earlier writings, and using the native
device of exaggeration in quite the modern manner.

But it is as a lyrist that Hopkinson did his most enduring work. He was a musician, the first native com-
poser indeed, a maker of songs with the accompanying
music. Such a burst of pure lyricism, as, for instance, his
"Song II" (1788), reminiscent undoubtedly of Matthew
Prior, was something new in American poetry, a lyric that
must be included in every American anthology.

1

My gen'rous heart disdains
  The slave of love to be,
I scorn his servile chains,
  And boast my liberty.
    This whining
    And pining
  And wasting with care,
  Are not to my taste, be she ever so fair.

2

  Shall a girl's capricious frown
Sink my noble spirits down?
Shall a face of white and red
Make me droop my silly head?
Shall I set me down and sigh
For an eye-brow or an eye?
For a braided lock of hair,
Curse my fortune and despair?
My gen'rous heart disdains, &c.

Still uncertain is tomorrow,
Not quite certain is today—
Shall I waste my time in sorrow?
Shall I languish life away?

All because a cruel maid,
Hath not Love with Love repaid.
My gen'rous heart disdains, &c.

IV

No stranger evolution from war than that which turned
the luckless adventurer, Thomas Paine (1737–1808), into
a world-figure of major proportions, one still affecting
areas of political and religious thinking even today. He
was from the English commonalty, bred as a stay-maker,
his parents humble Quakers who sought to instil into him
Quaker principles. But restlessness ruled him even from
his boyhood. Again and again he ran away to sea, shipping as a pirate, the first time at the age of sixteen or
seventeen. Returning to England, he failed in business, he
failed in his venture into married life, he was discharged
from a position he had gained in the revenue service. At
the age of thirty-seven, down and out apparently, he came
in contact with Benjamin Franklin. "As I always had a
taste for science," he wrote in later years, "I naturally
had friends of that caste in England, and among the rest
George Lewis Scott, Esq., through whose formal introduction my first acquaintance with Dr. Franklin commenced."
Impressed with the man, Franklin advised him to emigrate
to America, the land of the second chance, and despite
the fact that Paine exemplified the reverse of every one of
the old philomath's proverbs of thrift, he gave him letters
to friends in Philadelphia, one of them to his son-in-law
Richard Bache.

That Paine should have found employment at once in
Philadelphia as a journalist with a distinctive style and
remarkable fluency seems at first an impossibility. "One
cannot but wonder," writes his biographer, Moncure D.
Conway, "how Paine acquired his literary equipment, almost as complete in his first work as in his last." A natural
gift it must have been, for he had had little schooling. As
early as 1772, two years before his arrival in America, he

had written "an appeal for the excisemen" and had gained through it a "local reputation for writing—and especially for strong, sound reasoning."

But America seems to have been the making of the man. He was given, instead of the academy he wished to open, the editorship of the *Pennsylvania Magazine,* and, despite his meager education and his inexperience, he was widely read. Confidence in his own powers sat upon him as on a divinity, and with it an unlimited English facility in "muddling through" and a courage often amounting to rashness. He had arrived in America (1774) at a peculiarly critical moment. In his own words:

I happened to come to America a few months before the breaking out of hostilities. I found the disposition of the people such, that they might have been led by a thread and governed by a reed. Their suspicion was quick and penetrating, but their attachment to Britain was obstinate, and it was at that time a kind of treason to speak against it, They disliked the ministry, but they esteemed the nation. Their idea of grievance operated without resentment, and their single object was reconciliation. Bad as I believed the ministry to be, I never conceived them capable of a measure so rash and wicked as the commencing of hostilities; much less did I imagine the nation would encourage it. I viewed the dispute as a kind of law-suit, in which I supposed the parties would find a way either to decide or settle it. I had no thoughts of independence or of arms. The world could not then have persuaded me that I should be either a soldier or an author. . . . I had formed my plan of life, and conceiving myself happy wished every body else so. But when the country, into which I had just set my foot, was set on fire about my ears, it was time to stir. It was time for every man to stir.[3]

His first firebrand he hurled in March, 1775, his *African Slavery in America;* then in 1776 came his second bombshell, his pamphlet *Common Sense,* a document that advocated extreme measures—total separation from Eng-

[3] *The Crisis,* VII (Nov. 21, 1778).

land! No mere petty list of small grievances in this stirring document; it was the call to a crusade universal for Liberty. In later years it was to be republished, translated into French, as propaganda for the cause of "Liberty, Equality, Fraternity." "The cause of America," he declared in his preface to *Common Sense,* "is in a great measure the cause of all mankind. Many circumstances have, and will arise, which are not local, but universal, and through which the principles of all lovers of mankind are affected."

Tremendously was it successful. "I believe," wrote Paine to Henry Lawrence in 1779, "the number of copies printed and sold in America was not short of 150,000— and is the greatest sale any performance ever had since the use of letters—exclusive of the great run it had in England and Ireland." Its effect upon the wavering people of the colonies was electrical. It was issued in January, 1776: six months later came the Declaration of Independence, hastened undoubtedly by Paine's arguments.

War declared, Paine hastened to join the Colonial army, where he became aide-de-camp to General Greene. After the disastrous fall campaign of 1776 he sought to hearten the American patriots with another militant pamphlet, *The Crisis,* with an opening sentence that has become proverbial: "These are the times that try men's souls." Again Paine had said peculiarly the right thing at peculiarly the right moment. Washington ordered the pamphlet read before the American regiments, and compliments and honors came fast to Paine. Emboldened by success, he made of the pamphlet a periodical to be published when needful. Thirteen regular numbers and two supernumerary numbers and a *Crisis Extraordinary* appeared during the war, Number XIII opening with the sentence: "The times that tried men's souls are over and the greatest and completest revolution the world ever knew, gloriously and happily accomplished."

Paine's work for America was done. Stormy petrel that he was, he remained not at all for the slow work of reconstruction. He was off to Europe where was gathering another world-shaking revolution. Again was he to be in the ranks of the propagandists. Burke's criticism, *Reflexions on the French Revolution* (1790), he countered with his impetuous *The Rights of Man,* a work that gave him at once French citizenship (1792) and a seat in the National Assembly. His later adventures we shall not follow. Only one other of his works needs to be mentioned— *The Age of Reason.* On his way to prison Paine handed the manuscript of the first part of this volume to Joel Barlow. Half-starved and ill, Paine was removed from the prison to the house of James Monroe. "It was while thus a prisoner in his room, with death still hovering over him, that Paine wrote Part Second of *The Age of Reason.*"

Again a document universal, again a first trumpet-call for a crusade for what he considered Liberty, Equality, Fraternity. The revolution in America and in France, he believed, was to be followed by a greater revolution that was to clear the world of superstition and fanaticism. He had seen the vilest deeds of the reign of terror done in the name of religion, but worse than that, he has seen the revolution that was to bring to men the Golden Age turned into a school for utter atheism, and atheism was to him as repulsive as it would have been to his Quaker parents. In a letter to Samuel Adams, he wrote: "The people of France were running headlong into Atheism, and I had the work [*The Age of Reason*] translated and published in their own language to stop them in that carreer, and fix them to the first article (as I have before said) of every man's Creed who had any Creed at all, *I believe in God.*"

The book proved to be his ruin. America, fundamentally religious, received his extreme onslaught upon revealed religion as blasphemy, and erased him, so far as it was able, from its records, using him as its strongest synonym for *infidel* and *atheist*.

Upon these four works, *Common Sense, The Crisis, The Rights of Man,* and *The Age of Reason,* Paine's literary fame must rest. Strictly speaking, he was not a literary man at all. He was a propagandist in wartime, a hurler of militant pamphlets before the opening of the newspaper age, a journalist who thought only in superlatives and who knew nothing of prudence. Always was he at the level of the common people, with a plan for Utopia founded always on the corner-stones of democracy, brotherhood, justice, equality—principles gathered principally from the New Testament which he knew by heart. He was a phrase-maker, a soap-boxer with a panacea, a man who knew the common people from whom he sprung and could speak with ease their language. He wrote as he thought, pell-mell, often in defiance of grammar, of logic, of elegance, but always so as to be instantly understood. He came at the one time in all history when he could have been a moving force, and the unprecedented success of the revolutions of which he was a part makes of him more of a prophet and philosopher than he really was. More and more his works must be relegated to the reference shelves rather than to the alcove for mere readers.

v

The times that tried men's souls tried most sorely the souls of the Tories. Read Crèvecœur's newly discovered *Sketches of Eighteenth Century America,* first issued in 1925. And the Tories in many respects were the best element in the colonies, men of wealth and refinement and social standing, many of them educated in England, all of them belonging to what may be called the aristocracy in distinction from the commonalty, and from the "embattled farmers" in the soldier-ranks. They were tarred and

feathered like M'Fingal, they were driven into exile, many
of them never to return. They were able with their pens;
they had publishing houses and newspapers, notably those
of Hugh Gaine and of James Rivington in New York; and
they had writers of pamphlets and newspaper propaganda
like Hugh Gaine, James Rivington, and Samuel Sea-
bring, and satiric poets like Joseph Stansbury and Jonathan Odell. Most bitter was Odell. Note his treatment of
Washington:

> Hear thy indictment, Washington, at large;
> Attend and listen to the solemn charge:
> Thou hast supported an atrocious cause
> Against thy King, thy Country, and the laws;
> Committed perjury, encourag'd lies,
> Forced conscience, broken the most sacred ties;
> Myriads of wives and fathers at thy hand
> Their slaughter'd husbands, slaughter'd sons demand;
> That pastures hear no more the lowing kine,—
> That towns are desolate, all—all is thine;
> The frequent sacrilege that pain'd my sight:
> The blasphemies my pen abhors to write;
> Innumerable crimes on thee must fall—
> For thou maintainest, thou defendest all.[4]

And so on to the end of the poem.

Some hesitated long in pitiful indecision. To side with
either of the forces seemed to be ruin. There was John
Dickinson, one of the most brilliant men in the colonies,
a lawyer trained for three years in the Middle Temple,
England, an aristocrat with a notable estate near Philadelphia, a member of all the important congresses during a
stormy decade and the writer of many state papers and
legal documents connected with the period, President of
the Supreme Executive Council of Pennsylvania and later
Governor of the State. During the Stamp Act discussions,
according to Franklin, he was the only American whose

[4] Frederick C. Prescott and John H. Nelson, *Prose and Poetry of
the Revolution*, p. 111.

"words were listened to on both sides of the Atlantic." Though called by Moses Coit Tyler "the penman of the Revolution," his literary fame depends wholly upon a series of twelve letters which in 1767–1768 he published in the *Pennsylvania Chronicle*. Issued as a volume with the title *Letters from a Farmer in Pennsylvania to the Inhabitants of the British Colonies,* they were widely read. The title was attractive to agrarian America. Franklin advertised the book by having an edition published in London. Everywhere the newspapers reprinted the letters, and unquestionably they had a strong influence in molding the sentiment of the times.

But as inflaming products in the mad era before a war, they seem pitifully inadequate. They are without fire, without quotable brands for hurling, without the atmosphere of deep conviction. War propaganda is never dependent on cold reasoning. There was Paine, letter-perfect as an agitator, emotional, superlative, intimately acquainted with the *sans culottes* masses who were to be affected, a man who viewed precedents with contempt and who, whatever his real feelings in the matter, was able to convey the impression of earnestness and honesty. But Dickinson was a lawyer, obedient only to legal precedent. Right or wrong, the law must stand. And he found the English position concerning taxation legally unsound. His twelve letters attempt to explain with legal calmness to the generality untrained in the law the weakness of the English position. Far was it from him, however, to suggest revolution as the remedy. To him it was a law case to be settled in the courts. He was for limited monarchy, for America given her rights under the Crown. And he stood by his convictions. His was the only vote cast against the Declaration of Independence. But war once declared, he seems to have gone with the patriot majority.

What has undoubtedly preserved the letters and caused critics like Tyler to declare them the most important writings of the Revolutionary period is their literary style.

The author throws about them a rural atmosphere, tells of the joys of country life, and, having created his medium, proceeds to try his case legally with the farmers as jury:

I will now tell the gentlemen what is "the meaning of these letters." The meaning of them is, to convince the people of these colonies, that they are at this moment exposed to the most imminent dangers; and to persuade them immediately, vigorously, and unanimously, to exert themselves, in the most firm, but the most peaceable manner, for obtaining relief.

That the rural atmosphere was a literary fiction, the subtle device of a skilful lawyer, and that the arguments of all of them were for returning to the old *status quo* without recourse to force, seem not to have impressed its earliest readers. It is a document for lawyers, not for the masses at a time of crisis. Only as a legal expert, a man skilful in the composition of state papers, is Dickinson to be called "the penman of the Revolution." More accurately may he be called the engrossing clerk of the era.

CHAPTER III

PHILIP FRENEAU

I

THE FIRST real poet produced by the thirteen colonies was born in the midlands—in New York City—unpuritanic totally, uncavalier. Only one generation from France, he was totally un-English, totally Gallic in temperament and training. His father, an émigré from France, an importer of wines, was a man of moderate wealth, of refinement, of culture which expressed itself in a library unusually large for the time. The young poet was brought up with books, was fitted for college by the best tutors to be obtained, and, entering Princeton at fifteen, he was found to be so well prepared that the president of the college sent the parents a letter of congratulation.

Latin it was that seems first to have laid hold of the young student's imagination. Toiling over his Seneca, he found a passage that awakened his creative soul. Thus he translated it:

> The time shall come, when numerous years are past,
> The ocean shall dissolve the bands of things,
> And an extended region rise at last;
>
> And Typhis shall disclose the mighty land
> Far, far away, where none have rov'd before;
> Nor shall the world's remotest region be
> Gibraltar's rock, or Thule's savage shore.

"Fired at the theme," he had planned a New World epic of the *Columbiad* type eight years before Barlow had

begun his *Vision of Columbus.* It resulted only in fragments to strew his published volumes later, but it is tremendously noteworthy that America had an undergraduate poet in 1770 dreaming of epics made of such
native themes.

Graduated in 1771, he had his chance. He was chosen
with H. H. Brackenridge to be class poet, and the Columbus dream awoke: he would write on the "Rising Glory of
America." Never commencement exercise based on broader
foundations. The young graduates bewail at every step
their limitations of space. The plan they suggest is the
plan of a *Columbiad.* They would begin with *all* the tale
of Columbus; they would rehearse the story of Cortez
and Pizarro; they would discuss at learned length the
origin and the characteristics of the Indians; they would
tell the story of the early colonies and would trace the
course of settlement and review the progress and the
promise of agriculture and commerce; they would peer
into the future and mark the time

> When we shall spread
> Dominion from the North and South and West,
> Far from the Atlantic to Pacific shores
> And shackle half the convex of the main.

But, alas, the time! An epic cannot be condensed into a
commencement poem. Suddenly Freneau (and we must
not read the poem from later reprints where the author
frankly admits that he added new lines for "a supposed
prophetical anticipation of subsequent events") bursts into
true prophetic rapture. Remember, this was in 1771 when
the wild Western frontier was almost within sound of
the Atlantic:

> I see, I see,
> A thousand kingdoms rais'd; cities and men
> Num'rous as sand upon the ocean shore.
> The Ohio then shall glide by many a town
> Of note; and where the Mississippi stream,

By forests shaded, now runs weeping on,
Nations shall grow, and states not less in fame
Than Greece and Rome of old. We too shall boast
Our Alexanders, Pompeys, Heroes, Kings,
That in the womb of time yet dormant lye
Waiting the joyful hour for life and light,—
O snatch me hence, ye muses, to those days
When, through the vail of dark antiquity,
Our sons shall hear of us as things remote,
That blossom'd in the morn of days.

It is not a great poem if we measure it by absolute
standards—too rhetorical it is for modern readers—but
it is a very great poem if we view it in connection with
the conditions that produced it. Full as it is of Latin influence and commencement-day zeal, it is the first real
poem that America ever made, the first American poem
that was impelled hot from a man's soul. It is more than
this : it is the first fruit of a new influence in the world of
letters—the first literary product of that force which had
set in motion the American and the French Revolutions.
The vision overcame the young poet :

Alas !
How could I weep that we were born so soon
Just at the dawning of these mighty times
Whose scenes are painting for eternity.

II

Teaching for a time followed college in the usual way.
And with all his soul he hated it. He was a poet, but fate
had cast him among a people utterly barren of poetic ideas.
"Barbers cannot possibly exist as such," he complained,
"among a people who have neither hair nor beards. How
then can a poet hope for success in a city where there are
not three persons possessed of elegant ideas?"
He even dreamed of escaping the democratic mob in a
flight to Europe :

Long have I sate on this disastrous shore
And, sighing sought to gain a passage o'er
To Europe's courts, where, as our travellers say,
Poets may flourish, or—perhaps—they may.

Then suddenly broke about the young dreamer's ears
the storm of the Revolution. His Huguenot blood was
quickly fired. Hatred of the British had come with his
French soul, and quickly the insolence of the invading
troops kindled him to rage. During the autumn of 1775
satire after satire, published in pamphlet form, came from
his pen. The democratic mass could read the stuff. This
was poetry. And Freneau ground it out in quantities. In
August and September he wrote no less than six long
poems, four or five of which were issued as separate
works. War propaganda; to none of them did he sign
his name.

III

But the period of this first outburst was short. Late in
1775 he secured a position as secretary to a sugar-planter
in the West Indies. A final shot at his critics, "Mac-
Swiggen; a Satire," and he was off to a new world. There
is a touch of pathos in the lines:

I to the sea with weary steps descend,
Quit the mean conquest that such swine might yield,
And leave MacSwiggen to enjoy the field.

In distant isles some happier scene I'll choose,
And court in softer shades the unwilling Muse.

The change was a salutary one. Amid the novel scenery
and dreamy beauty of the tropics, the young poet forgot
his rage, forgot the narrow carping of his critics and the
world that had had so little use for the higher ranges of
poetry. The change awakened anew his slumbering genius.
During the next year or two in the seclusion of an old

sugar plantation on the island of Santa Cruz he did his most significant work—"The Beauties of Santa Cruz," "The House of Night," and the "The Jamaica Funeral" (1776), poems uneven always, crude very often, quotable perhaps only in a few stanzas, yet poems unquestionably that cannot be overlooked, poems with original notes, wild "sports" from the old trunk of standard poetry.

In "The Beauties of Santa Cruz" he pours out his first rapture over the tropic isles: the teeming vegetation, the plant forms so novel to a Northerner—the mangrove, the palmetto, the tamarind—the luscious fruits and brilliant flowers, the sudden and fierce hurricanes, the sensuous beauty of the Southern night, when

> The drowsy pelican wings home his way,
> The misty eve sits heavy on the sea.

All this thrilled and stirred the soul of the young poet. "Surely," he cried, "such were the isles that happy Flaccus sung." And again:

> O grant me, gods, if yet condemned to stray,
> At least to spend life's sober evening here.

The summer isles "betwixt old Cancer and the midway line" have never had a more inspired laureate. From the poem there breathes the soul of those tropic seas, a century later to be painted in azure and vermilion by Lafcadio Hearn. At times a lilting music most charming, as this from his description of the West Indian hurricanes:

> O'er the wild main, dejected and afraid,
> The trembling pilot lashed his helm a-lee,
> And swiftly scudding, asked thy potent aid,
> Dear Pilot of the Galilean sea.

Freneau now entered the region of pure invention. With his "House of Night" he became one of the pioneers in

that dimly lighted region which was soon to be exploited
by Coleridge and Poe. The poem is the first distinctly
romantic note heard in America. Moreover, one may
search in vain in the English poetry of the early Romantic
Movement for anything that can equal it in strength of
conception and in sustained mastery over the vaguely
terrible. It is a "vision of the midnight hour," in which
the poet is led to a mysterious "dome" where he becomes,
despite himself, a witness of the death of the grim monster
Death himself. The atmosphere of the poem is vague and
awful. Note the following random stanzas numbered as in
my edition of Freneau's poems, Volume I, pages 212–239.
The entire poem has 136 stanzas.

3

Let others draw from smiling skies their theme,
And tell of climes that boast unfading light,
I draw a darker scene, replete with gloom,
I sing the horrors of the *House of Night*.

50

Much spoke he of the myrtle and the yew,
Of ghosts that nightly walk the church-yard o'er,
Of storms that through the wint'ry ocean blow
And dash the well-mann'd galley on the shore,

109

O'er a dark field I held my dubious way
Where Jack-a-lanthorn walk'd his lonely round,
Beneath my feet substantial darkness lay,
And screams were heard from the distemper'd ground.

110

Dark was the night, but at the inchanted dome
I saw the infernal windows flaming red.

118

Trembling, across the plain my course I held,
And found the grave-yard, loitering through the gloom,
And, in the midst, a hell-red, wandering light,
Walking in fiery circles round the tomb.

127

Each horrid face a grizly mask conceal'd,
Their busy eyes shot terror to my soul.

At least this shows what might have been had the poet
lived in a literary atmosphere with adequate literary companions and competent criticism.

In "The Jamaica Funeral" he outlines his early philosophy of life. He is growing in poetic power and is fast
breaking from the influence of his early master, Thomas
Gray. It is Gallic philosophy that he outlines, one tinctured
with rebellion and the germs of Deism. He is a bacchanalian without apology. Is there not the atmosphere of
the *Rubaiyat* in a stanza like this?

Count all the trees that crown Jamaica's hills,
Count all the stars that through the heavens you see,
Count every drop that the wide ocean fills;
Then count the pleasures Bacchus yields to me.[1]

IV

Captured by the British on his way home from the
tropics, thrown into a prison-ship in New York Harbor
where for two months he suffered the brutalities common
in every war, discharged at last more dead than alive, he
was now a man of Berserker rages. His poem descriptive
of his captivity came hot from his soul. In a sort of fury
he bade farewell to the Muse of his choice and turned to

[1] An imitation it may have been of a poem attributed to Anakreon in
which he declares his numberless amours: "Εἰ φύλλα πάντα ξεύξρων,"
etc.

the bitter Muse of satire, who alone could "suit the taste."
During the next three years he wrote the greater number
of those propagandic satires and songs which have earned
for him the title of "Poet of the Revolution." Every movement of "the insolent foe" called out a scathing criticism;
every heroic deed of the struggling patriots called out a
lyric. His poems of this period are in themselves a history
of the last years of the war. His heart was in his work;
the prison-ship had blotted for a time all memories of the
old fight with his critics, his dreams of poetry on the
tropic isles, everything save the one thought of his "injured country's woe." He lampooned Cornwallis, Clinton,
Tarleton, and the Royalist printers, Rivington and Gaine.
He made tender lyrics for the patriot dead at Eutaw
Springs:

> They saw their injur'd country's woe;
> The flaming town, the wasted field;
> Then rush'd to meet the insulting foe;
> They took the spear—but left the shield.

He celebrated the naval victories of Barney and of Jones,
and he called down maledictions on the ship that bore the
"worthless Arnold" from American shores in a lyric
which, though modeled on Horace, lacks nothing in originality, certainly nothing in timeliness and stinging force.

These are more than the fleeting voices of a newspaper
Muse. Scott declared "Eutaw Springs" to be "as fine a
thing as there is of the kind in the language." The lyric
"On the Memorable Victory, Obtained by . . . John Paul
Jones . . . ," written when America was full of the first
news of the battle, is one of the glories of American
literature. It moves with leaps and bounds; it is full of the
very spirit of battle:

> They felt the fury of her ball:
> Down, prostrate, down the Britons fall;
> The decks were strew'd with slain;

> Jones to the foe his vessel lash'd,
> And, while the black artillery flash'd,
> Loud thunders shook the main.

It is not impertinent to observe that the British poet Thomas Campbell (1777–1844) was but four years of age when this ballad was written.

With half a dozen others as strong, Freneau was our earliest and in many respects our most virile balladist when dealing with the theme of naval battles. About all the lyrics the odors and atmospheres of the ocean. And in them an excitement contagious. Campbell in later years read this elder poet of the ocean, for one entire line of his he appropriated without acknowledgement.

Crude as stanzas of Freneau's may be when weighed in the romantic balances of the next poetic generation, they nevertheless have life in them, actuality, fire. For instance, when reading such a ballad as "On the Death of Captain Nicholas Biddle," the gallant American fighter who from the deck of the *Randolph* poured death into the British ship *Yarmouth*—

> Tremendous flash!—and hark, the ball
> Drives through old Yarmouth, flames and all,

and who at the moment of victory was blown up by his own magazine, one has for the moment the feeling of having been actually present at the tragedy. Vivid and contagious, too, such lyrics as "On the New American Frigate Alliance" with such lines as "She walks the ocean like its queen," and "She stays to guard her native shore"; or the "Song on Barney's Victory over the Ship General Monk," that rollicking sailor rouse after victory; or, best of all, perhaps, "The Invitation," which is full of the very salt and tang of the ocean. It was not Scott or Cooper who added the domain nautical to literature: it was Freneau.

V

The Revolution over, the poet, after following with invective the departing foe and after showering with ridicule and scorn Rivington and Gaine and the discomfited Royalists, found his occupation gone. The impetuous tide of his hate and his outraged sense of justice and of freedom had made him for a time forget his early dreams. He had realized that no poet can build a permanent fame upon satire, but the times had forced his pen. The enemy vanquished, there was no more need for satire. Once started, however, there was no stopping. His countrymen, delighted with the lampoonery and the bitter blows which they could fully appreciate, demanded more. Freneau turned upon them with bitterness: "For men I keep a pen," he cried, "for dogs a cane!" He would use the cane no longer. But who in all the land was there to listen to aught but ridicule and rant?

> Expect not in these times of rude renown
> That verse like yours will have the chance to please;
> No taste for plaintive elegy is known
> Nor lyric ode—none care for things like these.

Democracy, the mass, the American people, were mere children when it came to culture:

> Let but a dancing bear arrive,
> A pig that counts you four, or five—
> And Cato, with his moral strain
> May strive to mend the world in vain.

He would leave the unpoetic shore and seek the ocean. He would return to the ancestral profession, import wines from the Canary Islands, and he would serve as the captain of his own vessel. A second farewell to the muses:

Then, Sylvius, come—let you and I
On Ocean's aid once more rely,
Perhaps the Muse may still impart
Her balm to ease the aching heart.
Though cold may chill and storms dismay
Yet Zoilus will be far away.

Thereupon he became our poet of the sea. For years he was a merchantman captain on the Atlantic, wrecked time and again during voyages to the Canary Islands, the Southern ports, and the West Indies. No poems written in America are more full of the presence and soul of the open ocean. When one reads "The Hurricane," for instance, first published under the title, "Verses made at Sea in a Heavy Gale," knowing from the foot-note that "Captain Freneau's ship survived the violent hurricane off Jamaica, July 30, 1784, when no more than eight out of 150 sail of vessels in the ports of Kingston and Port Royal were saved," the poem becomes a living thing.[2]

The poem "Hatteras" opens with the realistic line: "In Fathoms five, the anchor gone." There is a vagabond flavor in his very titles—"Stanzas written at the Foot of Monte Souffriere, near the Town of Basseterre, Guadaloupe," "Stanzas written at the Island of Madeira," "On the Peak of Teneriffe," "Stanzas written in Blackbeard's Castle," "Lines written at Sea," the last with the opening stanza:

No pleasure on earth can afford such delights
As the heavenly view of these tropical nights:
The glow of the stars, and the breeze of the sea,
Are heaven—if heaven on ocean can be.

And is there not an epigrammatic quality about this nautical summing-up in the poem "The Bermudas"?

[2] To the poem Freneau added this locating foot-note: "Near the east end of Jamaica, July 30, 1784."

When verging to the height of *Thirty-two*,
And east or west you guide the dashing prow;
Then fear by night the dangers of this shore,
Nature's wild garden, plac'd in *Sixty-four*.
Here many a pilot his lost freight bemoans,
And many a gallant ship has laid her bones.

VI

Here was a man equipped by Nature for a poet, a man
with a message, yet dwarfed and silenced by his times and
his environment. America was not ready for her singer.
It took half a century more to make way in the wilderness for the new message that had been whispered to
Freneau in his college room. Had he been a supreme
genius, he would perchance have been heard despite all
difficulties, he would have trampled down the barriers
about him, perhaps, and compelled his age to listen; but
the task was beyond him. America to this day has produced
no poet who, single-handed and alone, could have performed such a labor of Hercules. A creator is as great as
his audience. Freneau therefore turned deliberately to the
world of affairs and suffered his dream to fade.

In June, 1786, the very year that witnessed the Kilmarnock Edition of Burns, there appeared from the press
of Francis Bailey of Philadelphia an edition of Freneau's
poems. Bailey, editor of the paper in which much of the
work had appeared, published it with hesitation: its author
was at sea; for more than a year the manuscript had been
in his hands. From his advertisement it appears that his
only hope for the success of the volume lay in its satire and
its songs of the Revolution, which, as they had appeared
"in newspapers and other periodicals in the different states
of America during the late war," had been read with
"avidity and pleasure."

According to a family tradition, on the day of Washington's inauguration, when his magnificent flotilla en-

tered the Bay of New York, Freneau at the end of a deep-sea voyage also sailed into the bay "with a cargo of monkeys." Whether true or not, it is an excellent piece of symbolism. For through the influence of Madison, Freneau was added to the Jeffersonian junto at Philadelphia and soon was entrusted with the editorship of the Anti-Federalist newspaper, the *National Gazette,* to hold his own in the Peter Porcupine atmosphere which enveloped the city like a miasma. So thoroughly did he do the work assigned him that his name became with Paine's a synonym for all the extremes of French democracy and ungodliness. The literary aristocracy of New England looked upon him as in a later generation they were to look upon Poe and Melville and Whitman. His fervid work for Jefferson and the Anti-Federalists, his outspoken advocacy of all the ideals of the French Revolution, his Tom-Paine-like religious philosophy which could express itself in such stanzas as these lines first published in the *National Gazette* defining the journal's standards and later applied to his volume of collected poems:

> "Virtue, order, and religion,
>   Haste and seek some other region;
>   Your plan is laid, to cut them down,
>   Destroy the mitre, rend the gown,
>   And that vile hag, Philosophy, restore"—
>   Did ever volume plan so much before?—

all this was a thing of horror to the New England Brahmins, especially at Yale. And the prejudice still lingers there.[3] Even the serene Washington was ruffled by the man's unreasoning democracy. "That rascal Freneau," he declared, left two copies of his despicable paper on his door-step every morning.

Freneau was at heart a poet; he worked with his emotions, as did Rousseau and Paine, and he worked without

[3] See Henry Seidel Canby, *Classic Americans from Irving to Whitman* (1931), pp. 55, 65.

stint. Into the marsh of politics he now threw his whole soul, and the result was ruin to all his literary hopes. Not without a struggle did they die. Even in the heat of his editorial life at the capital he had sought to make the paper also a literary organ. He reprinted from his poetry, added new work, wrote essays really excellent. But his age was not ready for such work. It called for satire blow on blow, for lampoonery and jingles.

His editorial career in New York and his publication in New Jersey of a local sheet need not detain us. His last years were dismal and pathetic. Verse continually came from his pen, especially during the War of 1812—the rhymed campaigns and the sea-fights which he issued in 1815 in two small volumes—but all that he wrote after his 1795 edition may be marked as inconsequential and worse. The *poet* Freneau was dead, killed by two revolutions, killed by his unliterary age. He lived in the flesh, however, until 1832. A man all his life of storm and tempest, he died most appropriately in a furious blizzard, having lost his way in the blinding snow—a tragic bit of poetic symbolism.

Ragged and unsustained, unbelievably feeble at times, nine-tenths perhaps of all he wrote mere trash, nevertheless Freneau was a genuine poet, the real father of American poetry. A half-dozen of his best lyrics—Poe can show no more—are worthy of any anthology. In many fields he was a pioneer. He was the first poetically to touch the Indian—five poems are devoted to this single subject; he was one of the first to picture the horrors of African slavery; he was the pioneer nature-poet in America, introducing the whippoorwill into "The House of Night," using the flora and fauna of his native land everywhere in his poems, and producing in "The Wild Honey Suckle" lyric what the majority of the critics believe to be the first genuine nature-note in our literature.

The prose of Freneau was produced largely during his newspaper career. Most noteworthy is the *Philosopher of the Forest* series, published in the *Freeman's Journal* between 1781 and 1788. In the tenth number of these essays he anticipates Chateaubriand in a picture of America in its idyllic period when "the children of Nature" had not been touched with the miasma of European civilization. In 1798, in the *Time-Piece,* he enlarged upon the idea:

Man in a state of simplicity, uncorrupted by the influence of bad education, bad examples, and bad government, possesses a taste for all that is good and beautiful. He is capable of a degree of moral and intellectual improvement, which advances his nature to a participation with the divine. . . . Pleased with himself and all around him, his heart dilates with benevolence and piety. . . . But where is man to be found thus noble, thus innocent, thus happy. Not in so many parts of the terraqueous globe as he ought to be; but still he is to be found wherever the rights of nature and the virtues of simplicity are not violated or banished by the false refinements, the base artifices or *corrupt-governments.* Unhappily for man, society has been almost universally corrupted, even by the arts intended for its very improvement, and human nature is gradually depraved in its very progress to civilization.

His "Letters on Various interesting and important subjects," by Robert Slender, many of them first issued in the *Aurora,* his "Tomo Cheeki" letters in the *Time-Piece,* and his "Hezekiah Salem" letters in the same newspaper, bantering the New England Federalists—all these deserve the republication they have never had. His titles are intriguing: "On the Culture of Pumpkins," October 23, 1797; "Rules How to get through a Crowd," October 23; "From Hezekiah Salem's Last Basket," November 1; "A Few Words on Duelling," November 10; "The Howling House," November 13; "A Scrap, from a Keg of Hezekiah Salem's Sermons," November 17. While these various essays do not make him, as H. H. Clark has contended, "the father of American prose," [4] they do place

[4] Harry Hayden Clark, "What Made Freneau the Father of American Prose?" *Transactions of the Wisconsin Academy of Sciences, Arts, and Letters,* Vol. XXV.

him on an equality with the best prose-writers in America before the advent of Washington Irving.

A victim he was of an unpoetic age and an unpoetic people. Swept from his course by war and revolution, brutal silencers of poets, and then by journalism, husher of so many lyric voices; alone in a headlong business-land without adequate readers, adequate publishers, adequate critics, literary companions, he surrendered so completely that in 1795 he omitted the greater part of "The House of Night" from his new edition. So fare all real poets in a land of newspaper readers and Franklinian philosophers.

CHAPTER IV

THE YALE POETS

THE FIRST dream of an American literature came in the 1720's to an English philosopher who lingered in America for three years. A generation later it came again to groups of students at Princeton and Yale dreaming over their Homers and their Vergils but powerless adequately to translate their dreamings into poetic actuality. Their attempts at verse, however, in the late 1760's mark our literary beginnings, at least in the field of poetry.

I

The residence in America from 1729 to 1731 of George Berkeley,[1] eminent English scholar, philosopher, and divine, must always be reckoned with as one of the major forces in the intellectual life of eighteenth-century America. Discouraged with the conditions moral and political in his native Europe, he had come to believe that the one hope for preserving the highest achievements of civilization lay in transferring them to a totally unsullied world where the race might be given a fresh start, unhampered by its past mistakes. With a promise from the English Government of twenty thousand pounds for the establishment of a college in Bermuda, he sailed for Rhode Island, bought ninety-six acres of land for a farm near Newport, erected a dwelling, surrounded himself with a library, and soon was in contact with the intellectual

[1] Benjamin Rand's *Berkeley's American Sojourn* (1932), is the latest authority.

leaders of America, especially the presidents of the colleges. His dream, as he sat by the savage Narragansett, he embodied in a lyric which is a part of the intellectual history of the New World:

> The Muse, disgusted at an age and clime
>   Barren of every glorious theme.
> In distant lands now waits a better time,
>   Producing subjects worthy fame:
>
> In happy climes, where from the genial sun
>   And virgin earth such scenes ensue,
> The force of art by nature seems outdone,
>   And fancied beauties by the true.
>
> In happy climes, the seat of innocence,
>   Where nature guides and virtue rules,
> Where men shall not impose for truth and sense
>   The pedantry of courts and schools:
>
> There shall be sung another golden age,
>   The rise of empire and of arts,
> The good and great inspiring epic rage,
>   The wisest heads and noblest hearts.
>
> Not such as Europe breeds in her decay;
>   Such as she bred when fresh and young,
> When heavenly flame did animate her clay,
>   By future poets shall be sung.
>
> Westward the course of empire takes its way;
>   The four first Acts already past,
> The fifth shall close the Drama with the day;
>   Time's noblest offspring is the last.

In Berkeley's dream, this Golden Age in America was to be brought about not primarily by the churches, but by the colleges. His dream of St. Paul's College in Bermuda was never realized. The British Government failed to supply the necessary funds, and after three years he returned

home to England. But the influence of his visit America still feels. Professor T. E. Jessup, an Englishman, gives this summary of his visit:

America cannot well forget the impetus he gave to her cultural life by his personal presence, his writings, his invited counsel to the leaders of higher education, and his gifts to her first universities. The libraries of Harvard and Yale were handsomely enriched by him; Yale still has three Berkeley scholars in classes provided for out of an estate gifted by him for the purpose; the colleges that are now the Universities of Columbia and Pennsylvania were shaped in part after his ideas; and several schools and even two cities bear his name.[2]

Especially noteworthy has the effect of the Berkeley Foundation been at Yale. The roll of Berkeley students has been a remarkable one. Among them one may find such names as Jared Ingersoll, John Trumbull, Joseph Buckminster, Abiel Holmes, and a notable list of college presidents headed by Eleazer Wheelock, Dartmouth; the Reverend Aaron Burr, New Jersey; Samuel Johnson, Columbia; Timothy Dwight and Napthali Daggett, Yale; Samuel Austin, Vermont; and Sereno Dwight, Hamilton.

In the germinal period that was to culminate in the Revolution, such men of culture and intellect and force were needed. Through them largely came a new awakening in American life, and this awakening was brought about, even as Berkeley had dreamed, not by the churches which so long had ruled the intellectual life of the colonies, but by the colleges. The eighteenth century in America indeed may even be denominated the "age of the advancing college." Had an American Academy been established during the first decade of the Republic, the 1790's, to include all the prominent authors of the nation and limited in its membership to thirty men, this might have been its enrollment:

[2] *A Bibliography of George Berkeley* (1934), preface.

	Date of Birth	*College*
John Adams	1735	Harvard
Thomas Jefferson	1743	William and Mary
Jeremy Belknap	1744	Harvard
H. H. Brackenridge	1748	Princeton
Lemuel Hopkins	1750	
John Trumbull	1750	Yale
James Madison	1751	Princeton
Philip Freneau	1752	Princeton
David Humphreys	1752	Yale
Timothy Dwight	1752	Yale
Joel Barlow	1754	Yale
Royal Tyler	1757	Harvard
Alexander Hamilton	1757	King's
Noah Webster	1758	Yale
Fisher Ames	1758	Harvard
Matthew Carey	1760	
Richard Alsop	1761	Harvard (nongraduate)
St. John Honeywood	1764	
Theodore Dwight	1764	
William Dunlap	1766	
Alexander Wilson	1766	
John Q. Adams	1767	Harvard
Joseph Dennie	1768	Harvard
Joseph Hopkinson	1770	Philadelphia
Elihu H. Smith	1771	Yale
Charles Brockden Brown	1771	
Thomas G. Fessenden	1771	Dartmouth
William Cliffton	1772	
William Wirt	1772	
Robert Treat Paine	1773	Harvard

College men nearly all of them, and to be a college man anywhere in the eighteenth century meant easy familiarity with the Greek and Latin classics. Too much cannot be made of this classical training which made American students early acquainted with literature on its highest levels. Many of these students, as we shall see, awakened over their *Georgics* and their *Bucolics,* their satires of

Horace, their Greek dramas, and their Homeric epics, awakened to poetry as a living thing which touched their own lives. Even a man as prose-minded and as practical as James Madison had been touched deeply for a moment by the "elegant" Muses. Two years after his graduation from Princeton he wrote to a college friend:

I myself used to have too great a hankering after those amusing studies. Poetry, wit and criticism, romances, plays, &c., captivated me much: but I began to discover that they deserve but a moderate portion of a *Mortal's* time and that something more substantial, more durable, more profitable befits our riper age.

In the rival literary societies in the colleges, as, for example, the Clios and the Whigs at Princeton, literature as the subject for debates and endless discussion ran parallel with politics, religion, and morals. A few like Freneau, Brackenridge, and Barlow could even dream of literature as a profession. Almost all of them at one time or another had sharpened quills over original couplets and had even planned Homeric epics. Among them especially one may count two young tutors at Yale, John Trumbull of the class of 1767 and Timothy Dwight of the class of 1769, both of whom had been enabled to complete their college work because of the Berkeley Foundation. It is not wide of the mark indeed to attribute to the Berkeley influence the gathering of the group of poets dubbed sometimes the "Connecticut Wits," sometimes the "Pleiades of Connecticut." Yale men for the most part, and all of them grounded and drill-mastered in the Greek and Latin classics.

Trumbull and Dwight were the pioneers of the group. Both of them were children of the manse, who learned the classics in their cradles. Stories of their precocity one hesitates to repeat. Trumbull is said to have passed his entrance examinations to Yale at the incredible age of seven, and Dwight almost as early. Both were held back, however, until they were thirteen, and both made collegiate records so brilliant that they were retained by the college as tutors, Trumbull until 1773, Dwight until 1779. After a pastorate at Greenfield, Connecticut, Dwight became the President of Yale in 1795, retaining the office until his death in 1817.

The scholarly energy of the two men was unceasing. Their regular courses in the narrow curriculum of the college they supplemented with studies of their own in the English classics and the eighteenth-century contemporary writers. As tutors, they enriched their student-work with matters then considered nonscholastic. Trumbull, in the preface to his poem *The Progress of Dulness,* was a full century ahead of his time:

> The mere knowledge of ancient languages, of the abstruser parts of mathematics, and the dark researches of metaphysics, is of little advantage in any business or profession in life; it would be more beneficial, in every place of public education, to take pains in teaching the elements of oratory, the grammar of the English tongue, and the elegancies of style and composition.[3]

Once again was Trumbull in advance of his day. At the Yale commencement of 1770, when he was awarded his Master's degree, he set forth in polished couplets "the advantages of the fine arts" despised by the Puritans and, in a burst of prophecy, equaled Berkeley and Freneau in his delineations of "the Future Glory of America":

> See, this blest land in orient morn appears,
> Waked from the slumber of six thousand years,
> While clouds of darkness veil'd each cheering ray;
> To savage beasts and savage men, a prey.
> Fair Freedom now her ensigns bright displays,
> And peace and plenty bless the golden days.
>
> .   .   .   .
>
> For pleasing Arts behold her matchless charms,
> The first in letters, as the first in arms.

[3] Edition of 1820, pp. 9–10.

See bolder genius quit the narrow shore,
And realms of science, yet untraced, explore,
Hiding in brightness of superior day,
The fainting gleam of Europe's setting ray.

Sublime the Muse shall lift her eagle wing;
Of heavenly themes the sacred bards shall sing,
Tell how the blest Redeemer, man to save,
Thro' the deep mansions of the gloomy grave,
Sought the low shades of night, then rising high
Vanquish'd the powers of hell, and soared above the sky;
Or paint the scenes of that funereal day,
When earth's last fires shall mark their dreadful way,
In solemn pomp th' eternal Judge descend,
Doom the wide world and give to nature, end;
Or ope heaven's glories to th' astonish'd eye,
And bid their lays with lofty Milton vie;
Or wake from nature's themes the moral song,
And shine with Pope, and Thompson and with Young.

This land her Swift and Addison shall view,
The former honours equall'd by the new;
Here shall some Shakspeare charm the rising age,
And hold in magic chains the listening stage;
A second Watts shall string the heavenly lyre,
And other muses other bards inspire.[4]

Thus the young tutor Trumbull, not yet twenty-one.
That he himself was not the epic seer prophesied in his
poem was soon evident. His literary talents ran "toward
the left," toward gentle satire and pulpiteering criticism.
First of all he would lampoon, most tutor-like, the college
world that he knew so thoroughly—the stupidity of the
students and the absurdity of the curriculum. The theological schools were filling Connecticut with replicas of Tom
Brainless, an eighteenth-century Elmer Gantry:

What though his wits could ne'er dispense
One page of grammar, or of sense;

[4] "Prospect of the Future Glory of America" (Sept. 12, 1770).

What though his learning be so slight,
He scarcely knows to spell or write;
What though his skull be cudgel-proof!
He's orthodox, and that's enough.

Settled finally as pastor of a church, he

On Sunday in his best array,
Deals forth the dulness of the day,
And while above he spends his breath,
The yawning audience nod beneath.

Two hours his drawling speech holds on,
And names it preaching when its done.[5]

Thus glib-tongued Merc'ry in his hand
Stretch'd forth the sleep-compelling wand,
Each eye in endless doze to keep—
The God of speaking, and of sleep.

Excellent work, considering the world from which it
came. Despite his Calvinistic audience, his scholarship,
his Puritanism, he leaned at times decidedly toward the
left. In his *Progress of Dulness* are passages that strike
fire even today. The college career of the young clod educated beyond his intellect and "The Adventures of Miss
Harriet Simper" are still modern instances.

The outbreak of the war found him a law student in
the office of John Adams, and apparently it left him there.
Not a Tory at all, and, so far as activities were concerned,
not a Whig, he did nothing until Silas Deane, reading to
him the pompous proclamations of the absurd General
Gage, aroused him to write a satire on the situation,
M'Fingal, two hundred lines modeled after the pattern set
by the English humorist and satirist, Samuel Butler. Instantly the poem struck fire; an imitation was what the
Whigs in America wanted. The Hudibrastic rocking-horse

---

[5] This couplet was omitted in the edition of 1820.

meters and the smart "wise-cracking" couplets amused them. A supreme genius could not have satisfied them more. *M'Fingal,* the first part of it, became a vital part. of the Revolution. As propaganda, it is to be rated with Paine's pamphlets.

A curious document it seems now, however, analyzed in the cold light of a hundred and fifty years. It was not a spontaneous outpouring of personal convictions and emotions; it was a *tour de force,* an attempt to be literary after classical patterns and at the same time to be popular and propagandic. The parts that pleased the people of the 1770's were unquestionably the horse-play scenes such as the hauling of the squire to the top of the liberty-pole with a hook in his waistband and the holding of him there until he satisfied the mob with his recantations:

> Good Gentlemen and friends and kin,
> For heaven's sake hear, if not for mine!
> I here renounce the Pope, the Turks,
> The King, the Devil and all their works;
> And will, set me but once at ease,
> Turn Whig, or Christian, what you please.

The tarring and feathering of M'Fingal is told with Old Testament unction:

> . . . he in peril of his soul
> Stood tied half-hanging to the pole;
> Then lifting high the ponderous jar,
> Pour'd o'er his head the smoking tar.
> With less profusion once was spread
> Oil on the Jewish monarch's head,
> That down his beard and vestments ran,
> And cover'd all his outward man.

II

The third canto, not published until 1782 and so not at all helpful during the Revolution, is the best part of the

epic satire. Like Brackenridge's *Modern Chivalry,* it
turns a flood of vaudeville upon the victorious Whigs.
Not with rancor, however.

As attacks upon "the insolent foe," as Freneau's satires
were attacks, the poem was a failure. No part of it was
written in bitterness of soul. It is a literary piece made in
cold blood according to rule. Not a line that would make
even a British red-coat of the Revolution hot and angry.
It is unlocalized: with small changes it could be made to fit
a war in Europe. And completely is it European in poetic
feeling and poetic art. Everywhere the shadowings of
classic models. Part of the time the Tory M'Fingal is
Milton's Satan thrown from Heaven and rising uncon-
quered from the burning marl, and part of the time he is
Don Quixote with his squire Sancho Panza. And precisely
like Milton's central figure, the Tory Devil is the hero of
the piece. Invariably he has the best of the argument. His
philosophy is often brilliant:

> All punishments, the world can render,
> Serve only to provoke th' offender;
> The will gains strength from treatment horrid,
> As hides grow harder when they're curried.
> No man e'er felt the halter draw,
> With good opinion of the law;
> Or held in method orthodox
> His love of justice, in the stocks;
> Or fail'd to lose by sheriff's shears
> At once his loyalty and ears.

Witty passages one may quote, some of them in general
currency as Butler's own, as, for instance, many of the
couplets containing the old Tory's philosophy of life; but
the poem as a whole is noteworthy only because of its
connection with the Revolution.

Trumbell in gentler times, with leisure and with an
adequate reading public, might possibly have risen to the
level of contemporary satire—no high elevation, but higher

than any he ever attained. Unquestionably he had standards of measurement in advance of his times. He was considered, even in the iron boundaries of Yale, a literary rebel. He had ideals of art and education quite at variance with his day, as witness his *Progress of Dulness*. But even he could not forget that he was in the eighteenth century. He hated literary lightness and he hated the incoming tide of sentimentality. Describing in his poem, Part III, the education of Miss Harriet Simper, rhyming "Pamela" with "really" and "fair one" with "heroine," he lashed everything that he called "light literature," especially all varieties of writing pleasing to the ladies:

> We own that ladies sometimes read,
> And grieve, that reading is confin'd
> To books that poison all the mind;
> Novels and plays, (where shines display'd
> A world that nature never made).

Better poetry by far his *Progress of Dulness* than his *M'Fingal*. Though a century and a half have passed, the piece still has a modern sound: it touches fundamental characteristics. It is the best satire produced in America before Irving.

But the popularity of *M'Fingal* was the poet's undoing. The public demanded it, and he republished it again and again. Editions appeared as late as the 1860's. As a result, the poet perished with this albatross of a comic epic hung about his neck. He wrote little in his later years. Generally is he rated now among the single-poem poets, and that single poem is remembered because of the part it played in the Revolution.

III

Timothy Dwight, the leader of the Yale school of poets, was never in danger of such a fate. Upon the pen of this grandson of Jonathan Edwards lightness never for an instant descended. Tremendously was he religious and tre-

mendously was he conscious of his divine mission for
leadership. When the epic urge came upon him as he pored
over his Homer as a college student, he launched out upon
an epic of his own, and it was indeed no "middle flight" he
planned to make. As with Milton, nothing seemed adequate as a theme save the wars of Jehovah Himself. Oblivi-
ous to the fact that an epic was enacting at his very door,
he searched Old Testament writ and paused at the Book
of Joshua, the most slaughterous in the Hebrew canon.
That he knew thoroughly his Homer is everywhere evident; like Homer, he would center not upon the conquest
as a whole, but upon a single demigod hero. To depart
from the biblical record troubled him not at all, and to
drag in similes from battles of the Revolution disturbed
not in the least his sense of humor, since humor had been
totally omitted from his equipment. That he toiled over
his poeticizing like a medieval monk over a missal is evident in every one of the 9,672 lines of the epic. He knew
the classic rules for poetry as completely as did Milton;
whatever else one may say concerning the poem, one must
commend its unity of scene and action and its carefully
drawn climaxes. Just when Dwight wrote the thing is
hard to determine, but it was early in his poetic career.
Youth is everywhere evident in its lines. It was a *tour de
force,* a scholarly exercise, a poetic study worth a Doctor
of Philosophy degree. That it was intended as a biblical
allegory—*The Conquest of Canaan* prefiguring the later
conquest of the New England Canaan—Dwight in later
years vigorously denied.

The scholarly world, especially the Yale Parnassus,
praised the poem as if a new Milton had alighted in Connecticut. The English poet Cowper dignified it with a
review. Joel Barlow put the poet into his *Vision of Columbus* (1785) as one of the glories of the New World:

> On glory's wing to raise the ravish'd soul
> Beyond the bounds of earth's benighted pole,

For daring Dwight the Epic Muse sublime
Hails her new empire in the western clime.
Fired with the themes by seers seraphic sung,
Heaven in his eye, and rapture on his tongue,
His voice divine revives the promised land,
The Heaven-taught leader and the chosen band.
In Hanniel's fate, proud faction finds her doom,
Ai's midnight flames light nations to their tomb,
In visions bright supernal joys are given,
And all the dread futurities of heaven.

Undoubtedly the poem has poetic excellencies, though few modern critics have paused to see them: the defects are too obvious. Some of the battle episodes, as, for instance, the single combat of the youthful Irad and the giant Jobab, with the youth victorious, have dramatic power. Some of the Homeric similes surpass Pope's:

As the dire comet, swift through ether driven,
In solemn silence, climbs the western heaven;
His sanguine hair, portending fearful wars,
Streams down the midnight sky, and blots the stars;
Pale death and terror light the dusky gloom,
And quivering nations read their sudden doom,
So in the flaming van great Joshua rose,
And shot red glories on the wondering foes.

More one cannot say. The poem is not original: it is "fired," even as Barlow has expressed it, "with the themes by seers seraphic sung"; it is bombastic with youthful extravagance. The hero Joshua in slaughterous power exceeds even the supermen of the *Arabian Nights*. Lightning from his eyes mows down whole squadrons:

Huge piles of slaughter gathering round his course,
On Shimron Joshua wing'd his mighty force.
Like two red flames his vivid eye-balls glow,
And shoot fierce lightnings on th' astonish'd foe;
Before, expanded, his meteorous shield

Blaz'd a broad ruin thro' the stormy field;
Round the wild war his flashing terrors fly;
Cars burst before him;—steeds and heroes die.

And again:

His sword, swift circling, hew'd his dismal way,
Fell'd ranks at once and broke the deep array.

A nameless critic in the Boston *Monthly Anthology* of
1805, signing himself "Remarker," was the first, so far as
I can find, to record the standard contemporary joke upon
Dwight's unwieldy epic:

The greatest defect of these poems [he wrote] is an entire
want of interest. We doze over the *Vision of Columbus,* and
if we are kept awake in perusing the *Conquest of Canaan* we
are indebted to the thunder and lightning, that roars and
flashes in every page, and which, like another Jupiter Tonans
the poet discharges in perpetual rumble and corruscation; so
that, as a wit once observed, it is scarcely safe to read this
poem without a conductor.

Voluminously Dwight wrote all his life long, often in
verse at volume length, but nothing of it has survived save
perhaps a single hymn, found in all the modern hymn-
books—"I love thy Kingdom, Lord." Once while chaplain
in the Revolutionary army he burst into a rhapsodic anthem, the future glories of America his theme, but there
is little poetry in the stanzas:

Columbia, Columbia, to glory arise,
The queen of the world, and child of the skies!
Thy genius commands thee; with rapture behold,
While ages on ages thy splendors unfold.
Thy reign is the last, and the noblest of time,
Most fruitful thy soil, most inviting thy clime;
Let the crimes of the east ne'er encrimson thy name,
Be freedom, and science, and virtue, thy fame.

> To conquest, and slaughter, let Europe aspire;
> Whelm nations in blood, and wrap cities in fire;
> Thy heroes the rights and mankind shall defend,
> And triumph pursue them, and glory attend.
> A world is thy realm: for a world be thy laws,
> Enlarg'd as thine empire, and just as thy cause;
> On Freedom's broad basis, that empire shall rise,
> Extend with the main, and dissolve with the skies.

Four other stanzas follow, equally superlative and equally grandiloquent. To this lyric, however, one unique tribute must be paid: in point of time it leads the long list of American national anthems.

The poet's volume, *Greenfield Hill* (1794), is of better quality. Written for the most part in 1777 while he was pastor at Greenfield, Connecticut, it attempts to do for America what Denham in his *Cooper's Hill* and Pope in his *Windsor Forest* did for England. Echoes everywhere there are of earlier poets—Thomson, Goldsmith, Pope, Gay, Beattie—but much of the poem is original, written in the presence of the scenes described. And intensely is it patriotic:

> The solid foundations, which appear to be laid for the future greatness and prosperity of the American Republic, offered very pleasing views of this subject to a Poet; and of these the writer has, in the Seventh Part of the Work, endeavored to avail himself.

This from his preface written for the edition published in 1794. In prophetic vision undoubtedly he exceeds Trumbull:

> All hail, thou western world! by heaven design'd
> Th' example bright, to renovate mankind.
> Soon shall thy sons across the mainland roam;
> And claim, on far Pacific shores, their home;
> Their rule, religion, manners, arts, convey
> And spread their freedom to the Asian sea.

And again:

> See this glad world remote from every foe,
> From Europe's mischiefs, and from Europe's woe!
> Th' Atlantic's guardian tide repelling far
> The jealous terror, and the vengeful war,
> The native malice, envy, pride, and strife,
> The plagues of rank, the rust of useless life,
> The cumberous pomp, of general want the spring,
> The clashing commerce, and the rival king.
> See, far remote, the crimes of balanced sway!
> Where courts contract the debt, and subjects pay.

Realistic picturings often there are that remind one of Crabbe, episodes of Negro slavery, Whittier-like snow scenes, stirring narratives of Indian fights. Perhaps the best of all is Part VI, "The Farmer's advice to the Villagers," a series of Franklin-like proverbs used as texts for ten-line lay-sermons on Yankee thrift and family management. These, for example:

> In merchant's books from year to year
> Be cautious how your names appear.

> With steady hand your household sway
> And use them always to obey.

> My country's youth, I see with pain
> The customs of their sires disdain.

But whatever the quality of the man's work as measured by present-day standards, the fact cannot be disregarded that for at least one generation he was the accepted poet laureate of New England if not of all America. Of him his Yale colleague Trumbull could write in all seriousness,

> Fame shall assent, and future years admire
> Barlow's strong flight and Dwight's poetic fire,

and Barlow in turn could admit him into his *Columbiad* as one of the glories of America pointed out to Columbus by Hesper.

IV

But Joel Barlow was a disciple of Dwight. At Yale during the closing years of the elder poet's tutorship, he had been inspired to poetry by his instructor, and to such a degree that, like the young Freneau at Princeton, he had dedicated his life to poetry as a profession. Graduated in the class of 1778 as commencement poet, he remained for two years at Yale as tutor and graduate student. Poetry seemed to possess the man. Like Freneau and young Trumbull, he would build an American epic in the Miltonic grand manner. One of his tutors, Joseph Buckminster, advised him to follow the example of Dwight and build with the only materials worthy his genius, biblical story: "The history of Joseph," he argued, "has never had justice done it in poetry that I have seen; of Cain and Abel, in which a little machinery and fiction would do very well; of Daniel, and a variety of others."

But the young poet had been led by the native Muses into fields more poetic. A subject had taken possession of him that was in every way Miltonic, the one that had started the young Freneau to epic expression, a subject indeed that was to rule his entire life. Why not make the aged Columbus, dying in prison, see in a vision the future glories of the America he had discovered? There was nothing in the whole new Western World that could not be admitted into such an epic structure—glorious! From 1779 until 1787 he worked upon it, publishing it at first with the title *The Vision of Columbus*—"the first important poem," says his biographer, C. B. Todd, "distinctively American in subject and authorship ever projected," a statement, of course, open seriously to question, but one nevertheless partly true.

The tutorship did not materialize. Affairs for the young poet were waxing desperate; his friends became anxious. His poet friend, Humphreys, now in the army, advised him to seek a chaplaincy in one of the regiments. "There is a hopeful genius . . . in this town," he wrote his superior officer, "who is so far gone in poetry, that there is no hope of reclaiming and making him attentive to anything else. . . . He is certainly a very great genius, and has undertaken a work which, I am persuaded, will do honor to himself and his country—if he is enabled to prosecute it in the manner he has proposed. It is entitled 'The Vision of Columbus' and in the course of the poem will bring into view upon a large scale all the events that have or will take place on the continent."

Securing the chaplaincy, for the next few months Barlow, with Dwight and Humphreys, was in the Revolutionary army, using every spare moment upon his epic and joining with them in the production of martial lyrics and patriotic songs.

Next we find him in Hartford as newspaper editor and publisher, but everywhere hailed as a poet, a man of genius, so commanding indeed that he was entrusted by the Congregational churches of Connecticut with the editorship of a new version of the Watts hymnal (1788). Fourteen psalms he paraphrased, five new hymns he created entire for the work, and many of the older hymns he dropped or revised—a job accepted by the churches not entirely, however, without criticism. Oliver Arnold, the wit of Revolutionary days, voiced the opposition:

> You've proved yourself a sinful cre'tur;
> You've murder'd Watts and spoil'd the metre;
> You've tried the word of God to alter,
> And for your pains deserve a halter.

Powerless with his pen to support his family, he turned at length to the law as a profession, still working at his colossal epic, and, with his old friends, "The Hartford

Wits," Trumbull, Dr. Hopkins, and Humphreys, issuing from time to time in the local newspapers the series of poetic lampoons known as *The Anarchiad*. In 1787 *The Vision of Columbus,* so long toiled over, was ready for the world and elaborately published. In Connecticut at least it was as if a new *Paradise Lost* had appeared. America now had a literature.

But a complete break was to come in the poet's life, one that was to sever him completely from the Connecticut "school" and change the entire current of his life. In 1788 he became the foreign agent for an Ohio land company, and during the next seventeen years he was abroad, most of the time in France. With Paine, he sided with the forces of the Revolution, and in 1792 he was made a citizen of France. Returning to America in 1805 so thoroughly Gallicized that his Yale friends avoided him, he took up his residence in Washington. Six years later he was sent by Madison as Minister to France, was involved in Napoleon's disastrous Russian campaign, and died from exposure in a little village near Cracow, Poland, in 1812.

Although some of Barlow's minor poems, like his really charming mock-heroic "Hasty Pudding" (1792) and his vigorous "Conspiracy of Kings," are at present the most readable part of his poetic output, his place as a poet must be determined by the quality of the master-work to which he gave the greater part of his literary life. The first draft of this colossal structure, *The Vision of Columbus,* was dreamed of by its author first of all as an epic, but quickly he abandoned this complicated form and made of it, to use his own words, "a poem on the subject of America at large, designed to exhibit the importance of this country in every point of view as the noblest and most elevated part of the earth, and reserved to be [the] last and greatest theatre for the improvement of mankind in every article in which they are capable of improvement. The poem will be rather of the philosophic than epic kind." Columbus was not to be shown merely a series of moving-pictures, but he was to be instructed in metaphysics, politics, cosmography, religion, statecraft. He was to be lectured to, preached to, catechized. Note the "Argument" of Book VIII, an argument not changed at all for the *Columbiad:*

The vision suspended. Causes of the slow progress of Science and its frequent interruptions. Its ancient compared with its modern establishment. Consequences of the latter. Causes of the apparent uncertainty in matters of theology. Superstition built on the passions; scepticism on the reasoning power. Necessity and happy effect of the united force of reason and the passions in the discovery of truth.

Revising this poetic hodgepodge for publication twenty years later, Barlow brought not only a widened critical experience, but a totally changed view of all things governmental and religious. His first version had been dedicated most fulsomely to "His Most Christian Majesty, Louis the Sixteenth, King of France and Navarre"—

The great Father of the House of Bourbon will be held in the highest veneration, till his favourite political system shall be realized among the nations of Europe, and extended to all mankind—

and it had been filled everywhere with praises of the monarchial system and advocacy of the divine right of kings.

But the poet of the *Columbiad* had passed through the French Revolution and had been with the party that had beheaded the divine Louis. He had even become a deist. As a result, his first task was to erase from the earlier poem all monarchial and religious utterances and to replace them with Liberty, Equality, and Fraternity. In *The Vision of Columbus* a passage like this:

Thro' each extended realm, in wisdom great,
Rose the dread sires, that claim the cares of state;

> Long robes of purest white their forms embrace,
> Their better hands imperial sceptres grace,
> There left the laws, that shining leaves infold,
> Where rights and charters flame in figured gold.

in the *Columbiad* is changed to:

> Thro' each colonial realm, for wisdom great,
> Elected sires assume the cares of state;
> Nursed in equality, to freedom bred,
> Firm is their step and strait the paths they tread;
> Dispensing justice with paternal hand,
> By laws of peace they rule the happy land;
> While reason's page their statute codes unfold,
> And rights and charters flame in figured gold.

The poet, experienced now, has found that his poem after all is an epic. In a learned preface he defends his stand. "In no poem," he declares, "are the unities of time, place, and action more rigidly observed: the action, in the technical sense of the word, consisting only of what takes place between Columbus and Hesper; which must be supposed to occupy but a few hours, and is confined to the prison and the mount of vision." Accordingly he fits the poem with an epic opening:

> I sing the Mariner who first unfurl'd
> An eastern banner o'er the western world.

And he fits it, too, with a formal dedication, not to the Muse but to "Almighty Freedom!"

> Strong in thy strength I bend no suppliant knee,
> Invoke no miracle, no Muse but thee.

Otherwise the poem is not greatly changed. The fundamental plan of *The Vision of Columbus* has not been disturbed, nor has the order or the content of his historical material. The *Columbiad* is but a thoroughgoing revision.

He has changed the key only to heighten the diction. Still is it a hodgepodge, its object not at all epic story but sermonic, moralizing: "My object is altogether of a moral and political nature. I wish to encourage and strengthen, in the rising generation, a sense of the importance of republican institutions; as being the great foundation of public and private happiness, the necessary aliment of future and permanent meliorations in the condition of human nature."

Tremendously impressed with the awesome thing, the first publishers determined to make the first edition of it the finest book ever printed in America. In Brown's *American Register* for 1807 appeared this impressive announcement:

The Columbiad

A poem by Joel Barlow. Royal 4to, embellished with twelve elegant engravings. Twenty Dollars.

This work is confidently offered to the public as the most elegant specimen of typography hitherto produced in this country. The high character of the poem, which, a late English critic says, "is now probably destined to stand the epic song of his [Mr. Barlow's] country," was considered by the publishers as deserving of the most costly decorations that could be procured. The first artists were therefore employed in the execution of the plates, printing, &c, &c. The printing is done in a masterly style by Messrs. Fry and Kammerer; the twelve engravings are by Auker Smith, Schiavonetti, Neagle, and Heath, from subjects painted expressly for this poem by the celebrated Smirke, and were in such high estimation with the amateurs of England that several proof copies were sold at 12 guineas a set.

No poem in all the world was ever welcomed with more heartiness. Its subscription pages contained the names of scores of eminent people on both sides of the water. New England at least hailed the book as a world classic to be added to the roll containing the *Iliad* and the *Odyssey*. Classic, however, the poem certainly is not. Barlow was a man of prose and reason rather than a poet. His lines are literary and labored, and all his moving-picture effects are accomplished by mere allusion. One must know intimately the history of America to understand these swiftly generalized glimpses. Nothing of the hodgepodgery of the earlier volume has been omitted. There is even a survey of European history beginning with the Roman era. No poet with so little of poetry ever received so much of glory.

v

David Humphreys, for a generation always mentioned as the fourth poet in the American choir, was also essentially a man of prose. The atmosphere of Yale, with Trumbull and Dwight on the faculty, set him also to the making of heroic couplets and inspired him also with dreams of poetry as a profession. But suddenly the war had broken upon him, and instantly the Muse and old Yale he bade farewell:

> Adieu, thou Yale! where youthful poets dwell,
> No more I linger by thy classic stream.
> Inglorious ease and sportive songs farewell!
> Thou startling clarion! break the sleeper's dream!

He had found his work. Step by step he arose in military importance until he was a member of Washington's staff with the rank of colonel. After the war he was sent as secretary of legation abroad and then as Minister to Lisbon and Madrid. Fourteen years was he abroad, his record brilliant.

In personality the man was unusually attractive. He was courtly and impressive in manner, and universally trusted. The love and respect everywhere felt for him blinded, perhaps, his own day to his poetic leanness.

In Europe his popularity as a poet exceeded Barlow's.

When in 1804 his volume, *The Miscellaneous Works of David Humphreys, Late Minister Plenipotentiary from the United States of America to the Court of Madrid,* appeared, two hundred of the five hundred and fifty subscribers were Europeans, most of them from the ranks of the nobility of the various nations.

His *Poem on the Happiness of America* (1786) went into ten editions. The *Columbian Magazine* found it beautiful because it dealt with American scenery that was beautiful. America, it declared,

stands high in literary reputation. Amidst the favourite pursuits of our countrymen, the Muses have had their votaries; nor have these coy maids been unsuccessfully courted. Their genius seems much delighted with our sylvan scenes. The face of nature, throughout the United States, exhibits the *sublime and beautiful,* in the most exalted degree. In almost every part of this country, we are surrounded with objects calculated to inspire the most elevated conceptions of the imagination. Our mountains, vallies, plains, and rivers, are formed on a great scale; the extent of the country itself is great; and the whole is rendered magnificently beautiful, by the creating hand of the Almighty Architect! And if we contemplate the eminently dignified part that has been recently acted on the vast national stage, with the scenes of magnanimity, wisdom, and patriotic virtue, which our gallant countrymen have exhibited thereon, we must allow, that nothing can afford more noble themes for our native bards.

The years in Europe brought him material prosperity. He was permitted to import from Spain the merino breed of sheep and was one of the first on a large scale to manufacture woolen goods. He became at last one of the richest men in America. In his final volume he expressed his mature philosophy. *A Poem on Industry* was the title. The richest fruit gained by the war, he declared, was Commerce. This from his introduction:

The main scope of the author's principal productions in verse, has been to indicate to his fellow-citizens, in a connected manner, the measures best calculated for increasing and prolonging the public felicity. . . . He proposes now to show the prodigious influence of national industry in producing public and private riches and enjoyment.

To Humphreys, then, poetry had become wool-growing, machinery, industry— "Come, then, oh Industry! possess my soul"—prophetic indeed of what the nineteenth century was to do to the Muses, but there was little else in the man to suggest the age to come. The fields where grazed his merino sheep, the first of the breed ever seen in America, the humble scenes of domestic life, he loved like a Whittier. But completely was he of the eighteenth century. To him poetry could be expressed only in "elegant" language. Nature impressed him, but always must it be dressed with "umbrageous trees," "Hyperborean" and "Vesperian" skies, and breathe with "gelid breath" "ambrosal balm." He has been, if possible, even more completely forgotten than Barlow.

CHAPTER V

THE FIN DE SIÈCLE

I

THAT ALL *fin de siècle* decades are yellow has become a
facetious axiom. Surely none could be yellower than the
decade that launched the American Republic. It saw in
Europe the French Revolution, the reign of terror, the
destruction of age-old monarchies, the rise of Napoleon.
In America it saw party strife to the verge of civil war:
Shays's Rebellion, the "whisky insurrection," war with
France averted only by a miracle.

The storm-center during the decade was Philadelphia,
just chosen as the American capital, or, as reported by
Freneau:

> From Hudson's banks in proud array,
> (Too mean to claim a longer stay)
> Their new ideas to improve,
> Behold the generous Congress move!

The move was inevitable: the city had been the revolutionary center, and it had become the national metropolis,
outranking New York. As the new capital, it rapidly took
on cosmopolitan characteristics. Foreign legations began
to appear, and old-world travelers of many nations curious
to see the workings of the new experiment in government
in the wild hinterlands of the New World.[1] Congressmen

[1] See Jane Louise Mesick, *The English Traveller in America, 1785–
1835* (1922). See also Timothy Dwight's *Travels in New-England and
New-York* (1821–1822), IV, 216–257.

and government officials, some of them picturesque specimens, swarmed in from the thirteen states and beyond.
The quiet Quaker town had become a roaring metropolis.

Other elements gave color to the decade. In 1792 and
again in 1798 the city was nearly depopulated by the yellow fever. But far more potent in its lasting results was
another infection that swept the city and soon all the cities
in the new Republic—polemic journalism. An evolution
it was from conditions peculiarly American. Partisanship
had reached limits of frontier ferocity, even to pistol battles like that between Editor Oswald and Editor Carey in
which the latter all but lost his life. In old Quaker Philadelphia a half-dozen fighting journals, and behind each of
them a militant personality: Cobbett, Oswald, Fenno,
Bache, Carey, and "that rascal Freneau."

Most picturesque of all, perhaps, was the British refu-
gee, William Cobbett, who, exalting everything British at
the expense of everything American, exasperated Philadelphia beyond endurance. Right and left he shot his quills
with damnable accuracy. His newspaper, *Porcupine's
Gazette and Daily Advertiser,* he supplemented with a
barrage of pamphlets: *A Little Plain English, A New
Year's Gift for Democrats, A Kick for a Bite.* Carey
shied at him with counter-pamphlets, one of them "The
Porcupiniad," but nothing stopped the quill-fire until he
attacked the popular Dr. Rush, charging that his blood-
letting practice killed most of his patients. Sued for libel
and held on a judgment for $5,000, he went to New York,
emitting as he went a Parthian volley of quills. Further we
need not follow him.

II

The effect upon the rising literature of the new nation
was disastrous. A tremendous fact had been discovered:
the literature of democracy is the newspaper. The republican masses would read the weekly paper, would read po-

litical satire if it jingled merrily and was brutal in its personalities, but it would read nothing else. Hence, more and
more a literary descent to the majority—to "the republic
of letters" whose classics are feuilletons.

The division into political parties had been fundamentally a social matter: aristocracy versus the mass, the *sans
culottes* versus the old régime. The colonies had been settled by an agrarian middle class, but they had evolved social gradations amounting almost to European caste. In
New England an aristocracy of education—the divine
right of the intellectually prepared. At the top the clergy,
with colleges founded for their training. At every point
religion. God they visualized as a feudal overlord, with
the clergy an elect nobility—in time a hereditary oligarchy,
the "Brahmin caste." Next in order the "saints" of the
church membership, the kernel of wheat in the bushel of
chaff; then the "sinners," the "non-elect," the "mob." In
the midlands an aristocracy not so professionally religious,
one centered in wealth and refinement, an aristocracy with
family traditions. In the South an aristocracy of the feudal
type, one evolved from local conditions—plantations,
manor-houses, slaves, conditions suggesting the English
nobility; religion aristocratic after the British fashion.

The Revolution had cut deep into these aristocracies. In
the main, the uprising had been nonaristocratic—an agrarian and mercantile population hit in the pocket-book by
foreign-made taxes and insistent upon a hearing. It had
been an uprising of the *people*. The aristocracy had furnished the "Tories." Rebellion is the work of youth, of
those who have at stake only their mere lives. Property
and traditions and institutions and hard-won rights are
conservative, prone to abide by the old régime.

After the Revolution the same lines of cleavage. The
new Constitution was felt by the conservatives to be a
revolutionary document. It gave, they argued, too much
power to the *sans culottes,* to the untrained masses so
easily manipulated by demagogues. Government by the

majority, everybody permitted to vote, meant "beggars on horseback"—anarchy. The result had been the Federalist Party, strongest in New England, led by men like John Adams and Fisher Ames of Boston, all of them college men, Harvard aristocrats. A writer in the Boston *Anthology* could boast that New England, "with less than double the population of either London or Paris, can boast of possessing more universities than either England or France." They feared the *people,* the populism which had so recently been made dramatic in Shays's Rebellion and the "whisky insurrection." They had not fought through the seven years that tried men's souls just "to make the world safe for democracy."

III

Wild news from France, too, kept taut the nerves of the new nation. There was a democracy in full control, beggars on horseback, with the aristocracy on the guillotine. Behold how it works! how,

> With laughing lips and eyes serene,
>   The aristocracy of France
> Went gaily to the guillotine.

The French Revolution at the beginning had seemed almost a home affair, the logical sequel of the American struggle. Freneau had voiced it as early as 1790:

> From the bright spark that first illumed these lands
> See Europe kindling as the blaze expands.
> Each gloomy tyrant, sworn to chain the mind,
> Presumes no more to trample on mankind.

And again in 1791:

> From the spark that we kindled, a flame has gone forth
> To astonish the world and enlighten mankind:
> With a code of new doctrines the universe rings,
> And Paine is addressing strange sermons to kings.

Paine in 1792 had echoed the lines in *The Rights of Man:* "From a small spark, kindled in America, a flame has arisen not to be extinguished. Without consuming, like the *Ultima Ratio Regum,* it winds its progress from nation to nation. . . ."

But in 1793 a spark from the European conflagration alighted in old Philadelphia in the person of "Citizen" Genêt, delegated Ambassador from Revolutionary France. A howl of joy from what today would be called the American "reds." Instantly everyone was a "Citizen"; all Philadelphia was talking "Citizen Genêt." On the third of June the republican element staged for him a flamboyant "republican dinner" where enthusiasm became explosive. Bache's *Aurora* records that "After three of the toasts the artillery fired salutes with two twelve pounders, fifteen rounds each"; that Pinchon's "Ode to Liberty," translated into English meters by Freneau, was received with roaring applause; and that Freneau's national anthem, "God Save the Rights of Man," was sung "with great effect." A better ode it is than the British national song to the same music, yet hardly worthy of an artillery salvo as applause. This the second stanza:

> Let us with France agree,
> And bid the world be free,
> While tyrants fall!
> Let the rude savage host
> Of their vast numbers boast—
> Freedom's almighty trust
> Laughs at them all!

But exultation was short-lived. The French tragedy moved rapidly. Instead of "Freedom's almighty trust," there began the "reign of terror," and the American Federalists and many of the early republicans deserted in a body. International complications became grave. There was a threat of war, and, but for Washington, war undoubtedly would have come. As a result, a newspaper torrent

of invective. One might make a "schimpflexicon" of abuse
of Washington that would give the impression that the
great man was a veritable Nero.

A tumultuous decade.

IV

In such an atmosphere had begun the new nation and
the new American literature. Everywhere unrest, everywhere criticism. "A people independent a century before
they are of age," roared the British Southey. "See what it
is to have a nation take its place among civilized states
before it has either gentlemen or scholars."

The previous period had ended abruptly with a magazine—the *American Museum* (1787–1792). For the first
time an attempt to gather up the literature of the past, to
present in rounded form the writings of a period. Mathew
Carey, an Irish immigrant less than three years in America, was the founder. To Carey, who was primarily a
publisher, a magazine was a repository. The prose and the
poetry that had helped to win American independence he
found scattered through newspapers and pamphlets; it
should be saved. Hence his *Museum,* an eighteenth-century
Golden Book.

In number after number the Revolutionary classics, all
of them entire: Trumbull's *M'Fingal,* Paine's *Common
Sense* and *The Crisis,* Washington's important papers,
Hopkinson's *Miscellaneous Essays,* Dickinson's *Letters
from a Farmer in Pennsylvania.* Poetry of the newspaper
variety seemed especially to attract him. One-fifth of every
number of the *Museum* was in verse. Carey loved the
florid, the sentimental, the moralistic. The young Dr. Joseph Brown Ladd (1764–1786), a Della Cruscan before
Della Crusca, he published *in extenso.* Twenty-eight of his
poems he published in his first three volumes.

He went a step farther. The English publishers, imitating the Germans, were issuing books of choice selections

from the poets: why not an American anthology? Accordingly he issued three collections of American poetry, the first, *Select Poems, Chiefly American,* published before 1791; the second, *Beauties of Poetry, British and American, containing Some of the Productions of* [names of twenty-four British poets and twenty-four American poets], 1791; and third, *The Columbian Muse, a Selection of American Poetry, from Various Authors of Established Reputation,* 1794, a book made from the American part of his second anthology, with additions. All of the poems had previously appeared in the *Museum.*

The work of the second anthologist, Dr. Elihu H. Smith, whose *American Poems, Selected and Original* appeared in 1793, we shall note later. The view of both anthologies was retrospective. Their work ended a literary period.

v

The new era took from the first the color of the times. It was dominated by party dissension. When Washington in 1796 presented his "Farewell Address to Congress," a fatherly document from a full heart, he stressed with especial emphasis the dangers of unbridled politics, "the fury of party spirit."

Had he been thinking only of the literary future of his country, his words would have been the same. Years before this, Oliver Goldsmith had listed it in one of his prefaces as the most insidious of all dangers to literature:

But there is an enemy in poetry still more dangerous, I mean party; party entirely distorts the judgment and destroys the taste. A mind capable of relishing general beauty, when once infected with this disease, can only find pleasure in what contributes to increase the distemper.

Literature, so far as America had achieved a literature, had been the product of the midland and the northern aristocracies. The republican mass wrote nothing, read nothing but newspapers. "Remarker," writing for the Boston *Anthology* in 1805, could be even more superlative:

> It is not for the want of learning or genius, that the American poets are so little regarded, and that the public quietly endure such contemptuous criticisms of their works. It is because, amidst the mutual clamors of contending parties, not one reader in a thousand cares three cents about the poetical or literary honor of his country.

In the presence of the rising new journalism, "the mutual clamors of contending parties," and the literary grossness of the republican mass, even the Yale poets lost their poise. The college youths who had dreamed over their Vergils of the rising star of a new American literature—epic dreamings, glorious, of the rising young Republic—awoke in anger and answered the ranters in kind. Joseph Dennie, outlining the policy of his Philadelphia *Port Folio* ruled that the only force that could be appreciated by "the ignorant swine of democracy," "the forces of ignorance and delusion," "those now under the democratic dogstar" was "the caustic cayenne of lampoons."

> Let the contemptuous critick shed upon an addled head the bitterest ink of satire, and lampoon into utter oblivion, or expose unto general contempt the miserable trespasser, who has equally offended good Taste by his Fustian, good Sense by his Folly, and good Government by his Faction.[2]

But the thing that, especially in New England, turned literature completely out-of-doors was a new phase of the French Revolution. The new government, extemporized from the ruins of the monarchy, was throwing out Christianity as rubbish and was offering as a substitute a new

[2] *Port Folio*, Oct. 15, 1808.

thing they christened "deism." Most monstrous! The young Virginian, Thomas Jefferson, had been infected, it was believed, while American representative in France, and he was charged now with spreading the contagion. After Paine's *Age of Reason,* New England was in a white funk. Nor was it wholly the ministers who were concerned.

Hopkins and Elihu H. Smith were physicians; Trumbull and Theodore Dwight were lawyers; Richard Alsop was a wealthy merchant; David Humphreys, soldier, diplomat, manufacturer, was one of the wealthiest men of the new Republic; and Joel Barlow, at least in his later years, was a diplomat. But the native New Englander, whatever his profession, is always a preacher, and what are satires but sermons?

The result of it all was that literature everywhere lost itself in a swamp of religious polemic and ranting satire. The Yale poets, led by Dr. Dwight, now president of the college, set out to annihilate "Tom" Paine. No allegory now, no beating about the bush with epic satire. Dwight was fundamentally a theologian, and he *knew* he was right. Like a veritable Thor armed with a hammer, he would fight the advancing forces of "Tom-Paineism" and deism till all the world, especially his Yale students, should see the Truth. His poem, "The Triumph of Infidelity," printed in 1788, was to be no shot in the air. Prefixed was a printed personal letter to Voltaire. This and his homiletic bombshell, "The Nature and Danger of the Infidel Philosophy Exhibited in Two Discourses Addressed to the Candidates for the Baccalaureate in Yale College" (1798), his "The Duty of Americans at the Present Crisis" (1798), his published sermons, especially the five volumes of his *Theology, Explained and Defended* (1718–1719)—173 sermons preached to the Yale students who were forced to take notes—all these he hurled with slaughterous fury into the ranks of atheism, he the Joshua in a new conquest

of Canaan. The poet, placed by all the contemporary critics
and anthologists as the leading American poet, had become
wholly a theologian.

The entire school of the "Connecticut Wits" perished
in the same Serbonian bog. A new nation, a new world, a
new epic making before their eyes, and to voice it only
feeble revampers of the most deplorable area of British
satire—Charles Churchill, "Peter Pindar," the makers of
"The Rolliad." One single meter seemed to cling to American poetry like an epilepsy—the see-saw teeter, the rattling rhymes, and the smart "wise-cracks" of *Hudibras.*
The trail of Butler indeed sprawls over the whole area of
early American verse. One may find it as far back as 1708
in the poem "The Sot-Weed Factor," published in a
volume entitled *The Maryland Muse.* Later times have
never used the measure better. Note a passage like this describing an old Quaker,

> Who neither swore nor kept his Word,
> But cheated in the Fear of God;
> And when his Debts he would not pay,
> By light within he ran away.

Volumes of ranting satire the Connecticut school
emitted before it died. Satire was a variety of preaching.
The Reverend Worthy, in *The Power of Sympathy,* could
recommend it as proper reading even for women. "Satire,"
he ruled, "is the correction of the vices and follies of the
human heart: a woman may therefore read it to advantage."

Thus perished the school of poets who had caught a
vision in their college days of "the Rising Glory of America." They died of satiritis.[3] A dozen volumes they emitted

---

[3] Note a few of the titles: *The Plagi-Scurrilliad,* by Mathew Carey,
1786; *The Albaniad, an Epic Poem,* by "Pilgarlic," 1791; *The
Spunkiad,* by an American Youth, 1798; *The Demos in Council, or
Bijah in Pandemonium,* Anonymous, 1799; *Olio, or Satirical Hodge-
Podge,* Anonymous, 1801; *A Parnassian Shop, opened in Pandaric*

before they died: satires like *The Anarchiad,* work perhaps of the combined Muses of Barlow, Hopkins, Humphreys, and Trumbull; and *The Echo,* parodies, burlesques,
and lampoons published first in the *American Mercury.*
Bitterest of all the group was Dr. Lemuel Hopkins, who
rolled at the same time pills purgative and poems satiric—
The Democratiad in 1795 and *The Guillotina, or a Democratic Dirge* in 1796. Worse than all was the Hudibrastic
hodgepodge, *The Political Greenhouse for the Year 1798,*
the work of Alsop, Hopkins, and Theodore Dwight. The
Connecticut Muse had become ferocious:

> And while a Jacobin remains,
> While Frenchmen live, and Faction reigns,
> Her voice, array'd in awful rhyme
> Shall thunder down the sleep of time.

The "awful rhyme," however, was by no means confined to Connecticut. The budding poetry of the whole
young nation was touched with the "yellows" in its opening decade.

Contemporary critics, especially those in the New England claque, might rate their effusions "among the hap-
piest imitations of Butler" and pronounce their "graver
poetry" to be of permanent value since it was "founded
upon the purest models of the silver age of English
poetry," but nevertheless none of it today emerges from
the anthology graveyards of Kettell and Griswold and
Duyckinck.

Twenty Leading Books of the 1790's

1789 *The Power of Sympathy,* Anonymous. Now attrib-
      uted to William Hill Brown.
1790 *Charlotte Temple,* Susanna Haswell Rowson. Writ-

Style, by Peter Quince, Esq.; *The Hamiltoniad,* by John Williams,
1804; *Fashions Analysis,* by Sir Anthony Avalanche, 1807. For a
fuller list see *The Cambridge History of American Literature,* I,
462ff.

ten and published in England. First American edition, 1793.

1791   *Travels through North Carolina and South Carolina, Georgia, East and West Florida,* William Bartram.

1791   *The Rights of Man,* Part I, Thomas Paine. Part II published the following year.

1792   *The History of New Hampshire,* Jeremy Belknap. Vol. I, 1784.

1792   *Modern Chivalry,* first version, H. H. Brackenridge. Later additions and revisions in 1793, 1797, 1804, 1805.

1792   *The Conspiracy of Kings,* Joel Barlow.

1792   *The Foresters, an American Tale,* Jeremy Belknap.

1792   *Miscellaneous Essays and Occasional Writings,* three volumes, Francis Hopkinson.

1794   *American Biography,* Vol. I, Jeremy Belknap, editor.

1794   *Edwin and Angelina; or, the Bandit,* Elihu H. Smith. Opera performed; printed in 1797.

1794   *Greenfield Hill,* Timothy Dwight.

1794   *The Fatal Deception,* William Dunlap. Acted; written in 1790; acted again as *Leicester, a Tragedy,* 1806.

1795   *The Age of Reason,* Thomas Paine.

1795   *Poems Written between the Years 1768–1794,* Philip Freneau.

1796   *Hasty Pudding,* Joel Barlow.

1796   *The Lay Preacher,* Joseph Dennie.

1798   *Alcuin; a Dialogue on the Rights of Women,* Charles Brockden Brown.

1798   *Wieland,* C. B. Brown.

1798   *Reuben and Rachel,* Susanna Haswell Rowson.

CHAPTER VI

THE FIGHT FOR THE NOVEL

THE NOVEL in America is as old as the Republic—not a trace of it before 1789. England in half a century had produced school after school of novelists—Richardson, Fielding, Smollett, Fanny Burney—but no response in the Western colonies. Prose fiction in the Northern area was classed with the theater and card-playing and dancing. The South was more tolerant. Even before the Revolution the importation there of novels and romances *à la mode* surpassed in quantity everything save Bibles and religious commentaries. Judging from book-store records, Williamsburg and Charleston and other centers were aware early of the best-sellers in the English market such as Longsword's *Crysal, or the Adventures of a Guinea,* Hawksworth's *Almaran and Hammet,* and the many oriental tales freely current like *Solomon and Almeda,* and *Theodorus and Constantia.* All of these were read alike by men and women. Of Richardson, however, little trace: the South preferred Fielding and Sterne.

In New York conditions were much the same. Prejudice, if any existed, was unorganized. The majority in the swiftly growing metropolis read not at all; the others, as in the South, followed the English fashions. In Philadelphia and Boston, however, prejudice had hardened into a convention. The era of moral solicitude was at its high noon. The clergy in command sent novel-readers to hell. Nevertheless, English fiction found its way even into Puritan Boston. Novels were "bootlegged in" with every importation of books, and read, especially by literary-

minded "females," in fearful secrecy even as boys in the
1860's read dime novels.

The works of Richardson seem to have been neutral
ground. They were classified not as novels, but as books
of moral instruction. Even the clergy read them. Jonathan
Edwards read *Sir Charles Grandison* and considered his
time well-spent. Philadelphia discovered Richardson early.
Four years after *Pamela* had left its author's pen, Franklin
issued an edition, the first novel published in America.[1]
Only five other American reprintings of English fiction before the Revolution: *Robinson Crusoe* (1768), *Rasselas*
(1768), *The Vicar of Wakefield* (1772), *Juliet Grenville*
(1774), and Sterne's works (1774).

Fiction like this could be tolerated even by Dr. Dwight,
who had ruled in high-priestly tones that "between the
Bible and novels there is a great gulf fixed." "Novels" to
him, and to the clergy generally, meant the current best-
sellers of London, the fads of the moment that deluged
the book-stalls and overflowed even into Boston and Hartford; the oriental romances and the Gothic romances and
later the love novels of the feminine "school."

Best-sellers beget best-sellers always in increasing ratio.
To read current fiction is to be inspired sooner or later to
write current fiction. The first symptoms in America of
the infection, soon to become an epidemic, one finds in the
magazines which sprang up so thickly after the clearing
away of the Revolutionary battle-smoke. Carey's *Columbian Magazine* (1786–1792) had fiction in every number,
much of it of native origin. Always anonymous, always
sensationally moral, tale after tale with such titles as "The
Dangers of Sporting with Innocent Credulity; Exemplified in the History of Miss Harriot Aspin." There was even
one short novel, "Amelia, or the Faithless Briton; An
Original Novel Founded on Recent Facts" (1798), the
parent, perhaps, of the coming *Charlotte Temple*. In all

[1] Such satirical analogues or allegories as Hopkinson's *The Old
Farm and the New* are in reality not novels.

of the tales the assertion that the tale was founded on
actuality—a sop to the current criticism that fiction is but
a mass of lies—and always the moral purpose of the story
standing out like a preacher's text.

I

The first native novel to be issued in book form came
from the press of Isaiah Thomas of Boston in 1789—
*The Power of Sympathy: or, the Triumph of Nature;
Founded in Truth; In Two Volumes.* In 1878 (I know of
no earlier reference) F. S. Drake, in his *The Town of
Roxbury,* assigned the authorship of the novel to Sarah
Wentworth Morton, wife of Perez Morton, known to her
generation as "Philenia," Della Cruscan poet, and until
recently classed generally as America's first novelist. It
is now maintained that the author was William Hill
Brown, a neighbor of the Mortons, a young literary
enthusiast who, despite the fact that "during his short life
from 1765 to 1793 he turned out at least one other novel,
two plays, and a considerable number of poems, essays,
and sentimental tales," [2] has disappeared completely.

Aware of the fact that Boston would tolerate no fiction
that was not the record of actual happenings and not the
embodiment of moral teachings, he set out, it would seem,
to record a happening in his own neighborhood.

The husband of "Philenia," Perez Morton, grandson of
Jonathan Edwards, had had, it seems, Lovelace adventures. His wife's younger sister, Miss Frances Theodore
Apthorp, had come to live in the family, had been taken
advantage of by Morton, and, after the birth of a child,
had committed suicide. An investigation made by the city
officials, however, had pronounced Morton innocent of any

[2] Emily Pendleton and Milton Ellis, *Philenia, the Life and Works
of Sarah Wentworth Morton* (University of Maine Studies, 1931).
Milton Ellis, "The Authorship of the First American Novel," *American Literature,* January, 1933.

crime, and the scandal had been hushed up with alacrity. Perez Morton was an important man in the city. Then had come the novel, which seemingly was written by one with intimate knowledge of the tragedy. Instantly the book was suppressed to the point almost of complete extermination, and in all probability it was done by the family.[3] That Mrs. Morton, who in the face of all the evidence sided with her husband, could have written the book is highly improbable.

Most skilfully was the novel rigged for the shallows it was bound to encounter. The first safeguard was in the title: *Founded in Truth*. Turning the leaf, the reader is confronted with a dedication that would have disarmed even Cotton Mather. Eleven varieties of type there are in the amazing thing:

To the young ladies of United Columbia, these volumes, intended to represent specious Causes, and to Expose the fatal Consequences of

SEDUCTION;

To inspire the Female Mind with a principle of Self Complacency and to Promote the Economy of Human Life, Are Inscribed, With Esteem and Sincerity, By their Friend and Humble Servant, The Author, Boston, Jan. 1789.

Still more completely, as the tale proceeds, is the reader disarmed by warning after warning against the fiction that was being so freely imported from England for the use of the ladies. "Novels," says the leading character, "not regulated on the chaste principles of friendship, rational love, and connubial duty, appear to me totally unfit to form the minds of women, of friends, of wives."

Having prepared this elaborate camouflage, the author proceeds to tell what in modern terms would be called a

---

[3] "This work created quite a sensation and was suppressed by interested parties."—J. Sabin, XV, 377.

sex story. The book was aimed at the fearful eighteenth-century sin of SEDUCTION, but a seduction must be preceded by a wooing, feigned perhaps on the part of the Lovelace of the tale, but genuine always on the part of the radiantly beautiful young victim. And what is a tale of wooing but a love story? No elements are wanting. Sensation in abundance: at the end three women dead from SEDUCTION, the heroine in her death agony preaching a sermon in rounded eighteenth-century periods most eloquent:

O SEDUCTION! how many and how miserable are the victims of thy unrelenting vengeance! Some crimes indeed cease to afflict, when they cease to exist, but SEDUCTION opens the door to a dismal train of innumerable miseries.

What an awful thing must be LOVE! Starved colonial maidens, totally unacquainted with life and with love, drenched such novels with tears, and as the richly deserved fate of the Lovelace villain was seen approaching, they shuddered in delicious terror. In *The Power of Sympathy* the seducer is compelled to make a Dantesque descent into hell, and in the lowest pit of all is made to look upon a boiling mass of beings writhing in sulphurous agony. "Quivering with horror, I inquired who they were. 'These,' answered my guide, 'are the miserable race of SEDUC-ERS. Even the damned look on them with horrour.'" Thereupon the young novelist breaks out into five pages of most damnable verse describing the Court of Vice, with all the Vices hushed and abashed when SEDUCTION enters the circle. But not even yet is the author satisfied. He must present as a tailpiece a picture of poor Harriet's gravestone with long lacrimose inscription in still more damnable verse.

Typical of a whole school that was to follow. Its sentimentality, its Della Cruscan floridity of style, its total absence of actuality and verisimilitude make it everything a novel should not be. It may be classed as American humor today, so extreme is it in its overdoneness, yet there is in it all an element of pathos: a novel having to disguise itself in this tawdry stuff in order to gain even the privilege of publication. It explains the general feebleness of American fiction for a century, especially in the New England area. The novel was forced to come into our literature, when it did come, by stealth and subterfuge. It crept in disguised as history, like the novels of Cooper and Simms; as sermonic illustrations, like the tales of Hawthorne; as humanistic propaganda, like *Uncle Tom's Cabin*. It slipped in around the pulpit, like Judd's *Margaret* and Ware's *Aurelian,* and through the doctor's office, like Holmes's *Elsie Venner*.

II

The second episode in the history of American fiction also demands more space than the quality of the work deserves. Like *The Power of Sympathy,* it is an early symptom of a disease that was soon to be epidemic. The fact that three generations of readers have made of *Charlotte Temple* a best-seller—the most sensational bestseller, perhaps, before *Uncle Tom's Cabin*—compels an unpleasant thesis: the subliterary nine-tenths has from the first compelled the current of our American fiction.

The arrival in 1793 of the young English novelist, Susanna Haswell Rowson, was perhaps the most significant literary event of the pregnant 1790's. She had come with an English reputation. She was an important member of the feminine group that in England was making colorful the fiction of the closing century. Already her list of novels numbered among them the best-seller of her generation, even in England, where its popularity is partly to be accounted for by the fact that its heroine and victim was supposed to be a well-known member of the British nobility. "It is said," observes her biographer, Elias Mason, "that the monumental tablet in Trinity Churchyard, New York, originally bore the quarterings of the noble house of Derby, and that the name of Charlotte Temple has been substituted for that of Charlotte Stanley."

The story of the author's own life, too, had appealed to the British reader. Born in America, the daughter of an English naval officer stationed in the colonies, she had suffered as a prisoner of war and finally had reached England in utter poverty. Fortune, however, had favored her. She had found employment in a family of the nobility where she soon attracted the attention of notable personages, notably the Duchess of Devonshire and the Prince of Wales. Like Fanny Burney, she made use of her experiences, recording them faithfully, and, patronized by the Duchess and her friends, embodied them in a fiction which she entitled *Victoria, a Novel; The Characters taken from Real Life, and calculated to improve the morals of the female sex by impressing them with a just sense of the merits of female piety* (1786). As with Miss Burney's novels, it was felt by the general reader that a glimpse was being afforded at life below stairs by one within the secret environs of nobility and perhaps even royalty.

But Mrs. Rowson, despite her eight novels and despite the fame of her *Charlotte*, had not come to America as a novelist. She had married a trumpeter in the Royal Horse Guards, a picturesque personage whom manager Wignell, in England for "talent," had signed up for his Chestnut Street Theater. And his wife he had also engaged, but as an actress. Again she achieved fame. For four years she took leading parts at Annapolis, at Philadelphia, at Baltimore, and at Boston. Four plays she also wrote, some of them successful on the stage. Then at Boston another transformation. Abandoning the stage, she served for forty years as preceptress of fashionable schools in the city, providing all of them with text-books and feminine reading matter of highest morality. Two or three more novels she also wrote, all of them pietistic in tone, one of them recounting the adventures of her own early creation, Charlotte Temple.

Worthless stuff for the most part, twenty volumes of it in all, and all twenty would have been forgotten a century ago, and its author along with it, but for one single fact: one of the books was *Charlotte Temple*. Its popularity had begun in England. Then Carey republished it in Philadelphia with the title *Charlotte*.[4] Then edition had followed edition. The thing had become a best-seller with amazing popularity. According to her biographer, "Twenty-five thousand copies were sold in a few years after its first publication"—a figure quite remarkable considering the size of the American reading public at the time. A passage in *The Personal Memoirs of Joseph T. Buckingham* declares that this bit of fiction "over which thousands have sighed and wept, and sighed again . . . had the most extensive sale of any work of the kind that had been published in this country." "Editions almost innumerable have appeared," her biographer Nason wrote in 1870, "both in England and America. During the first quarter of the present century this little book distanced in popular favor, Horace Walpole's *The Castle of Otranto;* Henry Mackenzie's *Man of Feeling,* Ann Radcliffe's *Romance of the Forest,* published in 1791; Regina Maria Roch's *Children of the Abbey;* Frances Burney's celebrated *Evelina;* and every other competitor in the field."

Unquestionably the sales of the book have gone into figures sensational. It became, declares Sabin, "the most popular romance of its generation." Francis W. Halsey, who edited the work in 1905, correcting, according to his count, 1,256 errors which had crept into the text, listed 104 editions issued during a century, "with many editions

[4] *"Charlotte. A Tale of Truth,* by Mrs. Rowson of the New Theatre, Philadelphia. Author of *Victoria, The Inquisitor, Fille de Chambre,* &c. In 2 Volumes. Philadelphia. Printed by D. Humphreys for M. Carey. No. 118, Market Street, 1794."

still missing." Its own generation received it without criticism, praised it indeed for its "Truth" and its morals—all save Peter Porcupine, who, in a pamphlet entitled "A Kick for a Bite," accused the gentle author of coloring her facts to fit her fiction, of "insincerity," as he expressed it. But the last word was the woman's: "The literary world" she wrote in her next introduction, "is infested with a kind of loathsome reptile. One of them lately crawled over the volumes which I have had the temerity to submit to the public eye."

How explain these 104 and more editions of a book in most respects so feeble, this popularity that has lasted even to our own day, for the book has never been out of print since the London first edition? To answer is to frame an indictment of the great mass of the American people for four generations. It was the first American best-seller, the first volume pitched precisely to the note demanded by the unlettered mass. It is emotional, it is sentimental, it has a skilfully camouflaged sex *motif* and it seems to admit its reader into the love secrets of the nobility, and, like Richardson's fictions, it skilfully leads the inexperienced reader to identify himself with the persecuted heroine. Verisimilitude it has, undoubtedly, but the Truth it so loudly proclaimed as its chief merit most certainly is not in it. From Richardson she had caught the trick of the detailed catalogue method, the seeming realism of enumerated details until the reader unconsciously has surrendered to be led whither the novelist may desire. But read with critical eye, the characters are seen to be mere lay-figures in costume, the dialogue impossible to the bounds of the ludicrous, the style inflated with elaborate circumlocutions and rounded periods of "elegant" writing. Everywhere the mawkishly melodramatic: maidens dying of "Seduction" soar into flamboyant rhetoric, and the villain is unrelieved in his utter blackness. And the reader is made to feel that the dose has been good for him: the *motif* of it all is primarily sermonic.

But even Mrs. Rowson cannot be dismissed with un-
mixed criticism. In more fields than one she was a noteworthy pioneer. She was the first prominent writer to
bring to the reading public the American Revolution as
a literary background, and she was a pioneer in the use
of the American Indian as the subject for fiction. She was
a realist, too, in many of her chapters. She was one of the
earliest of our dramatists. And she wrote a national anthem, "America, Commerce and Freedom," that is superior
in literary merit to Hopkinson's "Hail Columbia" of a
later day. Her novel *Reuben and Rachel* is better work
than many of Cooper's romances dealing with Indian life.

III

The influence of the volume was immediate. The ladies
had discovered a secret: this "tale of Truth" with its
moralistic *motif* was fiction that could pass even the religious censorship. Feminine novels, therefore, published
for the most part by subscription, began to increase rapidly
in numbers and to be imported without fear of criticism.
Royall Tyler, in the introduction to his *Algerine Captive*
(1797), declared—speaking from the standpoint of his
fictitious hero—that his first observation upon returning
from abroad after an absence of seven years "was the
extreme avidity with which books of mere amusement
were purchased and perused by his countrymen." The land
was filled, he declared, with "modern travels and novels almost as incredible." The era of feminine fiction had begun.

From a literary standpoint, the best of the seduction
novels was *The Coquette: or, the History of Eliza
Wharton, A Novel Founded on Fact* (1797), by a lady
of Massachusetts, Hannah Foster. According to the bibli-
ographer Oscar Wegelin, the thirtieth edition of the novel
was published in Boston in 1833.[5] Its great popularity has
come perhaps from the fact that it is a novelization of the

[5] *Early American Fiction* (1902), p. 14.

tragedy of Sarah Whitman and Pierpont Edwards, son of
Jonathan Edwards. One finds in the novel unexpected ex-
cellences. It is a study of a crime in *The Ring and the Book*
manner: the story from three different standpoints. The
principal characters each write explanations of the matter
in revealing letters. First we have the seducer's version:
"I fancy this young lady is a coquette; and if so I shall
avenge my sex by retaliating the mischiefs she meditates
against me. . . . I have never yet been defeated. If a lady
will consent to enter the lists against the antagonist of her
honor, she may be sure of losing the prize." Then we have
the viewpoint of the friend in letter after letter uttering all
the warning she knows, painting seduction in blackest dyes.
Then the amorous flitterings of the enamoured "coquette"
(in modern times, "flapper") drawing nearer and nearer
the fatal web. Then her final cry: "May my unhappy story
serve as a beacon to warn the American fair of the dangerous tendency . . . of men." Redolent the book with
eighteenth-century ethics. When the seducer has ruined
the girl, he has a moment of remorse and even a thought
of marrying her, but then to him comes this bit of Chesterfieldian logic: "I confess the idea of being thus connected
with a woman whom I have been able to dishonor would
be rather hard to surmount. It would hurt even my delicacy to have a wife whom I know to be seducible." And
this even though she was greatly his superior in family and
accomplishments.

Seduction became a theme even more popular than the
Mrs. Radcliffe horror *motif*. One could hardly open a
magazine without finding a seduction tale, always
"founded on the truth."

IV

Soon the novel became the only reading matter in the
hands of the women, and pulpit and press and rostrum
awoke in consternation. A Boston *Anthology* reviewer of

The Gamesters, or Ruins of Innocence (1805), by Caroline Matilda Warren, burst out in Puritan wrath. The novel, he declared, was a feeble specimen "of the vermin infecting the ladies of the time." Dennie, in his *Port Folio,* declared that American literature had had poured upon it "a veritable influx of feebleness,—these Angelinas and Celestinas who have exchanged a washing-tub for a writing desk. . . . Novels are flowing," he declared,"*a fluminibus stultitiae* into the *oceanum oblivionis,* sometimes so thick and fast as to threaten taste and her temples with a deluge, and actually have polluted a few of her fountains, and thrown down some monuments in their course." He could praise, however, the feminine school of Great Britain, the literary women who were painting in ocher and vermilion the *fin de siècle* sunset— Madame D'Arblay, Mrs. Radcliffe, Mrs. Hamilton, Charlotte Smith, Hannah More, Maria Edgeworth—but he was positive that

Nothing in the shape of these *all accomplished* females has yet appeared in America; and we hazard nothing in predicting that one thousand years in the chronology of this new country will probably roll away prior to the appearance of even the outline, the shadow, the semblance of such a character.

Mrs. Bloomsgrove, in the *Memoirs of the Bloomsburg Family* (1791), not a novel at all but an educational treatise, declared that "nothing can have a worse effect on the mind of our sex than the free use of those writings which are the offspring of modern novelists."

As the new century grew into its second decade, the pounding of pulpits and rostrum-desks became thunderous. The Reverend James Gray, addressing the graduates of the Young Ladies' Academy, Philadelphia, used his whole hour upon this single subject. Novels, he thundered,

are a species of artificial stimulant, . . . chamber cordials not conducive to the health of our minds . . . especially when taken during the vernal equinox of our existence when the sun is passing the line which separates childhood from maturity.

The battle entered even the universities. Samuel P. Jarvis, in his Phi Beta Kappa address delivered at Yale in 1806, went into superlatives:

The taste for novels and all other kinds of light reading has arisen to an astounding and alarming height. Like the lean kines of Pharaoh, they have swallowed up all other reading, and like them too, they have not looked the better for it. The evil consequences attendant upon novel reading are much greater than has generally been imagined.

One whole novel was written with no other purpose than to make ridiculous the romances of the time, Mrs. Tabitha Tenney's *Female Quixotism: Exhibited in the Romantic Opinions and Extravagant Adventures of Dorcasina Sheldon* (1803), dedicated "to all Columbian Young Ladies Who read Novels & Romances." "The ladies of late," she says in her preface, "seem almost to have appropriated this department of writing." Life was being misrepresented and romanticized, she believed, in a body of trash that was like the romances of chivalry read so abundantly by Don Quixote. She would take for her heroine a grotesquely plain country girl, saturate her with the current tales of romance, make her change her name from Dorcas to Dorcasina, add as a helper and Sancho Panza an ignorant country girl, and send her out in quest of amorous adventures. "A true uncolored history" it was to be, according to its author's explanation, and she was writing the tale for no other purpose than "That, by observing their [romances'] baneful effects on Miss Sheldon, who was in every other respect a sensible, judicious, and amiable girl, you may avoid the disgraces and disasters that so long rendered her despicable and miserable."

A hodgepodge of adventure follows. Built after the *Don Quixote* model, the novel cries aloud for humor, cries aloud for realistic treatment of the Sancho Panza character, Betty, for fights ferocious that will stir the reader to sympathy; but none are vouchsafed by the gentle novelist. The *motif* borrowed from Mrs. Lennox, who years before had written *The Female Quixote, or the Adventures of Arabella,* is excellent, but nothing else.

v

Satire and sermon accomplished nothing. Charles Sprague, in his Phi Beta Kappa poem, "Curiosity," delivered at Harvard in 1829, might picture in lurid colors feminine America bedrugged by "The damned henbane of Radcliffe and Chapone," but the magic jar had been opened.

Despite the general prejudice against feminine higher education, women more and more were leading the men in culture and in literary creation. Much better were they educated than any similar class of women in England. They had more leisure than the men, more opportunity for writing, more knowledge of what the reading public demanded. The Old Testament idea of the proper sphere of women was rapidly passing. Schools for daughters were being established. As early as 1770 John Trumbull had prophesied that intellectual women were to be among the glories of the Golden Age which he believed was soon to come:

> Her Daughters too the happy land shall grace
> With powers of genius, as with charms of face;
> Blest with the softness of the female mind,
> With fancy blooming and with taste refined,
> Some Rowe shall rise, and wrest with daring pen
> The pride of science from assuming men;
> While each bright line a polish'd beauty wears,
> For every muse and every grace are theirs.

But the severest strictures came from Boston. The *Monthly Anthology,* reviewing *The Gamesters; or Ruins*

of Innocence; An Original Novel Founded in Truth
(1805), by Caroline Matilda Warren of Boston, went to
the extremes of Peter Porcupine:

Among the ephemerae of this species that continually flit
from the press and expire, this is unquestionably the most
puny. It appears to have been conceived by an intellect in a
state of stagnation. . . . The avidity with which it was run
after by the town the moment it was hatched reminded us of
Sir Joseph Banks in the pursuit of a butterfly. . . . In what
way the ladies have been infected by this vermin we confess
ourselves unable to determine, for it appears on examination
not only too inanimate to buzz but too insignificant to sting.
. . . As we experience no particular exultation in swinging
a club to dislocate a flea, we resign this minimus—to be em-
paled on a pin for the scrutiny of the curious.

And again, reviewing *Emily Hamilton, a novel Founded
on Incidents in Real Life By a Young Lady of Worcester County:*

We do not recollect any American female, except
Mrs. Rowson, who has written a novel which can be read
with any pleasure; and we are not disposed to encourage the
exertions of females to become known as authors, unless
convinced that the amusement and instruction which they
can furnish will extend beyond the circle of their own partial
friends.

Not until 1830 was America ready for a *Godey's Lady's
Book.*

CHAPTER VII

CHARLES BROCKDEN BROWN

THE 1790's midway: America lay in sections, each self-contained, each in feeling and ideals independent. In the North, New England—intellectual, aristocratic, fearful of the democratic mass, its poets soured into political satirists. In the midlands, Philadelphia and New York—Philadelphia run to a thistle-crop of political newspapers, literature of democracy; New York, cosmopolitan, commercial, tolerant, irreligious. Below them the solitary South. Each lacked elements possessed by the others, but of exchange almost nothing.

To coalesce units so diverse was to be a work not of decades, but of centuries. Even in the 1790's, however, the blending was to begin. In literature the earliest flux—catalytic agent—was a young poet, youngest member of the Connecticut school, Elihu Hubbard Smith,[1] born in 1771, the same year as Charles Brockden Brown. Yale, of course, Timothy Dwight instructor and model, and poetry dreamed of as a life-work. At fifteen he had earned his first degree. A graduate year with the old college president–poet, and he, even as in earlier times Trumbull and Barlow, was writing classic imitations and lyrics. And the culmination was—an opera (strange product for a "Hartford Wit") : *Edwin and Angelina, or, The Banditti,* finally in print in 1797.

But the choice of profession was not in the boy's hands. He was to be a physician, and no sooner had he entered upon his studies than he discovered his peculiar aptitude

---

[1] See Marian Edgerton Bailey, *A Lesser Hartford Wit, Dr. Elihu H. Smith* (University of Maine Studies, 2d series, 1928).

for the work. He finished his course with brilliance and at once was sent to Philadelphia for graduate work in the university medical department. A "Connecticut Wit" in Old Philadelphia: there were surprising results. He brought new life into the exclusive literary club of the city and he made a friendship that was to be a noteworthy event in the history of American literature: Charles Brockden Brown, a brooding, solitary soul, a genius who had not found himself. From the first, the two were joined by a strange affinity. Both at this early stage of their lives were poets. Smith, under the pseudonym of "Ella," poured out verse lyric and dramatic: Brown, judging from his "Devotion; an Epistle," a poem of 536 lines first printed in the *American Register,* Volume III, was lyric, intense, unfettered by models.[2]

Brown was completely a Philadelphian—old Quaker stock, mystical of soul, noncombative, introspective. In Quaker fashion, when adolescence had set his blood on fire, he had turned rebel and for a moment was possessed by French deism, by Godwinism with its Wollstonecraft corollary of women's rights, by Utopianism extreme even in that golden age of American Utopian dreams. Another shaping element had been his frail physical endowment. Never had he been a boy among boys: he had been a wanderer by himself, a porer over books. For a time he studied Greek and Latin in a select Quaker school, but in reality he was self-educated, his reading running into strange areas. Poetry had possessed his imagination. "At the age of sixteen," records his biographer, William Dunlap, "he sketched plans of three distinct epic poems, one on the discovery of America, another on Pizarro's conquest of Peru, and a third on Cortez's expedition to Mexico. With these he was much engrossed, and for some time thought life only desirable as a means for their accomplishment."

[2] For extracts from this poem see *Wieland,* edited by Fred Lewis Pattee, p. xv.

But as in the case of young Smith, the counsel of the
home had been Franklinian. He must have a profession.
Accordingly he began to study the law, but literature still
held him fast. "He studied," said Dunlap, "with assiduity,
the writings of the best English authors." And soon he
found himself the center of a group of young students as
eager for culture as he. A club, of course, had to come—
"The Belles Lettres" club with nine members—for was this
not America? And prose essays were written, not briefs.

More and more he found the law disgusting, and at
last he refused to continue his studies. Then, according to
Dunlap, "Dissatisfied with himself and with the most
gloomy prospects of the future scenes destined for his lot
in life, Charles, as if to avoid the presence of his disappointed friends, rambled from home without any apparently defined object." According to a tradition hard to
verify, he wandered into the mountains of Pennsylvania
where he gathered materials that were to enter his later
fiction. At this critical moment had come the advent of
Dr. Elihu Smith and the friendship that was to turn into
new channels the current of his life.

With the departure of Smith from Philadelphia, there
followed a period in Brown's life impossible to reconstruct with any certainty. Smith finished his medical
studies at Philadelphia in June, 1791, and for two years
practiced his profession in Connecticut, perhaps at Litchfield.[3] There is a tradition that Brown visited him at Litchfield and that while in Connecticut he met Dr. Dwight and
others of the Yale group of poets.

C. W. Everest, author of *The Poets of Connecticut*
(1843), adds this fact:

In 1793, appeared from the Litchfield press, "American
Poems, Selected and Original," edited by Dr. Smith. . . .
It was the first general collection of poetry ever attempted

---

[3] According to C. W. Everest, Dr. Smith had settled in Wethers-
field, Connecticut, near Hartford. Smith's native town was Litchfield.

in the country, and the literature of that day is indebted to its editor for the preservation of many interesting effusions which otherwise would doubtless have been lost.

Never project more ambitious. With a list of subscribers not exceeding two hundred and fifty, he projected a series of best-poems-of-the-year volumes to extend indefinitely:

To bring together, in one view, the several poetical productions of the different States. By this means a more certain estimation can be made of the comparative merit of their various writers; a more thorough acquaintance may be obtained of the state of belles-lettres in the individual parts of the Union; and hereby will be promoted a more intimate combination of literary interests.

An honest attempt undoubtedly, notwithstanding the fact that the young Connecticut anthologist gave just half of his space to the "Hartford Wits," twenty-two pages to Governor Livingstone of New Jersey, a scanty bit of space to Hopkinson and Freneau representing Philadelphia, and that he was content to leave Boston represented by "Philenia" and "Allen." No specimens from the South.

Volume II never appeared.[4] The young doctor was a century ahead of his time. The public was not ready to contemplate its poetry—at least not for a price.

Then had come the third period in the literary life of the two—Dr. Smith's removal to New York City for the practice of his profession, Brown's visits to the city where he made the acquaintance of Dunlap with whom he lived for months, and his final removal to the city to share the rooms of Smith.

[4] That this was not the first collection I have elsewhere shown. The editorship of Smith has never been fully proved. In the "Postscript" to the preface of the volume, a second volume was promised "in the course of the next two years," but "Many disappointments, the ill health of one of the Editors, and other circumstances, too complicated and painful to mention, have contributed to render their part of the work less perfect than their expectations and promises." Possibly the sick man may have been Brown.

From 1797 to 1801 Brown lived in New York City and, with Smith and Dunlap, was associated constantly with the best literary society afforded by the metropolis. With Smith as nucleus, there began a literary club—The Friendly Club—a group that in the free atmosphere of New York could discuss without prejudice literary and political conditions in England and in France. Dunlap and Smith were enamoured of the drama. Smith, to whom literature meant only poetry, wrote at least one poetic prologue to be recited at a notable presentation. To share in the young doctor's enthusiasms, members of the Connecticut school of poets, notably Alsop and Hopkins, visited the city and even attended meetings of the Friendly Club. It made for the enlightenment of both sections.

For Brown, however, the drama was not a compelling literary form. He had discovered Godwin's *Caleb Williams*—humanitarianism, philosophy, romance—and eagerly he sought to create after the same pattern. Small success at first: "When I revolve the transcendent merits of *Caleb Williams,* my pleasure is diminished." But furiously he worked on. He would write a novel, its name *Sky-Walk or the Man Unknown to Himself*—a Hawthorne touch, surely. The prospectus of it, issued March 17, 1798, set forth the principles that were to animate not only his forthcoming novel but all his later work:

To the story-telling moralist the United States is a new and un-trodden field. He who shall examine objects with his own eyes, who shall employ the European models merely for the improvement of his taste, and adapt his fiction to all that is genuine and peculiar in the scene before him, will be entitled at least to the praise of originality. . . . He, therefore, who paints, not from books, but from nature, who introduces those lines and hues in which we differ, rather than those in which we resemble our kindred nations beyond the ocean,

may lay some claim to the patronage of his countrymen. The
value of such works lies without doubt in their moral tendency.
The popular tales have their merit, but there is one thing in
which they are deficient. They are generally adapted to one
class of readers only. . . . The world is governed, not by the
simpleton, but by the men of soaring passions and intellectual
energy. By the display of such only can we hope to enchain
the attention and ravish the souls of those who study and reflect. . . . To gain their homage it is not needful to forego
the approbation of those whose circumstances hindered them
from making the same progress. A contexture of facts capable of suspending the faculties of every soul in curosity may
be joined with depth of views into human nature and all the
subtleties of reasoning.

The novel never was published: the manuscript is
thought to have been destroyed with the effects of the publisher, who died of the yellow fever. We know only the
title, but even this is illuminating. His subtitle, "An
American Tale," his employment of European models
"merely for the improvement of his taste," his striving for
originality, his American setting, his title, " 'Sky-Walk,'
a popular corruption of Ski-Wakkee, or Big Spring, the
name given by the Lenni Lennaffee or Delaware Indians
to the district where the principal scenes of this novel are
transacted"—all this is significant. His "The Man Unknown to Himself" is pure Hawthorne ten years before
Hawthorne was born.

The loss of the novel troubled him not at all. He was
off on another and more ambitious venture. By September
5th he could write to Dunlap, "This afternoon I revised
the last sheet of *Wieland*. It will form a handsome volume
of three hundred pages."

But tragedy was upon him. Before the book was off the
press, malignant yellow fever had broken out in New
York, and a reign of terror such as he later described in
Ormond and *Arthur Mervyn* took possession of the city.
Dr. Smith joined the medical forces fighting the disease

and himself fell a victim. Brown, whose room he shared, refused to leave him, and after the doctor had died was himself stricken, though not with the malignant form of the disease.

By late autumn he was again at work, however, with redoubled energy. In the *Weekly Magazine* appeared the first instalment of *Arthur Mervyn,* a romance centering about the Philadelphia epidemic of 1793 which he himself had witnessed. Soon another novel, *Ormond,* was racing with the press. Hardly was it finished when he was rushing pell-mell into a widely different literary venture. To his brother he wrote in mid-December, 1798: "Proposals have been issued here for the publication of a Monthly Magazine, of which I am to be the editor, and whose profits are to belong to me. The uncommon zeal of my friends here promises success to this project. If it answers expectation, it will commence in February or March."

It was April 1, 1799, before the new periodical appeared, the *Monthly Magazine and American Review,* a work that kept even Brown's headlong pen going at top speed during the next year and a half. Fiction seemed for a time to obsess the man. At one period—1798–1799— he had in progress as many as five uncompleted novels. In the first number of the *Monthly* appeared a fragment entitled *Edgar Huntly*—that part (chapters 16 to 19 inclusive) which deals with Indian adventure.

That he had added a new *motif* and a new background for American fiction Brown seems to have been aware. In an editorial note in the magazine he says:

The following narrative is extracted from the memoirs of a young man who resided some years since on the upper branches of the Delaware. These memoirs will shortly be published. . . . Similar events have frequently happened on the Indian borders; but, perhaps, they were never before described with equal minuteness. As to the truth of these incidents, men acquainted with the perils of an Indian war must be allowed to judge. Those who have ranged along the foot of the Blue-Ridge from the Wind-Gap to the Water-Gap will see the exactness of the local descriptions. It may also be mentioned that "Old Deb" is a portrait faithfully drawn from nature.

In the thin atmosphere of New York he struggled on with his magazine for a year and a half; then in December, 1800, appeared his valedictory. He had begun the magazine, he declared, when no similar publication was known to exist in the United States. But the "apathy and disregard to literature and science" had rendered the continuance of the work impossible.

The thin population of the United States renders it impossible to procure sufficient support from any one city, and the dispersed situation of readers, the embarrassments attending the diffusion of copies over a wide extent of country, and the obstacles of a prompt collection of the small sums which so cheap a publication demanded had been fatal to the work.

III

In the third period of Brown's life—at home now in Philadelphia—he was a magazine editor, an editorial writer, and a critic. No more poetry and, with the exception of two short left-over pieces of inferior merit, no more novels. The atmosphere of his native city seemed not favorable to novels. They brought, moreover, no money. He missed, too, the inspiration which had come from Dr. Smith and Dunlap. "From the regions of poetry and romance," records Dunlap, "from visionary schemes of Utopian systems of government and manners, Mr. Brown, like many others, became a sober recorder of things as they are." The novelist died with the eighteenth century.

From its morning of gloom, Brown's life was now turning toward a noon of exceptional happiness. He had married the brilliant sister of John Blair Linn, the

poet; there were children in his home; his fame as a
writer was gradually increasing. But his health, always
precarious, now took an alarming turn. Tuberculosis had
fastened upon him, and quickly it had turned into a "galloping consumption." He died February 19, 1810, aged
thirty-nine years.

Brown was our first national man of letters, the first
writer of note not narrowly bound to a provincial area,
the first all his life to pursue literature as a profession.
Under the leadership of Smith he came into intimate
knowledge of three widely differing literary provinces in
the Republic. He had felt the quality of New England, its
prejudices and its classicism; he had lived for four headlong years in the creative atmosphere of New York, where
fiction was not proscribed; and finally he had gone home
to Philadelphia with its magazines and its criticism.

Forever must he rank as our first novelist and, along
with his contemporary in Philadelphia, Joseph Dennie,
as our first literary critic. He was the first American
writer, too, to exert an influence upon European writers.
To quote Thomas Wentworth Higginson, books published
between 1798 and 1801 made their way across the ocean
with a promptness that now seems inexplicable; and
Mrs. Shelley, in her novel, *The Last Man,* founds her
description of an epidemic on "the masterly delineations
of the author of *Arthur Mervyn.*" Shelley himself recognized his obligations to Brown; and it is to be remembered
that Brown himself was evidently familiar with Godwin's
philosophical writings, and that he may have drawn from
those of Mary Wollstonecraft his advanced views as to
the rights and education of women, a subject on which his
first book, *Alcuin,* provided the earliest American protest.

Time has decreed that he is to be considered only as a
novelist, as the author of four romances, *Wieland, Arthur
Mervyn, Ormond,* and *Edgar Huntly,* written, all of them,
in creative excitement when he had suddenly found himself translated from the solemn Quaker level of his native

city into the vast freedom of New York. They are improvisations, and youth is written on their every page.
Fatally easy is it to criticize them. He lacked repose, he
lacked finish, he lacked the patience that could recast and
replan, and he had a stilted Della Cruscan inflation of
style that was extreme even in the ornate period in which
they were written. Instead of "the wind blew," he wrote
"the elemental music was remarkably sonorous"; "he
fell in love" becomes "he had not escaped the amorous
contagion"; blunders from lack of revision, such as the
Conway episode in *Wieland,* where he changes in the midst
of the narrative the name of one of his characters; episodes dragged in and sewed upon the main tale like patches
of a different color, such as the Indian adventures in
Edgar Huntly—all these have been dwelt upon. There is
another defect, however, more damning. The Englishman
John Davis, in his *Travels in the United States* (1798),
was the first to point out his utter lack of humor:

Nature has utterly disqualified him for subjects of humor.
Whenever he endeavors to bring forth humor, the offspring
of his throes are weakness and deformity. Whenever he attempts humor, he inspires the benevolent with pity, and fills
the morose with indignation.

But in the England of the 1790's literature was running
at a level not at all higher. Fiction there was at its yellow-
est moment. Mrs. Radcliffe was the best-seller, and her
type of romance was thus described by Joseph Dennie in
1803:

Horrible description predominates. The authors go out in
the walks of nature to find some dreadful incident. Appalling
noises must be created. Ghosts must be manufactured by the
dozens. A door is good for nothing, in the opinion of a romance writer, unless it creak. The value of a room is much
enhanced by a few dismal groans. A chest full of human bones
is twice as valuable as a casket of diamonds. Every grove

must have its quiet disturbed, by the devil, in some shape or other. Not a bit of tapestry but must conceal a corpse; not an oak can grow without sheltering banditti.

With this school he had no patience. Dennie later, in the *Port Folio* issue following Brown's death, discussed the matter with convincing clearness:

Disgusted with the dull, insipid tales of the German school, the ghosts, the castles, and the hobgoblins of modern romance, he [Brown] searched the mysterious volume of nature and found prodigies more to his liking. Somnambulism and ventriloquism furnished fields equally large and commodious for fancy to expatiate and capable of the same embellishment of incident,—the strong objection to which German writers are liable, that such novelties do not exist in Nature.

More was he influenced by Godwin, though not to the degree of imitation. Godwin had sounded a new note in fiction. In the original preface to *Caleb Williams* he had written: "The question now afloat in the world respecting things as they are is the most interesting that can be presented to the human mind." The novelist, he contended, must dominate his reader, hold him by a very powerful interest, even terrorize him. The novel must have a moral purpose, and the reader must be changed because of his reading. It must be a tale "that shall constitute an epoch in the mind of the reader, that no one, after he has read it, shall ever be exactly the same man that he was before." And yet, though woven of the most amazing and horrible and uncommon of materials, the novel must move at every point "within the laws and established course of nature as she operates in the planet we inhabit." It was his task as a novelist, he contended, "to mix human feelings and passions with incredible situations, and thus render them impressive and interesting."

CHAPTER VIII

"THE BOSTON STYLE"

I

THE FIRST mannerism peculiarly American, one seemingly evolved from native conditions, was the tendency toward flamboyant expression. The eighteenth century in England, the century of manner and manners, had planted the seeds, and in the new soil of America they burst into amazing efflorescence. Poetry and oratory, and to a large extent the essay, tended toward a vocabulary and an artificiality of manner and ornament that, when viewed over the fashions of the present day, seem impossible, seem indeed deliberately made ludicrousness.

A literary episode at the yellow end of the century gave the thing a name—Della Cruscanism! A mere fad in England, a decadent affectation of the *fin de siècle,* it was quickly killed by William Gifford in a single caustic criticism, but in America it grew into a veritable jungle. Poets everywhere, especially those in the Boston area, became worshipers at the new shrine.

In England the fashion had been started by Robert Merry, a British émigré in Italy who had signed his poetic effusions "Della Crusca." To one of these Mrs. Cowley had responded, signing herself "Anna Matilda":

> O! seize again thy golden quill,
> And with its point my bosom thrill:
> With magic touch explore my heart,
> And bid the tear of passion start.
> Thy golden quill Apollo gave—

> Drench'd first in bright Aonia's wave:
> He snatch'd it, flutt'ring thro' the sky,
> Borne on the vapour of a sigh.
> It fell from Cupid's burnish'd wing.

Merry had replied with an amorous gush of superlatives, italics, and capital letters. First published in the *London World,* it was widely copied and widely imitated.

It was two years before it reached America. Really it was no new thing. Early America reveled in the florid. Dr. Joseph Ladd, a Rhode Island youth, was a Della Cruscan before Della Crusca. His *The Poems of Arouet,* published the year of his death in a duel in South Carolina, 1786, are poetical epistles to his lady-love, Amanda, in diction florid and elevated. Carey, in his *American Museum,* published him for a time in almost every number. But real Della Cruscanism in America, by name at least, began in 1790 when Sarah Wentworth Morton—"Philenia"—ended her epic pamphlet, *Ouabi,* with a three-page epistle entitled "Lines Addressed to the Inimitable Author of the Poems under the signature of Della Crusca":

> Across the vast Atlantic tide
> Down *Apalachia's* grassy side,
> What echoing Sounds the Soul beguile,
> And lend *the lip of grief* a smile!
> 'Tis DELLA CRUSCA'S heavenly song,
> That floats the western shores along.[1]

It awoke the *Columbian Centinel:*

To afford the afflicted soul, the balm of consolation, who better qualified than the amiable Philenia? *Della Crusca* and *Anna Matilda* have ameliorated the Eastern world—a news-

---

[1] The *American Museum* (1791) published four of the Della Crusca —Anna Matilda effusions, and Carey's *The Beauties of Poetry, British and American,* pp. 84–93, published seven. Philenia's address to Della Crusca was published in the *Museum* and also in *American Poems* (1791), p. 184.

paper was the medium of their correspondence. *The Centinel,*
emulating the example, solicits the correspondence of Philenia
and Alfred, that the Western Hemisphere, may be alike bene-
fited.

"Alfred"—we know only the poet's pseudonym—was
the first to respond. Love had flouted him and penury had
chilled his soul:

> Ah, fatal *Love!*
> Now *Hope* has clos'd her sun-bright eye,
> And midnight glooms my midday sky.

"Philenia," herself a "child of woe," hastens to comfort
him, but seemingly in vain. Then had come the Ella-Birtha
series,[2] Ella doubtless being Dr. Elihu Smith, editor of
American Poems; and finally, most popular of all, the
Philenia-Menander correspondence in the columns of the
Massachusetts Mercury. Menander, we know, was Robert
Treat Paine, Jr. His biographer, Charles Prentiss, a loyal
Bostonian, made much of the episode:

Philenia had, however, the most exalted opinion of Paine's
poetic powers: and Paine thought he could not say too much
of a lady, who was so highly celebrated for her manners,
beauty, colloquial talents, and literary attainments; and who
had ascended to such an altitude on Parnassus, as to leave all
American female competitors at a humble distance.

Their exchange of superlative compliments stands
unique in the myriad columns of American poetry. This
gush, for instance, from the pen of "the American Sappho." I give but fragments:

> Blest Poet! whose Eolian lyre
>   Can wind the varied notes along,
> While the melodious Nine inspire
>   The graceful elegance of song.

[2] Published in the *Gazette of the United State.* Partially reproduced
in *American Poems* (1793).

Who now with Homer's strength can rise,
  Then with the polished Ovid move;
Now swift as rapid Pindar flies,
  Then soft as Sappho's breath of love.

.   .   .   .   .   .

'Tis for thy eagle mind to tower
  Triumphant on the wing of Fame;

.   .   .   .   .   .

Divine Menander, strike the string;
  With all thy sun-like splendor shine;
The deeds of godlike heroes sing,
  And be the palm of Genius thine! [3]

Young Paine's Muse now awoke in full voice. The series
proceeded from purple now to purpler.

The episode is pathetic. The old city, eager for a real
poet, hailing these two as "the American Sappho" and "the
American Simonides," certainly needed a revision of its
poetic standards.

Not totally without poetic merit was "Philenia," however. [4] Her "Song for the Public Celebration of the National Peace" is perhaps the best national ode written before the War of 1812. Not so much, however, can be said
of Paine. Melodrama sat upon him like a red cockade.
That he had his baptismal patronymic, Thomas, changed
by legislation ostentatiously to Robert Treat, Jr. is a revealing touch. Poetry, always at the windy heights of his
famous *Odes and Songs,* he poured out in a sort of
corybantic extempore. And Boston and Harvard crowned
it with honors and even with cash. For his Harvard
rhymed dissertation, *The Invention of Letters* (1795), he
received $1,500; for his Phi Beta Kappa effort, *The
Ruling Passion* (1797), $1,200 clear; and for his patriotic

---

[3] Much of the correspondence was reprinted in the *Works in Verse
and Prose of the Late Robert Treat Paine, Jun. Esq.* (1812).
[4] See Emily Pandleton and Milton Ellis, *Philenia, the Life and
Works of Sarah Wentworth Morton* (University of Maine Studies,
1931).

lyric, "Adams and Liberty," he received $750—"more than eleven dollars," says Kettell, "for each line of the piece, a munificence of reward for literary labor, which has rarely been equalled in any age or country." And in praise the city was even more munificent. Completely unreliable, dissipated, worthless by every possible measure, he was given by the old Puritan City as much help and praise as if he had been a veritable Pindar. After his death his poems were collected with religious care and published in an edition *de luxe*. A remarkable volume, surely. The biographical introduction stands undoubtedly as the best specimen of Della Cruscan prose evolved during a whole "elegant" period. Everywhere "sublime stanzas": "once engaged, he was an electric battery; approach him, and he scintillated; touch him, and he emitted a blaze." His death came from "pouring too copiously libations to Bacchus."

"Philenia," too, they rated as a major poet. All the Boston bards wove laurels for her wearing. This from "Ironicus" in a Boston paper of her day:

> Philenia's great, Philenia's wise,
> Philenia, daughter of the skies!
> Whose songs, whose music, and whose lyre
> Charm each fond soul, and all inspire.

"Oblivion has fallen upon her," mourned Joseph T. Buckingham, who in his youth had worshiped at her shrine. "Fifty years ago—one little half century—the Poems of Philenia were as popular as those of the most popular of the magazine poets of the year 1850. About twenty-five years ago they were published in an imposing octavo, by one of the Boston booksellers; and the question was then often asked, who is Philenia? Who is Mrs. Morton."

II

From Boston the contagion spread rapidly. American poetry had always been inflated and gorgeously adjectived, but now it became so smitten with the Della Cruscan yellows that it troubled even the poets themselves. Dr. Dwight made haste to declare that the Yale area had not yet been infected. It was a Boston disease:

"The Boston Style," is a phrase, proverbially used throughout a considerable part of this country to denote a florid, pompous manner of writing; and has been thought by persons at a distance to be the predominant style of its region. It cannot be denied that several publications, written in this manner, have issued from the presses here, and for a time been much celebrated. Most of the orations delivered on the 5th of March may be produced as examples. Still it has never been true, that this mode of writing was either general in this town, or adopted by men of superior talents. The most respectable writers, here, have been distinguished for the chasteness, and simplicity of their compositions.[5]

Boston, however, found the roots of the disease in England. According to "Remarker" in the *Monthly Anthology* (1808), the prevailing floridity came from Johnson, Gibbon, Burke: imitating them, "our writers seem to think a fine style consists of fine words, and consequently accumulate ungraceful ornaments with a lavish hand." A British critic in the *London Quarterly* retorted with a fling at "Republican rhetoric."

According to Joseph Dennie, the first real broom, in America at least, raised against the fantastic school was Royall Tyler's. In his "Colon and Spondee" column in the *Farmer's Museum,* Tyler for months clubbed the new affectation in savage glee. His travesties and parodies are a part of the history of American poetry. Our native verse, he declared, was really suffering; it was dying of inanition. What it needed was the judicious use of more and better epithets.

These should be gorgeous, splendid, far fetched, and obnubilous; that is to say, almost unintelligible. The fault of the

---

[5] *Travels in New England and New York,* I, 520.

American Parnassian weaver is, that he makes both warp and
filling of strong, plain, good sense, when the stuff will find a
much readier market, if he will merely warp with sense, and
fill with epithet. . . . Messrs. COLON & SPONDEE, have, at a
great expense, erected an Epithet Jenny, with which they card,
spin, and twist all kinds of epithets; single threaded, double
twisted, and long rolled epithets, by the hank, or pound. A
few real gold and silver wire, and spangled ditto, for the
manufacturers of epilogues and theatrical addresses. Ditto
tinsel for songs.[6]

Then imitating Della Crusca himself, he indited an ode
inviting the great lyrist to leave his native Europe and
come to the land where a superlative welcome awaits him:

> Rise Della Crusca, prince of bards sublime,
> And pour on us whole cataracts of rhyme.
> SON OF THE SUN arise, whose brightest rays
> All merge to tapers in thy ignite blaze.
> Like some colossus, stride the Atlantick o'er,
> A LEG OF GENIUS place on either shore,
> Extend thy red right arm to either world;
> Be the proud standard of thy style unfurl'd;
> Proclaim thy sounding page, from shore to shore
> And swear that sense in verse, shall be no more.[7]

He volunteered to furnish Della Cruscan instruction to the
rising school of young poets, guaranteeing to all who finished his course an *entrée* into all the magazines. This he
furnished as a sample lesson:

In seven words of New England poesy, in the New England
Primer, are the following lines.

> The cat doth play,
> And after slay.

This happy description we have amplified, and bespangled with
epithets in the following best manner of Charlotte Smith.

[6] *The Spirit of the Farmer's Weekly Museum* (1801), p. 27.
[7] *Ibid.,* p. 28.

Sonnet to an Old Mouser

Child of lubricious art! of sanguine sport!
Of *pangful mirth!* sweet ermin' sprite!
Who lov'st, with silent, *velvet step,* to court
The bashful bosom of the night.

Whose elfin eyes can pierce night's sable gloom,
And witch her *fairy prey* with guile,
Who sports fell frolic o'er the grisly tomb,
And gracest death with dimpling smile!

Daughter of ireful mirth, sportive in rage,
Whose joy should shine in sculptur'd base relief,
Like Patience, in rapt Shakespeare's deathless page,
Smiling in marble at wan grief.

Oh, come and teach me all thy barb'rous joy,
To sport with sorrow first, and then destroy.[8]

With gravity he advertises to sell a catalogue of epithets which he, with infinite labor, has finally completed. A page of samples he exhibits:

> Whispering showers
> Simpling tides
> Quivering bosoms
> Filmy curtains
> Musky air
> Gelid caverns
> Plumy race
> Lucid tears
> Dappled skies
> Velvet.sod
> Tiptoe pleasures
> Pebbly ways
> Blossomed sprays, etc.

[8] *The Spirit of the Farmer's Museum* (1801), p. 29.

Children, he declares, must be brought up on them if the poetry of the future is to be what it should be. A mother, of an evening, should say, "Come Anna Matilda, cast a glimmering glimpse on this paper, and let me see if you can spell *murky hours*. Laura Maria, what filmy vapors keep you so long on the pebbly way? Why don't you come to your leafy bed."

The founding of the Anthology Club and its organ, the *Monthly Anthology,* brought the warfare against the "Boston style" into Boston itself. At first it could only deplore, as, for instance, in the issue of March, 1805:

Genius without judgment is useless or ridiculous; there can be no good poetry where there is not good sense. Broken metaphors, gorgeous epithets, and forced thoughts are the artificial flowers that adorn their gaudy parterres, and are substituted for the simplicity of nature and the justness of truth. Nor are our prose writers entirely free from these defects. From want of true taste, and misconception of real elegance, they are forever torturing their faculties for novel expressions, and newly-invented combinations.

Later it could condemn even the national lyric, "Hail Columbia," as "nonsense and rodomontade." Soon it was parking its batteries even in the Yale area. Richard Alsop's *Echo,* which had been established to help "check the progress of false taste in American literature," especially the "pendantry, affectation and bombast which pervaded most of the pieces published in the gazettes," had, it declared, turned into a piece of bombastic inflation much worse than the disease it had sought to correct.

III

But the disease was wider than Boston, wider than Della Cruscan influences. One has but to examine the great mass of elegy following the deaths of Franklin and of Washington to realize that it was and is a national charac-

teristic. The death of any great national hero in America
has always called out floods of poetry rich in superlatives.
After the death of Franklin, Philip Freneau professed to
have heard the old philosopher complaining from his
grave:

> Philosophers are fam'd for pride,
> But, pray, be modest—when I died
> No sighs disturb'd old ocean's bed,
> No "nature wept" for Franklin dead!

The verse connected with Washington's last decade and
his death is amazing both in quantity and variety.[9] An
anthology of it would belong in the museum of American
literary curiosities. A New Hampshire poet issued *A Versification of President Washington's Farewell Address to
the citizens of the United States;* St. John Honeywood
issued a soaring Pegasus flight on the "Address"; Francis
Glass started a life of Washington in Latin—*Vita Wash-
ingtonia.* Newspapers and magazines sobbed and soared
with the sentimentalizings and exaggerations of the
"Lauras" and "Alonzos" and "Philomels." Robert Treat
Paine led the Boston choir at this altitudinous pitch:

> Could Faustus live, by gloomy Grave resigned;
> With power extensive, as sublime his mind,
> Thy glorious life a volume should compose,
> As Alps immortal, spotless as its snows.
> The stars should be its types—its press the age
> The earth its binding—and the sky its page.

As late as 1818 Solyman Brown, A.M., in his *Essay on
American Poetry,* a critique in rhymed couplets, was not
less extreme:

[9] See *Washington. First in the Hearts of his Countrymen. The
Orations by Men Who Had Known Washington in Person and Who
Thus Could Speak with Authority,* edited with a preface by William
Buckner McGroarty; introduction by Charles H. Callahan (1932).

What form is that, that strides along the line?
Is it a mortal—or some power divine?
Some guardian Angel of a Nation's peace,
Some Seraph, sent to bid the slaughter cease?
No!—'tis Columbia's son—the heir of fame,
Creation's Hero! WASHINGTON his name.

But even the Bostonian Federalist, Fisher Ames, could fire the altitudinous Brown to superlatives:

What voice resounds in yonder crowded hall?
What lips are those from which such accents fall?
That form—Demosthenes! is that thine own?
Or Chatham's, thundering at Oppression's throne?
Not thine, Demosthenes!—nor Chatham! thine;
In AMES, alone, your blended virtues shine.

An equal amount of flamboyancy one finds in the various attempts of republican poets to make for the new land an adequate national anthem. One might fill a volume with samples. The first candidate for the honor came as early as 1777 from the pen of Dr. Timothy Dwight:

Columbia, Columbia, to glory arise,
The queen of the world, and child of the skies!

A war-rouse in battle pitch. Then in 1794 Robert Treat Paine's Della Cruscan rhapsody:

When first the Sun o'er Ocean glowed,
   And earth unveiled her virgin breast,
Supreme mid Nature's vast abode,
   Was heard the Almighty's dead behest:
   Rise, Columbia, brave and free,
   Poise the Globe, and bound the Sea!

A generation later the poets were still in mid air. Read Drake's "The American Flag":

When Freedom from her mountain height
Unfurl'd her standard to the air,
She tore the azure robe of night,

And set the stars of glory there.
She mingled with its gorgeous dyes
The milky baldric of the skies,
And striped its pure celestial white
With streakings of the morning light;
Then from his mansion in the sun
She call'd her eagle bearer down,
And gave into his mighty hand
The symbol of her chosen land.

The first successful anthem, "Hail Columbia," was written in 1798 when war with France was believed to be unavoidable. Party feeling between those who sympathized with France—the Jefferson faction—and those who opposed her—the Federalists—was extreme in its intensity. Between the two stood Washington, inflexible for peace and neutrality. As an aid to him and the cause of harmony generally, it was proposed to Joseph Hopkinson, son of Frances Hopkinson, that he compose a patriotic song to be set to the music of "The President's March" and to be sung in the theater on a benefit evening when all Philadelphia would be present. The result was the patriotic lyric that all Americans know—by title.

Rotundity and sonorousness fill it like a fife-and-drum duet. This is the third stanza:

Sound, sound the trump of fame!
Let *Washington's* great name
    Ring through the world with loud applause,
    Ring through the world with loud applause;
Let every clime to freedom dear,
Listen with a joyful ear.
    With equal skill and godlike power,
    He governed in the fearful hour
    Of horrid war; or guides, with ease,
    The happier times of honest peace.

It is a barrage of adjectives, heavily chromatic.

IV

By no means, however, were altitudinousness and super-latives confined to poetry. Until late in the nineteenth century the oratory of the nation North and South began with magniloquent exordiums and ended with climactic perorations. From Patrick Henry to Daniel Webster the language of oratory was far removed from the language of every day.

American political life, the great American occasions, the frontier pulpit and rostrum, all demanded "eloquence" with sonorous periods. For half a century on the Fourth of July the American eagle screamed all day long from every stump in the Republic. Elocution and oratory flourished in the schools: the school readers were treatises on public speaking. The oratundo, the periphrastic that never called a spade a spade, the martialing of phrases into periods, everywhere this was eloquence. And vigorously was it defended:

The literature of a young and free people, will of course be declamatory, and such, so far as it is yet developed, is the character of our own. Deeper learning will, no doubt, abate its verbosity and intumescence; but our natural scenery, and our liberal political and social institutions, must long continue to maintain its character of floridness, and what is there in this that should excite regret in ourselves, or raise derision in others? Ought not the literature of a free people to be declamatory? Should it not exhort and animate? If cold, literal, and passionless, how could it act as the handmaid of improvement? [10]

The Boston *Anthology,* however, was inclined to be critical. In 1805, reviewing a sheaf of typical orations, it was inclined to deplore the American tendency toward the out-Heroding of Herod:

[10] Daniel Drake, M.D., "Discourse on the History, Character, and Prospects of the West: Delivered to the Union Literary Society of Miami University . . . , September 23, 1834."

Though there is no country so fruitful in orations as our own, yet are our orators widely distant from perfection in this species of composition. Unnatural thoughts, extravagant metaphors, and violent exclamations, conveyed in a style inflated and incorrect, are the rhetorical flowers, with which these patriotick effusions are commonly decorated.

Ten of these orations, sumptuously published, most of them at the orator's own expense, it reviewed in three numbers of the magazine, the last of them with this pertinent explanation:

Perhaps no nation can furnish so great a number of public discourses during the same period, as are produced among us, commencing with fast-day sermons and ending with July orations. This season, which in our variable, capricious climate partakes of winter, summer and spring, might be correctly designated the *season of orators*. Many of these are annually delivered on the same subject; and the most ingenious writer would vainly endeavor to produce any novelty, without deserting entirely the particular object of his discourse.

Especially rotund and grandiloquent was the legislative oratory of the period. William Wirt, in his *Letters of the British Spy* (1803), declared that "In the national and state legislatures, as well as at the various bars in the United States, I have heard great volubility, much good sense, and some random touches of the pathetic: but in the same bodies, I have heard a far greater proportion of puerile rant, or tedious and disgusting inanity." To Wirt the chief defects of the early orators of the republic were three: lack of general knowledge, lack of "close and solid thinking," and lack of original ornaments. But to Wirt "original ornaments" consisted of "those novel and beautiful allusions and embellishments, with which the very scenery of the country is so highly calculated to inspire orators." Even as he demanded "the primitive simplicity of the patriarchal age," he himself in the same volume and

the same essay was employing the same honeyed floridity
of style:

What is this divine eloquence? What the charm by which
the orator binds the senses of his audience—by which he at-
tunes and touches and sweeps the human lyre, with the re-
sistless sway and master hand of a Timotheus? Is not the
whole mystery comprehended in one word—SYMPATHY?
I mean not that tender passion which quavers the lip and fills
the eye of the babe when he looks on the sorrows and tears of
another; but that still more delicate and subtle quality, by
which we passively catch the very colours, momentum and
strength of the mind to whose operations we are attending;
which converts every speaker to whom we listen, into a
Procrustes; and enables him for the moment, to stretch or
lop our faculties to fit the standard of his own mind.[11]

v

The cause of this widespread literary malady has been
variously assigned. A rich new country, says one group of
critics, will naturally be efflorescent. The Great Plains, the
Rocky Mountains, Niagara Falls, and the Mississippi must
naturally call forth superlatives. It is simply the color of
American ignorance, says another group. A new country
requiring of all severest labor has little time for anything
not instantly practical. Poetry therefore became the plaything for adolescents, for physical weaklings, for college
students preparing for the ministry. Let William Biglow
serve as a typical case. Thus he describes his evolution up
from poetry:

In ballads first I spent my boyish time;
At college, next, I soared in doggerel rhyme;
Then of a school the master and adorner,
I scribbled verses for a Poet's Corner.
But when, ere while, I strove, with *slender means,*

[11] *Letters of the British Spy,* First ed., 1803, Letter III.

Newspapers to endite, and Magazines;
The public frowned, and warned me, at my peril,
To drop the pen, and reassume the *ferule*.

.   .   .   .

And now, enchanting poetry, adieu!
Thy syren charms no longer I pursue . . .
Farewell! On others inspiration flash,
Given them eternal fame—but give me cash.

To the adolescent poetaster, beauty in poetry meant mere floweriness.

To another group, first voiced, perhaps, by an early writer in the *North American Review,* the root of the matter lay "in the American passion for Liberty":

The general tone of our popular composition has been showy and declamatory, a natural result of the influence of a free and independent form of government upon the buoyant spirits of a young, enterprising, and prosperous people.

Samuel F. Jarvis, however, Phi Beta Kappa orator at Yale in 1808, found the cause in the American spirit of lawlessness. Charles Brockden Brown threw all the blame upon the colleges, and many of the Phi Beta Kappa orators of the period were with him. Properly administered classical training would have checked literary extravagance, would have taught conciseness, restraint, chaste beauty without gaudiness. But the colleges had not accomplished this: the best-trained scholars of the whole period were as guilty of the mannerism as the totally uncolleged herd. William Hickling Prescott roundly criticized Brockden Brown for his periphrastical expressions. Yet Prescott, even as he criticized Brown, was well-nigh as pariphrastic. Instead of saying "the man was born a Quaker," he writes: "His parents were of that estimable sect who came over with William Penn, to seek asylum where they might worship their creator unmolested, in the meek and humble spirit of their own faith."

Whatever the cause, the fact remains that none of our literary creators, cultured or uncultured, felt wholly comfortable when he had called a spade merely a spade.

One final cause, I think, has never been mentioned. Children in the lower schools were taught from the first that the difference between literature and the common run of expression was wholly a matter of style, the adding of ornaments, the doffing of the week-day working-dress of language and the putting on of the Sunday raiment. I have before me a heap of early school readers of the period. From them I select Daniel Staniford's *The Art of Reading; Selected and Original Pieces calculated to improve the scholar in reading and speaking with propriety and elegance.* In 1816 it was in its eleventh large edition. Open at random to a specimen selection which the pupil was to use as a model:

THE WISDOM OF PROVIDENCE DISPLAYED IN THE SEASONS

Dreary winter is past; its severe cold is mitigated; the returning zephyrs dissolve the fleecy snow, and unlock the frozen streams, which overflow the extensive meadows, and enrich the teeming earth. At length the rapid streams begin to glide gently within their banks; the spacious meadows soon receive their usual verdure, and the whole face of nature assumes a cheerful aspect. By the refreshing showers, and vivifying power of the genial sun, we behold the rapid and amazing progress of vegetation. Etc.

What has the child learned about literature? That every noun must have a beautiful adjective and every verb a beautiful adverb. But the glory of literature as exhibited in this particular text-book was oratory. Let me, in this Washington bicentenary period, select a specimen from one of the funeral orations delivered during the mourning year 1800 and presented to the child as a model:

Great, Immortal Washington! Too soon for man, hast thou ascended to glory! Humanity mourns, virtue rejoices in

thy worth. Angels shout "Welcome! great Hero, to thy
Home! Thy benevolence embraced mankind! thy services
blessed the world. Too good for earth, to heaven art fled,
and left the world in tears. Weep, generous Nations! weep,
the sad, the swift remove of him, whom Heaven, indulgent,
sent to man: recalled from earth, adorned with bright
religion's gems. Thou favorite Child of Heaven! stripped of
thy mortal form, clad in thy native divinity, hast thou ascended
to heaven, there to enjoy the presence of thy God!"

What wonder that the young learner associated literary
excellence with overdecoration. And with the poetry of the
time before him, what wonder that "the ostentatious display of blue hills and crashing torrents and petrifying
suns" seemed necessary if one was to write literature truly
"elegant"?

CHAPTER IX

TRAVELERS AND EMIGRÉS

I

DURING THE 1790's America swarmed with émigrés from
the French Revolution.

The number of foreign exiles who at this time are moving
in Philadelphia society gave a cosmopolitan character to the
City, and lent to it the air of foreign capitals. Talleyrand,
Beaumais, Vicomte de Noailles and his brother-in-law La-
fayette, Volney, the Duc de Liancourt, and General Moreau,
and at a later date Joseph Bonaparte and Murat, were but a
few of the distinguished members of the French colony.[1]

Chief among them was Talleyrand, who arrived in 1794,
traveled to some extent through the states, and returned
the following year to lecture before the French Institute
upon his experiences. One passage at least in his initial
paper deserves reproduction. Civilization in America, he
declared, is "exhibited in space as well as time—as the
traveller moves westward from state to state he appears
to go backward from age to age."

The same year came an equally famous English émigré,
one destined to remain in the new land, Joseph Priestley,
philosopher and scientist. The young nation showered upon
the man all the honors in its possession, raised for him a
purse, opened for him lectureships, founded for him a
chair of chemistry in the University of Pennsylvania, but,

[1] A. H. Smyth, *Philadelphia Magazines and Their Contributors*
(1892), p. 89.

brushing them all aside, he retired to the country home of his son at Northumberland, Pennsylvania, and there, in studious seclusion, passed the remainder of his life. Though voluminous in his publications, he touched American literature only through the influence of his fame and his personality. Disciples gathered about him, among them the Englishman Thomas Cooper, whose *Information Respecting America* is one of the earliest of the books written for circulation among prospective emigrants. His observations upon the state of American literature in 1794 deserves quoting:

> Literature in America is an amusement only. . . . The Americans are inferior to you in the opportunities of knowledge; their libraries are scanty, their collections are almost entirely of *modern* books; they do not contain the means of tracing the history of questions; this is a want which the literary people feel very much, and which it will take some years to remedy.[2]

During the same year America seemed for a moment about to acquire a whole school of major poets. Coleridge, leaving the university with his course uncompleted, had come in contact with Robert Southey, who had been infected from the French Revolution area with the idea of a new organization for social betterment. Together the two had worked out plans for what they called a "pantisocracy," a community where everybody, according to the etymology of the word, was to be ruler. The locality chosen was to be in Pennsylvania, on the banks of (to use Coleridge's pronunciation) the "Suse-kee-hárner," near Priestley. The dream was so glorious that Coleridge, then in clearest voice, burst into rapturous lyricism:

> O'er the ocean swell,
> Sublime of Hope, I seek the cottage dell,
> Where Virtue calm with careless steps may stray;

[2] *Some Information Respecting America, Collected by Thomas Cooper, Late of Manchester* (1794), p. 64.

And dancing to the moonlight roundelay,
The wizard Passions weave a holy spell.
O Chatterton, that thou wert yet alive
Sure thou would'st spread the canvas to the gale
And love with us the tinkling team to drive
O'er peaceful Freedom's undivided dale.

Whether Wordsworth was involved in the plan is uncertain. The community was to begin with twelve married couples, and the two founders had no wives. This was easily remedied. Byron, in a stanza of *Don Juan,* gave this version of what happened:

All are not moralists, like Southey, when
    He prated to the world of Pantisocracy;
Or Wordsworth unexcised, unhired, who then
    Seasoned his pedlar poems with Democracy;
Or Coleridge, long before his flighty pen,
    Let to the Morning Post its aristocracy;
When he and Southey, following the same path,
Espoused two partners (milliners of Bath).

The Pantisocracy died at the hymeneal altar. Doubtless the money side of the question for the first time became evident, or was it that the young poets awoke to the fact that married life is not at all a pantisocracy—the rule of everybody. The affair has left behind only conjectures. What would have been the outcome had they established themselves as they planned. What would Oliver Goldsmith have become had his plan for settling in the new country not by merest accident miscarried totally? And what of Robert Burns, who was near the emigration point when his Kilmarnock Edition rescued him for Scotland?

II

From the bibliography in Jane Louise Mesick's volume, *The English Traveller in America, 1785–1835,* the only complete study of the subject at present available, I have

isolated the twenty leading volumes of travel in America
written by British travelers during the period between the
two revolutions:

1789   W. Matthews, *Historical Review of North
            America,* 2 vols. (Dublin, 1789).

1792   Thomas Coke, *A Journal of the Rev. Dr. Coke's
            Fourth Tour on the Continent of America*
            (London, 1792).

1793–1797   William Priest, *Travels in the United States of
            America; Commencing in the Year 1793 and
            Ending in 1797* (London, 1802).

1794   Thomas Cooper, *Some Information Respecting
            America* (Dublin, 1794).

1794   Henry Wansey, *An Excursion to the United
            States of North America in the summer of
            1794* (Salisbury, 1798).

1795   William Winterbotham, *An Historical, Geo-
            graphical, Commercial and Philosophical View
            of the American United States,* 4 vols. (Lon-
            don, 1795).

1795–1797   Isaac Weld, *Travels through the States of North
            America and the Provinces of Upper and
            Lower Canada during the Years 1795, 1796
            and 1797* (London, 1799).

1797–1811   John Bernard, *Retrospections of America.* Pub-
            lished in 1887; edited by Laurence Hutton and
            Brander Matthews.[3]

1798–1800   Richard Parkinson, *A Tour in America in 1798,
            1799 and 1800,* 2 vols. (London, 1805).

1803   John Davis, *Travels of Four Years and a Half in
            the United States of America During 1798,
            1799, 1800, 1801 and 1802* (London, 1803).

1804–1806   Robert Sutcliffe, *Travels in Some Parts of
            North America, 1804, 1805, and 1806* (New
            York, 1811).

1806   Thomas Moore, *Odes and Epistles* (London).

[3] First published as "Early Days of the American Stage" in Tallis's
Dramatic Magazine, 1850–1851. Republished with additions from
manuscripts prepared by Mrs. Bayle Bernard (his daughter-in-law)
by Hutton and Matthews.

1806   Priscilla Bell Wakefield, *Excursions in North America* (London, 1806).

1806–1808   John Lambert, *Travels through Canada and the United States of North America in the years 1806, 1807, 1808*, 2 vols. (London, 1816).

1807   Edward Augustus Kendall, *Travels through the Northern Parts of the United States in the Years 1807 and 1808*, 3 vols. (New York, 1809).

1808   Thomas Ashe, *Travels in America Performed in 1806* (London, 1808).

1807   Charles William Janson, *The Stranger in America* (London, 1807).

1807–1811   John Melish, *Travels in the United States of North America in the Years 1806 and 1807 and 1809, 1810 and 1811*, 2 vols. (Philadelphia, 1812).

1809–1811   John Bradbury, *Travels in the Interior of America in the years 1809, 1810, 1811* (London, 1819).

1810   F. Cuming, *Sketches of a Tour to the Western Country* (Pittsburgh, 1810).

A valuable list of books, a shelf of authorities essential to the student of the first two decades of the Republic. Most of them were written by travelers who had come to America through sheer curiosity and who sought to give to the people at home a faithful picture of what they saw. It was not these books that raised the storm in America: it was the reviews of these books in the English *Quarterly Review* and other British journals.

III

The first criticism from abroad that had touched American pride had come as a result of Thomas Moore's brief visit in 1804. The young Irishman, newly famous for his volume, *Odes of Anacreon,* had been appointed Registrar of the Admiralty at Bermuda and, after performing "the

necessary duties in person" for four months, was on his
way home. He had gone to America, he later wrote, "with
prepossessions by no means unfavorable," but after his
horrible jauntings through the states,

> O'er lake and marsh, through fevers and through fogs,
> Midst bears and Yankees, democrats and frogs,

he was leaving it in an Irish rage.

He had sailed from Bermuda May 1, 1804, and had
landed in New York about a week later. On June 16 he
had arrived in Philadelphia, which, thanks to Dennie, was
all agog to receive him. For months Dennie had been printing his poems in the *Port Folio* and offering him the most
cordial invitations. Now the town outdid itself. "My
reception at Philadelphia," Moore wrote on June 26, "was
extremely flattering: it is the only place in America which
can boast any literary society." And again:

> In the society of Mr. Dennie and his friends at Philadelphia
> I passed the few agreeable moments which my tour through
> the states afforded me. Mr. Dennie has succeeded in diffusing
> through this cultivated little circle that love for good litera-
> ture and sound politics, which he feels so zealously himself,
> and which is so very rarely the characteristic of his country-
> men. They will not, I trust, accuse me of illiberality for the
> picture which I have given of the ignorance and corruption
> that surround them. If I did not hate, as I ought, the rabble
> to which they are opposed, I could not value, as I do, the
> spirit with which they defy it; and in learning from them
> what Americans *can be,* I but see with the more indignation
> what Americans *are.*

And again:

> The rude familiarity of the lower orders, and indeed the un-
> polished state of society in general, would neither surprise
> nor disgust if they seemed to flow from that simplicity of
> character, that honest ignorance of the gloss of refinement,
> which may be looked for in a new and inexperienced people.

But when we find them arrived at maturity in most of the vices, and all the pride of civilization, while they are still so far removed from its higher and better characteristics, it is impossible not to feel that this youthful decay, this crude anticipation of the natural period of corruption, must repress every sanguine hope of the future energy and greatness of America.

The *Port Folio* junto, headed by Dennie, outdid itself in literary entertainment; the Philadelphia aristocracy, which in 1778 had so captivated the element of nobility in the British army, dined and fêted the young poet as if he were a veritable scion of royalty. He was taken out to see the Indian chief Seenado and was delighted with the old savage. His "manners," he declared, "were extremely gentle and intelligent, and almost inclined me to the Frenchman's opinion that the savages are the only well-bred gentlemen in America." A sheaf of poems written during his progress through America appeared in 1806, and they were indeed not flattering pictures:

> Is this the region then, is this the clime
> For soaring fancies? For those dreams sublime,
> Which all their miracles of light reveal
> To heads that meditate and hearts that feel?
> Alas! not so. . . .
>
> Yet, yet forgive me, oh ye sacred few,
> Who late by Delaware's green banks I knew;
> Whom known and lov'd through many a social eve,
> 'Twas bliss to live with, and 'twas pain to leave.

As a token of his appreciation, he sent from time to time original poems to be first published in the *Port Folio*, poems like these: "When Time who Steals our Hearts Away," "Lines Written on Leaving Philadelphia," "Dear, in Pity Do not Speak," "Good-night, Good-night, and is it so?" "When the Heart's Feeling," "Loud Sung the Wind," and "Sorrow Long has Worn my Heart."

It was the golden event in the long history of the *Port Folio* group. As late as 1826, John E. Hall, the last editor of the magazine, published *The Philadelphia Souvenir,*[4] an anthology of *Port Folio* verse that was to be, according to its editor, "a sort of *cairn* to the memory of the circle of friends which Mr. Moore has commemorated in his immortal poems."

The way it struck the other half of Philadelphia was voiced by Charles Brockden Brown, who had himself been in the group which welcomed Moore. This in his literary magazine (1806), with the title "Anacreon Moore vs. America":

Even his warmest admirers say no more of him, than that he drinks genteelly, plays well on the pianoforte, and writes very fine verses, and sings his own verses scientifically—these do not imply any great capacity for impartially surveying the manners of a nation.

This little cock-sparrow of a songster came hopping across the Atlantic, to sing his amours in the wilds of America. As we had seen nothing of the kind so chirping and so light, he was much noticed and admired, and every one was delighted to hear the little bird chirrup his Greek. He could make rhymes on any or every *little* thing; a nose, an eye, a cheek, a curl, a lip, the tip of an ear, a little fly, a flea, or a gnat's toe-nail enchanted him. He looked like a being born in a jelly glass, handed round on a cake, fed on sugar plums, and educated among the dreams of fancy; the little spirit could hide himself under a lady's eyelash and expire with delight— Always singing, sighing and evaporating.

He must have found plenty of excellent Madeira; many admirers of such writers as Anacreon, Tibullus, and Secundus; many who conceive the highest human excellent to consist in keeping up a contest of singing, drinking, and jesting till midnight, over a dinner table, in producing an extemporary epigram, or quoting a luscious description. They must be

[4] *The Philadelphia Souvenir: a Collection of Fugitive Pieces from the Philadelphia Press with biographical and explanatory notes, & original contributions by the editor* (1826).

learned; that is, they must be able to retail sentences of Greek
and Latin in common conversation. They must be polite;
that is, they must give suppers, and preside at them with well-
adjusted elbows, a cravat fresh from the laundress, and indefatigable attention to the great man who is their guest. They
must possess a refined taste; that is, they must be able to
select the best Madeira and champaign; poetry, that is, song
writing, and music. That is, song singing must be the business
of their lives.[5]

The lively editors of *Salmagundi* made merry with the
little man. This from William Irving, poet of the group:

> A little pest, hight Tommy Moore,
> Who hopp'd and skipp'd our country o'er;
> Who sipp'd our tea and lived on sops,
> Revell'd on syllabubs and slops,
> And when his brain, of cobweb fine,
> Was fuddled with five drops of wine,
> Would all his puny loves rehearse,
> And many a maid debauch—in verse. . . .
> And can it be this book so base,
> Is laid on every window case?[6]

Ingersoll in 1810, in his *Inchiquin Letters,* was more
severe:

One of the last and most contemptible of those who have
endeavored to defray the expenses of a tour through the U. S.
by the publication of a volume of travels, is an individual distinguished for his genius and erudition, a scholar and a poet,
over whose mind therefore, illiberal prepossessions should
have less sway, than over the mere itinerants and travel-
wrights of the age. I allude to Anacreon Moore, who is so
entirely a slave of prejudice when his pen is exercised on this
country, that it is bereft of all its magic, and he dwindles into
a poor epitome of common-place calumnies. He left England
to take upon him some little office in the "still-vex'd Ber-
moothes"; and not liking the situation, came friendless and

[5] *Literary Magazine,* September, 1806.
[6] *Salmagundi,* March 7, 1807.

penniless to the American continent, with no other recommendation than his enchanting talents for music; with which
passport he sang his way through some of the chief towns,
loitering where he was bidden, and almost piping for a meal;
of course without any means of knowing or appreciating the
inhabitants. Yet on his return necessity drove him to manufacture a paltry, malignant duodecimo, disgraceful alike to
his head and his heart; in which after dealing out his ingratitude in as much prose as he could produce on the occasion, he falls away into rhyme, as grovelling as his usual
strains are lofty, and spits the remainder of his contemptible
venom in doggerel and recitative.[7]

IV

From a literary standpoint, the best of the English volumes is that by John Davis, who spent four years tramp-
ing through fifteen states from Philadelphia to South
Carolina, paying his expenses by serving from time to time
as a tutor. With the curiosity of a modern realist, he entered, as he expressed it, "with equal interest the mud-hut
of the negro and the log house of the planter." And he tells
us what he saw. Though dedicated to Jefferson, the book
was not always pleasing to the American democrats, and
not always was it written with accuracy. Wild nature, as he
saw it in the southern hill-lands, enchanted him. At the
sight of the Ashley River and the Natural Bridge he burst
into song. He wrote, too, an "Ode to the Mocking Bird."
A sprightly volume, often humorous, full of anecdotes, it
reminds one of Parson Weems's writings. For a time
indeed he worshiped at Weems's church at Pohick, and
he has left us a lively picture of the old preacher. Always
he posed as a man of letters, a novelist, a critic, but his literary surveys are always more amusing than informative.
This, for instance, concerning Dennie and his *Port Folio:*

The editor of the *Aurora* calls the *Port Folio* the *Portable
Foolery;* and his facetiousness is applauded by one party, and

[7] An excellent paper on the Moore episode is that by Charles Henry
Hart—"Tom Moore and America," *Collector,* February, 1896.

scorned by the other. But a better quibble on the word would be to name it the *Court Olio;* for it mingles the dresses at *St. James* with speculations on literature. It being rumored that Mr. Dennie had been denominated by the British Reviewers, the *American Addison,* the following ludicrous paragraph appeared in the *Aurora Gazette.* "Exult ye white hills of *New Hampshire,* redoubtable *Monadnock* and *Tuckaway!* Laugh ye waters of the *Winiseopee* and *Umbagog Lakes!* Flow smooth in heroic verse ye streams of Amoonoosuck and Androscoggin, Cockhoko and Coritocook! And you *merry Merrimack* be no more merry."

v

The warfare with the British reviews began in November, 1809, when the newly founded *Quarterly Review,* in an article purporting to be a review of Abiel Holmes's *American Annals,* struck out in the savage cut-and-slash fashion of the times upon everything American. Deriving its facts from the prejudiced volumes of Ashe, Janson, and Weld, it made of America a veritable convict colony, a land of savages, a land whose very soil was so cursed that everything European that touches even humanity is dwarfed and enfeebled. "There is scarcely any medium in America between over-godliness and a brutal irreligion." And it ended in that intolerable English note of patronizing advice which is more anger-provoking than charges of imbecility:

This is an unfavorable picture, yet surely not an unfair one, nor has it been drawn by an unfriendly hand. Let but the American government abstain from war, and direct its main attention to the education of the people and the encouragement of arts and knowledge, and in a very few generations, their country may vie with Europe.

The warfare, which lasted until long after Lowell's paper, "On A Certain Condescension in Foreigners," was on in full force. Soon Sydney Smith was roaring, "In the four quarters of the globe, who reads an American book? or goes to an American play? or looks at an American picture or statue?" [8]

The attack seems to have been general. It had long been the belief that everything, including humanity, deteriorated when transplanted in America. Bülow, an officer in the Prussian service, having been twice in the United States, once in 1791–1792 and again in 1795–1796, published a series of observations on America in the Hamburg *Spectator of the North*:

> The Americans bear very little resemblance to the English. Their form of stature is altogether different. . . . There are, indeed, strong, nervous men to be met with in America, but they are generally the first generation from European parents. Upon these the climate has not produced its full effect. The Americans of the 2nd and 3d generation are tall, but surprisingly thin and weak in the bones.[9]

Even his own native Germans he found affected:

> The Germans in Pa. are above all the worst enemies to literature. The only German books sold among them, and at a profit of 70%, are song books imported from Frankfort on the Main.

VI

The first American counter-attack came in 1810 in the shape of a small volume with this title-page:

> Inchiquin, The Jesuit's Letters, During a late Residence in the United States of America: Being a fragment of a Private Correspondence, Accidentally Discovered in Europe; containing a favorable view of the manners, literature, and

---

[8] *Edinburgh Review*, January, 1820.
[9] *Port Folio*, Aug. 21, 1802. Under the caption "Interesting Travels in America," translated from the German of Bülow, this volume was published in weekly instalments in the *Port Folio* from May 8, 1802, to Jan. 29, 1803.

state of society of the U. S. and a refutation of many of the
aspersions cast upon this country, by former residents and
tourists. By Some unknown Foreigner. . . . New York,
1810.

Charles J. Ingersoll, author of the volume, was a Philadelphian, born in 1782, and liberally educated with a culminating finishing course in England. His tragedy, *Edwy
and Elgiva,* written during his twentieth year, was enacted
on the Philadelphia stage in 1801, but he was no dramatist. He was a critic, a political economist, a historian. In
literary history, however, he is remembered only for his
Inchiquin Letters, his answer to the English reviewers.

Impersonating a foreign traveler, Inchiquin, a Jesuit,
he makes a survey of America, touching most carefully
the places criticized by the English reviewers. America is
far from perfection, he finds. The new city of Washington is by no means an adequate capital, but the excellencies
of the new land are nevertheless far in excess of its de-
plorabilities. It is a land with a homogeneous population:

It has been ascertained by actual enumeration that the importation of foreigners for ten years preceding 1805 did not
exceed four thousands. About nine-tenths speak precisely the
same language, which is a national unity probably not to be
found without some variation of dialect among the same number, so largely diffused, in any other quarter of the world.

In the matter of education it greatly surpasses Europe,
for instance: "In the little state of Ct. alone there are no
less than 1200 public schools which contain about 40,000
scholars at a time."

And as to the lack of literary development:

Though the literature of this country seems to have incurred
the scorn of Europe, there certainly are two works, which
as literary compositions on national subjects are at least comparable, if not superior to any that have appeared in Europe

since the independence of the U. S.: I mean Mr. Barlow's epic and Mr. Marshall's history.

Not a deadly engine, surely. Doubtless it would have gone the way of hundreds of such ephemeral works had not a *Quarterly* reviewer, his attention doubtless caught by the word "Jesuit," let loose upon it all his batteries of sarcasm. The result we shall record later.

VII

The first in America to be a poet subdued to truth by science, a realist and yet a poet, a product of the eighteenth century yet so nature-intoxicated as to forget utterly his models, was the Scotchman, Alexander Wilson, who reached America in 1794, aged twenty-eight. He had been a weaver, then a peddler miserably poor, but a poet. Poetry was in the air of Scotland: Burns was alive. Even the plowboys read lyrics and heroics and made them. Young Wilson had enough for a volume, but of funds for printing it—not a shilling! All Scotland he canvassed along with his peddler wares for subscribers, and at last it was published in 1789—*Poems, Humorous, Satirical, and Serious.* Other poems followed, one at least praised by Burns. Says Alexander Grossart, his editor and biographer, in 1876: "With the exception of Allan Ramsay, Fergusson, and Burns, none of our Scottish vernacular poets has been so continuously kept 'in print.'" In his later years, however, the poet was inclined to deplore this earlier verse. "I published these poems when only twenty-two, an age more abundant in sail than ballast."

Inspired criticism. Never Scotchman more restless, per-fervid, o'er-crowded with sail. He was in sympathy with the revolution in France; he wrote local satire so biting that it landed him in jail, so biting indeed that it was con-demned to be burned in the public square. As a result, he was off, as Burns a little earlier had been tempted to go, to America where a man could be free—to write what he pleased. Accordingly he

> Ploughed the Atlantic waves,
> And left a land of despots and their slaves.

He was in America twenty years: he died at forty-eight. Poverty had pursued him even in America. For ten years school-teaching was his major work, first in the South, then in New Jersey, then near Philadelphia. A Scotchman teaching the Pennsylvania Dutch! Hear him sing:

> Or all professions that this world has known,
> From clowns and cobblers upwards to the throne;
> From the grave architect of Greece and Rome,
> Down to the framer of a farthing broom;
> The worst for care and undeserved abuse,
> The first in real dignity and use,
> (If skilled to teach and diligent to rule)
> Is the learned master of a little school.

Never for a moment was he idle. Birds had become his avocation. With gun in hand, he tramped over all Pennsylvania:

> Many a tour the lonely Tutor takes,
> Long known to Solitude, his partner dear;
> For rustling woods, his empty School forsakes.

And now with his last school and academy near Gray's Ferry he found himself neighbor to one of the foremost naturalists in America, William Bartram of the famous botanic garden, a man who knew more of American birds than Wilson at that time, more indeed than any other man in the world. Never contact more fruitful; it seemed the pollen that burst the sleeping naturalist and poet into bloom and fruitage. In 1803 there came to him like an inspiration the vision of an illustrated ornithology to include every important American bird. It meant not only knowledge of birds but the mastery of color painting and of engraving. Not a moment did he hesitate, and now that he had a definite object his progress was all but miraculous.

The following year, October, 1804, he started on his first long tour for bird-study and specimen-collecting, a pedestrian trip of 1,300 miles to Niagara Falls and return, an excursion which he cast into poetic-journal form with the title *The Foresters*. In 1809 it ran for ten weeks in Dennie's *Port Folio*—2,219 lines, a poem to compare, at least in interest, with Wordsworth's *The Excursion*. Next came the seemingly impossible task of securing four or five hundred subscribers to his colossal bird-book at a subscription price of $120 per set of nine volumes. Much of the rest of his life he spent in endless journeyings, telling hundreds of times his story, subscription-book in hand. A swing through the whole extent of New England secured only 41 subscriptions, a tour of the South about the same number. Then against the advice of all his friends, he plunged alone into the Middle West as far as Cincinnati, then down through Kentucky and Tennessee to New Orleans where he found 60 subscribers, then across to Florida and home through the Southern states. The subscription roll, as finally published, numbers 450, with Jefferson's name at the top. The publication dragged on, though its author toiled night and day upon its engravings and its multitudinous details. The first volume appeared in 1808, the second in 1810. The ninth volume he did not live to complete. "There are," says his biographer, William Peabody, "few examples to be found in literary history of resolution equal to that of Wilson. Though he was made fully aware, both by his friends and his own reflections, of the difficulty of the enterprise in which he engaged, his heart never for a moment failed him."

VIII

Wilson's literary work may be discussed under three heads: his journals and letters; his literary prose in parts

of his *Ornithology;* and his poetry. His journals, his letters to Bartram, Alexander Lawson, and others recounting
his adventures while touring the country for birds and
subscriptions, are graphic and headlong. He recorded like
a scientist, omitting nothing. Had he issued this section of
his writings in 1806–1813, his *Ornithology* never would
have been published. His pictures of the New England
Yankees, the Southern Crackers, the Pennsylvania Germans, the frontier settlers along the Ohio are not flattering
at all to American vanity. His poetical journals are vivid
often with pictures like Dutch genre sketchings. This of a
hotel in Easton, Pennsylvania:

> The wretched fare its scurvy walls afford;
> The black wet bread, with rancid butter spread,
> The beastly drunkards who beside us fed;
> The beds with fleas and bugs accursed stored,
> Where every seam its tens of thousands poured:
> The host's grim sulkiness, his eager look,
> When from our purse the glittering gold we took.

It has become the fashion of late to idealize the frontier
as it lay west of the Allegheny barrier in the early nineteenth century. A reading of these journals and such
journal-poems as "The Foresters" should be set as a preliminary study for such idealists.

The bird descriptions and characterizations in the
Ornithology have long been famous, and deservedly so.
No one has written so enthusiastically, so poetically, yet so
accurately of the bald eagle, the blue-jay, the Carolina par-
rot, the various woodpeckers, the blue-bird, the owl, the
robin, the wren, the indigo-bird, the catbird, the barn-
swallow. They are like character studies for a bird novel.

The Reverend William B. O. Peabody, in his life of
Wilson for Sparks's *Library of American Biography*
(1851), touches very lightly the poetry of the naturalist:
two pages and a half out of 169, and these pages inclined

to the apologetic. "His accuracy in matters of fact was such, that he seems to have been hardly willing to see them colored in the least by imagination." Of *The Foresters* he could write: "It had considerable merit, though strongly marked with the prevailing faults of his poetical style." In other words, Wilson was a pioneer, like his English contemporary, Wordsworth; a voice of the new era; and his critic, a Boston clergyman, was still living in the dead century. Not wholly, however, was Wilson free from the Pope influences. *The Foresters* he cast into heroic couplets, and at times most decidedly he lapses into the Popeian dialect: the gun is "a levelled tube"; the hunters instead of shooting, "With sudden glance the smoky vengeance pour." But no eighteenth-century poet—Pope, Thomson, the graveyard bards—could have admitted into their work "hunks of bacon," "snorting hogs," or a bit of realism like this:

> The table cleared, our Journal we survey,
> And minute down the wanderings of the day;
> For fresh materials at our host inquire,—
> Who broiled his brawny limbs before the fire.
> "What township's this, old daddy?" "Why—hm—well;
> Township? The dickens, Sir, if I can tell;
> It's Pennsylvania though." "Right, daddy Squares.
> Who are your nearest neighbors?" "Why, the bears."
> "No mill or school-house near you?" "Yes, we've one
> Beyond the church a piece, on Panther's Run."
> "Is church far distant, daddy?" "Why—hm—no;
> Down Susquehanna, twenty miles or so."
> "You go to preaching, then?" "Be sure, that's clear;
> We go to mill and meeting twice a-year."
> "No curiosities about?" "Why—yes,
> You've brought a few of them yourselves, I guess."
> "What, dollars?" "Aye, and fi'-pennybits, I swear
> Are downright rarities among us here."
> Thus passed the evening, till the time of bed,
> When to a kennel we at last were led;

There, slumbering, shivered till the dawn of day,
Then cursed this scurvy cave, and marched away.[10]

This in 1808. Be it noted that Crabbe's *The Parish Register* appeared in 1807 and his *The Burough* in 1810.

Wilson had the scientist's disdain for mere authority. He followed only nature. "My harp is new strung," he wrote in 1802. The beauty of the new world had awakened the poet within him:

I believe a Scotsman better fitted for descriptions of rural scenes than those of any other nation on earth. . . . There is not an ignorant plowman in Scotland but who has a better taste and relish for a pastoral . . . than most of the pretended *literati* of America. . . . My heart swells, my soul arises to an elevation I cannot express, to think I may yet produce some of the glowing wilds of rural scenery—some new Paties, Rogers, Glauds, and Simons, that will rank with these favorites of my country when their author has mixed with his kindred clay.

America, he believed, was all unsung, and he would be the first to put its marvelous beauty into verse:

Sweet rural scenes! unknown to poet's song,
Where Nature's charms in rich profusion lie;
Birds, fruits, and flowers, an ever-pleasing throng,
Deny'd to Britain's bleak and northern sky.
Here Freedom smiles serene with dauntless eye,
And leads the exil'd stranger thro' her groves;
Assists to sweep the forest from on high,
And gives to man the fruitful field he loves,
Where proud imperious lord, or tyrant, never roves.[11]
Come roam with me Columbia's forests through,
Where scenes sublime shall meet your wandering view:
Deed shades magnificent, immensely spread,

[10] Alexander B. Grosart, *The Poems and Literary Prose of Alexander Wilson* (1876), Vol. II, p. 132.
[11] *Ibid.*, p. 177.

Lakes, sky-encircled, vast as ocean's bed,
Lone hermit streams that wind through savage woods,
Enormous cataracts swoln with thundering floods;
The settler's farm with blazing fires o'erspread,
The hunter's cabin and the Indian's shed,
The log-built hamlet, deep in wilds embraced,
The awful silence of th' unpeopled waste:
These are the scenes the Muse shall now explore,
Scenes new to song, and paths untrod before.[12]

For the first time in American poetry a description of the
Indian summer, that season so peculiarly American:

The sultry heats of Summer's sun were o'er
And ruddy orchards poured their ripened store;
Stripped of their leaves the cherry av'nues stood,
While sage October ting'd the yellow wood,
Bestrew'd with leaves and nuts the woodland path,
And roused the Katydid in chattering wrath;
The corn stood topped, there punkins strewed the ground,
And driving clouds of blackbirds wheeled around.
Far to the south our warblers had withdrawn,
Slow sailed the thistle-down along the lawn,
High on the hedge-rows, pendent over head,
Th' embow'ring vinec their purple clusters spread,
The buckwheat flails re-echoed from the hill,
The creaking cider-press was busier still;
Red through the smoky air the wading sun
Sunk into fog ere half the day was done;
The air was mild, the roads embrowned and dry,
Soft, meek-eyed Indian Summer ruled the sky.[13]

For the first time in American poetry "the catalpa," "the
Bob White," "the dog-wood," "the magnolia," "the catbird," "the jay." The prose of the *Ornithology* volumes is
enriched often with bird-lyrics, one of them, "The Blue-
Bird," the best known perhaps of all Wilson's poems.

A solitary soul he was, utterly alone, unmarried, an

[12] *Ibid.*, p. 112.
[13] *Ibid.*, p. 113.

exile in the vastness of the New World. His poems alone
reveal the depths of his life. In "The Solitary Tutor" such
lines as these:

> Wild Fancy formed him for fantastic flight,
> He loved the steep's high summit to explore,
> To watch the splendor of the orient bright,
> The dark deep forest and the sea-beat shore.
>
> . . . .
>
> Thus peaceful pass his lonely hours away.

But never had he leisure for gloom. Let us leave him with
this camera snap:

> While I travel thro' the woods sae lanesome and drear,
> It aye gi'es me pleasure my ain voice to hear;
> An' sae aneath my pack, as I lightly trudge alang,
> I wake the wild wood's echo wi' an auld Scottish sang.

In 1804 Brown published in his *Literary Magazine*
Wilson's "A Rural Walk," "The Solitary Tutor," and "A
Talent for the Observation of the American Scene."

CHAPTER X

THE EMERGING WEST

AMERICA, a land covered by "the damned shadow of Europe"—the definition comes from a petulant burst of Hawthorne's. A critic grubbing for the primal germs European, for shaping influences and models, finds all he is seeking for until he reaches the 1790's. Then suddenly elements unique, evolutions untouched by foreign influences, personalities and ideals unshadowed by Europe. The trans-Allegheny West had emerged.

The quarter of a century from the close of the French and Indian War to the inauguration of Washington and the advent of the new Republic was the most vital and germinal period in American history. The bare prose narrative of it is an epic. In 1769 Daniel Boone had migrated from North Carolina through the Cumberland Gap into Kentucky; the same year William Bean of Virginia penetrated into the wilds of Tennessee. The westward march had begun.

As the piled wagons from New England, from the middle states, from Virginia and the South had disappeared behind the Allegheny wall, they had not looked back. They were gone. They were severed from civilization as the East knew it, at first almost totally. They were forced in the wilderness to build utterly anew.

The settlers of the original colonies, all of them, it is true, had lived on a raw frontier, away from civilization, but it was a frontier vastly different from that which lay beyond the Allegheny barrier. It was open to the sea. To the early settler who could look daily at the ocean, who scanned every morning the horizon to see if perchance there might be a sail, there was always, at least in suggestion, a way of escape, if need be, back to the mother-land. Ships constantly were coming and going, and every ship brought Europe. Every harbor along the coast was a potential doorway to Europe. But to the thousands of wagons and horsemen and foot-goers that for a century poured through the mountain-gaps to the West there was no backward look. No Europe was behind that frontier.

What was happening on that long savage line beyond the ranges, the eastern seaboard did not care. The harbor cities were trading with Europe, reprinting and importing English books, and soon were republishing the English reviews. Along the Ohio and in the wilds of Kentucky, however, a new breed of men was evolving:

> The cowards never started;
> The weak died on the way.

Adventurers, trail-breakers, Indian-fighters, hunters, land-clearers, farmers—self-reliant they became as Indians, and as independent. During the Revolution their acts were sudden and decisive. At King's Mountain they killed or captured the whole enemy force; at Kaskaskia, with incredible toil and daring, they made possible the annexation of a veritable empire. In the second war with England a wild horde of them, led by Andrew Jackson, all but annihilated Pakenham's veteran army at New Orleans.

By 1790 Tennessee had a population of 35,681 and Kentucky a population of 73,677. Two years later Kentucky was added to the Union, and four years later still, Tennessee. Ohio was admitted in 1802. By 1815 the Union consisted of eighteen states and four territories. More and more the West and its ideas had to be reckoned with; "the Valley of Democracy" was adolescent and growing.

I

Into literature this newest America came late. Earliest to picture in the form of fiction actual life in the far West, a book sometimes called the first *American* novel, is the curious volume, an early candidate for a place among the curiosities of American literature, *The Emigrants, or the History of an Expatriated Family; Being a Delineation of English Manners; Drawn from Real Characters; Written in America by G. Imlay* (1793).[1] Though written in Richardsonian letters, the work is not a novel. In his preface the author calls it a history:

In this history I have scrupulously attended to natural circumstances and the manners of the day; and in every particular I have had a real character for my model. The principal part of my story is founded upon facts, and I was only induced to give the work in the style of a novel, from believing it would prove more acceptable to the generality of readers.

It is a prolonged tract thrown into story form, its object, as its author confesses, to expose the marriage laws of England. It was published in England for Englishmen. The American part of the book is a romanticized account of the emigration of the characters to the New World to repair their fortunes, their picturesque journey across Pennsylvania, their meetings with famous border characters—Boone, Richard Henderson, Sinclair, General Wilkinson, George Rogers Clark, Crevecœur. A glorification it is of frontier life, and the noble savages who were "chasing the antelope over the plains." Thomas Moore, the poet, condemned it with heat: "such romantic works . . . would seduce us into a belief, that innocence, peace and freedom had deserted the rest of the world for Martha's Vineyard and the Banks of the Ohio."

The author of the work, Captain Gilbert Imlay, a wan-

[1] Edith Franklin Wyatt, "The First American Novel," *Atlantic Monthly* (October, 1829), CXLIV, 466.

derer and an adventurer to a degree almost exceeding
belief, common-law husband of Mary Wollstonecraft, soldier of fortune, explorer of the wild West, though born
apparently in New Jersey, can hardly be called an American. No stranger figure in the history of any literature.
His *Topographical History Description of the Western
Territory of North America* (1792), exhibits as much his
own flamboyant personality as it does the territory described.

II

A more convincing study of frontier living is J. Hector
St. John Crèvecœur's *Letters from an American Farmer,*
first issued in English in London in 1782 and 1783, and
then thrown into French by its author and issued in Paris
in 1784. Tinted undoubtedly with the Rousseau sentimentality, it has pages vividly realistic, picturings uncolored,
interpretations clear and definitive of the American frontier of its day. America for a century and a half made
small note of the early volumes. Mathew Carey's reprint
in 1793 of the London edition fell dead from the press.
It remained for Europe to recognize the book and even to
hail it as a volume to go down the years as a classic.

Born near Caen, France, in 1735 of a distinguished
family, Crèvecœur had been given every advantage for a
thorough education, even to a "finishing course in England" where he learned to speak with facility the English
language. Leaving England in 1754, he enlisted in the
French army and under Montcalm went through the last
years of the French and Indian War. Then, finding military life unfitted for his oversanguine idealism, he was
discharged at length from the service and for some years
was an unsettled wanderer. In December, 1765, however,
he became a naturalized citizen of New York State, and
in 1769 he married an American girl and settled down
as a farmer in Pine Hill, Orange County, New York. But

the idyllic farm-round he so poetically describes in his published volume seems not at all to have chained him to his
farm. To judge from his journalizings, he visited sooner
or later every section of the colonies and even beyond.
Then had come the Revolution and in 1779 his arrest as a
spy and imprisonment for months by the British. Finally
in September, 1780, permitted to sail for France, he had
been able to dispose of his *Letters* in London for thirty
guineas, and, reaching Paris, had found a publisher for an
enlarged version of the work in French. And suddenly he
had found himself famous. It was the one moment and the
one place in all history for such a volume. A second edition came immediately. He was hailed not only as a philosopher who had discovered the real secret of human
felicity, but as a practical farmer who could advise the
agriculturists of his native Normandy.

In 1783, the American war ended, he returned for his
family, but tragedy and ruin greeted him. His wife had
died, his children had been scattered, his farm buildings
destroyed. About to return to France, however, he was
made French Consul at New York, an office which held
him in America until 1790. Returning to France in that
year, he lived in practical retirement until his death in
1813.

In 1925 appeared the second part of Crèvecœur's *Letters from an American Farmer,* papers found in the family
archives in France and issued in distinctive form by the
Yale University Press. A remarkable volume! In quality
and in interest many of the letters surpass any of those in
the original series. More than half of them are documents in the history of the Revolution, so realistic and so
gruesomely truthful that undoubtedly they were thought
in 1782 unfit for publication, especially in England. The
brutalities and the unspeakable outrages upon suspected
"slackers" and Royalists, many of them totally innocent
of wrong, were not regarded as good reading for the homeland. "Now it can be told," and these revealing letters now

appear for the first time. Other parts of the newly discovered letters are as distinctive. There are beautiful passages of prose, passages unsurpassed by any writer in America before Irving; there are careful observations upon manners and movements which render their author one of the first of our social historians; and there are touches at times of real poetry.

Another work by Crèvecœur also has had an obscure history, his *Voyage dans l'haute Pennsylvania et dans l'Etat de New York,* published in Paris in three volumes, a work translated into German in 1802, but, so far as I can find, never rendered into English.

Thus the man stands between two literatures, one foot on either shore of the Atlantic. American literature must always claim him, but fundamentally was he a Frenchman of the Rousseau era. A sentimentalist he was, and a dreamer; a restless soul, an innovator, a poet. According to Bernard Fäy, "The reader felt that it [his book] was a confession, a perpetual effusion. Some passages had a tender and touching charm of which something remains even today." And again: "It is in Crèvecœur that we must seek the concept that was held about 1785 of 'The state of Nature' as the philosophers would have had it." [2]

But "the state of Nature," as Crèvecœur conceived of it, was an artificial concept even as it was with Rousseau. Fundamentally he was an aristocrat. His American colonists living in a Forest-of-Arden world, as he described it, were literally creations completely Gallic and wholly in the manner of the Rousseau-tinted times. At heart he was a Royalist. His typical American was but a transplanted European of his own class—an aristocrat who is joyous because he has brought into the American forest all his Old World winnings with none of the aristocratic inhibitions chaining him down.

[2] Bernard Fäy, *The Revolutionary Spirit in France and America* (1927), p. 234.

Americans are the western pilgrims, who carry along with them that great mass of arts, sciences, vigor, and industry which began long since in the east; they will finish the great circle. . . . They brought along with them their national genius, to which they principally owe what liberty they enjoy, and what substance they possess. Here he sees the industry of his native country displayed in a new manner, and traces in their works the embryos of all the arts, sciences, and ingenuity which flourish in Europe.

The new American democracy, coarse and strong, evolving with pain and travail in the wilds of Kentucky and Ohio and along the river valleys to the Mississippi, the democracy from which was to emerge Andrew Jackson and Abraham Lincoln, he caught glimpses of in his restless trampings, but it was only to turn away from it with disgust. Nothing here for hope and dreamings; but right here indeed, had he but realized it, in this New World "Valley of Democracy," on which, to quote Hawthorne, "the damned shadow of Europe had never fallen," he might have discovered the veritable "state of Nature" fundamentals from which was to evolve a new concept of civilization. With his European aristocratic eyes, however, he saw on the frontier only wallowing bestiality:

That new mode of life brings along with it a new set of manners which I cannot easily describe. These new manners being grafted on the old stock, produce a strange sort of lawless profligacy, the impressions of which are indelible. The manners of the Indian natives are respectable, compared with this European medley. Their wives and children live in sloth and inactivity; and having no proper pursuits you may judge what education the latter receive. Their tender minds have nothing else to contemplate but the example of their parents; like them they grow up a mongrel breed, half civilized, half savage, except nature stamps on them some constitutional propensities.

He saw only manners. This was "the state of Nature," surely, but it did not square with his theories. Men living in the American wilds must have European manners.

There are moments, however, when he forgets his simple-life pose and writes of what he has actually seen on his little farm and on his extended wanderings. Had he thrown overboard completely his ruling thesis and written only of the life he had actually observed in the new land without glorification and with nothing omitted, he would never have gained, perhaps, his contemporary vogue in France, but he would have come down to our own day with greatly more of value. As it is, these oases in his artificiality have made of him the chief writer of literary prose in prenational America, Franklin alone excepted. Pausing at times to describe the wild life about him, the "lining" of bees, the habits of native snakes, the beauties of the seasons, he becomes our first nature writer. His description of the snow-storm in the recently discovered papers reminds one of Whittier's "Snow-Bound" of later years. Moreover, in these rescued manuscripts, rejected perhaps by the first printers because they told too much of British war methods, we have a glimpse of actuality behind the scenes not recorded by the historians. "He can describe," says Stanley Williams, his biographer, "unforgettably a Negro under torture, travellers arriving for the night; children coming home from school in a snow-storm; a woman's cry as the raiders enter her home for massacre; or a family frolic."

A sentimentalist, a hopeless theorist, a wavering soul neither British nor American in the Revolutionary struggle, a Royalist who wrote in the tones of the Revolution, a painter of rainbows that led at least one European group of colonists to their ruin in the western forests, he is valuable now only for these touches of realism, vivid and still vital, brilliant exotics in the dry wilderness of the eighteenth-century classicism.

III

The first actual recording of the new forces emergent in the West was by a Princeton scholar, a poet, a dreamer of an American epic over his Homer, like his contemporaries at Yale, young Trumbull and Dwight—Hugh Henry Brackenridge. The first fruits of it had been the resonant commencement ode of 1771, "The Rising Glory of America," written for the most part by his classmate Freneau, but delivered by him on the day of graduation as the more gifted orator of the two. Oratory indeed, to the end of his life, was to be his most conspicuous endowment. The idea of poetry as a profession, however, had died hard in both of the young graduates. They had taught school, as they waited for the Muse. In charge of an academy in eastern Maryland, "in the midst of a wealthy and highly polished society," says his biographer, "greatly respected as a man of genius and scholarship," Brackenridge was on the highroad to success until the advancing forces of the Revolution put to an end his school. For the use of his pupils he had turned the first tragic episodes of the struggle into poetic dramas—*The Battle of Bunker's Hill* and *The Death of General Montgomery*, works chiefly notable for their timeliness: the first American dramas, indeed, with the Revolution their subject. Like his Connecticut contemporary poets, he had then joined the army as a chaplain, and, mustered out in 1779, he had established in Philadelphia the *United States Magazine*, notable now chiefly as containing the earliest versions of some of Freneau's best poems, notably "The House of Night." Then had come his study of law at Annapolis in the office of Samuel Chase, later to be a justice in the United States Supreme Court, and his final settlement in a law practice in Pittsburgh, then a mere hamlet on the frontier. Here for some twenty years (1781–1801) he made his home.

In literary history he is like Crèvecœur today—a man
of a single book, and that book a classic not because of
what its author believed to be its main purpose. *Modern
Chivalry,* often falsely catalogued in libraries as a novel,
is a mass of lay-sermons chiefly political and satirical
which grew by accretions year by year, infinitely varied
like a newspaper column and having as its theme "all
created things and certain others." Written not at all was
it for profit. According to its author, "Five booksellers
have made a fortune by it; for I have never asked for a
cent from any of them for the privilege of printing an
edition." The earliest version came out in Philadelphia in
1792. Part III was published in Pittsburgh the following
year, and Part IV came still later. For every edition new
matter and various changes. Nowhere such bibliographi-
cal hodgepodge.

The general plan of the work is simple. The author
makes use of the *Don Quixote* method of arriving at his
materials. Captain Farrago and his servant, Teague
O'Regan, go wandering about the country from Pittsburgh even to the national capital, have various adventures, see varieties of people including the President,
note curious manners and customs, and conclude each
episode and adventure by a lay-sermon summing up of
the philosophy of the matter by Captain Farrago, who
in reality is the author himself. Noteworthy indeed much
of this practical wisdom. Franklin-like, he counsels
always prudence and frugality and common sense. From
his speeches one might cull a veritable *Poor Richard's
Almanac* collection of homely wisdom. For example:

It requires some experience of liberty to know how to use it.

In order to speak short upon any subject, think long.

A rat can gnaw a bowstring of Philoctetes.

Recollect that you were not made for the party, but the
party for you.

The passions having their vent in a Gazette, saves battery and bloodshed.

Talk much about a thing, and you will put it into the people's heads.

So inconsistent is the multitude, that they blame today, what they themselves had caused yesterday.

Riding, by which a man is carried swiftly through the air, though it contributes to health, yet stores the mind with few or no ideas.

Unlike Crèvecœur, Brackenridge was of humble birth. His father, a Scotch farmer, had migrated to America when the boy was a child and had worked hard for a mere living. Scotch-Irish-like, he had had ambitions to see his son in the pulpit, hence strenuous efforts by both parents and boy to acquire the necessary education. By school-teaching and by tutoring he had worked his way through Princeton. Despite his scholarship, he was all his life a commoner at heart. With Freneau and Jefferson he was a democrat, opposed with all his soul to the Federalist aristocracy central in New England. In sympathy was he with the French Revolution until it became a "reign of terror." Removed to the frontier at Pittsburgh, he saw in his legal practice the raw materials of democracy, but instead of turning away from them in disgust, as did Crèvecœur, he realized their latent strength and sought to eliminate their excesses. Hence his *Modern Chivalry,* the first balanced treatment of democracy in America, the first supremely important book to come from the area beyond the Allegheny wall.

In *Modern Chivalry* we have two contrasted ideals—the conservative East, embodied in the wise Captain Farrago with his caution, his store of parallel cases drawn often from erudite volumes, his cool common sense; and opposed to him we have the new West, vibrant with physical life, irresistible, extravagant, unconventional,

seemingly immoral, wholly uncultured, independent even
to license, embodied in the red-headed Irish bog-trotter,
Teague O'Regan. And of the two, Teague alone is alive.
Brackenridge was writing the book with all seriousness.
It was not a novel for amusement or financial profit: it
was a series of republican tracts, sermonic in this intent.
"We do not write," said its author, "altogether for grave
or even grown men; our book is not for a day only. We
mean it for the coming generation, as well as the present;
and intending solid observations, we interlard pleasantry
to make the boys read."

This "pleasantry" becomes the life-blood of the book.
Manifestly he was drawing from actuality the uncouth,
adolescent Jackson-Lincoln race evolving in the valley
unshadowed by Europe. To read it is to understand from
whence came the Mark Twainness of Mark Twain and
the unique tang of the Pike County ballad. Though using
throughout the *Don Quixote* machinery, the book nevertheless is completely American, the first peculiarly American work on our shelves.

First there is Teague; a mere grotesquerie he seems at
first sight, a caricature illustrating with comic exaggeration all the failings of the western democracy. He sug-
gests Scarron's *Roman Comique* and Lesage's *Gil Blas*.
But the rascal comes to life. The women fall in love with
him, the men elect him to any office he aspires to, colleges
add him to their faculties, learned societies elect him to
membership, and but for the restraining logic of Farrago,
exerted after every outbreak of the youth's ambition, he
might have gone who knows to what extreme. Teague at
one time is made to believe that he has actually been
elected to succeed the Devil, and starts to reign in that
exalted capacity. One realizes quickly why the book was
so popular with the unliterary class.

Again, the book is made of wild-western materials. We
are present at elections and are made to realize what
really counts in the primitive game of political electioneer-

ing. Two men are candidates, one of them grave and wise, the other with two kegs, and, mounting a stump, the two-keg man thus harangued the electorate:

Friends, I'm a good dimicrat, and hates the Brattish— I'm an elder of the meetin, forby, and has been overseer of the roads for three years.—An' ye all know, that my mammy was kilt o' the Ingens—now all ye that's in my favour, come forit and drenk.

The election was unanimous, a fact that tremendously impressed Teague and sent him galloping into a new adventure from which he had to be rescued by the captain.

Western outspokenness touches even the explosive stuff of religion. He condemns the general run of the clergy in the same terms that he condemns rascally lawyers:

Te clerchy, said an honest German; te clerchy is te pickest rokes from de two. An honest Sherman minister as knows nottin is petter as tem. Te lawyers is worser as te dyvil, mit tare pooks, and sheets te beeples for te money. Larning is gute for nix, als to make roques. It is all gontrive to sheet te beeples.

He can endure even Tom Paine, synonym throughout all Christendom for arch-atheist and infidel:

I have no respect for those narrow minded bigots, who are constantly alarmed at the progress of science. They are only sceptics of another kind. They unconsciously betrayed doubt, and want of confidence, by their efforts to avert investigation. These are the men who uphold witchcraft, and the revolution of the sun, through fear that the contrary man be inconsistent with particular passages of scripture.

Everywhere pictures of the trans-Allegheny West, and always with no squeamishness in the handling of coarseness. The new humanity, trained on the frontier, rather attracted him:

The stripling of these woods is distinguished from the city beau; but it will not become me to say who has the advantage; whether the attitude of the presented rifle, or that of the segar in the teeth, is the most manly? Which looks best, the hunting shirt open at the neck, or the roll of muslin that covers it and swells upon the chin? These are things to be canvassed by the curious. I am of the opinion, however, that it is better to be clear-sighted than purblind, and to be able to see a deer in the thicket, than to have need of a glass before the nose, to direct the steps where there is nothing to stumble over.

And he adds as a foot-note:

There can be no doubt of the improvement in form and feature of those born and brought up in a healthy wooded country, of hills and valleys, with a fertile soil, like that on the Ohio river and its tributaries. Abundance of wholesome food, labor moderate, and exercise in the open air, will account for the physical improvements in the natives of the west.

Nothing seems to have escaped him. "The vehicle which I have chosen," he remarks, "of supposed travels and conversations affords great scope and much freedom and furnishes an opportunity to enliven with incident. Doubtless it is of the same nature with many things in the novel way, written by philosophic men, who chose that form of writing, for the purpose of merely convey-ing sentiments, which in a didactic work, under the head of tract or dissertation, could not easily gain attention, or procure readers."

But it is preëminently the humor that brands it with the herd-mark, *Western*. First, there is the border type of mirth, the type illustrated in the chapter headings, which undoubtedly Irving read and laughed over before writing his *Knickerbocker's History*. One may choose at random:

CHAPTER XXII. Curious dream of the captain, from which he is awakened by a real occurrence—Battle between Teague

and the hostler about the best mode of currying a horse—
National vanity of foreigners—Reflections.

CHAPTER XXIII. The captain proposes to Teague to pass the
night in the open air according to the usages of chivalry—
Teague objects and they repair to a house near the road—
Of what befel them at the widow's.

CHAPTER XXIV. Which recounts the wicked theft of a
clergyman's credentials by a yarn merchant—The trial by
preaching—Farrago shows himself a wise compounder of dif-
ferences.

But western exaggeration had begun its work. Here
are the amazing adventures of two Lindberghs of the
1790's; the balloon was then a newly invented wonder:

Passing a cloud, I put out my hand, and took a piece of it,
and squeezed it like a spongue, and the water ran out freely.
As we ascended to a considerable height, the sun went north
about, but never set. At a distance of about fifty miles above
the earth, we saw a beautiful white bird setting on the corner
of a cloud, and took it to be one of Mahommet's pigeons. If
we had a gun we could have shot it. Passing by the moon we
saw a man selling land at auction. He wished us to give a bid,
but we declared we had no desire to buy lands in the moon.
We came across a comet, it appeared to be asleep; it had a
tail like that of a red fox, but much larger.

About a hundred leagues from the earth, the balloon struck
against a wasps' nest and we were in great danger from their
stings; fortunately we were blown off by a sudden flaw of
wind.

Coming near a hail bank, we filled a hat; some of the hail-
stones were as large as goose eggs.

About a thousand miles above the earth, we passed through
a field of turkey buzzards.

And so on to Venus where a vast wedding was in progress, to Mars, and then to Saturn where they found the
rings too large to bring back as relics. There is sometimes
a Shakespearean atmosphere about his findings in the
wildwood, as for instance the discovery in "the Mad-

cap settlement" that one Harum Scarum, notorious as a fighter and duelist, had posted billets on the trees with this inscription:

Take notice, that I, Harum Scarum, gentleman, do hereby post and publish the beasts of these woods to be scoundrels, liars, and cowards, of which let all men take notice; that no man of honor may keep company with them, but consider them as poltroons and rascals.

The Mad-caps, seeing these as they were rounding up their cattle, "were put into great passion" and gathered to fight Captain Farrago and his men:

The Captain saw the necessity of some active measures on his part, and collecting his men, began to form. He had with him the player on the bagpipes, and Tom the Tinker, who turned a piece of tin into a kettle drum, and beat on it the rogues march, which was the only point of war that he could beat. Will Watlin had a saplin of hickory, and O'Fin his flail, which he had brought along with him, not knowing but he might get a job of threshing by the way.

He had now got a job, it is true; but not of the same kind that he meant—wheat at six-pence a bushel—but people's brains to beat out, or their bones to break; a thing as unprofitable as it is unlawful. The Captain being a military man, was thinking of the science and manœuvres put in practice by the ancient and modern commanders, by which they gained battles. He deliberated whether to advance in a single column, until within a certain distance, and then halt with the head, while the rear wheeled round and struck like a serpent with its tail, in the manner Epimanondas gained the battle of Leuctra. Or whether he should imitate Hannibal at—I forget at what battle, with the Romans, and oppose a semi-circle, with a convex to the enemy; and which yielding in the centre changed to a crescent, and received the adversary in its horns, which encompassing the flanks, cut them to pieces; or whether he should pierce the enemies centre by successive masses, thus cutting him in two and destroying each part separately. He was debating with himself whether he should advance to a certain height, or rely upon an ambuscade among the bushes in the plain, when, in the meantime, Clonmel the ballad singer struck up a song in the centre, and the Mad-caps began to listen ; and though they had as many arms as a learned lawyer puts in his declaration,—"swords, staves and knives,"— they dropped them all, and seemed to return good humor.

An episode, it would seem, from *Knickerbocker's History of New York* written ten years later. Clonmel's ballad, a true Western river carrouse of the "half-horse half-alligator" type tempered by Scotch-Irish Presbyterianism, is the first note to come East of what was to be the wild-western Pike County balladry :

What use is in fighting, and gouging and biting,
    Far better to let it alone ;
For kicking and cuffing, and boxing and buffing,
    It makes the flesh ache, and the bone.

But give me the whiskey, it makes one so frisky,
    But beating and bruising make sore ;
Come shake hands, my cronies, come near my dear honies,
    And think of your grudges no more.

We are a set of poor fellows, just escaped from the gallows,
    And hunting a wolf or a bear,
And what with a tail on, except the camelion,
    Can live upon fog, or the air ?

Some venison haunches, to fill up our paunches,
    Come see if you cannot produce,
A barbecued pig, a nice mutton leg,
    Or turkey, or bit of a goose.

We have store of good liquor, so bring something quicker,
    And club your potatoes and yams ;
We'll make a great feast, and turn all to a jest,
    So away with your frowns and your dams.

Clonmel's ballads grow always from actual conditions. No European echoes in these homespun products :

Come gather away to the new town,
There's nothing but lilting there,
  And piping and singing and dancing,
Throughout every day of the year,
  No maid that comes here but gets married,
Before she is here half an hour;
  The brown, the black, or the hair red,
To live single is not in her power.

  We get our provisions for nothing;
Just knock down a wolf or a bear,
  The wear and the tear of our clothing,
A dress'd skin, or just in the hair.
  No trouble, no bubble, no sweating,
Like people that live in the smoke,
  We catch the fresh fish with the netting,
And roast them just under the oak.

And so stanza after stanza to the rollicking end:

  Oh, what is life but a blister,
Put on we cannot tell where;
  And sorrow herself is a sister,
To thinking and much taking care.
  So let us be jovial and jolly,
And make out as well as we can!
  Who knows whether wisdom or folly,
Makes the better or the happier man.

For literature the new land demanded newspapers, and newspapers that stirred things vigorously. "A newspaper is a battery, and it must have something to batter at"— and who better than the lawyers? "The chief foes of democracy are lawyers," shouts Harum Scarum, the frontier democrat. "So much for lawyers; they are under way, and down they go. . . . The more free the people, the more prolific are these fellows; it is the rank growth of freedom, shewing the productive energy of the soil." Down with the law! The press was a weapon for the blackguarding of rascals, and editors like Peter Pole Cat and Peter Porcupine were precisely what the people wanted.

Hear John Robeson, the carpenter, from his stump-rostrum:

I am for supporting the press. The objection is, that it is a black-guard press. But while there are black-guards to write and to read, must they not have a press? Is it only men of polished education that have the right to express their sentiments? Let them write in magazines, or have gazettes of their own, but not restrict the right that people of a less cultivated understanding, have to amuse themselves and others with their lucubrations. You call us the Swinish multitude; and yet you refuse us the food that is natural to us. Are there not amongst us those that have no relish for disquisitions on the balance of power, or form of governments, agricultural essays, or questions of finance, but can relish a laugh raised at the expense of the master of a family; or a public character in high station; if for no other reason, but because it gratifies the self-love of those who cannot attain the same eminence. Take away from us this and what have we more? What is the press to us, but as it gratifies envy? Is there to be an end to the lies, ribaldry and abuse, so necessary for the amusement of the people? One might as well attempt to put down bull fights in Spain.

A hodgepodge undoubtedly, this chaotic book. All America is in it: prose and poetry, philosophy and horse-play, dialect and Addisonian diction, humor and pathos. A dozen frontier characters stand clean-cut, and a dozen frontier characteristics. But never lost in the miscellany is the author's central thesis: democratic power unbalanced is the despotism of the many instead of one. "Democracy to be safe must be balanced" Teague O'Regan, Harum Scarum, Will Watlin whose specialty was "taming wild geese and brewing beer out of wasps' nests," Tom "the tinker hankering after insurrection," O'Fin the politician—yes, all of these, but balanced always by the common sense and the poise and the wisdom of the

Captain Farragos. To understand the America of the two decades before Jefferson, the president, one must read diligently in Brackenridge's *Modern Chivalry:*

I shall have accomplished something by this book, if it shall keep some honest man from lessening his respectability by pushing himself into public trusts for which he is not qualified; or when pushed forward into public station, if it shall contribute to keep him honest by teaching him the folly of ambition, and farther advancement; when in fact, the shade is more to be coveted, and the mind, on reflection, will be better satisfied with itself, for having chosen it. This is in great part, the moral of this book; if it should be at all necessary to give a hint of it.

CHAPTER XI

THE OPENING CENTURY

THE OPENING fifteen years of the new century were the most unliterary in our annals. Fisher Ames, in an essay issued in 1809, could even allege that, "excepting the writers of two able works on our politicks, we have no authors." [1] Ingersoll in 1810, conscious of "the scorn of Europe," could hold up in rebuttal only Barlow's *Columbiad* and Marshall's *Life of Washington*.[2] New England could point only at the "Hartford Wits."

American poetry was consumptive and hopeless. Consider William Cliffton, whose poetic remains were gathered in 1800:

> In these cold shades, beneath these shifting skies,
> Where Fancy sickens, and where genius dies;
> Where few and feeble are the Muse's strains,
> And no fine frenzy riots in the veins,
> Where still are found a few to whom belong,
> The fire of virtue and the soul of song;
> Whose kindling ardor still can wake the strings
> Where learning triumphs, and when Gifford sings,
> To thee the lowliest Bard his tribute pays,
> His little wild-flower to thy wreath conveys;
> Pleas'd, if permitted round thy name to bloom,
> To boast one effort rescued from the tomb.[3]

---

[1] "American Literature," in the collected volume of Ames's *Works* (1809), p. 459—"the first elaborate and really thoughtful essay on American Literature."

[2] Charles J. Ingersoll, *Inchiquin, the Jesuit's Letters,* Chapter VII.

[3] *Epistle to W. Gifford, Esq. Written at the request of Mr. Cobbett, and prefixed to his edition of that gentleman's Elegant poem, "The Baviad & Maeviad."* Philadelphia, 13th May, 1799. 152 lines.

Consider Freneau:

> On these bleak climes by fortune thrown,
> Where rigid reason reigns alone,
> Where lovely fancy has no sway,
> Nor magic forms about us play—
> Nor Nature takes her summer hue,
> Tell me what has the muse to do?

Freneau, always suggestive when in the mood of prophecy, believed that the age of poetry was over. Much he wrote after his 1809 collection, but nothing of significance. This was his swan-song:

> To seize some *features* from the faithless past;
> Be this our care—before the century close:
> The colours strong! for, if we deem aright,
> The *coming age will be an age of prose:*
> When *sordid cares* will break the muses' dream,
> And Common Sense be ranked in seat supreme.

The opening decade of the new century, with the new Republic in full swing, with the great new world of the western frontier opening its untold possibilities for man, with Jefferson for a handful of gold adding to the Republic the vast Northwest Territory, with the very air electric with a new hope: America should have been a nest of singing birds. But instead of Elizabethan joy, Hudibrastic whimperings:

> Our learned world is chiefly fed
> With flummery and gingerbread,
> Whipped syllabub and pepper-pot
> By Jacobins served piping hot,
> Vile fricassees of foreign trash,
> Sour krout and gallimaufry hash
> And stuff more gross than what the group
> Of Macbeth's witches formed for soup.
> This vilest baggage in creation
> Has taught the great men of our nation,

> In wealth though wallowing, to neglect
> And starve down works of intellect.[4]

A land infinite in epic possibilities, infinite in vitality, yet a land that during the life of one whole generation produced not a single classic destined to endure. Endlessly it talked of native literature, *American* literature, "the Republic of Letters"—one saw it everywhere. The nation had won its independence from England, why not make independence complete? Freneau, who hated the British with Gallic intensity, was one of the earliest voices:

> Can we never be thought to have learning or grace
> Unless it is brought from that horrible place?

The literary juntos of Boston and Philadelphia defended the English models, even while deploring their decline from classic standards. What better advice was ever given the beginner in letters, men like Dennie would urge, than Dr. Johnson's—the giving of one's days and nights to the study of Addison? But a younger generation had arrived—intolerable.

> The age of good English poetry ended with the reign of Queen Anne; the British muse has from that period been declining in a gradual nervous decay; her young offspring, the American Muse, inherited from her parent the same disorder; and both are now in the last stage of an incurable hectic.[5]

For all the literature of "the Republic of Letters" it had supremest contempt:

> If the flowers of poetry are not to be found in the academic bowers, it is vain to expect them on the dunghills of democracy. . . . So great has been the democratic rage of late years that every production of the *Sansculotte* school has been extolled, cherished, and circulated.[6]

[4] Peter-Pepper-Box (Thomas G. Fessenden), *Pills Poetical, Political, and Philosophical* (1802), p. 94.
[5] *Monthly Anthology*, 1805.
[6] *Ibid.*

I

The eighteenth century died hard. The universities nursed the moribund thing with solicitude. In America at least it did not die until well beyond the first quarter of the new century. At every commencement either a poem or a Phi Beta Kappa oration explaining American literary conditions, deploring them, and suggesting remedies:

The Present State of Literature, a Poem Delivered at New Haven, at the Public Commencement of Yale College, September 10, 1800, by Warren Dutton.

Want of Patronage the principal cause of the slow progress of American Literature, an Oration delivered before the society of Phi Beta Kappa on the Anniversary at that institution by Samuel F. Jarvis, New Haven, 1806.

Upon the importance of Literature to Our Country, Pronounced before the Phi Beta Kappa at their Anniversary at Cambridge, 27 August, 1807, by Theodore Dehon, A. M.[7]

The Literary Delinquency of America, by William Tudor, Delivered before the Phi Beta Kappa anniversary meeting at Cambridge, 1815.

The Circumstances Favorable to the Progress of Literature in America, Edward Everett. Delivered before the Phi Beta Kappa. Harvard, 1824.[8]

One might lengthen the list to the extent of a chapter.

The oration by Jarvis was gloomy and at times bitter: "There is no light in which our country can be contemplated with less satisfaction to genuine patriotism than in her literary relations." A leading cause, he declared, was "want of discipline in our schools and the almost universal pursuit of wealth by our Citizens." The remedy was rigor: there are needed "curbs for the mulish mouth of headlong youth." Another cause was the growing lack of respect for the clergy: "It is an axiom that literature will never flourish but in those countries where there is a

[7] Published entire in the *Monthly Anthology*.
[8] William Hopkins Tillinghast, *Bibliography of the Phi Beta Kappa Fraternity* (1891), p. 42.

learned clergy, and never will there be a learned clergy, unless they are regarded with reverence and supported with dignity." But the chief reason for literary barrenness, he believed, was the refusal of the rich to patronize arts and letters: "It is idle to believe that America will ever become a literary nation unless some permanent establishment can be made for the support of the learned; and this can be effected only in two ways: either by the generosity of individuals, or the munificence of government."

A clear voice from the moribund eighteenth century.

Tudor also was pessimistic, but there was less of the clerical in his arguments and less of the rigor of classicism:

If all the elements of our literature were collected into a mass it would amount merely to the accidental efforts of a very few adventurous individuals. Who is there among us who has dared to write a book that has received from our literary republic one smile to reward his labors? How few of our works have survived the question of our own criticism! The explanation of our delinquency is to be found principally in our dependence on English literature. We are not only dependent and wanting in literary enterprise, but we are deficient in genuine intellectual courage.

We are told that the literary market is full, that we cannot consume our literary importations—that there is no demand for American literature. There is not a stall for our literary wares in the whole market of letters. One reason is that our best writers have been unfortunate in their choice of depositories—newspapers and pamphlets. Such forms are sure to be short-lived and almost always contain nothing but controversial material.

Another powerful objection is the vehicles chosen for our literature—they are almost always short and allow but a very narrow view of the subject.[9]

[9] Reviewed in the *North American Review*, Vol. II, under the title, "The State of American Literature." Tudor was editor of the magazine.

After 1820 the outlook from the college platforms grew more cheerful. John C. Gray, in his Harvard Phi Beta Kappa address, August 30, 1821, could even congratulate the nation on the outlook for American letters: "Our writers are every day increasing in numbers and in merit. Our standard of excellence is rapidly rising, our readers are constantly becoming more correct and more severe in their requisitions." Edward Everett, returning from his years of study at Göttingen University, was even more optimistic. He was amazed, he said, at "the astonishing development of intellectual energy in this country." Doubtless he defined "this country" as New England, with Harvard at the center, but his optimism was soon affecting wider areas.

One other voice of the period must not be overlooked. More important perhaps than any of the Phi Beta Kappa orations was Everett's essay on "The Importance and Means of a National Literature" in *The Christian Examiner* of January, 1830. Robert E. Spiller, comparing this address with Emerson's "The American Scholar," finds it

inferior in literary quality to the more famous address on the same topic, but it contains the outlines of the same philosophical position and a statement of an identical demand for American mental self reliance which was attained by the Emersonian methods of study and meditation. There is reason now to regard Emerson's essay as a declaration of New England's rather than America's self-consciousness. The frontier, agrarian, and industrial movements have given to American literature ideals and forms which are not included within the metaphysical limits of that document.[10]

II

The eighteenth century died hard, especially in New England. Federalism was its last stand. Jeffersonian

[10] *New England Quarterly Review,* Vol. III (1930).

Democracy was sweeping in like a tide, irresistible. The new West was coming into sight. Virgin lands compel democracy. Relentless, surrounded with the wreckage of the older culture, it bursts all bounds. America was predominatingly agrarian. "Not more than 350,000 of the seven millions composing the population of the American states," wrote Inchiquin in 1810, "reside in large towns. The remainder live on farms or in villages. Most of them are proprietors of the soil." And again:

There is no populace (plebs). All are people (populus). What in other countries is called the populace, a compost heap, whence germinate mobs, beggars, and tyrants, is not to be found in the towns; and there is no peasantry in the country. Were it not for the slaves of the south there would be but one rank.

Upon them all was the compulsion of work, the compulsion of making a living—"the mother of democracy."

For the first time in ages a continent completely new to be won to civilization. No old order to be displaced, no conquered races to be amalgamated. Everywhere newness and vastness. "On one side the sea," wrote Inchiquin, "and on the other rich waste lands present inexhaustible fields of adventure and opulence."

Such conditions will create no classic literature; they will evolve a literature of their own. The very atmosphere of America compelled it. Eighteenth centuryism expressed itself in the classic essay, the "finished" oration, the "elegant" poem mindful of ancient laws; American democracy evolved the newspaper, the epic of democracy, written on flying sheets, to be read in a day—and forgotten in a day.

"From the reverend doctor Miller's Retrospect of the Eighteenth Century," quoted by Isaiah Thomas in his *History of Printing* (1810), note this paragraph:

Our own country in particular, and especially for the last twelve or fifteen years, has exhibited a spectacle never before

displayed among men, and even yet without a parallel on
earth. It is the spectacle, not of the learned and wealthy only,
but of the great body of the people; even a large portion
of that class of the community which is destined to daily labor,
having free and constant access to public prints, receiving
regular information of every occurrence, attending to the
course of political affairs, discussing public measures, and
having thus presented to them constant excitements to the
acquisition of knowledge, and continual means of obtaining
it. Never, it may be safely asserted, was the number of
political journals so great in proportion to the population of
a country as at present in ours. Never were they, all things
considered, so cheap, so universally diffused, and so easy of
access. And never were they actually perused by so large a
majority of all classes since the art of printing was discovered.[11]

"Newspapers," wrote Noah Webster in his paper, the
American Minerva, in the mid-nineties, "in a great degree
supersede the use of Magazines and Pamphlets. The
public mind in America, roused by the magnitude of
political events, and impatient of delay, cannot wait for
monthly intelligence." Politics quickly became a warfare
waged on the lowest levels of personal vilification, as in
the newspaper war in Philadelphia between the *National
Gazette,* Fenno's *Gazette of the United States,* and Cobbett's *Porcupine's Gazette and Daily Advertiser.*

The American press from the Revolution to the present
day has been absolutely free. The President of the Republic has been as open to attack as the meanest citizen.
This from Fisher Ames concerning Jefferson:

If we had a Pindar, he would be ashamed to celebrate our
chief, and would be disgraced, if he did. But if he did not,
his genius would not obtain his election for a selectman in a
democratick town. It is party that bestows emolument, power,
and consideration; and it is not excellence in the sciences that
obtains the suffrages of party.[12]

[11] Vol. II, p. 404.
[12] *Works of Fisher Ames* (1809), p. 471.

"The vilest trash," wrote Freneau in 1800, "has here a currency above all the eloquence of Plato." Journalism without idealism was debauching the American people, he believed. Who would read classic literature with Porcupine's latest quill-volley on the table before him? In an editorial of his New York *Time-Piece* he wrote:

It is an easy matter to fill the columns of a Gazette, as the world now goes, with the history of military marches, details of battles and sieges, storms, shipwrecks, murders, and that endless variety of events that are continually rising and floating on the surface of human things; but all these things do little more than gratify curiosity and leave the mind benighted as to the interests of humanity and bettering the condition of human nature.

The *Monthly Anthology,* founded in November, 1803, complained that already the book product of the nation had been debauched by journalism. There were being published "essays which grew out of occasion and which were intended to be laid aside with the newspaper in which they appeared."

Every "ephemeral" contributor to the columns of a newspaper, after a time, comes forth "stitched in blue" or "bound in calf." So that a library, composed of modern publication, will soon exceed the ancient Roman laws, which according to Livy, *tam immensus aliarum superalias acervatarum legum cumulus,* that they were computed to be the burden of many camels. This is one of the evils incident to the early state of literature in all countries, and which can only be alleviated by time and experience. . . . At present there seem to be more writers than readers in this country.

It is noteworthy, however, that the newspapers of America were the first literary areas to free themselves from the influence of foreign models. The newspaper writer wrote to be understood; he wrote at the level of his readers; he wrote because he had something to say. The

Boston junto found even the new advertising significant:

American advertisements are universally written with a simplicity, a clearness, a precision, a brevity, and by consequence, an elegance, which we in vain look for in the advertising columns of an English, an Irish, or a Scottish newspaper.

III

One rank growth of the 1790's, decade of wild ideas and revolution, was the project of an independent American language. A writer in Brown's *Monthly Magazine*, July, 1800, discussed the theme at length under the title, "On the Scheme of an American Language":

Some of those among us, who devote themselves to letters, are extremely anxious that, as we are politically independent and distinct from other nations, we should like to be so in literature and language. They are ambitious of obtaining, not only a national individuality in policy and jurisdiction, not only a government that shall be American, but likewise an American *language*. For this end, they think grammars and dictionaries should be compiled by natives of the country, not of the British or English, but of the *American* tongue.

Already the movement had gained a strong leader, and for more than a decade he had been issuing propaganda. So completely had the idea converted Noah Webster that he had made of it a life-work. Even before the establishment of the new government he had formulated his plan. America, he argued, had gained her independence and was laying the foundations of an independent nation, therefore:

Let us then seize the present moment, and establish a *national language,* as well as a national government. Let us remember that there is a certain respect due to the opinions of other nations. As an independent people, our reputation abroad demands that, in all things, we should be federal; be *national*.

We have the fairest opportunity of establishing a national language, and of giving it uniformity and perspicuity, in North America, that ever presented itself to Mankind. Now is the time to begin the plan.

The English with others is suffering continual alterations. America placed at a distance from those nations, will feel, in a much less degree, the influence of the assimilating causes; at the same time, numerous local causes, such as a new country, new associations of people, new combination of ideas in arts and science, and some intercourse with tribes wholly unknown in Europe, will introduce new words into the American tongue. These causes will produce, in a course of time, a language in North America, as different from the future language of England, as the modern Dutch, Danish and Swedish are from the German or from one another.[13]

Not only should there be a new language based upon American newnesses, but there should be, he maintained, a simplification of the spelling. In this he went to radical extremes. He had published his advocacy of this newness, he declared, since

I very early discuvered, that altho the name of an old and respectable karacter givs credit and consequence to hiz ritings, yet the name of a yung man iz often prejudicial to his performances. By conceeling my name, the opinions of men hav been prezerved from an undu bias arizing from personal prejudices, the faults of the ritings hav been detected, and their merit in public estimation ascertained.

Pressing his theories still farther, in 1790 he issued a volume with the simplified spelling, *A Collection of Essays and Fugitive Writings on Moral, Historical, Political and Literary Subjects,* the first book of its kind ever attempted in America. Not wholly, he explained, could he follow the simplified spelling:

[13] Noah Webster, *Dissertations on the English Language: with Notes Historical and Critical* (Boston, 1789), pp. 406, 36, 20.

The reeder will obzerv that the orthography of the volum
iz not uniform. The reezon iz that many of the essays have
been published before, in the common orthography, and it
would have been a laborious task to copy the whole, for the sake
of changing the Spelling.

With fine courage he began at once the compiling of a
"Columbian Dictionary," a volume that was to break
completely from Doctor Johnson's standard work and
record the English spoken in America. But by 1800 he
had yielded to criticism and was preparing a school
dictionary less revolutionary.

Strictly speaking, Webster is to be counted with the
Connecticut group of writers. He was a graduate of Yale
in the same class as Joel Barlow—1778. While teaching
in a classical school in Goshen, New York, he completed a
series of text-books which were to exert a strong influence
upon American scholarship and American literature—his
English Grammar (1784) and *An American Selection of
Lessons in Reading and Speaking, Calculated to Improve
the Minds and Refine the Taste of Youth* (1787). The
stories he reproduced became household words. The
books entered all the schools. Millions were sold, the re-
sulting funds greatly helping the struggling author in the
lean period of his dictionary-making.

Receding at last almost wholly from his original plans,
he issued his first American dictionary in 1806, octavo
in size, a mere preliminary study. But though he had re-
ceded from his simplified-spelling theories, he departed
greatly from the conventional usages, and, as a result,
opposition came upon him like a flood. Dennie denounced
as "wigwam words" his admitted Americanisms like
"lengthy," "sot," "spry," "gunning," "belittle," "caucus."
The dictionary, he declared, was "a disgrace to letters.
It is a record of our imbecility, a map and a journal of
our tottering and imperfect step in the walks of literature." And again: "As the dictionary, I understand, is to
be the dictionary of the vulgar tongue in New England,

would it not be better to prefix to it the epithet *Cabotian* instead of Columbian? Sebastian Cabot first discovered these Eastern States." For a decade and more the dictionary furnished topics for literary-club meetings and letters to magazines.

But Webster worked courageously on. His completed work appeared in 1828 when its author was seventy years of age. "Twenty-five hundred copies were printed in America and three thousand in England." Gradually has the volume grown during the century that has followed, until the final edition (1935) is a monument to American scholarship.

IV

Akin to Webster's attempt to start the new American Republic with a total uprooting of all literary evils was the campaign of the same period against Latin and Greek in the college curriculum. Typical of the attacks everywhere upon the old curriculum was the volume that Dr. Benjamin Rush of Philadelphia discharged at the evil. Latin and Greek, he argued, "make for a scholarly vocabulary not understood by the rank and file of the uncolleged populace." "The popularity of the Methodist preachers," he believed, "may be ascribed in part to their speaking in a language that is intelligible to the common people."

It is equally plain that the corruption of our language by the constant substitution of words of Greek and Latin origin, to those which had become familiar and universal, from long usage, has greatly retarded the progress of knowledge of all kinds, but in the more especial manner, a great proportion of that species of it which is delivered from the pulpit.[14]

Literature had become aristocratic. Most of the American writers were college men, educated in the classics and

[14] Benjamin Rush, M.D., *Essays Literary, Moral, and Philosophical,* 7th edition (1806), p. 33. First edition published in 1798.

readable only by the sophisticated few. Even the Boston junto which conducted the *Monthly Anthology* was inclined to be critical. This from the review of John Blair Linn's poem, "The Powers of Genius":

Yet nothing now, too, is admired by many, but the *hoary*. Nothing but the classicks, the classicks, the classicks! A smooth gentleman, from Alma Mater, tutors you, forsooth, that this performance is classical and that is not classical; our posies are all senseless; forced exoticks nourished by foreign fire, painted leaves of tiffany wound on formal wire. When, oh when, shall the winter of criticism be passed and the springtime of passion return! when shall the library be deserted for the fields, and poetry ruminate in the shades, she loves to depicture! when, oh when, shall the idolatry of learning be superseded by the worship of truth! We are surfeited with the repetition of repetitions.[15]

Dennie rated such statements as sheer anarchy. To maintain the safe old traditions he proposed "A confederacy of men of letters not exceeding in number that of the French academy":

After sufficiently decrying the ordinary systems of education, they might revive classical discipline, create a passion for pure undefiled English, guide the taste and fortify the judgment of youth, multiply the editions of sterling authors, and *absolutely eradicate every bad book in the country*. By all the sharpness of Satire, aided by all the strength of Judgment, they might cut down that Bohun Upas of democracy, whose baleful power corrupts the life-blood of the nation, and plant in its place a TREE OF KNOWLEDGE, under which men might sit as under the beatific *Vine and Fig-tree* of the Gospel, and none to make them afraid.[16]

A tragic figure, Joseph Dennie. With the new springtime opening all about him, he was planning for midwinter eternal.

[15] Vol. II (1805), p. 531.
[16] *Port Folio*, new prospectus, 1806.

V

Despite unliterary conditions and unliterary readers, despite the fact that most books must be published at the author's expense or else by subscription, the output during the fifteen years was large. In a single year, 1805, the Boston *Anthology* reviewed eighty-seven American books, forty-five of them, however, pamphlet-sermons and Fourth of July orations. Kettell, in his *Specimens of American Poetry*, lists eighty-seven volumes of native verse issued from 1800 to 1815 inclusive. Poor stuff for the most part! Among all the poetry and prose of fifteen years I find only twenty-six books in any way notable:

1800   *Poems Chiefly Occasional*, William Cliffton.
        Life of Washington, M. L. Weems.
1801   *Tour Through Silesia*, John Q. Adams.
        Edgar Huntly, Charles Brockden Brown.
1803   *Terrible Tractoration, a Poem &c.*, Christopher Caustic (T. G. Fessenden).
        Letters of the British Spy, William Wirt.
1804   *The Life of George Washington*, John Marshall.
1805   *American Annals*, Abiel Holmes.
        History of the Revolution, Mercy Warren.
1806   *A Compendious Dictionary of the English Language*, Noah Webster.
1807   *The Columbiad*, Joel Barlow.
        Salmagundi, Irving and others.
1808   *The Embargo*, William Cullen Bryant.
        Female Quixotism, Tabitha Tenney.
        American Ornithology, Vol. I, Alexander Wilson.
1809   *Speeches and Writings*, Fisher Ames.
        A History of New York, Washington Irving.
        The Foresters, Alexander Wilson.
1810   *Inchiquin, the Jesuit's Letters*, C. J. Ingersoll.
1812   *The Works in Verse and Prose of the Late Robert Treat Paine.*
        Diverting History of John Bull and Brother Jonathan, J. K. Paulding.

1813   *The Sylphs of the Seasons*, Washington Allston.
       The Life of George Fred Cooke, William Dunlap.
       The Lay of the Scottish Fiddle, J. K. Paulding.
1815   *The Life of Charles Brockden Brown*, [Allen and]
       Dunlap.
       A Collection of Poems on American Affairs, Philip
       Freneau.

CHAPTER XII

RISE OF THE REVIEWS

I

THE HISTORIAN of American literature gets not far into the new republican century before he finds himself bogged in a slough until lately uncharted and unpenetrated—the literary magazines. The latest explorer to emerge, Frank L. Mott, author of *A History of American Magazines,* describes fifty literary periodicals (not newspapers) started in the single decade of the 1790's:

> Seven of them were started in the single year 1795, and there were few years thereafter which saw less than ten magazines begun. But only three of all those started in the closing years of the eighteenth century outlasted two years, and it was not until 1811 that an American literary magazine could celebrate a tenth birthday: in that year the *Port Folio* had rounded out a decade.

The history of American literature even to the present has been the history of literary magazines.[1] All the prominent writers of the new Republic—Freneau, Brackenridge, Noah Webster, Thomas Paine, Mathew Carey, Isaiah Thomas, Royall Tyler, Dennie, Fessenden, William Emerson—served literature at one time or another as editors. The dream of every literary youth, every

---

[1] See William Beer, *Checklist of American Periodicals, 1740–1800,* reprinted from *Proceedings of the American Antiquarian Society* (1923). See also P. L. Ford, *Checklist of American Magazines Printed in the Eighteenth Century* (1889).

literary club, was a magazine in which he could publish at his own freewill.

Publication of books was not easily achieved in the early decades of the Republic. Reprinting the best-sellers from England occupied to the full the publishers and booksellers. There was no money in native ventures. The unknown writer had to obtain a list of subscribers before a publisher would look at his volume. And the poor American author:

> Figure to yourself an author, with hat in one hand and— *"Proposal for Publishing"* in the other; running from bookseller to printer, from printer to stationer, from stationer to barber's shop—and the picture is an American. It is a fact, with but few exceptions, that belles lettres publications in this country have been money from the author's pockets. The mystery is simple and plain: no printer or bookseller undertakes a publication, without indemnity from the author: and having secured his pay—leaves the work to find its way into the city, or die in the hands of the publisher.[2]

From the writer's standpoint it seemed cheaper and more certain of results to start a little *Spectator*-like magazine of his own of the *Salmagundi* variety. The result, of course, was always the same: a few weeks or perhaps months, and then financial catastrophe. The list of such ephemeræ is a long one. Most of the major authors began their literary lives as editors of such homemade little periodicals.[3]

With the new century began the age of the literary review: in Great Britain, the *Edinburgh Review* (1802), the *Quarterly Review* (1808), *Blackwood's* (1817); and with these there began the *Edinburgh* type of reviewing, the long approach to the subject in hand, the cutting and slashing of the book and its author, and then the cocksure detailing of what should have been done.

---

[2] "Petronius," in the *Farmer's Museum* (Walpole, N. H., 1801).
[3] The most noteworthy was Richard H. Dana's *Idle Man* (1821-1822).

To the Anglophobians in America and the politically-minded, the circulation of these reviews on this side of the water was regarded as a menace. Solyman Brown in 1818 ranked them among the insidious forces tending to undermine the structure of our national independence. They had been established, he declared, "under the eye of the British ministry."

These unmasked batteries, erected on the Forth and the Thames, are in the republic of letters, what the English navy is upon the ocean—the terror of mankind. The two grand designs of these periodical publications, are to extol the literary productions of England, and ridicule those of every other country. These Reviews are sedulously circulated in the United States, for which they seem principally designed.[4]

Little cause was there, however, for alarm. The American *people*—the general populace—were not reading the *Edinburgh Review,* or any other review. The lovers of up-to-date "polite literature" read it and adopted its methods in their reviewings, but their numbers were small.

It is not the *vocation* of Americans to cultivate polite literature and the classics. They are too much absorbed in commerce, speculation and politics. Not even a magazine can flourish in New England; and until this year we have had nothing like a review. In New York there is one attempted; its appearance is promising; but it bears the marks of haste and party spirit; but such is the temper of the times.[5]

II

From 1801 to 1827 the most influential review in America was the *Port Folio,* founded by Joseph Dennie one year before the founding of the famous review in Edinburgh and edited by him until his death in 1812,

4 *An Essay on American Poetry* (1818), p. 10.
5 *Farmer's Museum,* 1801.

then continued under able editors until snuffed out by
the vigorous airs of a new literary period. For the magazine was an eighteenth-century voice; its editor signed
himself "Oliver Oldschool, Esq.," and until its first
editor's death the periodical refused utterly to be modern,
even though edited in the capital of the most modern of
all the states. From the first the thing was a paradox: a
New England Yankee editor instructing Philadelphia;
an anti-democrat shrilly vocal in the heart of the American Republic; an editor aspiring to make of his magazine
an American *Edinburgh Review,* yet doing his editing
with a "Peter Porcupine" quill; a literary sheet made by
lawyers—Philadelphia lawyers; and, most paradoxical of
all, with all these characteristics, a magazine that could
become the most important literary influence in America
for a generation. There was but one explanation: its
editor, Joseph Dennie.

Dennie was of Boston birth (1768–1812)—of "that
merchant aristocracy," says his biographer, Harold M.
Ellis, "which became dominant in the New England
capital with the decline of the theocratic system soon after
the beginning of the century." Harvard had difficulty in
digesting him: individualism all his life long sat upon
him like a red cockade. He had been schooled during the
Revolution: revolt was in the atmosphere; he had
breathed it as a boy. Forced to choose a profession, he
picked the law as least objectionable of the professions
open to a gentleman, but there was no eagerness in his
study. In the lawyer's office where he had been set to read
the stereotyped forms of the driest of professions, he
read much poetry and much Addisonian belles-lettres.

From Boston Dennie removed to Walpole, New Hampshire, to open a law office and assume the editorship of
the *Farmer's Museum,* a rural sheet soon to become the
leading literary journal in New England. A group of
young lawyers, mostly college graduates, furnished him
companionship in the little town, some of them like Royall

Tyler, Thomas Green Fessenden, and Jeremiah Mason later to become nationally prominent. Walpole became a literary center. The effusions of Dennie and Tyler, published under the heading, "From the Shop of Colon and Spondee," may be claimed as the progenitors of the modern newspaper column. Tyler furnished for the most part the "Spondee" verse and Dennie the "Colon" prose.

Success came in a flood: newspaper editorships were offered the young editor in five different cities. He was offered a clerkship in the office of Timothy Pickering, Secretary of State in Philadelphia; William Cobbett— "Peter Porcupine"—made him a surprising offer for the copyright of his volume, *The Lay Preacher*—a thousand dollars, according to contemporary rumor; and John W. Fenno offered him the editorship of the *Gazette of the United States*.

In Philadelphia he found himself in a new world, even as Franklin had found himself in earlier years. A brief period of editorship of Fenno's *Gazette,* and then a venture of his own. In 1801 this literary announcement:

A young man, once known among village-readers as the humble historian of the hour, the conductor of a *Farmer's Museum, and Lay Preacher's Gazette,* again offers himself to the public as a volunteer editor. Having, as he conceives, a right to vary, at pleasure, his fictitious name, he now, for higher reasons than any fickle humor might dictate, assumes the appellation of OLD-SCHOOL.

Seemingly the man was unfitted for such an editorship. Into Philadelphia, with its victorious Jeffersonians, he had brought the fighting spirit of the New England Federalists, and in Philadelphia he quickly found a tense newspaper atmosphere of vituperation such as one associates with the small-town journalism of the frontier, not with refined literature. And fundamentally Dennie was a refined *litterateur,* a dreamer with vision, not a mere newspaper satirist. In October, 1808, he published in an elaborate supplement to his magazine a "Project of an Original Review," an all-American review of the *Edinburgh* type, one which he hoped would "at no distant period be established and successfully supported in the metropolis of the United States." A remarkable document, the work of a man with creative vision, but no review came from the project. The *Port Folio,* now a weekly, now a monthly, became more and more a hybrid affair, part literary review, part "Peter Porcupine" gazette.

In every way was it typical of what was being evolved in the American crucible. The mass was arising into dominance; democracy had been born in the forests of the new world, and it was learning to read; moreover, it was learning its power. The reading of the democratic populace is forever the columns of the newspaper, not the essays of the literary review, and Dennie was powerless to recognize the inevitable. He had announced in his preliminary prospectus that he would "bind the rod of the moralist with the roses of the muse," but the rod in his hand was a cudgel none the less. A journal that was to lead the thinking and the taste of a people should be "conducted by men who are avowed Partizans and Martinets in Religion, Politics, and Literature, men who would uniformly act in a spirit of Scottish clanship, always prepared at every hazard to defend themselves and assail the foe."

A New England Federalist aristocrat, uncompromising, unconquerable, editing a literary review which he hoped to make the *Edinburgh* of America! No magazine anywhere so extreme, so arbitrary. "So far," he declared, "from courting the mob, our Editors should treat the herd of swine and their feeders with the most ineffable contempt, and be satisfied with the general applause of scholars and gentlemen, men of honor, and cavaliers." His ideal editor, he declared, he found in the office of the Charleston, South Carolina, *Courier:*

A gentleman and a scholar. Hence he can arrange with the precision of a Linnæus, the catalogue of his friends and foes. The first are the men of genius, talents, principle and property. The last are the democrats, the fanatics, the knaves and the fools. . . . He will be contemptuously careless of the "distant din" of democracy; and he will treat the French republican party as *natural brute beasts,* as an impious, impudent, and savage gang, whom every man of genius and virtue is bound to meet with defiance on his brow, and the horse-whip in his hand.

Radical always, temperamental, impetuous, opinionated, the man was peculiarly fitted for partisan warfare. He was without the comparative degree: he worshiped or he damned. Yankee Federalism was to him a gospel, and even the election of Jefferson and the total collapse of the New England party did not silence him. The shooting of Hamilton by Burr enraged him beyond reason. He printed the *Port Folio* with turned column-rules, and at length became so incendiary in his editorial writings that he was put under arrest on the charge of "seditious libel." Defended in his trial by Joseph Hopkinson, he was finally acquitted only to redouble the virulence of his attacks.

But there was another side to Dennie. Peculiarly did he have the power to surround himself with powerful and devoted friends—Joseph Hopkinson, John Quincy Adams, Richard Rush, Charles Brockden Brown, John Blair Linn, Alexander Wilson, Royall Tyler, Charles Jared Ingersoll, Gouverneur Morris, and others, all contributors to the *Port Folio.* A remarkable group it was, and it should have made possible Dennie's dream of an all-American *Edinburgh Review.* But America was not ready. It was a patchwork of small provincial areas, mostly agrarian. The magazines drew their subscribers only from their own local areas—nowhere, says Mott, over 150 miles in diameter—and even in this prepared circle they drew only from the educated few.

What it was possible to do, however, the *Port Folio*

did. Until Dennie's death in 1812 it was a dominating force in our national literature. Its subscription list had grown amazingly, covering, indeed, the entire country. The higher classes of the reading public prized it for its originality, its fearlessness, its consistency, and, to a lesser extent, for its "polite" literature, and many of the subliterary classes prized it for its "Colon and Spondee" humor.

When not touched upon his prejudices, Dennie was a critic of considerable acumen. His "An Author's Evenings," contributed to also by Tyler, and in parts his "Colon and Spondee" column, can even now be read with pleasure and profit. Such reviews, too, as his five lay-sermons on Anne Radcliffe's romances are, at least in certain passages, worthy of a critic like Hazlitt.

It is worthy of note, too, that his was the first voice in America to praise Wordsworth's and Coleridge's *Lyrical Ballads*. While Charles Brockden Brown, in his Philadelphia magazine, was writing, "I know few performances so truly worthless as Wordsworth's *Lyrical Ballads*," Dennie, in his issue of June 13, 1801, was printing entire a long commendatory review from the British *Critic,* with this editorial note:

We have had frequent occasion in the course of our literary selections, to express the warmest admiration of the genius, spirit, and simplicity of "Lyrical Ballads," a volume which contains more genuine poetry than is to be found, except in the volumes of Shakespeare and Chatterton.

Thus Joseph Dennie, last of the literary monarchists in the new Republic, unmodified voice from the departed eighteenth century, New England Puritan remodeled to the standards of Philadelphia estheticism. Dead at forty-four, victim, perhaps, of his own capacity for good fellowship, burnt out by his own intensity, unquestionably he is to be voted with the few most brilliant American literary editors. In point of time he was the first. A victim of his times, cultivator of arts and letters in a peculiarly barren era, to him American literature owes much. For his own generation unquestionably he was the leading literary personality. A. H. Smyth, in his history of the Philadelphia magazines, has not been too generous with his praise:

> With genuine editorial tact and skill he drew to himself all the literary ability of the city, which was then "the largest and most literary and most intellectually accomplished city in the Union," to quote the words of a later editor of the *Port Folio,* Dr. Charles Caldwell. There was scarcely a more picturesque figure in Philadelphia in the first decade of this century than presented by the editor of the *Port Folio*. It would be necessary to go to London and to Oliver Goldsmith to find another to outshine this Oliver Oldschool as Buckingham saw him slipping along Chestnut Street to his office "in a peagreen coat, white vest, nankeen small clothes, white silk stockings and pumps, fastened with silver buckles which covered at least half the foot from the instep to the toe." [6]

III

The second reviewer in the new decade was also a man of genius and, even as Dennie, a victim of his times—Charles Brockden Brown. While in New York City, on the advice of "the Friendly Club," who promised contributions, he had started the *Monthly Magazine, and American Review* (1799) two years before the *Port Folio* in Philadelphia. No man ever worked harder than he to raise the level of American literature with his magazine, and no one ever was more unsparing of himself or his time. "There can be very little doubt," writes Mott, "that he wrote a very large part of the contents himself. . . . Over a hundred and fifty American publications are noticed more or less critically." But New York was no place for a literary review. Starved out, Brown changed

[6] *The Philadelphia Magazines and Their Contributors* (1892), p. 93.

the magazine to a quarterly with a new name, the *American Review and Literary Journal,* but this, too, after eight issues, died of starvation.

Returning home to Philadelphia, Brown found more congenial soil. Dennie's idea of an all-American review seems to have been in the air. Boston in November, 1803, was starting the *Monthly Anthology,* and in October of that year Brown began the *Literary Magazine and American Register.* His program, as he announced it, was ambitious. It was "To collect in one focal spot the rays of a great number of luminaries . . . to afford useful information and rational amusement . . . to be an American Review in which the history of our native literature shall be carefully detailed . . . to give from time to time some account of selected works which we deem above the common level of American poetry." The field was clear for such a work. There was not, he announced, "at present any other monthly publication in America."

The *Morning Chronicle* gave the new magazine a left-handed welcome. "Every attempt," wrote the editor, "to diffuse miscellaneous information and entertainment by publications of this sort has hitherto been found unprofitable to those who have made the effort." He could only hope that Brown's volume would be able to "remove the stigma consequently attached to the taste and literature of this country."

Brown did his best. With twice the energy of Dennie, with none of Dennie's procrastination and conviviality, he put his whole soul into his editing. Peculiarly was he fitted for such work. Like Poe in later years, he believed that the future of American literature was with the American magazines. This was his argument, not unlike Poe's:

Those have a much more extensive circulation than any other kind of works; they are cheaper in proportion to their bulk, and, besides a good deal of original matter, they contain, under various forms diurnal, weekly, monthly, quarterly and annual, the essence of all other publications, together with the whole contemporary history of the world. The paper and printing employed in periodical works greatly exceed those consumed in all other publications put together. Other works would be in some measure useless and unread without their assistance.

There is somehow an air of distinction about his magazine. For one thing, he was more careful in his selection of poetry than was Dennie for his *Port Folio*. He selected not so much, and he seems, more often than other editors, to have found excellent poems.

But despite its excellence, the *Literary Magazine* had to be abandoned. In the days before advertising, the subscription list was the sole source of income, and the public in America attracted by such a magazine as Brown's was small and fickle. It died in December, 1807. Then Brown had a new idea: he would start a semiannual review, the *American Register,* a semi-yearly book of everything American. Five hundred pages there were in each issue—a veritable encyclopedia—treating with care every phase of the preceding six months. It is history, but it is also criticism. His survey of literary conditions, for example, during the year 1806, a long careful study, makes him the first historian of American literature. A document is it that later critics cannot neglect. Had he lived to make for each year the careful year-book survey that he made for this year 1806, greatly lightened would be the work of the modern historian of our letters.

But Brown was more than a literary historian, more than a mere editor. He and Dennie are to be rated as the two pioneer American critics. His reviews have often distinctive passages. For example, this concerning the art of fiction-writing, a rule that may be framed as the first American word concerning short-story art:

Much has been written to explain and to teach the art of story-telling; but no science is more difficult to attain, nor can it be taught by any settled rules. If the teller can but contrive to keep the attention of his audience awake to the end of his tale, he has certainly gained a great point, let the method be what it will; and if he can add to their attention some emotions of pleasure, or of surprise, he may justly be deemed a good story-teller.[7]

Often his reviews are quaint in their epigrammatic turnings, as when before a table full of new novels he classified them as "by females, by males, and by writers whose sex was indeterminate."

Though he died at thirty-nine, his last years a slow and losing fight against consumption, Brown is to be rated with Dennie among the greatest magazine editors of early America.

IV

In the opinion of Philadelphia at least, early Boston was not a magazine city. Dennie, whose Boston magazine, the *Tablet,* had lasted only three months, satirized it as the graveyard of magazines. The awe-inspiring nearness of Harvard College, the intellectual leadership of the clergy, and the uniform gloom of decaying Puritanism were thought to be chilling influences.

But Boston had Isaiah Thomas, who published what he thought he could sell, even the scandalous fiction, *The Power of Sympathy,* and a lively drama when no theater was allowed in the city. From his press had come the sprightly *Massachusetts Magazine* (1789–1796), with its still readable essay columns and its quite un-Boston-like elements of lightness. Says Frank Luther Mott:

Fiction was also a staple in this magazine, brief "fragments," oriental tales, and "characters" written especially for the *Massachusetts* filling many pages; indeed this periodical

[7] *Literary Magazine,* July, 1805.

is one of the best in which to study the early development of
the American short story.[8]

In poetry it was abundant and flowery. It was far
gone, however, with "the Boston literary disease." It was
in the *Massachusetts Magazine* that the Della Cruscan
correspondence had appeared between "Menander" and
"Philenia."

But all the early Boston magazines sink into insignificance before the *Monthly Anthology,* established in
November, 1803. Phineas Adams, a Harvard graduate, a
teacher in the Boston schools, started the bantling, and
several editors with scissors and pen struggled for six
numbers to keep it alive. Its literary ambitions, however,
soared into the clouds. It was to contain "lucubrations on
manners and literature, on the improvement of taste and
the encouragement of genius," and it was "to offer such
essays as are furnished with sentimental instruction and
rational amusement." It was provincial, even parochial, in
its outlook, but it was alive. For six numbers it feebly
wailed, and then unceremoniously it was laid as a found-
ling at the door of the father of Ralph Waldo Emerson.
A hopeless affair it must have seemed to the Reverend
Doctor as he examined it through his clerical spectacles.
Everywhere anonymity. It had filled its columns very
largely from other journals, but it had opened them wide
for such unknowns as "Literary Wanderer," "Remarker," "The Botanist," "The Family Physician," all
of whom amused, and rebuked, and instructed, and sometimes preached. Its editor, "Sylvanus Per-Se," however,
was no minister. In quite un-Bostonian tones he could
say, "We have endeavored to add to the general stock of
innocent gaiety." After messing together Sanskrit
translations, "Matilda" effusions, and attempts at lightness, he had won no subscribers. Why the Reverend Emerson took in and coddled the little un-Emerson-like found-

[8] *A History of American Magazines* (1930), p. 109.

ling so near starvation no one knows. This in his preface, later written:

Although we have the feelings of a parent for the publication before us, yet it may be proper to declare to the world that it is not indebted to us for birth, nor was it born in our house. We knew neither its father nor its mother, nor hardly of its existence, until naked, hungry, and helpless, it was brought and laid at our door. . . . In proportion as it engaged our care it won our affections. . . . The grand object of giving to our charge these expensive advantages, is to make him extensively and permanently useful.

Emerson's idea of "expensive advantages" was soon apparent: the organization of a club of Boston savants to be known as "The Anthology Club" and to act as godfathers and guardians. The crude literary infant was spanked into respectability and educated to "the quality of Boston." Four editors in succession took charge: Samuel Cooper Thatcher, William Smith Shaw, James Savage, and Alexander H. Everett. The Reverend J. S. J. Gardiner, Rector of Trinity Church, was elected the first president of the club. "The number of resident members," wrote William Tudor in his *Miscellanies* (1812), "varied from seven or eight to fifteen or sixteen. It was one of the rules that every member should write for the work: the contributions were in some cases voluntary, in others they were assigned by vote, which was the general practice in regard to review."

Among the members were Reverend Joseph S. Buckminster, Reverend William Emerson, Reverend Joseph Tuckerman, William Tudor, Reverend John T. Kirkland, and George Ticknor.

Tremendous seriousness sat like a sermon everywhere upon the little magazine, so much so that the editor in 1804 was forced to outline the general policy of the board:

It has been, more than once, hinted to the Editor that the currency of this publication is much impeded especially in Boston by its want of the recommendation of amusing anecdotes and wonderful stories. In reply, *he would observe that tales ingeniously related and forcibly inculcating some virtuous sentiment, and anecdotes, amusing to a refined and correct taste, will always be objects of his attention.* But he heartily disdains to insult his patrons, by offering them witless jests, silly puns and non-sensical bon-mots from which the popularity of periodical works too often arises. The primary and invariable purpose of his present undertaking is, to open to public notice some specimens of literary skill in this country,—to offer such essays as are furnished with sentimental instruction and rational amusement,—to remark on the progress of science and the fine arts, and, with various tongues, to plead in behalf of virtuous refinement. If this attempt will not gain extensive patronage, it is pleasing to find, that there are even a few, who bestow their approbation.[9]

But despite its moral and didactic tone, the magazine had no use for the sermonic. In January, 1810, it burst out petulantly against the plague of sermons:

America is harassed with a class of authors, more numerous here than anywhere else, who, having triumphed over an audience in some species of occasional discourse, oration, sermon, etc., or occupied the poet's corner of a weekly newspaper, think they can write and continue to do so, thus flooding the market with a mass of worthless material. The Anthology feels it its duty to help eradicate this type of writer, though it is a fatiguing and irksome task to plow through their products and write reviews of them.

Unlike the *Port Folio,* the magazine took note of all American publications and gave to the more important issues the fullest space possible. The critical attitude was like Brown's and Dennie's, a fulsome reverence for the eighteenth-century standards:

[9] *Monthly Anthology,* I, 242.

Poetry, at no time, has possessed more admirers, than in the present age. But it may be asked, is our taste, in this charming art, correct? Do we judge of a poem, as Aristotle, Quintilian, and Horace would have judged it? What would they have said of the extravagant encomiums passed on the vulgar emptiness of a Bloomfield, on the conceptions and sleep-inspiring versification of a Southey, on the unintelligible fustian of a Della Crusca, and on the numberless poetical "Gorgons, and Hydras, and Chimeras dire," which the monster-breeding breasts of our modern bards have produced? Modern poems are a species of romance in metre; and the sentimental trash of a circulating library, turned into verse, would possess equal merit. It is not to be wondered at, since the public taste is thus perverted, that poems of sterling merit, which bear the stamp of classical elegance and correctness should be left on our shelves. Our sickly appetite is too much cloyed with sweetmeats to relish substantial food. Hence our standard authors are no longer read by the profound critics of the day; and the whimsical novelties of lyrical ballad-mongers and trifling sonneteers are preferred to the majesty of Milton, and the vigor of Dryden, and the brilliant sense and correct harmony of Pope.

For the most part, however, the reviewers were careful to weigh American productions in American literary balances. The critic, for instance, who reviewed at length *The Miscellaneous Works of David Humphreys* declared at the start that he intended to judge the poet by contemporary American standards. "It would be absurd to compare him with the great poets of England," but "on the American Parnassus he makes no mean figure."

Local prejudice one finds often, for example in the review of Robert Treat Paine's *The Ruling Passion,* which is placed among the great American products full of "strong and vivid touches of a keen and harmonious pencil," and in the review, too, of Winthrop Sargent's poem, "Boston."

For the first time in an American review we find now the *Edinburgh* influence, the Jeffrey style of book review

—the leisurely approach and then the annihilating cut and slash. Noah Webster's dictionary it brutally handled; also Alsop's satire, *The Echo,* as issued by the Porcupine Press in 1807.

Barlow's *Columbiad* was also severely mauled; Philip Freneau's poems were called "a monotonous collection," "pretty good for the time and circumstances under which they were written, tolerably good for American poetry, and would be very good if we possessed no better poetry." But *The Power of Solitude: a Poem in Two Parts* (1804), by Joseph Story, even though a Boston poem, it demolished with *Edinburgh* thoroughness:

> Of late years, so much currency has been given to the in-sipid and quotidian trash of those, who never were poets of God's making, that we are almost tempted to renounce our objections to the harsh, abrupt versification of Cowper, and hail him as the restorer of the dignity of English verse. . . . The general insipidity of the volume before us we do not so much attribute to want of talents in the author, as to an im-becile surrender of his powers to the modern school of writers.

The estimates of the new British poets varied with the time and the reviewer. Scott was welcomed from the first. His *Marmion* was reviewed at length, and later his *Lay of the Last Minstrel* was elaborately weighed against it for merits. Then came the volume, *The Lady of the Lake* (1810), and the verdict that Scott was "the finest of English poets now living"— "We will not qualify the assertion with an exception in favor of Mr. Campbell." Undoubtedly it was the *Anthology* that first introduced Scott, the poet, to American readers.

The "Remarker" papers, contributed doubtless by various members of the club—a running department of current discussion like a modern editorial page—is especially noteworthy, the best series of literary periodical essays written during the period.

The chief glory of the *Monthly Anthology,* however,

is the fact that in May, 1815, it was continued as the *North American Review.*

v

In 1809 came the Philadelphia magazine, *Select Reviews and Spirit of Foreign Magazines,* a periodical wholly made up of "the cream of foreign publications." By 1809 no one could pass in America as well-read unless he knew the increasing number of scholarly reviews in Great Britain, Germany, and France. For three years Philadelphia was in touch with the best in Europe: had she not her *Select Reviews?* But in 1812 Enos Bronson, originator of the anthology idea, wearied of his work and his all too inadequate returns and sold the magazine to Moses Thomas, bookseller and publisher. The next step was to find an adequate editor, one who knew European literature and at the same time one who could strengthen the pitifully small subscription list with a well-known name. Who more sure to bring success than the brilliant young New Yorker whose amusing *Knickerbocker's History of New York* had been published so successfully in their own city? And, surprising even his own family, Irving accepted the editorship.

Success beyond anything thus far achieved by an American magazine seemed certain. It was an event that seemed national in its bearings. His *History of New York* had made him everywhere recognized as the most promising of the younger group of Americans, and his acceptance of the editorship seemed like an acceptance of literary leadership—the beginning of a new period. Most extravagantly was he congratulated. "I have been stayed with flagons and comforted with apples by these editors and newspaper writers until I am sick of puffing," he wrote from Washington in mid-December. "This Select Review has drawn upon me such an abundance of worthless compliments that I really stagger under the trash."

And again, in a note on the January, 1813, number of the magazine, he remonstrated against the shower of unwelcome compliments and extravagant panegyric. It was the first word of his editorship.

That he had entered upon the adventure with no thought of serious work is evident in all his letters. He had not begun upon it as a career. He wanted elegant leisure, time for desultory reading, for writing, perhaps, as the mood might seize him, and for the social dissipation that hitherto had been so much of his life. But he was practically without means. Here was an opportunity, a sinecure with a salary attached which not only would pay his expenses but shield him from the criticism such a life of elegant leisure invariably called forth from the America of that day. To his brother Peter in England he wrote, December 30, 1812: "I mentioned in former letters that I had undertaken to conduct the Select Reviews at a salary of 1,500 dollars. It is an amusing occupation, without any mental responsibility of consequence. I felt very much the want of some such task in my idle hours; there is nothing so irksome as having nothing to do." And to Brevoort in Paris: "I am handsomely paid, and the work is no trouble." It did not necessitate even a residence in Philadelphia: the magazine could be edited from his "old quarters" in New York in the center of the circle of relatives and friends he had known all his life.

The preparations he made for his task are significant: they help us to understand the later Irving. To his brother Peter in England he at once despatched orders for all the British magazines and new books of importance, and to Brevoort in Paris a similar order for "the different periodical journals of France, as well as those of note on the continent, such, for instance, as Kotzebue's, &c." For nearly two years he lived in the full tide of current European literature. When in May, 1815, he set sail for England for what proved to be an absence of seventeen

years, he certainly had been prepared for his sojourn by
an intensive course in contemporary European culture.

Of the two years of Irving's actual editorship we know
almost nothing. Few revealing letters have been vouchsafed us. To his nephew and biographer the central fact
of the period was the few weeks of his military experience at the close of the war: he dwells upon it with
minuteness, neglecting almost completely the far weight-
ier matter of the magazine editorship. The episode has
been neglected, and yet it is impossible to understand
fully the later Irving without it. A few details of external
evidence there are; the rest must come from an examination of the four volumes upon which he put the stamp of
his editorship.

That Irving almost immediately found the work no
sinecure appears in one of his letters. Before he had fairly
accepted the editorship, the owners and managers began
to dictate to him an editorial policy. The war with England had begun; it was being fought sensationally upon
the sea; there must be biographies of naval heroes, narratives of sea fights, and a miscellany of naval news after
the pattern of the British *Naval Chronicle*. Little was
said of literary criticism, and the literary opportunity was
the only feature that had attracted Irving. His first fight
was for a free hand. They demand "a vile farrago, a
congregation of heterogeneous articles that have no possible affinity to one another," he wrote. "I have written
to Philadelphia that I would not consent to have such a
fool's cap put on my head." What he effected was a
compromise. It was February before he got into action.
The January number, which was to contain his salutatory,
contained from his hand only an apology on the wrapper
and an announcement that the title of the next number
would "probably vary from that hitherto adopted."

To his new title, the *Analectic Magazine,* he finally
consented to have added *and Naval Chronicle,* but the

naval-chronicle material he ruled into a supplement to be bound at the end of each volume. The demand for naval biographies in the columns of the new magazine did not trouble him: he wrote at least four of them himself. The naval element soon became secondary: the public soon knew the periodical as the *Analectic,* a literary review.

That Irving lacked the temperament for holding steadily to "the irksome and ever recurring task of a periodical work," to quote his own words in a notice of Dennie's *Port Folio,* is manifest to all who read his letters. But it is also manifest that he did not do careless and ill-considered work upon the volumes that came fully under his editorship. The magazine from the start may be compared in value with the *North American Review,* later to be born in Boston. It contains original, independent criticism. Its standpoint was creative; it was designed at every point to elevate American taste and ideals. The reviews from European journals were selected not for entertainment alone but for the education of American taste. They reveal the source of much that went to the making of the later Washington Irving, and they account also in some degree for the rise of the new school of writers that was to rule the 1820's. They reveal everywhere Irving as the student of technique, of literary art, of elegant models. They reveal, too, the catholicity of the man. In his critiques of William Cliffton and of Robert Treat Paine he weighs them not in the balance used by *Edinburgh* reviewers: he presents them as logical results of American conditions, poets not to be judged by English classic models. Literary conditions in America in the early decades of the century he presents with precision:

There is no country to which practical criticism is of more importance than this, owing to the crude state of native talent, and the immaturity of public taste. We are prone to all the vices of literature, from the casual and superficial manner in which we attend to it. Absorbed in politics, or occupied by business, few can find leisure amid these strong agitations of the

mind, to follow the gentler pursuits of literature, and give it
that calm study, and meditative contemplation, necessary to
discover true principles of beauty and excellence in composition. . . .

The habits and fortunes of an author, in this country, might
yield some food for curious speculation. Unfitted for business,
in a nation where every one is busy; devoted to literature,
where literary leisure is confounded with idleness; the man
of letters is almost an insulated being, with few to understand,
less to value, and scarcely any to encourage his pursuits. It
is not surprising, therefore, that our authors soon grow weary
of a race which they have to run alone, and turn their attention to other callings of a more worldly and profitable
nature. This is one of the reasons why the writers of this country so seldom attain to excellence. Before their genius is dis-
ciplined, and their taste refined, their talents are diverted
into the ordinary channels of busy life, and occupied in what
are considered its more useful purposes. In fact, the great
demand for rough talent, as for common manual labour, in
this country, prevents the appropriation of either mental or
physical forces to elegant employments. . . . The fine writer,
if he depend upon his pen for a subsistence, will soon discover that he may starve on the very summit of Parnassus,
while he sees herds of newspaper editors battening on the
rank marshes of its borders.[10]

The editorship of Irving was ended really by the war,
first by his absence from New York as aide-de-camp of
Governor Tompkins, and secondly by the unsettled
financial condition of the country. When in January,
1815, he arrived in Philadelphia, the firm which had
published the magazine had failed and he himself was
compelled to "sign off what was owing him." Arrange-
ments were made, however, for continuing the publication. Irving promised an article which proved to be a
revision of the introduction to his edition of Campbell.
Four months later he was on his way to Europe, the
magazine editorship a closed episode.

[10] *Select Reviews*, I, 249, 252.

The extent of Irving's own contributions to the *Analectic* is problematical. The only external evidence is that furnished by his nephew Pierre in the official biography:

His contributions, extending through the years 1813 and 1814, consisted of a review of the works of Robert Treat Paine, then dead; a review of odes, naval songs, and other occasional poems, by Edwin C. Holland, of Charleston; a notice of Paulding's Lay of the Scottish Fiddle; of Lord Byron; Traits of Indian Character and Philip of Pokanoket, afterwards incorporated in the Sketch Book; and biographies of Capt. James Lawrence, Lieutenant William Burrows, Commodore Oliver Perry, and Captain David Porter. There was also a Biographical Sketch of Thomas Campbell the poet, revised, corrected, and materially altered from the former, published in the March number of 1815.

But even a casual examination of the four volumes will convince one of the incompleteness of this list. After the first volume Irving manifestly took his editorship with seriousness and worked with considerable diligence. It is clearly evident that he wrote the monthly foreign and domestic literary department, and there is small doubt that he wrote six long papers in addition to those attributed to him by Pierre.

Distinctive work, all these criticisms in the *Analectic Magazine*—unquestionably the most distinctive pieces of literary criticism written in America before 1830. To realize their originality and their daring, one must read them in the atmosphere in which they were produced. The review of Robert Treat Paine, though annihilatingly severe, was not patterned at all after the cut-and-slash work of the *Edinburgh Review* critics: it was an honest attempt to reform American poetry. Paine and Holland were typical American poets, over ornate even to ludicrousness, imitative, bombastic, and on every hand they were being praised in superlatives. It took courage to tell the truth; it smacked in wartime even of want of patriotism, but Irving told the truth. Even today, with the perspective of a century and more, one can hardly sum up better the weaknesses of these two very minor early poets. It was constructive criticism, the criticism that America needed, and it had its effect.

The criticism that he made of Scott for reproducing in his edition of Dryden the indecencies of the old dramatist smacks certainly of the later eighteenth-century ideals, and Irving's roots were all of them at this period of his career in the eighteenth century. Undoubtedly in later years, after his intimacy with Scott, he would hesitate about acknowledging this severe verdict of his younger self, but never did he recede from this early position. The review of the life of Cooke, perhaps, he forgot when he told his nephew of his contributions to the *Analectic*. There was no reason for suppressing it: much of it is in his most tripping *Sketch Book* style. It reproduces not only the condition of the early American theater as revealed by one who knew intimately and from first-hand experience of what he wrote, but it reveals fully the attitude of the more intelligent classes in America toward theatric art as America was then displaying it. The sketch of Byron has illuminating passages, as does the introduction to Campbell's poems, notably this much-quoted observation:

With respect to the living authors of Europe, however, we may be said, on this side of the Atlantic, to be placed in some degree in the situation of posterity. The vast ocean that rolls between us like a space of time, removes us beyond the sphere of personal favor, personal prejudice, or personal familiarity.

Certainly Irving would not suffer even from a complete republication of all these products of his early pen.

CHAPTER XIII

THE PERIODICAL ESSAY

I

THE EIGHTEENTH CENTURY in England, the cool fit after the age of creative heat, was intellectual, critical, primarily concerned with manner. To quote Poe, "It belongs to the first era of a nation's literature—to the era of impulse—in contradistinction to the era of criticism—to the Chaucerian rather than to the Cowperian days." [1] A century of literary weighing and gaging, of lay-preaching, of criticism—the measurement of manners. Even in poetry, manner first of all, style—"polish." For a century the term "elegant" was a *cliché* in critical essays. No vulgarity, no conventionality of term or expression, no excess. One might fill a rhetoric with the advice of the stylists from Dr. Johnson to Coleridge.

In the midst of this age of manners was born American literature—in America which had no manners. As a result, it was nursed by Federalists, defenders of the old order; nursed on for years after Federalism had lost its life-blood —and right there is the central tragedy of American literature.

The century in England had evolved for itself new literary forms: in prose, the Addisonian essay; in fiction, the Richardsonian novel; in criticism, the Johnsonian review. Most important was the essay, the periodical essay issued after the *Spectator* fashion. One may call the entire

[1] S. Foster Damon, *Thomas Holley Chivers, Friend of Poe* (1930), p. 140.

century the age of the periodical essay. In 1803 was issued *The British Essayists* in forty-five thick volumes, the contents of twelve periodicals after the model of the *Spectator*. And in Volume I a ponderous essay "On the Nature and Origin of the Essay."

America, as a matter of course, followed the literary fashions. What else was possible? In America also it became an age of the essay, but the essay form in the forests of the New World, like everything else, as England believed, suffered at length a sea-change, deteriorated, evolved into strangeness. It became democratized, vulgarized, lost at last as a literary form.

Requirements on the form came early. This in 1806:

It should be the aim of the periodical writer to introduce and diffuse a taste for useful and ornamental learning, in the engaging form of short and popular essays, which may be perused without much effort of intellect and without encroaching on the engagements of the high or stated employments of the middle class.[2]

Dr. Drake would add other requirements: to introduce and support a taste for elegant literature; to paint virtue in its most alluring form.

The evolution is interesting. In the Colonial era the essay had been a pamphlet, a literary hand-grenade in the battles of the Lord, unliterary, unelegant, concerned only with one overwhelming idea, the destruction of its opponent. With the arrival of the weekly newspaper in the Revolutionary era the pamphleteer found himself possessed of a more deadly grenade. The Revolution, on its literary side, was fought with pamphlets supplemented with newspaper articles.

During the stormy period before and after the adoption of the Constitution there was a sudden arrow-flight of essays which for a time all but obscured the sun. In quar-

[2] *The Literary Magazine and American Register* (1806), p. 219.

ters the barrage was peculiarly telling. On the Tory side during the Revolution there had been the "Westchester Farmer" letters of Samuel Seabury; on the Patriot side, the "Pennsylvania Farmer" papers of Dickinson. In the interregnum had come Hamilton's and Jay's *Federalist Papers*, political treatises still valuable. So far as they can be classed as literature, all of these later essays are *American* literature. So completely were the writers in earnest that they forgot their models and wrote themselves into their essays. Dennie's *Port Folio* in 1808 was inclined to count this as America's chief contribution to literature: "We have written and published *much*," it said. "From minds *keen to pursue, and vigorous to retain*, innumerable political essays have emanated, which frequently obtain a sort of sovereign influence over the publick mind."

With the "essay proper," the merely literary essay, America had done little. Aside from Francis Hopkinson, who dabbled in all things literary and artistic, and Philip Freneau in his *Philosopher of the Forest* and his "Robert Slender" papers, no one had attempted it. America was too headlong, too wind-swept by religion or politics or party warfare or revolution to pause for trifles. But with the 1790's came a new step in the evolution, a product peculiarly of the onrushing newspaper age—the serial essay devoted to things timely. Dennie described his *"Farrago"* series as "periodical pamphlets" and in 1807 applied the same term to Irving's *Salmagundi*. Now instead of the pamphlet the newspaper series. All at once elegantly written essay departments week after week, signed "Lounger," "Remarker," and the like. They satisfied their times to the full: they became the ruling literary form, the fashion of the day. There was nothing they could not treat, religious or secular, ancient or modern. A newspaper without its essay column was like a modern sheet without its editorial page.

The Reverend Nathan Fiske, under the signature of "The Neighbor" in the *Massachusetts Spy*, ran a series with the running title, *The Moral Monitor,* and in 1801 he reissued it in two volumes, with this paragraph in his introduction:

If I were to characterise the present period, I should call it *the period of essay writers.* America abounds with those useful vehicles of instruction and amusement, newspapers and magazines. Every magazine, and almost every newspaper, teems with periodical essays. As at the breaking out of a war, when men are enlisting for a campaign, every hat is ornamented with a cockade, or a feather, and even the boys are ambitious of appearing with the fashionable badge; so every newspaper of the present day, must have its literary mark of distinction, the feather, or cockade of the periodical essay. And so numerous are the fabricators of these ornaments, that the papers, multiplied as they are, may be supplied with duplicates—or, to change the metaphor, in this age of emulation, when the strife is, who shall excell in, cooking, or carrying to market, the most curious dainties to please the public palate, every vehicle of intelligence must be enriched with a dish of essays in succession, under some expressive signature or title; some, like solid beef, affording substantial nourishment; others, like sillibubs and nick-nacks, tickling the palate, or only tasting sweet in the mouth.

According to H. M. Ellis in his *Joseph Dennie and His Circle,* "Between 1785 and 1800 perhaps a hundred short series of lighter periodical essays were contributed to various New England journals." In Philadelphia fully as many, and outside these two cities as many more.

With the increasing numbers and the increasing influence of the newspapers, however, came swift degenerations. William Tudor, addressing the Harvard Phi Beta Kappa Society in 1815, declared that the leading cause of the contemporary feebleness of the American literary product was the fact that "our best writers have been unfortunate in their choice of depositories—newspapers and pamphlets. Such forms are sure to be short-lived and almost always contain nothing but controversial material."

The essay, once a pamphlet, then a newpaper letter, then a continued series, became at last an editorial. Charles Burr Todd, in his *Life and Letters of Joel Barlow,* could even give the date of the transition. In the Hartford *American Mercury* (1784) he says: "A series of careful essays on current political and social topics contributed by Barlow to this journal were the progenitors, it is said, of the modern editorial." Doubtful, but suggestive.

During the 1790's all the essayists who could procure subscribers enough to warrant republication of their newspaper work issued volumes of essays. These, perhaps, are the most noteworthy:

1790   *The Preceptor* and *A Collection of Essays and Fugitiv* [sic] *Writings* . . . , Noah Webster.

1792   *The Miscellaneous Essays and Occasional Writings of Francis Hopkinson, Esq.,* 3 volumes.

1796   *Miscellaneous Trifles in Prose,* Mathew Carey.
         The Lay Preacher, Joseph Dennie.

1798   *Essays Literary, Moral, and Philosophical,* Benjamin Rush, M.D.

1799   *Letters . . . by Robert Slender,* Philip Freneau.

II

Dennie it was, undoubtedly, who influenced most strongly the evolution of the essay from its sermon originals. Almost by accident had come the various steps in this development. Dennie, a lawyer, had consented, during a ministerial interregnum in the little town church, to read sermons to the congregation on Sunday mornings, and had given them lay-products of his own creation— "Farrago" essays—"mixed fodder" creations, which began with a biblical text and rambled into all fields religious and secular.

Later, attracted by journalism as a profession, he had removed to Boston and had started a paper of his own with the title the *Tablet.* It was to be a literary magazine, and, following what he considered to be the fashion of the day, "which requires variety and high seasoning," he had begun his series with a paper defining the literary form which earlier he had christened the "farrago," lay-preacher essay. Carefully he defined his literary form, the first attempt in America at critical definition. The essay, he wrote,

merits encomium for its conciseness, sprightliness and variety. From its size incapable of admitting widely expanded ideas, it exhibits in a page those useful truths for which the plodding students might toil through a volume. That condensation of thought, which Shenstone admired in Pope, and pronounced his chief beauty, in the succinct essay is everywhere prominent. Renouncing the sullen pomp of wisdom, it effects a vivacity, a gaiety, and an airiness peculiarly charming. This cheerful aspect may allure even the prodigal of moments; and though the essay may at first be read to waste time, it may at length contribute to its improvement. Every one from his own experience is sensible that even a hint may awaken the latent spark of wisdom and virtue.[8]

Very far, this, from Brander Matthews's definition of the "familiar essay" a century later: "It conveys no information, presents no serried argument, but exists for itself alone." But definitions vary with generations. Dennie's day was sermonic. Readers of his "Farrago" essays had complained, he declared, of their lightness, their lack of the heavily serious, and he had evolved for them his "Lay Preacher" series, each of them, even when he was analyzing *The Mysteries of Udolpho,* provided with a biblical text.

For thirteen numbers the magazine ran, and then it went the way of all Boston literary lightness. But the essays survived even the Boston East winds. In December, 1795, they were advertised as about to appear again, now

---

[8] H. M. Ellis, in the appendix of his *Dennie and His Circle,* has reproduced this first "Farrago" paper from Dennie's manuscript.

as a regular feature of the Walpole, New Hampshire, *Farmer's Museum*. In the column headed "Literary Intelligence" this note:

> We hear that the first attempt at vivacious and periodical essay writing, in America, will be exhibited, during the winter, under the title of "The Farrago."

In August, 1796, the series appeared as a volume, with the title *The Lay Preacher, or Short Sermons for Idle Readers*.

Removing to Philadelphia, Brown took with him his "Lay Sermon" literary form and used it during the whole period of his editorship of the *Port Folio*. In every number a periodical essay, and in some numbers two or three. The lawyers of the city furnished little else. Some of them were in charge of serial essay columns that dragged along for months. Brown was delighted with such material. In the prospectus for his new edition of the journal in 1806 he wrote: "The *Port Folio* appears four times each month. We have it in our power to publish four *original* essays during that period. In this important respect, we have a decided superiority over any magazine published in Europe."

In his own opinion, Dennie was first of all an essayist. His "Lay Sermon" series, he believed, contained his message to posterity, but posterity was not to live in the eighteenth century, and these slips of moralistic elegance could live in no other soil. They are the posings of a transplanted Puritan before what he considered the literary esthetes of old Philadelphia. If one were to seek essay models from among his writings, one would fare best in the "Colon and Spondee" columns. Here there is humor, here there is more of naturalness. It is a relief to descend from the forced elegance of the "Lay Sermon" essays, the conscious posings and primpings for the literary few, to the spontaneous naturalness of this democratic column.

CHAPTER XIV

THE BEGINNINGS OF NATIVE HUMOR

IN THE EVOLUTION of a native literature, original humor is the last element to come. It arrives only with independence grown habitual, with national uniqueness achieved, with localized individuality become as ingrained as the fundamentals of race.

In America the evolution was a part of the process of Americanization. Remove an English stock into the utter newness of a new world, keep it there for two hundred years, and it will evolve into a new type. Humor there was always on the American frontier line, and it grew into a native form unique.

The expression of this evolved American product in literary form, however, was quite another matter. The democratic mass did not throw themselves into print, and even if they had done so they would have received small recognition from the aristocratic few who made books and even newspapers. And the literary few seem from the first to have shied away from the native products. Until the mid-nineteenth century the complaint was general that American literature had in it no laughter. "Wit and humor are rarities in our country," ruled Dennie in 1808. Henry T. Tuckerman, in his *Boston Book* of 1836, announced "a dearth of excellent humorous articles written by Boston authors." And Dickens, it will be remembered, declared as late as 1842 that wit and humor in America were totally wanting. All of them, however, seem to have been speaking of the humor to be found in published literature.

As to the cause of this barrenness there has been difference of opinion. The younger critics have singled out Puritanism as the disease. But older critics seem to have made the same diagnosis. Dennie reminded his readers that the greater part of American literature had been written by "Praise God Barebones." Freneau voiced the midlands' opinion in galloping meter:

These exiles were formed in a whimsical mold,
And were awed by their priests, like the Hebrews of old,
Disclaimed all pretences to jesting and laughter,
And sighed their lives through to be happy hereafter.

But Puritanism by no means was the only cause. Literature from the first in America had been the product of an aristocracy by education, the voicings of men to whom literature was a serious thing, men who had been saturated in Greek and Latin and English.

By "people" I mean the great body of American farmers, merchants, mechanics, etc., who possessing habits of industry, and our primitive New England manners, may be considered as the *stamina* of republicanism. . . . I would make a distinction between the *people* and the *mob* or *populace*. By the latter I would designate certain of the lowest class in the community, who are alike destitute of property and of principle, and may emphatically be styled the *rabble*.[1]

In these two classes lay the bulk of the American population. These were "the swinish multitude," "the savages of democracy," so feared by the aristocratic Federalists. Unliterary they were to the last man, though most of them, at least in New England, could read the newspaper. Already they were a group unique. Nothing like them elsewhere in the world—a race for four generations edu-

---

[1] Christopher Caustic (Thomas G. Fessenden), *Democracy Unveiled* (1805), pp. 2, 3.

cated on the bare frontier, men independent, vigorous of
body and soul, individualists, intoxicated by Liberty.
From their numbers, even from the "rabble," had come
the armies of the French and Indian War and of the
Revolution. These it was who later penetrated into the
wilds of Kentucky and Tennessee, who floated on flat-
boats down the Ohio and the Mississippi and opened up
the great West. Unpolished specimens. David Crockett,
Andrew Jackson, Abraham Lincoln are typical representatives. And the East laughed at them and with them. And
it was laughter in a new key. Printed American humor
began with the laughter of the East at the incongruities
of the western receding frontier.

I

It had begun, however, even before the Revolution. Let
us say that it began with the creation in 1755 of the song
"Yankee Doodle." The case is typical: the sophisticated
East in the persons of British soldiers in smart red coats
hurling contemptuous doggerel—no matter where they
got it—at the uncouth, shirt-tail-out militia sent to their
aid. A tiny episode in the vastness of cocky insolence of
British soldiers in American areas, but it illustrates completely the evolution of our native humor—the sophisticated East laughing at the uncouth frontier product.

From the mass of legends which hopelessly conceal the
origins of everything connected with the thing I select
my own version. First, definitions. "Yankee": Indian barbarism—symbolic. Strange, wild newnesses America has
often made of her English words. Consider the noun that
went into the forest as "English" or "Anglais" and came
back as "Yankee." Strange survivals, too, there have been
—"Doodle": provincial for "simple fellow," "rural
clown."

Originating as a contemptuous skit, it probably for a

long period was unprinted. Someone made the earliest stanza, and doubtless someone else added the second and third and the others. This fragment is an early version:

> Father and I went to camp,
> Along with Captain Goodwin;
> And there we saw the men and boys
> As thick as hasty pudding.
> > Yankee Doodle do, etc.
>
> And there we saw a swamping gun,
> Big as a log of maple,
> On a little deuced cart,
> A load for father's cattle.
> > Yankee Doodle do, etc.
>
> And every time they fired it off,
> It took a horn of powder,
> It made a noise—like father's gun,
> Only a nation louder.
> > Yankee Doodle do, etc.

Not original the music, but certainly original the manner of rendering it. "To be sung," says an early version, "thro' the nose, and in the West County drawl and dialect." As to its adoption as an army piece, we know little. There is evidence that it was sung at Bunker Hill, and it is known to have been used as a "Rogue's March" by all the armies. All surrendered British forces—Burgoyne's, Cornwallis's—and all surrendered prisoners were forced to keep step to its republican time-beat.

Like all army doggerel, the thing grew by accretions. It is a true folk creation, a spontaneous piece of patchwork balladry. Stanzas and versions multiplied. Jonathan, in Royall Tyler's comedy, *The Contrast,* declared that he himself could sing only one hundred and ninety verses of it, "but our Tabitha at home can sing it all."

Variant versions there grew to be, like that, for instance,

in Farmer's and More's *Historical Collections of New Hampshire.* I quote but a fragment:

> There was Captain Washington,
>   Upon a slapping stallion,
> A giving orders to his men—
>   I guess there was a million.
>
> And then the feathers on his hat,
>   They look'd so tarnal fina,
> I wanted pockily to get
>   And give to my Jermima.
>
> And there they'd fife away like fun,
>   And play on cornstalk fiddles,
> And some had ribbons red as blood,
>   All wound about their middles.
>
> Old Uncle Sam come there to change
>   Some pancakes and some onions,
> For 'lasses cakes, to carry home
>   To give his wife and young ones.

Native American humor began, therefore, with "Doodle" characterization—a country bumpkin come to town and his activities reported from the superior heights of sophistication. Our first American type-character, he has dominated the whole line of our humorists.

Always a Yankee Doodle come to town— "Major Jack Downing" come to the city with a load of ax handles; "John Phœnix," military engineer, damned by his profession to live in California, amusing himself with the incoming horde of "Pikes"; "Hosea Biglow"; "Mark Twain" in *Roughing It* and *Life on the Mississippi;* "Artemus Ward," showman laughing at the Mormons and at "Old Abe" in the White House; "Josh Billings," "Yankee Solomon"; "Petroleum V. Nasby"; "Bill Arp, So-Called"; "Longstreet" of Georgia. Always the humorist in high glee over the uncouthness of frontier life or of frontier men.

Our "Uncle Sam" is a Yankee Doodle incarnated in a cartoon. In American humor, characterization must be central: always must it be realistic in details and in local setting. Consider again the Revolutionary seed-germ: "doodle" dialect—"I hooked it off"; "doodle" local color —"Siah's underpinning," "hasty pudding," "'lasses"; "doodle" point of view—Yankee thrift, "I wish it could be saved." And even at this early period exaggeration dominant. All the comparisons in terms of "whoppers"— "guess there was a million." Quickly was it to become a national characteristic. Subliterary was it for years, a literary genre confined to the almanac and the "funny" column of the weekly newspaper, and always anonymous. But as the frontiers pushed westward and the seeds fell into the enormous soil bordering the Mississippi, it burst into amazing extravagance, even into the Paul Bunyan legends that are bounded only by the infinite. Always, however, subliterary: it entered the parlors of culture like poor relations that must be kept out of sight.

It was *American* literature, however; "first fruits of our new soil." As late as 1852 a *North American Review* critic could write:

With but few exceptions, the only books which reflect the national mind are those which emanate from, or are adapted to, the unschooled classes of the people; . . . In the politer walks of literature, we find much grace of style, but very little originality of thought,—productions which might as readily be taken for the work of an Englishman as of an American.[2]

II

The second step in the evolution came in 1787. The type became for the first time objectively visible with the character Jonathan in *The Contrast*, the first home-made comedy of any importance to be played on an American

[2] January, 1852, p. 159.

stage. The play was anonymous, even when published in 1790 with Thomas Wignell on the title-page as editor. The author, however, was known—young Royall Tyler (1757–1826), Boston-born and Harvard-educated and for eight years a practicing lawyer in small New England towns. He was thirty years of age, infinite in good-fellowship, hilariously inclined—he had been rusticated at Harvard for a prank—and, despite his aristocratic legal training, no stickler for the conventions. He volunteered to defend in 1789 some of Dennie's Harvard classmates in a suit for assault, and partly as a result found it so difficult to practice law in Boston that he removed to Vermont. His play, *The Contrast,* a literary thing made with no dramatic experience, was the product of an impulse. In New York on militia business connected with Shays's Rebellion, he attended the theater, fell in with the actor Wignell, and almost by improvisation created a play that the actor was willing to put on the New York stage. Undoubtedly the two worked together, Tyler furnishing the literary basis and Wignell and his company the stage technique. We know the play only through the 1790 edition, and before 1790 it had been presented four times in New York and twice each in Philadelphia and Baltimore.

The debt of the play to English comedies, notably Sheridan's, is everywhere evident. The action involves two social strata, "the quality," who ape English monarchial society, and "the other folks," who ape the aristocrats. According to the prologue, "written by a young gentleman of New York" and delivered on the first night by the actor Wignell, the play was advertised as something peculiarly American:

Exult each patriot heart!—this night is shown
A piece, which we may fairly call our own;
Where the proud titles of "My Lord! Your Grace!"
To humble Mr. and plain Sir give place.
Our Author pictures not from foreign climes

> The fashions, or the follies of the times;
> But has confin'd the subject of his work
> To the gay scenes—the circles of New York.
> On native themes his Muse displays her pow'rs;
> If ours the faults, the virtues too are ours.
> Why should our thoughts to distant countries roam,
> When each refinement may be found at home?

As a whole, the work is an American mirror held up to the later English comedy of manners, notably *The School for Scandal,* but the character Jonathan is by no means an American Tony Lumpkin. He is a new growth of the New World, a character drawn not from literature but from the actuality of an evolved type. The first genuinely Yankee character on any stage, he has been the model for all Jonathan parts ever since. His prototype was the "doodle" of Revolutionary days who with his father went down to camp. Only psalm tunes could he sing, and this single ballad, if need be, in all its one hundred and ninety verses. Completely is he in key as he sings it; perfectly is he in make-up and in character. He is himself "Yankee Doodle." Come to town to see the sights, he sees "a great crowd of folks going into a long entry, that had lantherns over the door," and he follows them in. They took him "clean up to the garret, just like a meeting house gallery. And so I saw a power of topping folks, all setting round in little cabbins, 'just like father's corn-cribs';—and then there was such a squeaking with the fiddles, and such a tarnal blaze with the lights, my head was near turned." Soon "I vow, as I was looking out for him, they lifted up a great green cloth, and let us look right into the next neighbor's house. . . ."

JENNY. Well, Mr. Jonathan, you were certainly at the play-house.

JONATHAN. I at the play-house!—Why did n't I see the play then?

JENNY. Why, the people you saw were players.

JONATHAN. Mercy on my soul! did I see the wicked players?
—Mayhap that 'ere Darby that I liked so, was the old serpent himself, and had his cloven foot in his pocket. Why, I
vow, now I come to think on 't, the candles seemed to burn
blue, and I am sure where I sat it smelt tarnally of brim-
stone.

JESSAMY. Well, Mr. Jonathan, from your account, which I
confess is very accurate, you must have been at the play-
house.

JONATHAN. Why, I vow I began to smell a rat. When I came
away, I went to the man for my money again: you want
your money, says he; yes, says I; for what, says he; why,
says I, no man shall jocky me out of my money: I paid my
money to see sights and the dogs a bit of a sight have I seen,
unless you call listening to people's private business a sight.
Why, says he, it is the School for Scandalization.—The
School for Scandalization!—Oh, ho! no wonder you New
York folks are so cute at it, when you go to school to learn
it: and so I jogged off.

In 1790 Tyler removed to Guilford, Vermont, where
for the next eleven years he practiced law. He became a
member of the Literary Club of Walpole, presided over
by Dennie, and during the rest of his long life made literature his avocation, his plaything at odd hours. He wrote
two other comedies, *May-Day in Town, or New York in
an Uproar,* performed in New York in 1787, and *A
Georgia Spec, or Land in the Moon,* performed in Boston
in 1797. Neither has been published. In 1797 he published
what may loosely be called a novel, *The Algerine Captive,
or the Life and Adventures of Dr. Updike Underhill, six
Years a Prisoner among the Algerines.* The book is a
miscellany. The garrulous old doctor tells far more about
his early experiences in Vermont than he does about the
Algerines. His description of his adventures as a country
schoolmaster and his characterization of the old-school
doctors of a country district are the best chapters.

Tyler was undoubtedly the genius of the Walpole group.
His "Spondee" contributions in the *Farmer's Museum*

were for many of its readers, a group that soon was nation-wide, the life of the paper. Dennie, its editor, was "polished" and literary, a writer to be measured with eighteenth-century yardsticks, but Tyler was autochthonous in his outpourings. Literature was not his profession: he was a lawyer with a growing practice, finally to be chief justice of his state, and literature was merely a diversion, a thing to be enjoyed. Had he given to it the full measure of his powers, he might, perhaps, have commanded a chapter in the literary histories. In the mass of his poetry, much of it unrepublished, one finds convivial songs: this, for example, dashed off for a Fourth of July banquet:

> Here's Washington, the brave, boys,
>   Source of all Columbia's joys,
> Here's Washington the brave, boys,
>   Come rise and toast him standing:
>   For he's the hero firm and brave,
>   Who all our country's glory gave,
>   And once again he shall us save,
>   Our armies bold commanding.
>
> Here's to our native land, boys,
>   Land of liberty and joys,
> Here's to your native land, boys,
>   Your glasses raise for drinking;
>   And he that will not drink this toast,
>   May he in France of freedom boast,
>   There dangling on a lantern post,
>   Or in the Rhone be sinking.

Skilful was he in parody, in *vers de société* lyrics, and in hilarious satire made after his own patterns. His comic battles with the Della Cruscan bards fill a page in another chapter. Prose criticism he wrote, too, one volume of it collected and published with the title, *An Author's Evenings*. It need only be read by title and passed by. His fame is not there. What keeps him still before us are his droll Yankee picturings and characterizations done from

nature with little thought of rules or models. Note the
opening paragraph of his "Independence Day" lyric:

> Squeak the fife, and beat the drum,
> Independence Day is come!!
> Let the roasting pig be bled.
> Quick twist off the cockerill's head,
> Quickly rub the pewter platter,
> Heap the nutcakes fried in butter,
> Set the cups and beaker glass,
> The pumpkin, and the apple sauce,—
> Send the keg to shop for brandy;
> Maple sugar we have handy.
> Independent, staggering Dick
> A noggin mix of swinging thick.
> Sal, put on your russel skirt,
> Jotham, get your boughten shirt.
> Today we dance to tiddle, diddle.

In the opinion of Brander Matthews, American *vers de
sociètè* from the first has developed toward an independent
originality because it has depended less on "the mere
glitter of wit" and has shrunk less "from homely themes."

III

The clown and the fire-eater of the "Walpole Wits" was
Thomas Green Fessenden (1771–1837), in the words of
Dennie, "the author of those witty Hudibrastics under the
signature of 'Simon Spunkey' which once excited the
loudest merriment among the readers of the *Farmer's
Museum.*" In his day he loomed high. Dennie gave him
the title, "The American Butler"; "D. W."—undoubtedly
Daniel Webster—reviewed him at length in the *Monthly
Anthology* (1805); and Nathaniel Hawthorne made him
the subject of one of his studies in American biography.

He was a Dartmouth student in the Webster period of
the college, and from his undergraduate pen came some of
the most hilarious "skits" in the Hanover newspaper, the

Eagle, one of the seed-beds of the new evolving American humor. According to Hawthorne, the students, required to prepare and deliver English compositions, almost without exception merely echoed English originals:

> Mr. Fessenden had the good taste to disapprove of these vapid and spiritless performances, and resolved to strike out a new course for himself. On one occasion, when his classmates had gone through with their customary round of verbiage and threadbare sentiment, he electrified them and their instructor, President Wheelock, by reading Jonathan's Courtship.[3]

This earliest effusion from Fessenden's pen first appeared as a broadside, "perhaps as early as 1795."

> The *Rutland Herald,* April 4, 1796, advertised: "The Country Lover; or, Jonathan's Courtship. An excellent New Song. Founded on Fact. Tune Yankee Doodle." . . . Buckingham (*Specimens of Newspaper Literature,* II: 213) mentions "Jonathan's Courtship," which had been published in a pamphlet and secured for its author an uncommon share of popularity among the rural population.[4]

That the poem was known to Lowell before he wrote his Yankee ballad, "The Courtin'," one may learn from a mere glance at the two poems. Compare stanzas like these with the well-known Lowell classic:

> Now Jonathan did scratch his head
>   When first he saw his dearest,
> Got up—sat down—and nothing said,
>   But felt about the queerest.
>
> Yankee doodle, keep it up,
>   Yankee doodle dandy,
> Mind the music—mind the step
>   And with the girls be handy.

[3] Hawthorne's Works, Old Manse Edition, XVII, 38.
[4] Porter Gale Perrin, *The Life and Works of Thomas Green Fessenden* (1925), p. 33.

> Then talk'd with Sally's brother Joe
>   Bout sheep and cows and oxen,
> How wicked folks to church did go
>   With dirty woollen frocks on.

> Yankee doodle, &c.

> Sal cast a sheep's eye at the dunce,
>   Then turn'd towards the fire,
> He muster'd courage, all at once,
>   And hitch'd a little nigher.

> And now he wished he could retreat
>   But dared not make a racket,
> It seemed as if his heart would beat
>   The buttons off his jacket.

> Yankee doodle, &c.

Never poet more American. In a poem entitled "Poetical Dialogue," published in the *Port Folio,* August 26, 1805, he brands with scorn all petty dealers in "draggle-tailed distichs" about "sighing swains" and "love-lorn lasses" and the "whole tribe of moonstruck sonneteers."

Dennie agreed with him, even suggesting in a "Colon and Spondee" paper for the *Port Folio,* March 14, 1801, that all foreign birds and flowers be barred from American poetry after the first of May and that after that date "every rhymster, guilty of violations, should be exiled from the purlieus of Parnassus, as an alien, and enemy." This was his argument:

It has become a fashion among our American versifiers, to copy servilely, images and expressions, which, however pertinent in Italy or England, are most ridiculous, when associated with description of our own *home-bred* nature. . . . "It offends me to the soul," to hear a petty poetaster ring his changes upon borrowed bells, and, to the vexation of common sense, cover his papers, with a bead-roll of transatlantic phrases, unintelligible even to himself. . . . The expressive and picturesque word *intervale,* is as harmonious as *dale,* and not a villager but would understand its force. The names of some birds, selected from those multitudinous flocks, which cheer our forests, perhaps might steal as softly upon delicate ears as *Philomel.* . . . Oak and elm are as good wood to supply poetical fire as cypress and yew.

Taking his former chief at his word, Fessenden sent down an earlier poem of his college days completely in accord with the new demands, and in August the editor printed it with the title "Peter Periwinkle to Tabitha Towser; A most delicate love story": [5]

> My Tabitha Towser is fair,
> No Guinea pig ever was neater,
> Like a hackmatack slender and spare
> And sweet as a muskrat or sweeter.
>
> My Tabitha Towser is sleek
> When dress'd in her pretty new tucker,
> Like an otter that paddles the creek,
> In quest of a pout or a sucker.

And so on to the seventh stanza:

> My dear has a beautiful nose
> With a sled-runner crook in the middle
> Which one would be led to suppose
> Was meant for the head of a fiddle.
>
> The lips of my charmer are sweet
> As a hogshead of maple molasses,
> The ruby red tint of her cheek
> The gill of a salmon surpasses.

[5] Published in the *Farmer's Museum,* August 20, 1798. A week later in the same paper appeared "Tabitha Towser's comi-tragic response to Peter Periwinkle," over the signature "Z," undoubtedly the work of Tyler.

> Description must fail at her chin,
> At least till our language is richer,
> 'Tis fairer than dipper of tin
> Or beautiful china cream pitcher.

The entire poem, greatly lengthened, revised, and divided into two cantos, was reissued in the author's *Original Poems* (1806), which contained practically all of his rustic verse.[6] No "Philomels" in these homely lyrics. Once he introduces the whip-poor-will and explains in a footnote that it is "the nightingale of America." Tremendously were they popular. Of "The Country Lovers" Hawthorne wrote:

> The effort in question met with unexampled success: it ran through the newspapers of the day, reappeared on the other side of the Atlantic, and was warmly applauded by the English critics, nor has it yet lost its popularity. New editions may be found every year at the ballad-stalls.[7]

But rustic humor was, in quantity, the smallest part of Fessenden's poetical output. In 1801, as agent for a Yankee machine, he went to England, but with little success. The machine—evidently a republican thing—refused to work on British soil. It was four years, however, before its promoter left the island. He had become interested in Dr. Elisha Perkin's "metallic tractors," a quack apparatus for a time highly successful, and to promote it he wrote a Hudibrastic hodgepodge in four cantos, with foot-notes longer on each page than the poetry. Its title is all we need to quote: *Terrible Tractoration!! A Poetical Petition against Galvanizing Trumpery, and the Perkins Institu-*

[6] The edition contained the following New England verses: "Horace Surpassed; or, a Beautiful Description of a New England County Dance"; "The Rustick Revel"; "A Pastoral Dialogue; Scene, Vermont"; The Country Lovers; or, Mr. Jonathan Jolthead's Courtship with Miss Sally Snapper"; "The Old Bachelor; an Epistle to a Lady"; "Love's Labour Lost; Peter Pumpkin-Head defeated by Tabitha Towzer."

[7] Hawthorne's *Works,* Riverside Edition, XII, 246–263.

tion; In Four Cantos; Most Respectfully Addressed to the
Royal College of Physicians, by Christopher Caus-
tic, M.D., LL.D., ASS., Fellow of the Royal College of
Physicians, Aberdeen, and Honorary Member of No Less
than Nineteen Very Learned Societies.

The first American book it was—at least the first book
of American poetry—to be reviewed by the British press
as an English product. The reviews were favorable, some
enthusiastically so. A second edition was demanded. Recognized thus by England, the poet found himself immediately famous at home. An edition was printed in New
York in 1804 and another in Philadelphia in 1806. Fessenden was ranked for a time as the leading young American
poet. His great success he followed at once with *Original*
Poems, a collection of his early verses, issued also in London, this time with his name on the title-page with the
additional information that he was the author of the earlier publication. Immediately his English public dropped
him, and he returned to America to spend his life as a
country newspaper editor and lawyer. Much political satire
now came boiling from his pen, the most of it in *M'Fingal*
Hudibrastic couplets. His *Democracy Unveiled* (1805)
marks the extreme point of severity to which New England Federalism descended. The book, half of which is
foot-notes, is written in superlatives:

Your half-wits are, by nature, formed for Democracy.
Leaden-pated gentlemen, who vainly aspire to eminence in the
learned professions, quack doctors, illiterate clergymen, and
blundering lawyers, are the Democracy of nature, and their
opposites are, sometimes, styled the Aristocracy of Nature.
Between these two sorts of candidates for eminence there will
always exist a covert or an open war.

Political and social satire dies with its generation, save
as genius may lift it now and then from the local and the
transient into the universal. This Fessenden was powerless
to do. His copious foot-notes all need copious foot-notes

now. A few of his parodies are still readable, notably
"The Belgic War-hoop," his Della Cruscan imitations,
and such timely hits as his "Directions for Doing Poetry
in the Simple Style of Southey, Wordsworth, and other
modern metre mongers," but the thing that rescues him
for the twentieth century and perhaps beyond is his small
gathering of rustic poems completely American.

CHAPTER XV

NEW YORK

I

AMERICAN literature during the first twenty-five years of
the Republic was central in Philadelphia. Here literature
had been made a social refinement—it had run to "elegant"
magazines. Boston had been provincial, clergy-minded,
sermonic in its literary style, ponderous. Magazines and
lighter literature had not flourished in its hard soil. To
New York the old Dutch element still gave color. The
Hudson River aristocracy still affected its manners; foreign and domestic commerce, rapidly growing, gave it
worldliness. Puritanism and Quakerism it held in contempt. The British forces had been central in the city
during the Revolution, and the effects were still to be seen
and felt. Cosmopolitanism was coming in like a tide from
every quarter.

In 1810, however, the city could still be called a large
village. It was a commercial center, but the agrarian fringe
was close at hand. From the Battery almost could be seen
the windmills of the Dutch farmers. Through the Revolutionary period there had been much printing, but little of
literature in its more refined forms. All its writers worth
noting had come from without. Charles Brockden Brown,
when he arrived in the city in 1798 to live with his Connecticut friend, Elihu H. Smith, found that the literary
life of the city centered in a little circle of professional
men called the Friendly Club. William Dunlap, in his life
of Brown (1806), has preserved the membership roll:

"The Friendly Club," continued for several years to meet
weekly at the house of one or other of the members, discuss
literary or other subjects, and part of the time in conducting
a review. The members of this club were William Johnson, Esq.; Dr. Edward Miller; The Reverend Doctor Samuel
Miller; Doctor S. L. Mitchill; James Kent, Esq.; Anthony
Bleecher, esq.; Doctor E. H. Smith; Charles Adams, esq.;
John Wells, esq.; W. W. Woolsey, esq.; C. B. Brown, and
the writer. With most of the members of the Friendly Club,
Brown was in the habits of the strictest intimacy.

Yale alumni several of them, including Smith, whose
personality had drawn not only Brown from Philadelphia,
but, as more or less regular attendants upon the club
meetings, the "Connecticut Wits" Theodore Dwight,
Richard Alsop, and Mason Coggswell. A curious mixing,
one impossible at that time in any other spot in America
save in New York.

Unlike Boston and even Philadelphia, the city had no
squeamishness concerning things dramatic. It could tolerate even French comedy. Dr. Smith, safely away from
the Yale campus, could even be induced by the worldly
Dunlap to write an opera verging on melodrama, *Edwin
and Angelina; or The Banditti,* based undoubtedly on
Goldsmith's *Edwin and Angelina,* the second, third, fifth,
and sixth songs in the third act being almost literal quotations. It was performed at the New York Theater for the
first and only time on December 19, 1796. Smith it was
also who had written the poetic address to be delivered
by the chief actor. The influence of his old teacher,
Dr. Dwight, still upon him, however, he bore hard upon
the thesis that the fundamental aim of art is moral instruction:

> Great is the task and nice the art requir'd
> To raise such scenes as Dryden erst desir'd;
> But greater skill, and far more nice the art,
> To fix the impressive moral in the heart,
> To voice, form, feature, motion, accent, give

Appropriate force and bid the picture live.
This asks the poet's fire, the player's skill,
Minds that discern and souls that know to feel,
Applause, that cherishes as well as cheers,
And time that mends, and softens, and endears.

Not only dramatic poetry and operas and plays, but dramatic criticism came from the New York transplanting. In the opinion of Professor Arthur Hobson Quinn, in the Friendly Club group "we find the beginning of dramatic criticism in New York City of a very interesting character":

Dunlap tells us how John Wells, Elias Hicks, Samuel Jones, William Cutting, Peter Irving, and Charles Adams (son of John Adams) met after visiting a play, wrote critiques, and secured their publication in the daily press. They were really the precursors of the Drama League Committees of to-day.[1]

Largely by means of the Friendly Club was supported the *New York Magazine,* founded in 1790 and kept precariously alive for eight years. Reprint materials for the most part, the rest annonymous and feeble. In dramatic criticism, however, it was strong. The department, "The Theatrical Register," was undoubtedly conducted by Dunlap. According to *Norton's Literary Gazette* (1854), members of the Friendly Club—Bleecker, Smith, Brown, Dunlap, Hoffman, Kent "and several others, wrote in almost every number of the magazine."

II

The driving member of the group, the active leader, was William Dunlap,[2] dramatist, organizer, manager. His

[1] *A History of the American Drama* (1923), p. 80.
[2] The most helpful bibliography of Dunlap is that in Quinn's *History of the American Drama,* pp. 404–405. The publications of the Dunlap Society and Dunlap's own history of the American theater are indispensable authorities.

father, of Irish birth, an officer in the British army at Quebec had settled in Perth Amboy, New Jersey, where had been born his only son on February 19, 1766. The Revolution had removed the family, ardent in their British sympathies, into New York, which henceforth became their home. The loss of an eye in 1777 while playing had determined in a way the boy's future, had kept him from school and nursed his individualism. Largely was he educated at home by a tutor, and as a result his intellectual progress was desultory and temperamental. Experimenting with colors, he produced several portraits of Washington, became enthusiastic for art as a career, and as a result was sent to London in 1784 to study under Benjamin West. Soon, however, was he possessed by another enthusiasm. The playhouses of the city fascinated him, and for three years he neglected his art and did little save attend the theaters and read dramas. Returning to New York in 1787, he was undoubtedly better informed concerning European drama than any other man in America.

Tyler's comedy, *The Contrast,* he found was on every tongue. The Vermont wag, a greenhorn in the world of dramatics, by adding a single original element to the *School for Scandal* type of comedy—a "cute" Vermont Yankee—had captured the town. Young Dunlap also would capture the town. The result was the second native comedy, *The Father, or, American Shandyism,* first performed September 7, 1789. New York during a year or two, culminating perhaps with the removal of the capital to Philadelphia, was alive with literary promise: Tyler and Dunlap writing comedies, Charles Brockden Brown writing romance, Dunlap pouring out plays and dramatic criticism, the brilliant Dr. Elihu Hubbard Smith uniting the "Hartford Wits" with the Friendly Club school, and the Irving brothers debating literature as a profession.

Friendship with the leading actor and manager of the New York stage, Thomas Wignell, was the culminating force. Dunlap was no longer hesitant. Theatrics were to be his life-work. During the 1790's his plays, most of them adaptations from English models, were almost constantly on the American stage. His attitude, however, was fundamentally commercial. He wrote what he thought the public would come to see, and he played always to their taste and desires. When Mrs. Radcliffe was the literary sensation of the hour, he wrote in 1795 *Fontainville Abbey,* and the following year an opera, *The Archers; or, Mountaineers of Switzerland,* a story of William Tell and Arnold Winkelreid and the villain Gessler.

His first native tragedy, *André* (1798), undoubtedly his best drama, in construction and dramatic art must be ranked as the best play made in America in the eighteenth century—no great praise, but worth mention. The play failed because it aroused patriotic prejudices, not because it lacked art. With so many soldiers of the Revolution still alive, it was impossible to present *André* with sympathy.

One more phase of Dunlap's voluminous product is noteworthy—his adaptations of Kotzebue, in the preparation of which he studied intensively for a time the German language. Through his series of translations and adaptations there came into America through New York the first wave of that German type of romanticism soon to be so noteworthy.

Many of his plays, like *André,* for example, he threw into dramatic verse, unrhymed pentameter of the Shakespearean type. Never posing as a poet, he nevertheless wrote the best blank verse before Bryant. Intent always upon dramatic values, he sought not at all to be poetically "elegant." He was concerned only with the problem of making dialogue that would come from the mouths of his characters like their natural utterance, a reason perhaps why some of his poetry still has vitality.

His product was voluminous. "He produced," says Quinn, "more than fifty identified plays, twenty-nine of which were entirely or partly his own." Many of them did not get into print; some were issued anonymously. An important figure he was in the period, the father of the American stage-drama, our first professional playright, yet time has rendered him in our day little more than a name. Even the organization of his admirers into a club— the Dunlap Club, with funds for reproducing much of his work—has not rescued from oblivion much more than his mere name. He lives more in the literary influence he was able to exert upon his times, an influence in those pioneer days not small.

III

In 1807 there was still a remnant of the Hudson River aristocracy, that Royalist contingent with estates baronial in size and manor-houses English in atmosphere and style. In the assembly and theater season the younger element of these aristocracies was conspicuous. It had been at this Anglicised coterie that Tyler had aimed his satire. In Sheridan-like fashion he had brought out the contrast between their super-refinement and the super-coarseness of Jonathan, typical of the democratic mass. It had flattered their vanity.

But the city was changing rapidly. In ten years it had more than doubled its population: in 1810 it was 123,706. The Dutch element was rapidly being submerged. A social aristocracy more and more was arising from the merchant and the professional class that had poured into the city from abroad and from the other states. The city was becoming the leading American port, and wealth in amazing flood was pouring in.

A typical family was that of William Irving, a Scotchman from the Orkney Islands who had settled in the New York area before the Revolution—in 1763, to be exact. In spite of the war, with which he sympathized, he was able to educate his family of five boys and three girls even to the sending of the two oldest sons to Columbia College.

A Scotch home it was, as thoroughly Scotch in atmosphere as if it had been located in Edinburgh. The father, a deacon of the Covenanter type, brought up his children with Bible-readings and prayers and warnings against sin, especially the theater which to him was the doorway to hell. Wholesome reading matter in abundance, however, he furnished them from Milton and Bunyan and the eighteenth-century classics.

But the atmosphere of New York made for rebellion. It was worldly: the theater was a matter of course. Washington, the youngest of the family, frail in physique, petted, spoiled, stole out of nights and learned that the theater was not wicked at all, but gloriously entertaining. The theater fascinated the lad. Until he was of age, and indeed far beyond that time, the family humored him, made him a convalescent, sent him on tour after tour for his health. College for the young consumptive was out of the question, but not the gay life of a theater-lover and assembly-beau with almost every night a whirl of pleasure.

His brother Peter in 1802, when Irving was nineteen, established a newspaper, the *Morning Chronicle,* and edited it for four years. According to his earliest biographer in the London edition of the *Oldstyle Papers* (1824), it was "a political paper, and devoted to the views and interests of a party, yet some portions of its columns were occasionally embellished 'by hands unseen' with the flowers of poetry literature and sometimes enlivened by flashes of wit and humor."

One of the "hands unseen" was young Irving's. Under the signature "Jonathan Oldstyle" he contributed eight papers, purporting to come from the pen of an old inhabitant, deploring the doings of the younger generation. Six of the eight papers satirize New York theater conditions, a picture of democratic New York indeed deplorable. This of the gallery:

The noise of this part of the house is somewhat similar to that which prevailed in Noah's ark; for we have an imitation of the whistles and yells of every kind of animal. This, in some measure, compensates for the want of music, as the gentlemen of our orchestra are very economic of their favors. Somehow or another, the anger of the gods seemed to be aroused all of a sudden, and they commenced a discharge of apples, nuts, and gingerbread, on the heads of the honest folks in the pit, who had no possibility of retreating from this new kind of thunderbolts. I can't say but I was a little irritated at being saluted aside of my head with a rotten pippin; and was going to shake my cane at them, but was prevented by a decent looking man behind me, who informed me that it was useless to threaten or expostulate. They are only *amusing themselves* a little at our expense, said he.

In 1804 the family invalid, aged twenty-one, was sent abroad for his health and for a scheme of education that had been carefully outlined by his brothers, especially William. The scheme went for nothing: Irving went where he pleased and did what he pleased. He read up to date in the current literature of Europe, and he attended the theater as if he had been commissioned to bring home a report on the condition of dramatics abroad, especially in England.

Returning home after two years, he was soon the leading spirit in a hilarious little club, "The Nine Worthies," which held their meetings in the old mansion house of Gouverneur Morris on the banks of the Passaic about a mile above Newark, New Jersey—"Bachelor's Hall," later to figure as Cockloft Hall. Among the members were Irving's brothers and his brother-in-law, James K. Paulding.

The literary history of the period is a history of literary clubs. The elder Irving brothers had been members of an earlier organization, the Calliopean Society; they doubtless had been associated with the later club which had gathered about Dunlap and Dr. Elihu Smith. From most of the clubs in the various cities came magazines like the *Anthology Magazine* from the Boston Anthology Club, or volumes of club miscellanies like the papers from the Delphi

Club of Baltimore. From the Cockloft Hall group—
William Irving, James K. Paulding, and Washington
Irving came the *Salmagundi* (1807).

The episode has never been given adequate setting.
First of all, it was no boyish escapade: William, who
wrote the seven poems, was forty-one years old; Paulding
was twenty-eight; Washington Irving, twenty-four. Moreover, *Salmagundi* was a magazine that ran for twenty
numbers. Despite its levity, it had a serious intent. When
it announced that its purpose was "to instruct the young,
reform the old, correct the town, and castigate the age,"
it meant what it said. It was a thing with teeth and claws,
a thing serious, a journal of fierce protest, the last
back-to-the-wall stand of the defeated eighteenth century in
America. To consider it a mere *jeu d'esprit,* a bit of high-
spirited tittle-tattle over afternoon tea-cups, is to confess
that one has never read it. Its earliest readers, the ones
alone for whom it was written, opened it with apprehen-
sive shudders. The unknown satirists, who evidently knew
their New York even to its whispered scandals, were
armed with bludgeons as well as rapiers. There was the
case of Fessenden, so thoroughly done up in the tenth
number in the article (afterwards suppressed) entitled
"The Stranger in Philadelphia" that his literary career
was destroyed in a moment. They had reviewed his
"Dr. Caustic" work as by "Dr. Costive." He who had
been himself the most savage of satirists ended his literary
career with a whine like this:

It has been the hard lot of Dr. Caustick, after having passed
the British ordeals of literature, not only with impunity but
applause to have been exposed to be suffocated in American
coal pits of criticism.

Criticism of President Jefferson and the democratic
government, a ship "steered by its tail," was merciless
everywhere in the periodical: "I have seen beggars on
horseback, ragamuffins riding in coaches, and swine seated

in places of honor; I have seen liberty; I have seen equality; I have seen fraternity!—I have seen that great political puppet-show—an Election." This of the President of the Republic:

He is a man of superlative ventosity, and comparable to nothing but a huge bladder of wind. He talks of vanquishing all opposition by the force of reason and philosophy; throws his gauntlet at all the nations of the earth, and defies them to meet him—on the field of argument!—is the national dignity insulted, a case in which his highness of Tripoli would immediately call forth his forces;——the bashaw of America—utters a speech. Does a foreign invader molest the commerce in the very mouth of the harbours; an insult which would induce his highness of Tripoli to order out his fleets;—his highness of America—utters a speech. Are the free citizens of America dragged from on board the vessels of their country, and forcibly detained in the war ships of another power——his highness—utters a speech. Is a peaceable citizen killed by the marauders of a foreign power, on the very shores of his country——his highness utters a speech.—Does an alarming insurrection break out in a distant part of the empire——his highness utters a speech!

The country, observed the traveler "Mustapha Rub-a-Dub Keli Khan" writing home to his people, is ruled by its editors of newspapers, a tribe of "slang-whangers" who attack or defend the Bashaw:

Every slang-whanger resorted to his tongue or his pen and for seven years have they carried on a most inhuman war, in which volumes of words have been expended, oceans of ink have been shed; nor has any mercy been shown to age, sex, or condition. Every day have these slang-whangers made furious attacks on each other, and upon their respective adherents: discharging their heavy artillery, consisting of large sheets loaded with scoundrel! villain! liar! rascal! numbskull! nincompoop! dunderhead! wiseacre! blockhead! jackass! and I do swear, by my beard, though I know thou wilt scarcely credit me, that in some of these skirmishes the grand bashaw

himself has been wofully pelted! yea, most ignominiously
pelted!—and yet have these talking desperadoes escaped without the bastinado!

In 1807 this satire was alive. New York society read
the thing as we today, no matter how carefully we may
study the period, are powerless to read it. The personalities
were known. The psychograph in the eighth number, six
pages, drew to the life Joseph Dennie. Sophy Sparkle was
Mary Fairlie, later the wife of the actor, Thomas A.
Cooper. And there were the Misses Cockloft, Will
Honeycomb, Aunt Charity, Tom Straddle, Timothy Gib-
let, Diana Wearwell, Miss Dashaway, and Tucky Squash,
either known to all or else the subjects for shrewd guesswork.

Satire does not keep well. The next generation misses
the allusions, and the next wonders what the whole thing
is about. True, undoubtedly, of *Salmagundi*, but its creators did precisely what they set out to do: they castigated
the age—a useless task—and they presented "a striking
picture of the town" as it existed in 1807. But it has other
excellencies that keep it still alive while all else of its day
has gone to the scrap-heap: the satire of Washington
Irving is still readable, and with pleasure. Addisonian undoubtedly, yet unstrained, seemingly flowing with unconscious ease, and wholly free from the prevailing taint of
old rose and lavender. But it is more than this: there is
individuality in the style, a literary newness, an element
uniquely American. In this single volume lies implicit all
the later work of the man. In "Cockloft Hall," in Number 14, surely from the pen of Irving, we have the germ
of the later volume, *Bracebridge Hall;* Chapter CIX, "Of
the Chronicles of the Renowned and Ancient City of
Gotham," could be inserted almost without change into
the *Knickerbocker's History;* "The Little Man in Black" [3]

[3] See Fred Lewis Pattee, *Development of the American Short Story*
(1923), p. 19.

is in the vein of his later romanticism; whole paragraphs
one may cull that seem like clippings from the *Sketch
Book* to come. One agrees with Bryant, who was inclined
to "doubt whether he ever excelled some of those papers
in *Salmagundi,* which bear the most evident marks of his
style." And again: "Its style of humor is not that of Addison nor of Goldsmith, though it has all the genial spirit of
theirs; nor is it borrowed from any other writer."

IV

"It was not long after the completion of *Salmagundi,*"
wrote his biographer, Pierre Irving, "that Mr. Irving
resumed his literary labors." His brother Peter seems to
have suggested the subject. It was to be a burlesque, but
let Irving himself tell the story:

The following work, in which, at the outset, nothing more
was contemplated than a temporary *jeu d'esprit,* was commenced in company with my brother, the late Peter Irving, Esq. Our idea was to parody a small handbook which had
recently appeared, entitled *A Picture of New York.* Like that,
our work was to begin with an historical sketch; to be followed by notices of the customs, manners, and institutions of
the city; written in a serio-comic vein, and treating local errors, follies, and abuses with good-humored satire.

To burlesque the pedantic lore displayed in certain American works our historical sketch was to commence with the
creation of the world; and we laid all kinds of works under
contribution for trite citations, relevant or irrelevant, to give
it the proper air of learned research. Before this crude mass
of mock erudition could be digested into form my brother
departed for Europe, and I was left to prosecute the enterprise alone. I now altered the plan of the work. Discarding
all idea of a parody on the *Picture of New York,* I determined
that what had been originally intended as an introductory
sketch should comprise the whole work and form a comic history of the city.

In other words, the book came to life as he worked and compelled him. Excepting a few early chapters, the book is not at all a parody. It is a genuine history of New York substantially true as to its facts. Its creation cost Irving enormous toil: the books he consulted would form a library.[4]

The dominating influences, however, narrow quickly down to one; the others are guesswork. Irving knew his *Don Quixote* by heart. At one time he had contemplated writing a life of Cervantes. Lowell, with characteristic cock-sureness in his essay on *Don Quixote,* declares that Irving used this classic as his model.[5] Four times in the volume the Spanish classic is mentioned, as in this passage, for instance: "No sooner, then, did this scoundrel imputation on his honor reach the ear of Peter Stuyvesant than he proceeded in a manner which would have redounded to his credit even though he had studied for years in the library of Don Quixote himself." And again: "Like that mirror of chivalry the sage and valorous Don Quixote, I leave these petty contests for some further Sancho Panza of a historian while I reserve my prowess and my pen for achievements of higher dignity."

Everywhere one may find close resemblances. At the head of Book VI, Chapter VII, Irving has this: "Concerning the most horrible battle ever recorded in poetry or prose with the admirable exploits of Peter the Headstrong." In *Don Quixote,* Book I, Chapter VIII, there is this heading: "Of the good success which Don Quixote had in the terrible and never before imagined adventure of the windmills with other events worthy of happy remembrance." The same style of chapter heading throughout; the style of characterization is also similar. Peter Stuyvesant and Squire Anthony Corlear both prepare for battle in the same manner; Peter's journey into the land

[4] See the edition edited by Stanley Williams and Tremaine McDowell, American Authors Series (1927), introduction.
[5] *Essays,* VI, 135.

of the Yankees, attended by his esquire, is very like Don
Quixote's expedition. Moreover, Cervantes relates the ad-
ventures of Don Quixote from the manuscript of Cid
Hamet Benengeli.

The intent of the book was entertainment, not instruction, and it was not, like Don Quixote, fundamentally
propaganda. It is to be classed fundamentally as humor.
For the first time in all literature a history true in its main
bearings, yet so funny as to send its reader into roars of
laughter. A century after its creation it still "gets" its
reader. Who can read without laughter the Homeric account of the fearful battle between William the Testy
and the militant Swedes? The early reviews all stressed
humor as the leading characteristic. The Boston *Anthology* declared it

an amusing book . . . certainly the wittiest our press has
ever produced. . . . The people of New England are the subjects of many humorous remarks, but we are glad to observe
made with so much good-nature and mingled compliment and
satire, that they themselves must laugh.

It was humor with a new note. Its echoing of Cervantes,
of Swift, of Fielding, of Rabelais has been pointed out,
but the amazing thing about the book is not its echoings
but its originality. Upon European stock, who cares what,
he grafted the new laughter of America. No one, not even
Mark Twain or Artemus Ward, has ever used exaggeration more outrageously. The French critic Chasles, writing
in 1852, emits this solemn wisdom:

All he writes glows with the gentle, agreeable lustre of
watered silk. Correct and agreeable, he pleases, but does not
move you: the sensations which he exerts lack power.[6]

Surely the man had never read *Knickerbocker's History
of New York*. No watered silk there. After a century and

[6] Philarète Chasles, *Anglo-American Literature and Manners*
(1852), p. 37.

more it still has power to move its reader—to laughter, at least. Not at all consciously was its author following a model. All of us are a part of all that we have read and enjoyed, and Cervantes had been Irving's enthusiasm for years. But in the presence of his newly created characters, his delicious Dutch New Yorkers, he forgot his Cervantes, forgot his Addisonian elegance and even his parlor avoidance of all coarseness. He wrote, I believe, in a gale of laughter. Cervantes-like his style may be, at times, but it is Cervantes with American materials passed doubly through the alembic of the American manner and the Washington Irving personality. Native literature unquestionably, a mirror held up to the exaggeration and the romance and the picturesqueness of our own America. It is the most individual thing Irving wrote, the book of all his books the most American. Richard Henry Dana, in a *North American Review* critique, summed up the matter with something like finality as early as September, 1819:

He appears to have lost a little of that naturalness of style, for which his lighter works were so remarkable. He has given up something of his direct, simple manner, and plain phraseology, for a more studied, periphrastical mode of expression. He seems to have exchanged words and phrases, which were strong, distinct and definite, for a genteel sort of language, cool, less definite, and general. It is as if his mother English had been sent abroad to be improved, and in attempting to become accomplished had lost too many of her home qualities. . . . It was masculine—good bone and muscle—this is feminine, dressy, elegant and languid.

It has not been widely realized that the first edition of the *History* went through many changes at the hands of its author in later editions, and always for the worse. Especially thoroughgoing was the edition of 1812, in which whole chapters were added or dropped. Says his latest editor, Stanley Williams: "He later revised it again and again, amending, deleting, and writing new chapters. Yet for such refinements the book paid with something of its original force and gusto." Williams has reproduced in his American Authors Series edition the original text of 1809 [7]—a most valuable service. Again let it be added that it was the first *American* book, the first to make an impression upon Europe, a book that could give its author a substantial place among the early American authors had he written nothing beyond it.

v

A little flurry it was, however, in business-crazed New York. But for the *Sketch Book* a decade later and the books that followed it, the Cockloft group would have shared the oblivion which came to the Friendly Brothers and the earlier Calliopeians. Very soon the Irving brothers became immersed in business; William Dunlap became a manager of theaters, his plays increasingly commercial. Only one besides Washington Irving persisted as a man of letters and lasted with growing fame into the period beyond the War of 1812.

James K. Paulding alone of the literary New Yorkers was Dutch. His boyhood he had spent in the little village of Tarrytown in rural poverty, for his father, a sturdy patriot, had been ruined by the war. An elder sister of the lad had married William, brother of Washington Irving of New York, a union which had unforeseen literary results, since it sent young Paulding to the city when he was about eighteen, secured for him a clerkship, and associated him with the group that soon had him scribbling poetry and prose. In the *Salmagundi* partnership, Pauld-

[7] Indispensable for a study of this area of Irving's life are: Pierre M. Irving, *Life and Letters of Washington Irving*, 4 vols. (1862–64); George S. Hellman, *Letters of Washington Irving to Henry Brevoort*, 2 vols. (1915); George S. Hellman, *Letters of Henry Brevoort to Washington Irving*, 2 vols. (1916); *The Journals of Washington Irving*, edited by William P. Trent and George S. Hellman, 3 vols. (1819).

246 EARLY AMERICAN LITERATURE

ing furnished no fine frenzy like the younger Irving. He
was a country lad with Dutch traditions, and he had no
love for Englishmen—inheritance from his sturdy Dutch
father, the Revolutionary soldier. Reared a worker among
working people of an agrarian community, he was not, like
Irving, of the Federalist type, a hater of "the swinish
multitude." He sided with Jefferson. His papers in *Salmagundi* were realistic studies of the Dutch countryside,
as in "Autumnal Reflections" and "Sketches from Nature," characterizations of the Cocklofts and their
community—Dutch genre, especially the "Mine Uncle
John" and the "Aunt Charity" sketches—the work of a
novelist, preliminary studies. A promising beginning is
all that one may call it. But for its association with Irving's work and its steady publication as the first volume
of Washington Irving's complete works, it would have
perished in its first edition. The second series of *Salmagundi,* 1819–1820, done by Paulding alone, is today a
mere item for book-collectors.[8] But there was to be a second period in the literary life of Paulding, one to be
studied in a later chapter.

[8] The leading authorities on Paulding are *Literary Life of James K.
Paulding,* by his son, William I. Paulding (1867) ; Amos L. Herold,
James Kirke Paulding, Versatile American (1926) ; Oscar Wegelin,
A Bibliography of the Separate Publications of James Kirke Paulding
(1918).

CHAPTER XVI

THE LITERARY SOUTH

I

DURING the first generation of the Republic the South produced no literature peculiarly Southern. The papers of Washington during his presidency in Philadelphia, the papers of Jefferson colored throughout by his years in France, and the papers of Madison can hardly be called *Southern* literature. And not at all do they fall within the definition of *belles-lettres*. The South before 1815 wrote no poetry, no novels, no literature for entertainment. The South was not literary. In an early issue of the Boston *Monthly Anthology* it is stated that there were only ten printing presses in the whole state of South Carolina and that they published practically nothing but weekly newspapers and handbills. "The few books that are published are mostly on law or contain nothing but the doggerel hymns of some religious enthusiast."

In the first place, the geography of the South made not for literature. In contrast with New England, it had an out-of-doors climate, a sportsman's climate with mild winters. Moreover, the settlement of the region had been of a nature completely unliterary. The tendency had been not toward the making of towns and cities. Almost entirely was the South agrarian, divided into patriarchal landholdings modeled after the pattern of the great estates of England. It made of the plantation-masters an untitled nobility, at least a landed aristocracy with manor-houses and slaves.

All this called for executive oversight, for action, for

the realism of the life of affairs. From the South the leadership in the war and in the early Republic. It was inevitable. Poetry was for youth in love, not for Squire Westons. They wrote their poetry in fox-hunts. Not at all did they despise education: it fitted one for the law, for government, for oratory. Their sons learned law at the fountain-head, at the Inns of Court in London. And often they brought back literary ideals. There was William Byrd of Virginia, whose tombstone in the garden of his estate at Westover is inscribed with this tremendous epitaph:

Here lieth the Honorable William Byrd, Esq., being born to one of the amplest fortunes in this country, he was sent early to England for his education; where, under the care and direction of Sir Robert Southwell, and ever favoured with his particular instructions, he made a happy proficiency in polite and various learning. By means of the same noble friend, he was introduced to the acquaintance of many of the first persons of that age for knowledge, wit, virtue, birth, or high station, and particularly contracted a most intimate and bosom friendship with the learned and illustrious Charles Boyle, Earl of Orrery. He was called to the bar in the Middle Temple, studied for some time in the Low Countries, visited the Court of France, and was chosen fellow of the Royal Society. Thus eminently fitted for the service and ornament of his country, he was made receiver general of his majesty's revenues here, was thrice appointed public agent to the court and ministry of England, and being thirty-seven years a member, at last become president of the council of this colony. To all this were added a great elegancy of taste and life, the well-bred gentleman and polite companion, the splendid economist and prudent father of a family, with the constant enemy of all exorbitant power, and hearty friend to the liberties of his country. Nat. Mar. 28, 1674. Mort. Aug. 26, 1744. An aetat. 70.

One of the most admirably balanced and accomplished men of his generation undoubtedly. The exploit for which he is remembered today, however, is not on his tombstone. The first reference to it that I have ever seen is in Wirt's *The British Spy,* first published in the *Virginia Angus* in August and September, 1803 :

Richmond is built, as you will remember, on the north side of James river, and at the head of tide water. There is a manuscript in this state which relates a curious anecdote concerning the origin of this town. The land hereabout was owned by Col. William Byrd. This gentleman, with the former proprietor of the land at the head of tide water on Appomatox river, was appointed, it seems, to run the line between Virginia and North Carolina. The operation was a most tremendous one ; for, in the execution of it, they had to penetrate and pass quite through the great Dismal Swamp. It would be almost impossible to give you a just conception of the horrors of this enterprise. Imagine to yourself an immense morass, more than forty miles in length and twenty in breadth, its soil a black, deep mire, covered with a stupendous forest of juniper and cypress trees, whose luxuriant branches, interwoven throughout, intercept the beams of the sun and teach day to counterfeit the night. This forest, which until that time, perhaps, the human foot had never violated, had become the secure retreat of ten thousand beasts of prey. The adventurers, therefore, beside the almost endless labour of felling trees in a proper direction to form a footway throughout, moved amid perpetual terrors, and each night had to sleep *en militaire,* upon their arms, surrounded with the deafening, soul-chilling yell of those hunger-smitten lords of the desert.

Byrd's journal, *The History of the Dividing Line,* written in 1729, was first put into print in 1841.[1] A graphic bit of realism it proved to be, written with eighteenth-century precision and form. Nothing produced during its period in America was better fitted for publica-

[1] *The Westover Manuscripts: containing the History of the Dividing Line Betwixt Virginia and North Carolina; a Journey to the Land of Eden, A. D. 1733; and a Progress to the Mines. Written from 1728 to 1736, and now first published. By William Byrd of Westover. Petersburg, 1841.*

tion. Tyler called it a rare work, one "almost unique in our Colonial age—without question one of the most delightful of the literary legacies which that age has handed down to ours." Its charm comes from the fact that it was a spontaneous thing, made without thought of publication, without thought, indeed, of anything save the thrilling experience he was living from day to day. That its author never published it is a commentary upon the literary state of Virginia. Here was an accomplished author, who in England undoubtedly would have been able to stand with the literary masters, writing a classic and seeking no publisher.

The case is a typical one. First of all he was a Virginia gentleman. The publishing houses were in the North. Virginia, his native state, would not have read it. The South generally thought of publication only when there was something practical to be accomplished. They were interested in manners, in politics, in administration.

II

A mere list of the books written by Southerners during the century ending in 1815 tells the whole story of Southern literature. Almost without exception they are local histories, biographies of Southern men, or political documents. Of works exclusively belletristic there were none. The early South did not publish its poetry.

One may begin with Robert Beverley's *History and Present State of Virginia,* published in London in 1705, a straightforward, sensible account of the actual Virginia of his day, a piece of realism that romanticizes not at all. But it was written not as an addition to Southern literature, but as God's truth for the education of the mother-country.

Next comes John Lawson's *History of Carolina* (1709), also published in London, not a history at all, but a gazetteer, a guide-book, a journal written by a Scotchman who, as a public-land surveyor, had seen the state in all its areas.

One might fill a page with titles like these:

The Present State of Virginia and the College . . . , James Blair, Henry Hartwell, and Edward Chilton, 1727.
The Present State of Virginia, Hugh Jones, 1724.
The History of the First Discovery and Settlement of Virginia, William Stith, 1747.
A Narrative of the Proceedings, Francis Younge, 1726.

Of these and many more Moses Coit Tyler has spoken the definitive word. The South wrote no literature in the strict definition of the term "literature." David Ramsay, a native Pennsylvanian, a graduate of Princeton, then for the rest of his life a physician in Charleston, South Carolina, was undoubtedly the leading Southern historian of his epoch, with six volumes to his credit:

History of the Revolution in South Carolina, 1785.
History of the American Revolution, 1789.
Life of Washington, 1797.
History of South Carolina, 1809.
History of the United States, 1846.
Universal History Americanized, 12 volumes, 1819.

His volumes, sprightly as are some passages here and there, belong on the shelf devoted to the scientific and to the records of positive knowledge. And so do the valuable works of Jefferson, Madison, Marshall and the rest—legalistic in tone, the voice of affairs, documents in the day's work of practical administrators.

III

With the biographies one may linger longer. The printed biographies of Washington alone by 1815 would fill a bookcase. John Marshall's careful record based upon papers for the first time surrendered by the Washington heirs, the first unpartisan study of the great general and president, remains at the present time all unread and forgotten, while from the standpoint of mere Truth, mere recording of verified actualities, the poorest biography of them all is still republished and still quoted, its leading falsification on every American's lips.

The death of Washington, coming as it did to the nation with suddenness, had in it an element of the dramatic. The news came like a blow in the face. Everywhere it was the one topic discussed. The time was ripe for a popular biography, one keyed to the understanding and the sentiment of the whole American people, and the one biographer in the whole world capable of striking this happy mean and filling to the full this all but impossible demand was at hand. The Reverend M. L. Weems, "formerly Rector of Mount Vernon Parish," as he announced on his title-page, had a book ready for distribution, and its ingredients had been mixed with perfect knowledge. The hero it depicts walks from triumph to triumph like the good boy in the old-fashioned Sunday-school story book.

Its author, the first in the long line of American book-agents, was a native of Maryland, born in 1759 the youngest of a family of nineteen children. Early driven to self-support, he was able nevertheless to fit himself for the ministry and to preach, according to the testimony of his contemporaries, with conviction and power. But preaching was only an item in his multitudinous life. According to his biographer, he became in turn

preacher, publisher, writer of moral and patriotic biographies, tractarian, fiddler, wanderer, plying his trade of travelling book-agent in a broad radius from Philadelphia to Savannah. . . . Parson Weems knew the country and the common habits and speech of its people probably better than any other man of his day; and he himself was not the least remarkable of its products. He was equally prepared to speak before a fair or any other social or civic gathering, to take part in a wedding or funeral service, to preach before a congregation of any religious persuasion, always upholding the moralities and man's hope of salvation, and incidentally extolling the fine line of intellectual provender which he was ever ready to display.[2]

He had variety in his pack: he even had copies of that other best-seller of the early years, *Charlotte Temple.* And amazingly he succeeded. The Washington biography not only sold like a novel, but it became the matrix that made the deepest impression of the Washington myth. To millions today the word "Washington" instantly brings up the association word "cherry-tree." That there was no Mount Vernon Parish, that Weems had never been rector anywhere in the Washington area, that the episode of the cherry-tree was a fabrication of the author who knew his reading public and had in mind only the selling qualities of his book, the great American public cared not at all. The style and the anecdotes were entirely to their taste. Would you understand the American of the early nineteenth century, an America in its literary enjoyments not much above the age of twelve years, read Weems's life of Washington. At sheer random let me quote from the volume:

THUS bloody and miserable might have been the end of Washington or of Payne, had Washington been one of those poor deluded young men, who are determined to be *great;* and to be brought forward in *newspapers,* in spite of God or devil. But Washington was not born to exemplify those horrid tragedies, which *cowards* create in society by *pusillanimously* giving way to their bad *passions.* No—he was born to teach his countrymen what sweet peace and harmony might forever smile in the habitations of men, if all had but the *courage,* like himself, to obey the sacred voice of JUSTICE and HUMANITY.

[2] See Harold Kellock, *Parson Weems of the Cherry-Tree; Being a short account of the Eventful Life of The Reverend M. L. Weems, Author of Many Books and Tracts, itinerant pedlar of divers volumes of merit: Preacher of vigour and much renown, and first biographer of G. Washington* (1928).

By firmly obeying these, he preserved his hands unstained by the blood of a fellow man; and his soul unharrowed by the cruel tooth of never-dying remorse. . . . Sons of Columbia! would you know what is true courage? see it defined, see it exemplified in this act of your young but great countryman.

One needs no more.

And yet, despite the florid style and the goody-goody moral tone, the book has its merits. It is written with vivacity and complete conviction; its battle-stories are told with gusto that goes far toward counteracting its total lack of critical balance. But the great mass of its readers did not want critical balance. They wanted a good-man hero after their own definitions, and they got it. That the book has gone through thirty editions and that it is still selling are facts worth noting.

IV

The literary work from the South which attracted most the attention of the Northern literary clubs and reviews, however, was *Letters of the British Spy,* ten papers which had originally appeared in August and September, 1803, in the *Virginia Argus*. Their author, William Wirt, like Weems a native of Maryland, and like him without college education, had read law in a private office and at twenty had been admitted to the bar. Learning through a friend "of a very advantageous station for a lawyer in the State of Virginia," as he himself has recorded it, he removed to Culpeper Court-House and for the rest of his life was a resident of that state. His rise in his profession was rapid. In 1801 he was made chancellor; in 1807 he was so prominent in the Aaron Burr trial that he became a national figure. For a generation he was considered one of the most eloquent of the American orators, ranking even with Webster and Clay. In 1826 he was chosen to deliver before Congress the eulogy upon Adams and Jef-

THE LITERARY SOUTH

255

ferson, an oration that entered all the anthologies and
school-readers.

His first literary production, *The British Spy,* pur-
ported to be documents left accidentally in a Virginia inn
by a traveling member of the British Parliament. In his
own words:

> I adopted the character of a British Spy, because I thought
> that such a title, in a republican paper, would excite more at-
> tention, curiosity, and interest than any other: and having
> adopted that character, as an author, I was bound to support
> it. I endeavored to forget myself; to fancy myself the char-
> acter I had assumed; to imagine how, as a Briton, I should be
> struck with Richmond, its landscapes, its public characters,
> its manners, together with the political sentiments and moral
> complexion of the Virginians generally.

The success of the series when issued as a volume
amazed him. "The popularity of *The British Spy,* had
scarcely a parallel," writes his biographer, John P. Kennedy, "in any work, in the same department of letters,
which had, at that date, been contributed to American
literature. It may be regarded as having conferred upon
its author a distinct and prominent literary reputation."
Ten or twelve editions it took to satisfy the public demand.
For a time as a best-seller it vied even with *Charlotte
Temple.*

The reader today can only wonder at such a marvel, for
much of its contents, measured by modern standards,
seems mere trash. The title, a stroke of genius, undoubtedly gave it its first fling; the personalities, thoroughly
understood by its first readers, came next; and its floridity
of style and overflowing sentiment completed the matter.
It was precisely the proper mixture for the unliterary
class of America so excoriated by Dennie and the New
England Federalists in the year of grace 1803.

The author's Virginia, however, was infuriated by the
work, for in his seventh letter, professing to look at the

matter through the eyes of his British traveler, he had held his adopted state up to scorn. It was a state unintellectual, he declared; a state apathetic to everything literary. There are paragraphs, indeed, which might have come from the author four generations later of "A Sahara of the Bozart."

But the author himself was open to criticism. These were newspaper letters thrown off in the leisure moments of a tumultuous profession. That he himself was aware of their defects we know:

Some of the faults of the Spy I know and was conscious of them when they were sent to the press; such as the redundance of words, and the comparatively small bulk of the matter. Next to the exuberance of verbiage and the want of matter, is the levity, desultoriness, and sometimes *commonness* of the thoughts which are expressed. Upon the whole, the work is too tumid and too light; yet these, perhaps, are the very properties which gave it the degree of admiration which it excited.

Completely was he right; no other properties could have made of the work a best-seller. America tremulous with sentiment, emotional, evangelistic, for half a century loaded its school-readers with extracts from the volume, especially "The Blind Preacher," supposed for a generation to be the leading American essay.

Encouraged by his great success, Wirt in 1810 produced a second series of papers, this time with the running title, *The Old Bachelor*. The result was complete failure. They were conscious efforts, wrung out by sheer force. Today they are unknown, and they should be.

His third volume, and in many respects his best work, came in 1817—a life of his hero, Patrick Henry, done *con amore* and finished with much careful labor. It is chiefly known today, however, as the source of Patrick Henry's "Give me liberty, or give me death!" declaimed by thousands of school-boys for a century. Henry's original speech, which was influential in throwing Virginia into the war-column at a critical moment, seems to have been a spontaneous effort and it was not recorded. Years after the event, Wirt interviewed the few survivors who had heard the oration delivered, and from their reports and from his own knowledge of Henry's style and personality created the version now generally accepted as Henry's own words. It is Wirt's literary masterpiece rather than Henry's.

The man was a lawyer, not a maker of what the times denominated "polite literature." To him literature was a forensic matter, and his failure to win a permanent place among the American authors was a logical result. An anonymous writer, using Wirt's model, contributed a series of letters to the *Port Folio* in the autumn of 1804 discussing oratory, with the Boston orators as examples. The papers, which bore the title *The British Spy in Boston,* would be worthless but for a single paragraph at the end of Letter IV:

. . . of all the professions, which lead to the exertions of mind, that of the law gives the least chance of producing an author of extraordinary merit, on any subject detached from the theory and practice of his own calling. The technical style of its composition, the rules of court, the set habits and fixed formalities of pleading, shackling the mind, arresting the ideas, and imprisoning the free exercise of the imagination, giving constraint to all the graceful eccentricities of original genius.

Much light this throws not only upon the writings of the South, but upon a large part of the writings of the North as well.

V

One searches long in the wilderness of the early South before one finds a poet. Samuel Kettell, in his careful survey, *Specimens of American Poetry* (1829), found only one, and him he dismissed with a single sentence: "The

Hon. St. George Tucker was, we think, a Virginian." A
precarious hold he has had upon the anthologies by virtue
of his single lyric, one delighted in by John Adams:

> Days of my youth,
>   Ye have glided away:
> Hairs of my youth,
>   Ye are frosted and gray:
> Eyes of my youth,
>   Your keen sight is no more:
> Cheeks of my youth,
>   Ye are furrow'd all o'er:
> Strength of my youth,
>   All your vigor is gone:
> Thoughts of my youth,
>   Your gay visions are flown.

And so through two more stanzas. Parrington, a careful
scholar, devoted a page to his *Probationary Odes,* but attributed them, as Duyckinck had done previously, to
Freneau.[3]

Tucker, born in Bermuda in 1752, came to Virginia to
attend William and Mary College, entered the legal profession, became a professor in the college, and, in 1803,
Judge of the Court of Appeals. Decidedly was he a partisan of the Jeffersonian order, and after the literary
fashion of the times he launched out in Dr. Hopkins-like
satire. The volume, published anonymously in 1796,
opened with a barrage aimed at the whole line: "To all the
great folks in a rump." Ode II singles out Hamilton—
"To Atlas"; Ode III resumes the general barrage, this
time concentrating upon the Senate— "To a select body
of great men"; Ode IV turned all the guns upon John
Adams— "To a would-be great man." [4] Not bad satire,

[3] See *Main Currents in American Thought:* Vol. I, *The Colonial
Mind* (1927), p. 375.

[4] On page 5 of the 1796 edition an advertisement says: "The first
part of these Odes was printed in Freneau's *Gazette* June, July, and
August, 1793."

if one uses for comparison only the American products of
the period. To the delight of the general reader, he could
jingle most merrily. This in the John Adams ode:

> When you tell us of *Kings,*
> And such pretty things,
> Good mercy! how brilliant your page is!
> So bright in each line
> I vow now you'll shine
> Like—a Glow-worm to all future ages.
>
> On *Davila's* page [5]
> Your discourses so sage,
> Democratical numskulls bepuzzle,
> With arguments tough,
> As whit-leather or buff,
> The Republican BULL DOGS to muzzle.
>
> 'Tis labor in vain
> Your senses to strain
> Our brains any longer to muddle;
> Like Colossus you stride
> O'er our noddles so wide,
> We look-up like *frogs in a puddle.*

A lawyer and a politician writing verses and publishing
them anonymously as propaganda. Virginia and the South
had no poets until the recent years.

[5] In 1790 Adams had published in the Philadelphia *Gazette of the
United States,* "Discourse on Davila, a Series of Papers on Political
History."

PERIOD II
THE RISE OF ROMANTICISM
1815

CHAPTER XVII

INTRODUCTORY

I

THE FIRST period of republican America ended in 1815,
at the close of the second war with England and the beginning of the "era of good feeling." From 1783 to 1815,
thirty-two years: a generation, the first generation of the
Republic. That it produced no literature of note and that
it was, from the standpoint of literary creation, the
feeblest generation in American history has been the verdict of all our historians. It has been the fashion to slide
over the thirty-two years with a few paragraphs devoted
to Brockden Brown and the early Irving. But I have considered sixteen chapters not at all too much for the period.
Even from the literary standpoint I consider this generation most remarkable. Unconsciously, perhaps, yet none
the less effectively, its writers laid the foundations upon
which all of our later literature has been builded. They
translated American life for the first time into American
writings. They were the first to plant the seeds which were
to evolve from native conditions into genres and manners
and forms now regarded as peculiarly our own. In the
way of review, let us note nine fundamental accomplishments of this earliest generation.

1. It took the English eighteenth-century political essay
and adapted it to American conditions, as in the works of
the early presidents, in the so-called *Federalist Papers,*
and in great numbers of similar works—strong writings
which grew to be peculiarly our own.

263

2. In the two decades following the Revolution it evolved the polemic type of newspaper, a fact recognized by Charles Brockden Brown as early as 1799. As he expressed it,

There is one kind of authorship to which Americans have shown a stronger propensity than any other, and that is, the composition of political invectives for a newspaper. Those diurnal sheets are, perhaps, more widely diffused and read than in any other part of the world.

3. It evolved the genre peculiarly American known now as the popular newspaper "column," the earliest specimens of it in the "From the Shop of Colon and Spondee," weekly contributions of Dennie and Fessenden to the *Farmer's Museum* of Walpole, New Hampshire.

4. It established literary magazines, two of which—the *Port Folio* and the *Monthly Anthology and Boston Review*—were strong and original in all their departments.

5. It completed the evolution of the newspaper editorial from the primitive pamphlet, through the contributed letter to the weekly paper, to the periodical essay in a regular series, like the "Remarker" series in the *Monthly Anthology*.

6. It saw the beginnings of the American novel, and it saw, too, the entry of women in numbers into every field of literary creation, especially into fiction.

7. It produced the first American comedy.

8. It made the first American dictionary—Webster's well-known work.

9. It produced the earliest specimens of native American satire and American humor in Brackenridge's *Modern Chivalry,* Irving's *Knickerbocker's History,* and the writings of Tyler and Fessenden.

II

From 1815 to 1835 America was not thinking in terms of literature. "The character of our country's genius,"

declared G. C. Verplanck, addressing the students of Columbia University, "is eminently practical." It was the
era of national expansion; optimism like a spring morning
filled the whole land. The great West was opening its
vastness; settlers were pouring in covered wagons even
into the wild areas beyond the Mississippi. Nothing was
old, nothing was spent. Everywhere action, movement,
business. New inventions like Whitney's cotton-gin and
Fulton's steamboat opened new areas of action. Real estate was leaping overnight into fabulous figures. John
Jacob Astor was buying at farm rates what soon was to be
the heart of New York City. Immigration from Europe
was beginning; twenty-two thousand, over half of them
Irish, came in 1817. After that the deluge. There was the
great West wide open: if one failed in the East, there was
still hope in the unbroken West. Optimism triumphant;
"the era of good feeling"; along the whole limitless border
no backward look. Beyond was the golden fleece: why
linger over books?

No generation more epic in its accomplishment; the
bare history of it reads like romance: the defeat of England by the American Navy; the Louisiana and the Florida
purchases, which added an empire to the Republic; the
admission, by 1815, of eleven states into the Union, eight
of them beyond the Alleghenies; the pronouncement of the
Monroe Doctrine in 1823; the Lewis and Clark Expedition of 1804, which opened to view the vastness of the
Northwest; the election to the presidency in 1828 of
the Tennessee individualist, Andrew Jackson, instead of
the Harvard scholar and aristocrat, John Quincy Adams.
At last democracy completely triumphant.

No age was it for mere literature as a profession. Literature concerned only the few. In Boston it was a by-
product of the clergy, an echo of Harvard scholarship; in
Philadelphia it was a social refinement, a plaything for
lawyers and women; in New York it was an accidental
exotic exceedingly rare. To speak of a "Knickerbocker

school" of writers is nonsense. There was not in the city the slightest literary cohesion. In Baltimore and Charleston a cultivated few, but rarely publication.

By 1815 American literature was at a lower ebb than in 1790. Never has it fallen lower. There was no incentive. Publication on American presses was all but impossible. S. C. Goodrich could declare that

It was positively injurious to the commercial credit of a book-seller to undertake American works, unless they might be Morse's geographies, classical books, school-books, Watts' Psalms and Hymns, or something of that class. Nevertheless, about this time [1820] I published an edition of Trumbull's poems, in two volumes, octavo, and paid him a thousand dollars, and a hundred copies of the work, for the copyright. . . . I quietly pocketed a loss of about a thousand dollars.[1]

The cause of it all was dwelt upon at length by every American author. One can hardly open a magazine of the period without finding paragraphs like this:

Authors have been too few to create competition, and the public, to whom they addressed themselves, too much occupied with matters of direct practical interest to bestow any high consideration upon the talents which are exerted only in the embellishment of life. Hence we have never known till the present day any such thing as a professed author. All the talent and industry of the people have been called into the field of active employment, and the most of what has been written among us consists of such productions as were executed in the early days of our authors, before the serious business of life was entered upon; or in such leisure moments as were snatched from constant and laborious occupations. We have obtained therefore only the unripe fruits of their youth, or the imperfect performances of casual moments. The cultivation of literary talent has moreover been retarded by the state of dependence as to literature, in which we have continued, to the writers of Great Britain.[2]

---

[1] *Recollections of a Lifetime*, II, 111–112.
[2] Samuel Kettell, *Specimens of American Poetry* (1829), I, xlvii.

And again in the *North American Review:*

Who is there among us, who has dared to write a book, that has received from our literary republic one smile to reward his literary labours? How few works have survived the question of our own criticism? How little has our literature gained from the success of this fortunate number? Who now, we may ask here, in this winter and famine of reputation at home and abroad, will venture to give his days and his nights to the labours of the mind, that he may do something towards the literature of his country? Who that has talent among us, is wanting in that honest pride and dignified selfishness, which must deter man from trusting his intellectual labours to criticks destitute of independence, and to a publick too liberal and patriotick to allow of the excellence of domestic manufacture? [3]

And as late as 1831 the French traveler, Alexis de Tocqueville, could write:

America has hitherto produced very few writers of distinction; it possesses no great historians, and not a single eminent poet. The inhabitants of that country look upon what are properly styled literary pursuits with a kind of disapprobation; and there are towns of very second-rate importance in Europe in which more literary works are annually published than in the 24 States of the Union put together. The spirit of the Americans is averse to general ideas; and it does not seek theoretical discoveries. [4]

It was time for a renaissance of American letters. And in 1815 one was close at hand.

[3] Vol. II (1815), p. 34.
[4] *Democracy in America,* translated by Henry Reeve, with an original preface and notes by John C. Spencer (New York, 1838).

CHAPTER XVIII

"WHO READS AN AMERICAN BOOK?"

FROM this dead start of literature at its lowest ebb begins the second period in the history of republican letters. "The era of good feeling" stimulated boastfulness, spread-eagleism, superlatives—all of it to the disgust of the English. On the American side the War of 1812 loomed as a tremendous experience, an unprecedented victory—England beaten on her own element—and to be told by a visiting Briton that few people in England were conscious that there had been any war at all was maddening. The reports of travelers in America, mixtures of ignorance and contempt, were a constant irritation. For the most part they came to America in British magazines. The review of the *Inchiquin Letters* and the article in the *Quarterly Review* entitled "Mr. Faux's Travels" were like blows in the face. Everywhere mention of "the turbulent spirit of democracy," "the total disregard of religion," "the spitting, gouging, drinking, duelling, dirking, swearing, strutting republicans." The traveler visits Princeton College:

By this time there was a crowd of ragged students gathered about, and on its being whispered that I was certainly an Englishman, because I paid my bill, there was a cry of "Gouge him! Gouge him!" which certainly would have been done, had not the driver charitably whipped up his horses and out distanced the barbarians, who followed us for half a mile shouting and hallooing like Indians.

In answer came Dr. Timothy Dwight's *Remarks on the Review of Inchiquin's Letters, published in the Quarterly*

Review (1815), 176 pages of pamphlet wrath. In reply, too, came volumes from Paulding, notably *The United States and England* (1815). His *John Bull in America* (1815), however, is a humorous skit not at all destructive. Modeled after Irving's *Knickerbocker's History,* it purports to be a manuscript left by a British traveler and published to pay the traveler's board bill—a book of fun rather than satire, but Dr. Dwight was in deadly earnest. "English pens have been dipped in gall," he roared, "and their representations have been, almost merely, a mixture of malevolence and falsehood." So far as literature was concerned, the war with England lasted for years after peace was made, and the advantage, on the whole, was England's. After Sydney Smith's review in the *Edinburgh,* the American writers ran out of vituperative ammunition, like the irate fishwife after she had assaulted Dr. Johnson with a drench of Billingsgate: "He called me an isosceles parallelopipedon and what *could* I say?" This from Sydney Smith:

In the four quarters of the globe, who reads an American book? or goes to an American play? or looks at an American picture or statue? . . . Literature the Americans have none . . . it is all imported. . . . Why should the Americans write books when a six weeks' passage brings them, in their own tongue, our sense, science, and genius, in bales and hogsheads. Prairies, steamboats, gristmills, are their natural objects for centuries to come. . . . When these questions are fairly and favourably answered, their laudatory epithets may be allowed —but till that can be done, we would seriously advise them to keep clear of superlatives.[1]

All the more maddening because Smith was right and America knew it. The charges were true.

Out of the battle came the first regular "school" of American criticism: the editors of the *North American Review.* The *Monthly Anthology* had died of inanition.

[1] *Edinburgh Review,* January, 1820.

According to William Tudor, a member of the Anthology Club, the parent of the magazine,

> The publication never gave enough to pay the moderate expense of their suppers, and through their whole career they wrote and paid for the pleasure of writing. Occasionally a promise was held out that the proceeds of the work would soon enable them to proceed without assessments, but the observance never came.[2]

In 1805 it had 440 subscribers; in June, 1811, it died of pernicious anemia.

Resurrection, however, came in the spring of 1815, when Tudor, just home from Europe where he had traveled for a commercial firm, started the *North American Review*, tremendously impressed with the need of encouraging American writers, of combating British misrepresentation, and, in addition, of fighting French deism. Started as a bi-monthly, the *Review* was at first a mere prolongation of the *Anthology*. From Tudor's pen came three-quarters of the material in the early numbers. In 1818 the magazine became a quarterly, with Jared Sparks as editor and with the *Edinburgh Review* as the model. About it soon gathered a remarkable group, the second crop of Boston critics, most of them clergymen or lawyers in practice in that city: R. H. Dana, Willard Phillips, A. H. Everett, Walter Channing, J. G. Palfrey, E. T. Channing, Jared Sparks, Edward Everett, John Gardiner, and others.

Peculiarly was Boston the city for such a review. G. S. Hillard, in his biography of George Ticknor (1875), speaks of it as being from the first "a homogeneous community, nearly all of whom were of native birth and English descent":

> They were a people of primitive habits and a plain way of life. . . . It has always been deemed to be a sort of moral

---

[2] *Miscellanies* (1821), p. 4.

duty in New England for everyone to study some profession
or take up some calling. In Mr. Ticknor's youth the church
and the bar divided between them the young men of studious
habits and literary tastes.[3]

Criticism demands cultured readers and literary materials upon which to work. Boston must have possessed
both, for the *Review* flourished and still flourishes, though
now afar from Boston. Criticism, to be valid, must have
an object; the critic must be convinced, must be serious,
must be broad and tolerant, and yet must be firmly fixed in
what he believes to be the fundamentals.

Never a group of critics more in harmony. Their articles, always published anonymously, read as if written
by a single pen. Without an index it is impossible to determine the authorship of anything in the magazine.
Writes De Mille:

The work of these men is so homogeneous that one can almost treat them as a sort of composite critic. Alike in ante-
cedents, in training, in social background, in theological opinions, they are singularly alike in literary creed. Furthermore,
they were writing for a small and homogeneous public. Their
work is marked throughout by one set of attitudes, opinions,
prejudices, judgments. Never were critics more certain of
themselves.[4]

I

The *North American Review* had been founded with a
single objective: "its main object," wrote Tudor, "is the
encouragement of American literature." Sitting as they
did under the shadow of Harvard, the editors from the
first defined "encouragement" in terms pedagogical.
American literature was to be schooled under the rod,
taught literary manners, and advised as to literary forms
and literary themes. Moreover, the American *Edinburgh*

[3] George E. De Mille, *Literary Criticism in America* (1931), p. 21.
[4] *Ibid.*

Review was to be the defender of the coney herd of poets when they were attacked by the English press and the English traveler. And finally it was to see that the American Muses, both in poetry and prose, grew never unorthodox either in literature or religion. Tudor, in the very first volume, in three articles demolished William Cobbett: "Peter Porcupine—Peter Porcupine—he is constant only in violence—his style is imbued with his original profession—he knows but rancour, violence, and brutal abuse." Early he plunged into the thick of the "Inchiquin" fight: "In the whole history of literature it will be difficult to produce a more disgraceful paper." And again: the British newspaper is but "daily draughts of poison given the public." Scarcely a volume of the *Review* without its criticism of the English press.

The second duty laid upon itself by the *Review* was to make literary America realize its parlous condition. It allowed not England to criticize the literary poverty of the American cities, but it more than equaled the mother-country at times in the severity of its own generalizations. Channing's paper in Volume II, entitled "Reflections on the Literary Delinquency of America," is uniform with gloom: "Our whole literature is the accidental efforts of a very few adventurous individuals. . . . Our poetry is without a character."

Always the charge that American literature was but an echo of the English. In July, 1816, E. T. Channing, in a paper entitled "Models in Literature," lashed out even against the Greek and Latin classics as models. To write in the set forms of other lands and other centuries, he argued, left no room for the expression of national character. Hardly a magazine for years that did not echo this charge. But of things peculiarly American for the use of American writers it could think of but two: the American landscape and the American Indian. In the very first volume of the *North American,* September, 1815, the

Indian is held up to American writers as the most fertile of all literary fields:

> Our language being like that of another nation, we delight more in the acquisition of foreign literature, than in laboriously evolving one of our own by using our intellectual power. Our only real literature so far is the oral literature of the native Indians.

And again:

> These hills and forests hold romance; why may not majestic spirits have haunted them of old just as surely as they haunted the forests and mountains of Europe. Our country is alive with romantic possibilities if only one will grasp them before it is too late!

Everywhere the influence of Scott. The new romanticism these young classicists could not as yet abide, but wholly could they accept the glorified history of the creator of *Marmion* and *Waverley*.

Then, too, for a decade and more it was believed that our geography was to be our literary salvation. Having Niagara Falls and the Great Lakes and the Mississippi and the Rocky Mountains and California and Florida and the Appalachians and the two oceans, how could we fail to have a poetry to match them in grandeur and beauty? Lorenzo Knapp as late as 1829, in his *Lectures on American Literature,* blew on his pumpkin-vine horn a trumpet-blast that was to assemble a mighty constellation of poets singing, all of them, our American rivers and mountains and lakes. "What are the Tibers and Scamanders," he demanded, "measured by the Missouri and the Amazon? Or what the loveliness of Illyssus or Avon, by the Connecticut or the Potomack?"

But the leading encouragement to American authors came from the fact that the magazine reviewed practically everything American, even such minutiæ as the poems of William Person, who died during his college course at Harvard. The reviewer, J. Gallison, found him a genius and devoted thirteen magazine pages to his book. All too often the native writers were puffed to the verge of the ridiculous. Every attempt at literature for a generation and more called out an article done in the leisurely *Edinburgh* manner—four or five pages of generalizations about American literary conditions, then a rambling review of the book under consideration. Up to Volume LXVIII of the magazine, for example, Joel Barlow was reviewed six times, Brockden Brown seven times, Bryant nine times. Cooper's work was reviewed volume by volume as it appeared, by J. G. Palfrey, by William H. Gardiner, by Willard Phillips, by L. Cass, by Grenville Mellen, by O. W. B. Peabody, by W. H. Prescott, by F. Bowen, by A. S. Mackenzie, by F. Parkman, by C. M. Kirkland, by A. P. Peabody, and by H. T. Tuckerman. Irving during the same period was reviewed at length thirteen times, his reviewers being J. C. Gray, W. H. Prescott, A. H. Everett, Edward Everett, G. S. Hillard, Mrs. Kirkland, G. W. Greene, R. H. Dana, W. H. Gardiner, and George Bancroft. An index to the *North American Review* touches everything in the whole history of American literature.

II

Brilliant as certain passages surely are in the reviews by John Sylvester Gardiner and by A. H. Everett, the work of practically the whole *North American* school of critics has passed now into the limbo of the old-fashioned and forgotten. They were timid; they were bound by conventions that even genius could not break; in their rebellions they were unsupported by their people, most of whom were uncultured and even illiterate. More than any other single influence, however, their continued reviews did at last make possible an American literature unassailable by the *Edinburghs* and the *Quarterlies*.

Two critics only from the long roll of this early *North American Review* school have reached our own day— Richard Henry Dana, Sr., and William Hickling Prescott. Dana was the rebel among the Boston reviewers, the leader of the critical left-wing. He was a Wordsworthian in a period when Wordsworth was under fire; he would free poetry from the "gorgeous apparel" deemed necessary by the times, free it from its inflation and artificiality.

Alone of all the reviewers, Dana had chosen literature deliberately as a profession. He would be a poet as Wordsworth was a poet, and only a poet. Expelled from Harvard for a prank, but later given his A. B. degree as of 1808, he had read law for a time but had found it not at all to his liking. He would be a poet. But fate ruled otherwise. His cousin, Edward T. Channing, elected in 1818 to the editorship of the *North American Review,* engaged him as assistant, and as a result came four noteworthy reviews: Allston's *The Sylphs of the Seasons* (1817), Edgeworth's *Readings on Poetry* (1818), Hazlitt's *Lectures on the English Poets* (1819), and the *Sketch Book* (1819). Lectures unconventional they were, shots from the left-wing. First, a shy at the *Edinburgh* type of review:

And now to our author. He must excuse us, for even reviewers, like the ladies, must follow the fashion; and a review, nowadays, without a dissertation at its head, would look about as singular, as a slender maid of sixteen, in closewrapt muslin and simple, smoothly-parted hair, amidst expanded hoops and storied head dresses, on a St. James's Court-day.[5]

Allston he praised for daring at times to break from the beaten paths. The man, he believed, had not received due notice because of his novelty of treatment:

We are surrounded by a multitude of critics here, who set down everything new and peculiar, and not backed by author-

[5] *North American Review,* May, 1818.

ity, as in bad taste, and extravagant. Such critics are to poets what connoisseurs (a troublesome set of gentlemen, with whom, no doubt, our author is well acquainted) are to artists·; who gaze upon pictures all their lives, without its once occurring to their minds, that, to be a judge of paintings, one should study nature, from which they are taken. So with our critics: if a work comes out unlike what has been seen before, they have no mode of determining its merits; for their models are no longer guides.[6]

Byron's rebellion delighted him, but Pope he reviewed in terms of "taffeta phrases, silken terms precise"; Hazlitt "neither sees nor cares that they are paint and rags. Quite natural, too, upon my word!—Yes, the crackling, ill-savoured things, very like to honest out-of-doors flowers, and as fragrant of the fields as Pope himself."

And this of Coleridge in the days when Boston classed him as an intolerable rebel:

Mr. Coleridge's critique upon Wordsworth contains more of philosophy, subtle analysis, and good taste, than does any other criticism upon him, or, indeed, upon any other man whom we can call to mind. In fact, our better criticism owes its birth to that.

The "better criticism" of America owes its birth to Dana. He stood for realism before the shabby thing had received a name. His review of the *Sketch Book* in 1819 rests upon the thesis that genuine literature is a transcript of life in its actuality, "when unadorned adorned the most." *Salmagundi* imaged the real New York, "where the people—Heaven help them—are the most irregular, crazy-headed, quicksilver, eccentric, whim-whamsical set of mortals that ever were jumbled together." *Salmagundi* was a genuine picture made with enthusiasm; but in the *Sketch Book* "he appears to have lost that natural run of style which, in his lighter writings, is so pleasing. He

---

[6] *North American Review,* September, 1817.

has given up something of his direct, simple manner and plain phraseology, for a more studied and periphrastic mode of expression, artistic, to be sure, but general and less definite."

This out-of-stepness with Boston literary orthodoxy was the ruin of the young critic. Unpopularity had followed him ever since the day he had been thrown out of Harvard, and when in 1819 his cousin Channing resigned the editorship of the *Review* to enter upon his Harvard professorship, Dana, his logical successor, was dropped from the board. Young Edward Everett, just home from two years in Germany, was made editor.

Dana thereupon became a literary adventurer, edited a *Sketch-Book*-like periodical of his own, the *Idle Man,* wrote for Bryant's New York magazine, and delivered a course of lectures on Shakespeare. His literary ambitions, however, centered in poetry. His *The Buccaneer*—Byron adulterated with Puritanism—for a time was regarded as an American masterpiece. Beautiful stanzas one may quote from it—the opening stanza, for example:

> The island lies nine leagues away.
> Along its solitary shore,
> Of craggy rock and sandy bay,
> No sound but ocean's roar,
> Save, where the bold, wild sea-bird makes her home,
> Her shrill cry coming through the sparkling foam.

A lyric or two, like "The Little Beach Bird," may still be found in the anthologies, but the rest has faded into oblivion.

Dana, despite his own wishes, was by natural endowment a critic rather than a poet or a romancer; an editor of the Jeffrey type, but not strong enough to force himself upon the American literary aristocracy, the prejudiced group which alone read criticism. Had he been given the editorship in 1819 instead of Everett, undoubtedly he would have added blood and iron to the timid,

Europe-scanning *Review,* but undoubtedly he would have reduced the subscription list to the limits of ruin.

A moment one must pause before another of the early contributors, William Hickling Prescott, who made a practice during this early period of the *Review* of contributing one article every year. His paper entitled "Essay Writing" (1822) contended that the short story is a distinct literary *genre* and that the first author to work out the new form was Washington Irving—a landmark in the history of American criticism. His review of Leggett's *Leisure Hours at Sea* (Vol. XXII), his papers on "Novel Writing" (Vol. XXV), "Historical Composition" (Vol. XXIX), and "English Literature in the Nineteenth Century" (Vol. XXXV) are high points in the history of early American article-writing. Had Prescott not turned to the field of history, he might have made himself the leading American critic.

The coming of young Everett from Germany to the editorship of the *Review* not only doubled at once the subscription list but brought a new atmosphere into American criticism. Everett and Ticknor had matriculated at Göttingen in 1815, Joseph Green Cogswell in 1817— the pioneers of a notable army that was to follow. They brought German thought into the *Review;* they reviewed German books and explained German methods. Their induction into Harvard professorships was destined to revolutionize the old college. Charles Follen took the chair of German in 1825. George Bancroft, too, had studied at Göttingen, and for a time he also was enrolled as a Harvard instructor. Europe was pouring into New England like a tide.

The coming, in 1818, of Washington Allston after years abroad, where he had made himself one of the leading painters of his generation, brought to the Boston circle another atmosphere of culture. Much was made of his volume of poetry, *The Sylphs of the Seasons,* partly, it may be, because of his great fame as an artist and

partly because of his Boston relatives. For in Boston—
a village it was then—everybody not only knew everybody
in the town, but was "related" perchance to everybody
worth being related to. Allston's first wife, for instance,
was a sister of E. T. Channing, and his second wife
was a sister of R. H. Dana. As a result, perhaps, Dana's
review of the volume in the *North American* of 1817 is
too kindly. Griswold, who was not a relative, dedicated in
1842 his *Poets and Poetry of America* to Allston and
reprinted from his poems enough to fill twelve double-
column pages. E. C. Stedman in 1885, dwelling upon what
he termed the "earliest promise of a home school," rated
American poets of 1815 in this order: John Pierpont,
Richard Henry Dana, Washington Allston, Charles
Sprague, William Cullen Bryant, Richard Henry Wilde,
Edward Coate Pinkney. Truly, as Stedman remarked,
"fashion is a potency in art." Both *The Sylphs of the
Seasons* and the tremendous romance, *Monaldi,* from
which Griswold selected some four pages of specimens
for his *Prose Writers,* are dead today beyond all resurrection.

III

But the most original reaction to Sydney Smith's,
article was John Neal's. A young lawyer in Baltimore,
with a business "that had begun to give [him] a handsome
support," he was dining one evening with Henry Robinson, "an Englishman by birth":

The conversation turned, I know not how, upon American
literature, and he, being full of admiration for the *Edinburgh*
and *Quarterly,* asked, in the language of the day, "Who reads
an American book?" I know not what I said in reply; but I
know how I felt, and that, finally, I told him, "more in sorrow
than in anger," that I would answer that question from over
sea; that I would leave my office, my library, and my law-
business, and take passage in the first vessel I could find . . .

and see what might be done, with a fair field, and no favor, by an American writer.

Instantly he was off, not to fight the *Quarterly* or to defend American literature, but to write classics that would compel Sydney Smith to withdraw his impudent question. Arrived in London, he was for a time in doubt as to what he should write for his opening shot: "Should I try my hand first with magazine articles, or news-papers, or let fly two or three novels to begin with?" He chose the magazines, and his success exceeds belief:

And before six months were over, I had succeeded so far as to get papers about America and American affairs, Ameri-can literature, and American art, into *Blackwood*, the *New Monthly*, the *Old Monthly*, the *London Magazine*, the *New European*, the *Oriental Herald*.

The five long papers he was allowed to contribute to *Blackwood's* with the title "American Writers" must be classed among the curiosities of American literature. That the magazine could have been induced to accept from an unknown man with no literary reputation such an inco-herent, pell-mell-written, unscholarly criticism exceeds be-lief. Posing as an Englishman, using no reference books and no authorities, writing at top speed without revision or plan, he created what must be called a classic of its kind: the worst specimen ever put into English. In a total of some fifty-six thousand words, he devoted six thousand words to a glorification of his own work and as many more to proving that Washington Irving was his inferior as a writer.

Posing as an Englishman, he echoed with shrillness Smith's maddening question:

One is continually hearing, more or less, about American literature, of late, as if there were any such thing in the world as American literature; or any such thing in the United States

of North America, as a body of native literature—the production of native writers—bearing any sort of national character,
either of wisdom or beauty—heavy or light—*or* having any
established authority, even among the people of the United
States. . . .

With two exceptions, or at the most three, there is no
American writer who would not pass just as readily for an
English writer, as for an American, whatever were the sub-
ject upon which he was writing; and these three are PAULD-
ING, NEAL, and CHARLES BROCKDEN BROWN, of whom we
shall speak separately in due time.[7]

On every page the inference, if not the direct statement, that America had produced but one single author
worthy to stand with the English masters—John Neal.
In quantity and speed he was, he believed, a world
champion. "Neal has written more volumes . . . than,
perhaps, any other four of his countrymen," he declared,
—"one hundred octavo volumes to say the least." Each
one of them had been a whirlwind product: "With two
or three late exceptions, all that I have written, has been
dashed off, *with a rapidity which has no parallel in the
history of literature.*"

Logan, which re-appeared over the sea in four volumes, I
wrote in six or eight weeks, ending Nov. 17, 1821; *Randolph,*
published here in two volumes, I began Nov. 26, 1821, and
finished in thirty-six days; *Errata, or Will Adams,* in two
volumes, was begun Jan. 8, 1822, and finished in thirty-nine
days; *Seventy-six,* begun Feb. 16, 1822 and finished March
19, 1822—four days off—in twenty-seven days, republished
in London in three volumes; so that between October, 1821,
and March, 1822, I wrote and published no less than eight
large duodecimos, which in England would have been equal
to thirteen volumes.[8]

Never a man more positive in praise of his own excellencies. His egotism amounted to genius:

[7] *Blackwood's Magazine,* September, 1824.
[8] *Ibid.,* February, 1823.

LOGAN is full of power—eloquence—poetry—instinct, with a more than mortal extravagance: yet so crowded—so incoherent—so evidently without aim, or object, worthy of a good or a wise man—so outrageously over-done, that nobody *can* read it entirely through. Parts are without a parallel for passionate beauty;—power of language: deep tenderness, poetry—yet every page—almost every paragraph, in truth, is rank with corruption—the terrible corruption of genius.—It should be taken, as people take opium. A grain may exhilarate—more may stupefy—much will be death.

SEVENTY-SIX. I pronounce this to be one of the best romances of the age.

And concerning his poems, *The Battle of Niagara, Goldau,* and *Miscellaneous Poetry,* they contain

more sincere poetry, more exalted, *original,* pure, bold poetry, than *all* the works of *all* the other authors, that have ever appeared in America. A volume could be collected out of the whole, which would contain as much great poetry, as any single volume of this age. A few passages are equal to any poetry, that ever was written—to my knowledge. Cry out, if you will—say what you will. What I speak is the truth.

To read any of Neal's work with its slap-dash incoherence, its amazing digressions, its sheer ignorance, its almost total lack of critical power or stylistic beauty is like a journey through chaos. Not one of his books is worth placing on the shelves of any library save as a "believe it or not" specimen. Nor is my criticism the mere dragging of an ancient thing to the light to be slaughtered by modern standards. Here is a contemporary estimate, a clipping from the *United States Literary Gazette* (1825) —a review of the novel, *Randolph:*

It pretends to be a novel, and the various incidents have about as much coherence as the thoughts of a maniac. It is absurd, unnatural, impossible. . . . In general he talks about everything like a madman or an idiot.

An ignoramus, undisciplined, untaught, cock-sure, an individualist of the border type blundering into literature and attempting to "corner the market." His own explanation is sufficient:

Not having been educated, or brought up, as multitudes are, having had, in fact, no education at all, I have not many of *their* prejudices, whatever prejudices, of my own, I may have. My opinions are peculiar. I know it—I am proud of it.—My doctrines, whatever else they are, are not of the schools. I have been educated; or, in other words, kicked and cuffed about (figuratively, not literally)—in a school of my own— one that would make anybody wiser to the full extent of his capacity—the school of hardship, adventure—everlasting warfare with what are looked upon, by other men, as the giants of this world.[9]

It was this not-of-the-schools element in Neal that secured for him the columns of *Blackwood's*. This man and this unheard-of style were *American*—new birth of the American new soil. It was as if a wild Indian in full war-gear had arrived with a manuscript. Like Joaquin Miller of a later generation, he failed completely. Neither of the men had the judgment or the knowledge or the vision to capitalize their frontier independence. Neal had energy, courage even to utter rashness, and self-dependence to the verge of superlative conceit, but he had nothing to say. Whitman had much the same personality, but Whitman was able to evolve from the American situation a philosophy and an interpretation. Neal, on the contrary, was a mere literary David Crockett, a "Mike Fink" poet who believed he could roar himself into a classic. Undoubtedly he was the most picturesque literary character of a picturesque era. His autobiography belongs on the same shelf as Crockett's or Barnum's.[10]

[9] *Blackwood's Magazine,* February, 1823.
[10] John Neal, *Wandering Recollections of a Somewhat Busy Life; An Autobiography* (1869).

It must be recorded in his favor, however, that he was the first to write a history of American literature—his chaotic *Blackwood's* articles in which he attempted to present the American authors in alphabetic order, one hundred and thirty-seven of them, three quarters of them names one can find in no other book of reference. Then, too, Neal deserves praise for his advocacy of international copyright. Goodrich, in his autobiography, hailed him as a pioneer: "The earliest direct advocacy of international copyright that I have met with, is by John Neal, in the 'Yankee,' 1828."

America for a time was bluffed by the man. It took him at his own valuation. Griswold, in his *Poets and Poetry of America,* could rate him as a leading American poet and allow him thirteen double-column pages of specimens, and in his prose anthology give him half as much again. Poe, too, was "inclined to rank John Neal first, at all events second, among our men of indisputable *genius.*" [11] Lowell's estimate in 1848, however, still stands:

A man who's made less than he might have, because
He always has thought himself more than he was,—
Who, with very good natural gifts as a bard,
Broke the strings of his lyre out by striking too hard.

[11] *Marginalia,* No. 138.

CHAPTER XIX

ROMANTICISM

I

THE FRENCH REVOLUTION of the 1790's did not reach England in full force until the 1830's. Always a generation behind France in originality,[1] always the last to abandon the old regime, England, with back to the wall, fought for decades the inevitable, fought the new forces of democracy which were roaring in like a freshet. And as the ancient landmarks tottered about her, suddenly from the Celtic North a wizard with minstrel-harp who called all England to see a marvellous thing, a burning-bush in the desert sand—romance that radiates forever its shimmering glory and is not consumed. And while they wondered and dreamed of castles and tournaments and cloth of gold, the golden age of Toryism enthroned and glorious, the foundations of the ancient monarchy they stood upon were shaking all about them into ruins.

Thus Sir Walter Scott with his *Lay of the Last Minstrel*, his *Marmion* and *Lady of the Lake*, his *Waverley* and *The Talisman* and *Ivanhoe* and *The Heart of Midlothian*, fox-fire from the decaying monarchism of Europe.

II

Queer stuff for democratic America, yet it was in America that Walter Scott was to have his greatest fol-

[1] Samuel Rogers, in his *Table Talk*, records a remark by Edmund Burke that "England is a moon shone on by France."

lowing. Romance had never flourished in America. Six generations of writers, some of them voluminous, and scarcely a trace of it: there is no parallel in modern literary history. And this in the unexplored West of the New World, for centuries the world's chief portal of escape into epic living.

America from the earliest settlement had been Franklinian in its practicality. The religious life of the Puritans was fundamentally romantic inasmuch as it fixed its eyes upon "a better country," the idealized city of God; and yet, even as he dreamed, the old Puritan had his feet pretty firmly planted on the solid earth. "Common sense rules America," wrote James Fenimore Cooper in 1828, and common sense is the antonym of romance, as romance is generally defined. The frontier was settled in a tremendous Now, with grinding toil and baldest prose. Little of romance was there in the Revolution for those who fought the battles and suffered the hardships of war.

To the agrarian majority—practical, hard-handed, moralistic—literary romance as they conceived it was not only useless, but it was positively wicked. The Gothic infection from England in the last years of the eighteenth century found not the slightest lodgment: not even in Brockden Brown. His novel, *Wieland,* he declared, he wrote as a protest against Gothicism. All the effects accomplished by Mrs. Radcliffe he sought to produce without for a moment departing from the actual. He would simply record.

The first reception of Scott's poems in America, before the chorus of English praise had reached the native reviewers, was inclined to be hostile. A Boston *Anthology* critic in 1808 found the poem overdressed:

Every reader is surprised, at least, when he finds the poet relating, at every turn, the cloth his hero is dressed in, its texture and quality, and the place whence it was bought, and not even letting it slip his notice, if a lady puts off her veil to cool herself.

But soon the new romance overrode all criticism, even
that of the clergy, who had become hoarse in their de-
nunciation of fiction. Scott's novels were different, they
argued: Scott's novels were history; they recorded facts;
they were true. Moreover, their morality was beyond
question. Completely were they accepted. At the universities, the Phi Beta Kappa orators and poets, who so
fiercely had berated the Gothic romance, began to soften
their verdicts. Scott, they found, was an exception to
their rules. In 1829 Charles Sprague, Phi Beta Kappa
poet at Harvard, in his poem entitled "Curiosity," could
even paint a picture like this:

> 'Tis heaven, the upper heaven of calm delight
> The world forgot, to sit at ease reclined,
> While round one's head the smoky perfumes wind,
> Firm in one hand the ivory folder grasped,
> Scott's uncut latest by the other clasped,
> 'Tis heaven, the glowing, graphic page to turn,
> And feel within the ruling passion burn,
> Now through the dingles of his own bleak isle,
> And now through lands that wear a sunnier smile,
> To follow him, that all-creative One
> Who never found a "brother near his throne."

During the second decade of the new century editions
of Scott flooded the book-stands. Never writer so popular. In nine years, ending in 1823, a half-million copies
of the novels and poems had been sold in America, and
perhaps more.[2] The manor-houses of the aristocratic
South bought them in numbers. The feudal atmosphere
created by the great romancer they threw in their imaginations over their own feudal-like plantations.[3] The
North, even Puritanic New England, bought whole editions of the romances. In 1827 Nathaniel Appleton Haven,
speaking of the country as a whole, made the statement

[2] *The Cambridge History of American Literature,* IV, 541.
[3] See *American Literature,* II, 256.

that "The Waverley novels have composed nearly half the literature of the last ten years." [4] Five years earlier Miss Lydia Francis (later Mrs. Child), in the preface of her novel *Hobomok,* declared that to her it seemed ludicrous to attempt a romance "when *Waverley* is galloping over hill and dale faster and more successful than Alexander's conquering sword." Goodrich, speaking from the standpoint of a publisher, was equally superlative in his autobiography:

The appearance of a new tale from his pen caused a greater sensation in the United States than did some of the battles of Napoleon, which decided the fate of thrones and empires. Everybody read these works; everybody—the refined and the simple—shared in the delightful trances which seemed to transport them to remote ages and distant climes. . . . I can testify to my own share in this intoxication.

Into the remotest areas, into the red school-houses, the poems and romances soon penetrated. Young ladies in frontier farm-houses could repeat whole cantos of *The Lay of the Last Minstrel;* growing boys from Maine to Georgia spouted in school "The Combat" from *The Lady of the Lake.*

Stories of rival American publishers in the larger cities sending their agents to race across the Atlantic with the sheets of the new *Waverley* novel, hiring all the printers and presses of a city to produce an edition in a single day, then buying up, as once in Philadelphia, all the seats in the New York stage-coach to fill them with copies of the pirated edition—all this is a part of the picturesque Scott era in the history of our literature.

The popularity of Scott reached its height in 1825. He had won his readers early, but the old-guard of American writers was inclined to hesitate. American literature was still in the eighteenth century. Scott had appeared, as

[4] George Ticknor, *The Remains of Nathaniel Appleton Haven, with Memoir of His Life* (1827).

Carlyle was to express it, "in the sickliest of recorded ages, when British literature lay all puking and sprawling in Werterism, Byronism, and other sentimentalism, tearful or spasmodic (fruit of internal wind)." The older American writers, even far into the new century, were afraid of the new romanticism.

III

The most outspoken critic of Scott was James K. Paulding, who had been associated with Irving in the editing of *Salmagundi*. Irving, at first a classicist, escaped early into England, became intimate with Scott, and soon was as romantic as was his master. Paulding, however, remained in New York and fought the British. Never for a moment did he lower the standard of his classicism. Scott to him was a rebel, a literary "red," a man to be classed with Southey and Byron and the wild men of German Gothicism. His literary life until 1824 became a series of *Salmagundi*-like satires aimed at Scott and at Great Britain generally. Their titles reveal their nature and even their quality:

The Diverting History of John Bull and Brother Jonathan, by Hector Bull-us, 1812 [5]
The Lay of the Scottish Fiddle: A Tale of Havre de Grace; Supposed to have been Written by W——— S———, Esq., 1813, 1814.
The United States and England: Being a Reply to the Criticism on Inchiquin's Letters; Contained in the Quarterly Review for January, 1814, 1815.
Letters from the South, 1817.
The Backwoodsman; A Poem, 1818.

[5] "Several bibliographers and cataloguers place in the above list *Jokeby, a Burlesque on Rokeby, a Poem . . . in six cantos* under Paulding's name, but after considerable research I am convinced that it was written by John Roby, an English writer."—Oscar Wegelin, *A Bibliography of the Separate Publications of James Kirke Paulding* (1918).

A Sketch of Old England, by a New-England Man, 1822.
Koningsmarke, the Long Finne, A Story of the New World,
    1823.
John Bull in America: or, The New Munchausen, 1825.

All are satires, but never do they descend into vulgar
rant and badinage: it is of the *Salmagundi* type, gentle-
manly sarcasm inclining always to the ridiculous. *The Lay
of the Scottish Fiddle,* a lampoon upon Scott's manner
and a mock-epic of the British burning of Havre de
Grasse during the war, is feeble stuff on the whole, judged
from any standpoint. Now and then a poetic bit, as this
precursor of Drake's *The Culprit Fay:*

> As on the bank of some lone stream,
> Lit by the moonlight's quivering beam,
> The fairies in their gambols light,
> Are scar'd by some bewilder'd wight,
> The little caitiffs flit away,
> And leave undone their roundelay;
> Their faithful watchman of the night,
> The Fire-fly, shrouds his lamp so bright.

That Paulding was honest in his condemnation of Scott
is everywhere evident. Scott was a rebel who had escaped
from the eighteenth century; he was unrestrained, over-
ornamented, barbaric;

The savage prefers glass beads and tinfoil to polished
steel; and it would seem that our taste is nearly as much in
a state of barbarism; for we prefer the tinsel of Scott to the
classic gold of modest, unassuming Campbell. In the midst
of all the fury of declamatory verse, so profuse in our most
fashionable poetry, we detect a little freezing thought, that
makes one's teeth chatter; and yet the glitter of the phrase
makes amends for the poverty of the idea. We are monarchists in poetry, and bow to a pageant, because it appears with
outward splendor.

As late as 1823 he was still protesting. His novel
Koningsmarke he wrote as a burlesque of the Scott man-

ner. It is "a story of the *New* World" put into romantic costuming. Instead of "Norna of the Fitful Head," he has an old Negress, "Bombic of the Frizzle Head." He pauses in his narrative to condemn "extempore writing" even while writing extempore himself. Irving in England now, his *Sketch Book* enormously successful, expostulated mildly, but Paulding was honest in his criticism, and theoretically he was right. With the eighteenth-century critics, he stood for realism, for actuality uncostumed and unlighted. To make Scott the most popular author of the generation violated all his literary standards, or, to quote Paulding's own words:

I cannot help thinking it is placing him where he ought not to be, to put him on a level with Fielding, Smollett, Goldsmith, and Miss Edgeworth. He belongs, I imagine, to a different class of beings; to a class of authors, who, when the charm of novelty expires, and curiosity is satisfied in the development of the story, will never be much relished or sought after for other and more lasting beauties. . . . Each of these writers, without going out of the bounds of probability, or offending against "the modesty of nature," by extravagant and incongruous events, or boisterous, uncontrolled passion, has produced works, that appeal far more powerfully to the heart and the imagination than the dashing succession of characters and events, that only hang together by a chain of improbabilities, or by the thread of history, exhibited in the work of the Great Unknown.

During his whole career Paulding pleaded constantly for American themes and American fiction and poetry. In his notes to *The Lay of the Scottish Fiddle* he begs again and again for the use of American birds and American nature in poems and even prose American. First of all, originality; nature at first hand, not invention or romanticization. Never romance in the forests of an area as recent as the new Republic. America was but of yesterday:

Until we have a good number of ruins, with subterranean passages, and "Donjon Keeps" for our poets to commit

murders, and our travellers to locate legends in, I despair of
our excelling in these articles. . . . It would puzzle a Philadelphia lawyer to make a romance out of a log-hut.

Give us something new—something characteristic of your
native feelings, and I don't care what it is. I am some-what
tired of licentious love ditties, border legends, affected sorrows, and grumbling misanthropy. I want to see something
wholesome, natural, and national.

And again in *Salmagundi,* Second Series, August 19,
1820:

The best and most perfect works of imagination appear to
me to be those which are founded upon a combination of
such characters as every generation of men exhibits, and such
events as have often taken place in the world, and will again.
Such works are only fictions, because the tissue of events
which they record never perhaps happened in precisely the
same train, and to the same number of persons, as are exhibited and associated in the relation. Real life is fraught
with adventures, to which the wildest fictions scarcely afford
a parallel; and it has this special advantage over its rival,
that these events, however extraordinary, can always be
traced to motives, actions, and passions, arising out of circumstances no way unnatural, and partaking of no impossible
or supernatural agency.

The voice of a real critic, the last clear voice pleading
for eighteenth-century canons, the voice of a Jacob, but
the hands are the hands of Esau. His work in large areas
violates all of his own theories. He was finally compelled
to write himself with heavy hand the romances he so
uniformly had condemned: the times demanded it. During the first era of the gift-books he wrote no less than
seventy Irving-like tales and sketches in every key. Irving he followed like a veritable shadow: Hudson River
legends he wrote, Knickerbocker histories, colonial romances, Indian tales, sketches, a life of Washington, and
even Spanish romance. In everything he excelled except
in style. His humor seems forced, his narrative heavy.

Completely was he lacking in Irving's leading asset: mellow atmospheres and that glow of genial sunniness for which there is no critical name save Washington Irving.

IV

Up to 1810 Irving had been as completely a classicist as Paulding. Goldsmith had been his model, and Addison and Steele. His first draught of Scott, however, had been intoxicating. At J. O. Hoffman's country-seat on the Hudson he had read the new poem, *Lady of the Lake,* and had been thrilled by it. Then had come Scott's letter warmly praising his *Knickerbocker's History.* The rest was sheer accident. In 1815, balked in his plan to go to the Barbary States on Decatur's warship, he voyaged to England. In the words of his nephew-biographer,

Yielding to a roving propensity, "the offspring of idleness of mind and a want of something to fix the feelings," he had pulled up anchor in New York . . . to drift about Europe in search of novelty and excitement, ready, as he expressed it, "to spread his sails wherever any vagrant breeze might carry him."

Making his home most of the time with his married sister in Birmingham, for three years he drifted where impulse bore him. He visited Campbell; he spent a marvellous week with Scott at Abbotsford; he toured the Highlands. Then suddenly in 1818 had come a crisis: the hardware business which so long had supported him in idleness went into bankruptcy. He found himself wholly without means in a foreign land, and by temperament and training he was as unfitted for practical money-earning work as a bobolink. He was thirty-five years old, and he had done nothing save literary dabbling for mere amusement. Authorship as a life-work he had not yet considered.

He could think of but a single money-earning venture

—another *Salmagundi* magazine. As a result came the *Sketch Book,* issued in eight numbers and, when published as a volume by an inadequate firm, ending in failure almost total.

Then through the influence of Scott had come the miracle: the acceptance of the book by the leading publisher of London, with an honorarium the largest that had ever been paid an American author. Excitement in America? Not at all—at first. The little groups in Philadelphia and New York and Boston and the few literary journals viewed the matter with a shade of coldness. The book was a break from the eighteenth-century canons; it was a mere miscellany, a medley saturated with Scottism and rebellion. The attitude of the *North American Review* (1819) was typical. In a review written by Richard Henry Dana, the *Sketch Book* was declared to be inferior to *Salmagundi* and to the *Knickerbocker's History.* It was lacking in restraint and delicacy, as in "The Broken Heart" sketch and "The Wife"; it was oversentimental; it lacked verve and masculinity:

> The air about this last work is soft; but there is a still languor in it. It is not so breezy and fresh as that which is stirring over the others. He appears to us to have taken up of late some wrong notion of a subdued elegance. There is in his later style a too apparent elaboration, while, after all, its attained regularity of shape is not so pleasing as the easy irregularity of the former.[6]

The style, Dana believed, was a debauched one, over-ornamented, artificial, merely romantic. Without reserve, however, he praised "Rip Van Winkle": "We feel more at home in it with the author than in any of this collection." He found "The Author's Account of Himself" written with simplicity; and in the "The Voyage," the moralizing, abstracted state of mind at sea seemed to him impressive and true.

[6] *Poems and Prose Writings by Richard Henry Dana* (1849), II, 268.

Irving's next volume, *Bracebridge Hall,* announced
with all the trumpets of the great London publishing
house and paid for at English best-seller rates, was in the
full tide of the new romance—the "Sir Roger de Coverley
Papers" with Sir Walter lightings. Now he deals not at
all with the present but with the glorified past, not with
picturings from real life but with the artificial "drops"
and lightings of the romantic stage. The English reviews
treated the book on the whole as if it were a native
product and not an American bit of feebleness to be
damned unread. Mary Russell Mitford used no selections from Irving in her three-volume anthology of the
American shorter classics. "He is English," she ruled, and
save for a few bits about the Hudson there is indeed in
his work no hint of Americanism. All the British critics,
however, deplored his softness and lack of robustness.
This from Hazlitt:

He is deficient in nerve and originality. Almost all his
sketches are like patterns taken in silk paper from our classic
writers:—traditional manners of the last age are still kept
up (stuffed in glass cases) in Mr. Irving's modern version of
them. . . . He brought no new earth, no sprig of laurel
gathered in the wilderness, no red-bird's wing, no gleam
from the crystal lake or new-discovered fountain (neither
grace nor grandeur), plucked from the bosom of this Eden-
state like that which belongs to cradled infancy.

Blackwood's was even more severe. It found in all of
Irving's writings a languorous softness which relegated
them almost to the realm of feebleness, and it added: "Nobody has ever taken a strong hold of the English mind
whose own mind has not had for one of its first characteristics manliness."

The volume exhausted Irving's materials. Romance is
a stimulant that requires ever more and more. Restless,
unsatisfied, he turned now to Germany which had been the
fountain-head of the new romance. For months in Dres-

den he lived in the *märchenland* world of E. T. A. Hoffman, whose death a month before Irving's arrival was filling Germany with his wild tales.

The British publishers were demanding copy for another volume, and Irving, in need of the money, set out desperately to write it. But he had not kindled to the German romance. In Paris with John Howard Payne he was off on another venture—romantic drama for the London stage. Work thrown away. His new volume, *Tales of a Traveller,* disappointed the English public. It is a book of fragments, of literary torsos, of forced work.[7]

Then had come the next accident in the series: invited to Spain to translate the new life of Columbus, he had discovered the province of Granada and the ruins of the Alhambra. Again the wild dreamings of romance. For months he lived in the one area in Europe where one might find the veritable atmosphere of the *Arabian Nights.* As a result came *The Conquest of Granada* and the legends of *The Alhambra.*

When after seventeen years abroad he returned to America like a foreign immigrant, he was nearly fifty. His whole literary life had been lived abroad. A strange miscellany it was that he brought back as his life-work—fragments of romance. And nothing in all literature so quickly exhausts the soil. He was "written out." Professor Parrington has composed his literary epitaph:

[7] For critical studies of Irving's work, see A. Laun, *Washington Irving; Ein Lebens und Charakterbild,* 2 vols. (Berlin, 1870) ; Ferdinand Kunzig, *Washington Irving und seine Beziehungen zur englishen Literature des 18 Jahrhunderts* (Heidelberg, 1911) ; Otto Plath, *Washington Irving's Einfluss auf Wilhelm Hauff; In Euphorion, Zeitschrift fur Literaturgeschichte* (Leipzig, 1913) ; R. Sprenger, *Uber die Quelle von Washington Irving's Rip Van Winkle* (Northein, 1901) ; G. D. Morris, *Washington Irving Fiction in the Light of French Criticism,* Indiana University Studies, No. 30 (May, 1916), important bibliography of French reviews ; K. T. Gaedertz, *Zu Washington Irving's Skizzenbuch* (Stratford am Avon) ; *In Sur Kenntnis der altenglischen Buhne* (Bremen), 1888.

Irving in the end was immolated on the altar of romanticism. The pursuit of the picturesque lured him away into sterile wastes, and when the will-o'-the-wisp was gone he was left empty.[8]

That Irving himself realized his failure is evident to all who read his biography. In a letter concerning his *Tour of the Prairies* he described, perhaps unconsciously, his own soul:

We send our youth abroad to grow luxurious and effeminate in Europe; it appears to me, that a previous tour on the prairies would be more likely to produce that manliness, simplicity and self-dependence most in union with our political institutions.

Too late. *The Tour of the Prairies* has lively episodes and occasional vividness of picturing, but as an account of actual exploring it is sadly lacking. The present never kindled his imagination; always the glorified past, Indian summer in America's virile springtime.

The *influence* of Irving, however, cannot for a moment be made light of. His great European fame tremendously impressed the rising generation of American writers. He set the bells to ringing and he dictated the literary forms of two decades and perhaps three. In more ways than one he was a molding force:

1. He made the shortened form of fiction popular. With "Rip Van Winkle" he became the first prominent writer of the "American short story."

2. He was a leading influence in the stripping of the moral and the didactic from the prose-tale and the periodical essay.

3. He used with effectiveness American backgrounds and American legends. His seven Knickerbocker tales— "Rip Van Winkle," "The Legend of Sleepy Hollow,"

[8] *Main Currents in American Thought* (1927), II, 211.

"Dolph Heyliger," "The Devil and Tom Walker," "Wolfert Weber," "The Adventures of the Black Fisherman," and "Guests from Gibbet Island"—in the 1820's and the 1830's had a numerous progeny.

4. He added humor to the short story, and lightness of touch. Humor it was of the eighteenth-century type, but as Irving handled it, it seemed new and attractive.

5. And finally he threw over all his work a charm of style and an atmosphere of serenity and genial beauty. "To many critics this was Irving's chief contribution to American literature, and to some New Englanders at least it was his only contribution. To Emerson, Irving was 'only a word-catcher.' Perhaps he was, and yet it is by no means a calamity that our pioneer . . . writer should have begun with a literary style that has been the despair of all his followers." [9]

A life-work of fragments, of improvisations according to mood, task-work often thrown off for the moment, of style flowing and genial but all too often without substance —whipped sillabub when the new nation needed strong meat and a severe regimen. Realization of what he had done came too late to the dreaming, night-moth soul that had spent its life floating over European ruins. His final settling down to the biography of Washington for a life-work that had substance has in it a note of the pathetic. An old man's Washington, a beautiful and romanticized Washington, a Washington vaguely seen through a veil of heroic mist, an Addisonian Washington riding the whirlwind and directing the storm—a mythical Washington framed in a historical-romance picturing of the Revolution.

May it not be that the pitiful lack of masculinity, the softness and sentimentality of our mid-century literature, came from following too freely this first great model, this first American to win European approval?

[9] Fred Lewis Pattee, *Development of the American Short Story* (1923), p. 23.

CHAPTER XX

BRYANT

I

CRITICISM of William Cullen Bryant must begin with the statement that he was a New Englander. He is no more to be stamped with the hall-mark "Knickerbocker" than is Whittier. On both sides of his family distinctively New England stock; English with a sprinkling of Calvinistic Scotch.

The family early had moved westward from the Massachusetts Bay environment, the Scotch blood restless. When William Cullen was born the family had got to western Massachusetts, to the Berkshires, to a mountain-farm more remote from city influences than was the Whittier homestead. An atmosphere sternly Calvinistic was about the lad from his earliest years: the Bible read aloud in solemn tones; prayers morning and evening ringing always with the fervid poetic diction and resonant doom-notes of the Hebrew prophets. He was nurtured on Watts's hymns. He records that at the age of three, with the hymn-book in his hand and with such gestures as were prescribed for him, he could repeat with unction such tremendous stanzas as:

> Spare us, O Lord! aloud we pray;
>   Nor let our sun go down at noon;
> Thy years are one eternal day,
>   And must thy children die so soon?

The boy pleased his Calvinistic grandfather. At ten or eleven he received from him a ninepenny piece for a

rhymed version of the first chapter of Job. But there
was another influence in the home. The version of Job,
which pleased his grandfather because of its religious
content, was condemned by his father because of its inflated style. The father was a physician who had studied
medicine at Cambridge, had been surgeon on a merchant-
vessel, had lived for a year among the French of the West
Indies, then had rounded the Cape of Good Hope where
he had suffered shipwreck. Stormy petrel indeed in the
little Berkshire village. He brought a whiff of the world
—the French language, which he spoke with fluency;
manners which to the provincial little town seemed flaw-
less; fastidiousness in dress; liberality in religious matters; and a taste for the refinements of art and literature
which manifested itself in the constant addition of new
books to the family store. "In his library were the works
of most of the eminent English poets. He wrote verses.
. . . He was not unskilled in Latin poetry . . . Horace
his favorite."

The boy was fragile, precocious, overintellectual, pre-
disposed to consumption, the grim specter of which
haunted him even into manhood like a foreboding of
death. His little sister faded and died during that home-
period of his life when such experiences leave marks indelible. Everything—his stern environment, his frail hold
upon life, his constant reading in the elegiac school of
poets—inclined him to meditation and melancholy.

He appears never to have had a boyhood. Never in his
life was there a time when he was not pointed out as the
writer of remarkable poetry. At thirteen he was the author
of a book so successful that the following year a second
and enlarged edition was run off.[1] At fourteen he was
placed in charge of tutors, scholarly divines who put him

[1] *The Embargo, or Sketches of the Times; Satire; By a Youth of
Thirteen.* . . . (Boston, 1808), and *The Embargo; or Sketches of
the Times; A Satire; The Second Edition, corrected and enlarged,
together with The Spanish Revolution and Other Poems.* . . . (Boston, 1809).

through his studies in the college preparatory Latin and
Greek with a strenuousness that now exceeds belief.
Bryant has left a record of this period:

I was early at my task in the morning and kept on until
bedtime; at night I dreamed of Greek, and my first thought
in the morning was my lesson for the day. At the end of two
calendar months I knew the Greek New Testament from end
to end almost as if it had been English.

At fifteen he entered the sophomore class at Williams,
but after two terms there he became dissatisfied:

My room-mate, for the sake of obtaining a more complete
education than the course of study at Williams then promised
had resolved to leave the college and become matriculated at
Yale, in New Haven. His example and a like desire on my
part induced me to write to my father for leave to take the
same step, to which he consented.

But money was lacking. Yale had to be given up as a
possibility, and he spent the autumn that followed in a
welter of uncertainty as to his future.

Then had come into his life the first really molding
literary influence: his father brought home from Boston
The Remains of Henry Kirke White, edited with a long
introduction by Robert Southey. Red-letter day for the
restless young student: it was the first modern book of
poems the youth had ever seen. Here, he found, was a
kindred soul, a genius stricken with consumption before
life had fairly opened and crying out in agony of spirit.
"I read the poems with great eagerness," he recorded in
later years, "and so often that I had committed several of
them to memory, particularly the ode 'To the Herb Rose-
mary.'" This the opening stanza:

> Sweet scented flower! who art wont to bloom
> On January's front severe:
> And o'er the wintery desert drear

To waft thy waste perfume!
Come, tho shalt from my nosegay now,
And I will bind thee round my brow,
    And as I twine the mournful wreath,
I'll weave a melancholy song,
And sweet the strain shall be, and long,
    The melody of death.

Kirke White, as we read him today, has little save his adolescent melancholy and his echoes of earlier poets, but to the young Berkshire student who had been reared in daily contemplation of death from consumption, he was a twin soul. The declamatory, "Thanatopsis"-like poem "Time," the lyric "To an Early Primrose," the titles "Thanatos" and "Athanatos" all had their effect on the sensitive young poet.

There were other influences:

I remember reading, at this time, that remarkable poem, Blair's "Grave," and dwelling with great pleasure upon its finer passages. I had the opportunity of comparing it with a poem on a kindred subject, also in blank verse, that of Bishop Porteus on "Death."

Strange choice for a youth sixteen. Other books he found, "among them a thin volume of the miscellaneous poems of Southey." He reviewed his old favorite Cowper: "I now passed from his shorter poems, which are generally mere rhymed prose, to his 'Task,' the finer passages of which supplied a form of blank verse that captivated my admiration."

Here his fragment of autobiography comes to an end, but enough is given to explain the youthful Bryant: his early religious training, his brooding consciousness of death, his infection with the melancholy of Kirke White, his study of Southey and of the solemn declamation of Blair, with his

What is this world?
What but a spacious burial-field unwalled?

and finally his delight in the easy naturalness of Cowper's blank verse. At some time during this period he made attempts of his own—"exercises," he called them—and stored them away in his desk to be elaborated some future day into finished wholes.

II

College had proved impossible; literature as a profession was impossible; medicine and divinity were out of the question. Perforce he chose the law, and once having chosen it he gave himself up to the study of it with the whole-souled earnestness he had given to his Greek and Latin. His poem, "To a Friend on his Marriage," manifestly written during this period, though published in the *North American Review* in March, 1818, indicates that when he entered upon his legal studies he deliberately gave up all thought of poetry. He turned to his "harp, neglected long," only to celebrate his friend's marriage:

And I, that lov'd to trace the woods before,
And climb the hill a playmate of the breeze
Have vow'd to tune the rural lay no more,
Have bid my useless classicks sleep at ease,
And left the race of bards to scribble, starve and freeze.

Farewell.—When mildly through the naked wood,
The clear warm sun effus'd a mellow ray;
And livelier health propell'd the vital flood,
Loitering at large, I pour'd the incondite lay,
Forgot the cares and business of the day,
Forgot the quirks and Lyttleton and Coke,
Forgot the publick storms, and party fray;
And, as the inspiring flame across me broke,
To thee the lowly harp, neglected long, I woke.

When "Thanatopsis" appeared in the *North American Review* in 1817, he had completed his four years of legal study, had been admitted to the bar, and had practiced law in a country village for two years. He was twenty-three years of age and had settled down into his profession with no thought of change. To get the impression that he was toying half-heartedly with the law and that he was scribbling poetry when he should have been studying legal cases, one must overlook all that we know of the man.

Literary fame came suddenly and by accident. The story that his father found in his desk the fragments of his earlier poetical exercises and took them to the editors of the *North American Review* bears all the marks of truth. A glance at the poems in their earliest form is convincing. Never would author present his material in such dishabille: the four rhyming quatrains, boyishly inferior, printed as if they were a part of the blank-verse fragment, the abrupt beginning and the sudden ending of the main piece as if it were a part wrenched from a whole, and the second piece without even a title. This latter, "A Fragment," afterward to be expanded under the title "An Inscription for the entrance to a Wood," must surely have been written after reading Southey's collection of "Inscriptions," perhaps after that entitled "For a Tablet on the Banks of a Stream."

But exercises though they are, unfinished fragments, musings of a young student over his books, they have within them nevertheless the breath of life. As one comes upon them amid the general feebleness of the verse in the *North American Review,* the interminable translations of Boileau's satires into labored heroics, the hackneyed translations of Horace, the effusions like "Hope and Memory" and "The Cyprian Queen," and the pompous ode in school-boy Latin, it is like coming upon cold water in the desert.

But to compare the original version of "Thanatopsis" with the final text that we know is to learn a secret. Bryant

enlarged the poem and radically changed it. To call it an
example of precosity is foolishness. The original version
is a fragment echoing the spirit of Kirke White's "Time."
Soul was not added to the poem until 1821 when the poet
was twenty-seven years of age. Called upon to print his
poems after the Harvard rendition of "The Ages"
(1821), he molded the fragment into a whole, expanding
the original forty-seven lines into eighty-one and making
radical changes in the text. Among the additions were
the opening and the closing parts, the original having
opened with the lines,

> Yet a few days, and thee
> The all-beholding sun shall see no more,

and having closed with the line,

> And make their bed with thee.

He had discovered Wordsworth. "On opening Wordsworth," he once remarked to Dana, "a thousand springs
seemed to gush up at once in my heart, and the face of
nature, of a sudden to change into a strange freshness and
life." The original version of "Thanatopsis" is changed
completely in tone. Nature becomes now a teacher, a com-
forter, a religion. Unpoetic lines become distinctive. The
original version,

> The venerable woods, the floods that move
> In majesty, and the complaining brooks
> That wind among the meads and make them green,

is now expanded to,

> The venerable woods—rivers that move
> In majesty, and the complaining brooks
> That make the meadows green; and, poured round all,
> Old Ocean's gray and melancholy waste.

The original line,

> That veil Oregon, where he hears no sound,

now becomes,

> Where rolls the Oregon, and hears no sound.

The full influence of Wordsworth came later—best felt, perhaps, in "A Winter Piece," a poem that could not have been written by one who had not read Wordsworth's "Lines Composed a Few Miles above Tintern Abbey."

To both, Nature was a soothing presence which brought sanity and restoration. Bryant never passed beyond this conception; Wordsworth grew to have larger interpretations of Nature and so became a poet immeasurably superior.

Fame seemed to pursue the young Bryant. Seemingly without an effort on his own part he became with suddenness a poet of national prominence. The fragments published in the *North American Review* were discussed excitedly by the Bostonian junto, always eager for a native poet. At their call the young barrister emptied his first portfolio. "Translation of a Fragment of Simonides," and his lyrics "To a Waterfowl" and "To a Friend on His Marriage" appeared in the March, 1818, *North American Review*. For the July number he was asked to review the Reverend Solyman Brown's critical poem, "An Essay on American Poetry," and his response was a paper that deserves to be printed as the general introduction to all histories of nineteenth-century American poetry. No better study even yet of our early literary conditions.

The flattering attentions of America's leading review awakened the sleeping poet in the young lawyer. He was like the boy who has been compelled to renounce the object of his early infatuation and then suddenly finds himself again smiled upon. To R. H. Dana's little periodical, the *Idle Man,* he contributed "Green River," a note of protest against the profession where he was

. . . forced to drudge for the dregs of men,
And scrawl strange words with the barbarous pen,
And mingle among the jostling crowd,
Where the sons of strife are subtle and loud.

Two other poems followed—"A Walk at Sunset" and
"A Winter Piece." Then suddenly came a call most surprising: Harvard chose him to deliver the annual Phi
Beta Kappa poem. Unprecedented: the uncolleged youth
asked to address the most critical academic body in
America. And Bryant accepted the call. The theme he
used was that which the young Freneau had used at
Princeton and that which Barlow had used in his *Vision
of Columbus:* the long roll of the ages culminating in the
establishment in the New World of the hope of all lands:

Here the free spirit of mankind, at length,
Throws its last fetters off; and who shall place
A limit to the giant's unchained strength,
Or curb his swiftness in the forward race?

His effort was successful to the degree that a printed
edition of the poem was demanded, and as a result came
the significant collection issued in 1821 with the title
The Ages and Other Poems.

A tiny classic—the first book of poems that America
without apology could offer to the world. A young man's
book, and yet a book that had within it practically all the
best work its author was destined to produce in a long
lifetime. Had Bryant died in 1821, as Joseph Rodman
Drake died in 1820, America today would be still mourning her lost Wordsworth.

The rest can be told quickly. The law, his profession,
became intolerable. The poet within him refused longer
to be in chains. In 1825 he broke away from the profession which had held him for ten years and, removing to
New York City, toward which already the publishing
center of America was gravitating, he assumed the editorship of a struggling literary magazine which made haste

to fail, leaving him in the desolate mood described in his poem, "The Journey of Life." Then had come employment as assistant editor of the New York *Evening Post,* and finally in 1829 promotion to the editorship of the paper. During the next half-century Bryant lived in the maelstrom of a great city daily newspaper. End of our biography: the *poet* Bryant died in 1829 in the editorial office of the *Evening Post.*

III

The publication in 1826 of the poem "I Cannot Forget with What Fervid Devotion" is his valedictory. Rarely has the poet so disclosed his whole heart. To understand Bryant one must read it:

I cannot forget with what fervid devotion
    I worshipped the visions of verse and of fame;
Each gaze at the glories of earth, sky, and ocean,
    To my kindled emotions, was wind over flame.

And deep were my musings in life's early blossom,
    Mid the twilight of mountain-groves wandering long;
How thrilled my young veins, and how throbbed my full
        bosom,
When o'er me descended the spirit of song!
        .   .   .   .

Bright visions! I mixed with the world, and ye faded,
    No longer your pure rural worshipper now;
In the haunts your continual presence pervaded,
    Ye shrink from the signet of care on my brow.

In the old mossy groves on the breast of the mountain,
    In deep lonely glens where the waters complain,
By the shade of the rock, by the gush of the fountain,
    I seek your loved footsteps, but seek them in vain.

Another document in this period of struggle, another cry of the smothered poet within him, is the poem "Nature":

I broke the spell that held me long,
The dear, dear witchery of song
I said, the poet's idle lore
Shall waste my prime of years no more,
For Poetry, though heavenly born,
Consorts with poverty and scorn.

I broke the spell, nor deemed its power
Could fetter me another hour.
Ah, thoughtless! how could I forget
Its causes were around me yet?
For wheresoe'er I looked, the while,
Was Nature's everlasting smile.

Still came and lingered on my sight
Of flowers and streams the bloom and light,
And glory of the stars and sun :—
And these and poetry are one.
They, ere the world had held me long,
Recalled me to the love of song.

Thus where the cliff, abrupt and steep,
Looks down upon the sullen deep,
Far from his mother's side, the child
Sat playing on the verge, and smiled :—
She laid her bosom bare, and won
From the dread brink her truant son.

Thus gradually the poet died. The poems that still permit him to be rated with the American poets are those few desultory moments before he had lost his early vision in the maelstrom of New York.

Only a handful there are, not larger in bulk than Poe's anthology. Twelve poems, perhaps: "Thanatopsis," "The Yellow Violet," "Inscription for the Entrance to a Wood," "To a Waterfowl," "Green River," "A Winter Piece," "A Walk at Sunset," "Hymn to Death," "November," "A Forest Hymn," "The Death of the Flowers," and "I Cannot Forget with What Fervid Devotion." One more we may add, perhaps—"The Prairies"

—a moment of inspiration after entering a new and fresh world, and there are many who would plead for "To the Fringed Gentian."

Fragmentary—that is the first impression. Genius repressed, deliberately smothered out, a series of farewells to the Muse and momentary returns as to a stolen pleasure, then silence or worse than silence. Bryant's poems are a miscellany of glorious fragments, with here and there a real lyric. The bits of blank verse—"A Forest Hymn," "A Winter Piece," and the like—impress one as detached bits of an exploded whole, finished columns of a temple never completed, never even planned. What might have been if, like Wordsworth, he could have given his life entirely to poetry, it is useless to ask.

As it is, his few lyrics are the scant blossom of New England Puritanism before it was touched by the transcendental fertilizer, the tiny yellow violet of a cold spring:

> Of all her train, the hands of Spring
>   First plant thee in the watery mould,
> And I have seen thee blossoming
>   Beside the snow-bank's edges cold.

No native wild-flower, this violet, however; an Old World species, rather, grown stately, prim, pale by transplanting into new soil, old-fashioned, simple—no doubling and fringing, no flashy colorings to stir the passions. Puritanism breathed from its every petal, an eighteenth-century Puritanism unaffected by Wesleyanism, despite the influence of Cowper.

Only half-heartedly was he of the nineteenth century. He was of the classicists, law-bound as with iron, self-contained, reticent. Never could he let himself go, never could he write with passion, never could he lay bare his soul or cry aloud. Anything like self-revelation he shrank from. He would not republish from the *North American Review* his really beautiful "Lines to a Friend on His

Marriage." He could, however, treasure, as if it were
pure gold, the undistinctive translation from Simonides
that appeared in the same number. He aimed at the intellect of his reader, and always he left him cold. Like all
other New Englanders, constantly he preached, but always
with the calm voice of Isaac Watts.

In his treatment of nature he was influenced, as we
have seen, by Wordsworth, but it was a Wordsworth
tempered by New England Puritanism. He would retire
to the woods as to a sanitary resort. Self-realization, self-
improvement, self-salvation. Far from the haunts of men
for a few days or weeks he would repurify himself, wash
away the city stain, reorient himself, revive for his own
pleasure visions of his rural boyhood, and, in the solemn
cathedral of the forest, get nearer to God, whom, in the
jostling city crowd, he could not feel. His are the poems
of a solitary soul intent upon contemplation of life, a
soul which escapes now and then into the silences for itself
alone.

He was not of the nineteenth century at all. Wordsworth had gone through the same experience, but quickly
he had passed into the larger outlook of the new century.
To him Nature at length grew to have a social import.
He looked upon it,

> Hearing oftentimes
> The still, sad music of humanity.

Unlike Bryant, he could romanticize it, fill it with transcendental idealism and even pantheistic attributes. To
him at length it became but a natural step from Nature
as perceived by the senses to Nature as revealed by the
kindled poetic imagination and peopled even with creations of the primitive poets:

> Great God! I'd rather be
> A pagan suckled in a creed outworn;
> So might I, standing on this pleasant lea,

Have glimpses that would make me less forlorn,
Have sight of Proteus rising from the sea;
Or hear old Triton blow his wreathed horn.

Wordsworth was a romanticist, looking at nature to see the mystical unknown; Bryant was an eighteenth-century Puritan who went into the solemn forest to muse and save his own soul.

His real contribution to American poetry came from his personality rather than from his message: that majestic, solemn individuality which wrought itself without effort into all he did during the brief period of his inspiration. There is a bardic ring to some of his poems such as we find in no other American poet. Print his lines without their verse-form and often they might be mistaken for passages from *Ossian*. This from "A Walk at Sunset":

Oh, sun! that o'er the western mountains now go'st down in glory! ever beautiful and blessed in thy radiance, whether thou colorest the eastern heaven and night-mist cool, till the bright day-star vanish, or on high climbest and streamest thy white splendors from mid-sky.

His blank verse, solemn and resonant like the reverberations of organ-tones down the aisles of a cathedral, is perhaps the best yet written in American literature. He did but little, but that little is permanent. He used as background always materials of his own New England: the native water-fowl, the yellow violet, the primitive forest with its ice-storms and its Indian-summer glories.

In diction his style is often as inflated as Pope's. To him fishes are "the scaly herds." Once he advised Dana to change his title, "The Dying Crow," to "The Dying Raven." His editorship of the *Evening Post* was in one respect at least unique: he required classic English; he posted a long list of words and phrases that could not be used in the *Post,* and he enforced his rules. For years his paper contained the purest English to be found in the American journals.

His influence upon the New England group that arose
in the 1830's was peculiar. His success as a poet and the
chaste beauty of his nature-lyrics stimulated nearly all of
the group to their first efforts, but his distinctive poetic
notes were echoed by few. He led them undoubtedly to
native themes, but he imparted to none of them his
classicism. The influx of transcendentalism and of romanticism quickly overcame his influence. Scott was king.
Wordsworth, Byron, Shelley, Keats, and the German
romanticists were dominating forces.

He is a lone, cold summit on the horizon of our poetry,
solemn and grand in the morning twilight. He did but
little, but that little is unlike anything else in the range of
our literature.

CHAPTER XXI

COOPER

I

Open to the frontispiece of T. R. Lounsbury's life of Cooper, to that likeness caught with all the grim realism of the daguerreotype: an English county squire. The portly figure, the beefy face, the John Bull neck and chin: Squire Western looked like that. A choleric man who holds his opinions hard and tolerates no opposition; a man without humor, save as Squire Western had humor; a man built solidly for this present world: for the management of acres and the direction of fox-hunts and county fairs, and, if by chance he be thrown upon the sea, for the command of fighting armadas; a conservative man who loves old things—old conventions, old landmarks; a family man who would embody his idea of a home in a ducal mansion "with table dormant" and portraited halls, in manorial acres with lawns and peacocks—a full-important squire of the old English type.

No Natty Bumppo, this broadclothed Sir Roger, with the white gloves and the cane and the spectacles-cord over the flowered waistcoat. No poet either, no romancer with moth-wing soul, this man of beef and iron. And yet he is not English: he is American, a New World aristocrat, one of those manorial lords of the Hudson in the early decades of the first century of the Republic who were to the North what the slave-holding Cavaliers were to the South. He has been out of England for four generations, and he is American to the bone, yet he cannot escape his

314

ancestors. A Yankee American to the verge of phobia, and yet he is not a democrat—he abominates the "mob," "the swinish multitude." An aristocrat to his finger-tips, yet a republican. Strange paradoxes America has made of her Englishmen!

To understand the man we must begin with his father, Judge William Cooper, settler of forty thousand acres of virgin land in the heart of New York State just following the Revolution. "I have already settled more acres than any man in America," he wrote in justifiable pride, for he had started with nothing. He is robustly depicted in *The Pioneers,* an epic figure—settler, manorial lord, legislator, judge, athlete, fighter, Homeric in body as in soul. He offered a farm of one hundred and fifty acres to any man on the whole frontier who could throw him in a wrestling match, and only once did he lose. Impetuous as a kaiser, self-willed, arrogant, he was not to be crossed. A French nobleman, an officer, invited as his guest to "Mansion House," refused because he was away from his wardrobe, whereupon he was seized, borne by force to Cooperstown, and compelled to grace the table at dinner in the judge's own shirt. It is a flash-light glimpse. At every point this primal Cooper's conceptions were baronial. He erected in his border village the most lordly mansion west of the Hudson and equipped it with a dining-hall feudal, in its capacities, with a great organ and paintings and rich furnishings—"the window seats were filled with books."

In the words of *The Pioneers* he was "a great proprietor resident on his lands, and giving his name to, instead of receiving it from, his estates, as in Europe." He entertained with lavishness notable travelers from abroad, among them Talleyrand, and always were there present distinguished guests from Albany, Philadelphia, or New York. He was an orator of virility and invective, a border politician, a Congressman for more than one term, a local boss who ruled with power at the high noon of border individualism. A fighter, too—he died of a blow struck from behind on the capitol steps at Albany by an opponent who had been infuriated by his *ad hominem* invective. The Coopers ruled or ruined, and the iron sway of the King of Cooperstown included his own family. His wife, when the settlement was ready for its mistress, refused to leave her New Jersey home and her little social circle. The moving-van was at the door with most of the furniture upon it, but she declared that she would not go—no force could make her leave her chair. Whereupon her lord and husband loaded her, chair and all, upon the wagon and hauled her into Cooperstown, the future novelist, fourteen months of age, in her arms.

To dwell on this epic father is to throw light on the son who followed him. Note a letter like this, written to the novelist's elder brother who was then a student in Princeton:

I am anxious to hear of your advancement and calculate on your being the first of scholars, knowing that your abilities and memory are equal to any of your age; and you have every-thing to make you ambitious: here is a great country and no man has such an opportunity as yourself of being the first man in it. On your industry depends whether you are to be the greatly good and useful man—or nothing. I have it in contemplation to send you to Edinburgh or London for two or three years before you launch into life, and after you have the sanction of that first of schools, Princeton, to which you may, if you please, be an honor and make its tutors and governors proud to claim you as a product of that institution; and I will say it again—you have the ability and may if you will.

Here is not only the spirit of the Coopers, but the spirit of the New World.

II

To picture the boyhood of Cooper as spent in a remote settlement amid Indians and deerslayers is to go wrong at the start. When the lad first awoke to a realization of his environment, Cooperstown was a hamlet of seventy families centered about the Cooper mansion in feudal fashion, a town civilized and easily accessible from Albany and the Hudson.

The Judge had early founded an academy and had imported as teacher a scholar of unusual attainments, "Master" Cory, whom the novelist afterwards reckoned as one of the forces that had shaped his career. From the first, Cooper was thoroughly schooled. His environment was far from primitive. There were no Indians save drunken stragglers like the one depicted in *The Pioneers,* no deer-slayers save a squalid old man who sometimes came with furs and venison, no wild animals save in the remoter forests. Until he was nine all the molding influences about the lad—his brilliant elder sister who had him in charge, a maid who had been wooed by Talleyrand and who, in Philadelphia as her father's social helper, had rejected no less a suitor than the young Lochinvar, William Henry Harrison; the notable visitors constantly present in his home; the rigorous training under Master Cory; the country freedom that made for health and sturdiness of soul, and, more than all else, the dominating presence and example of his father—everything tended to develop within him the personality and the view of life of the younger son of a manorial lord.

It must not be forgotten, too, that at nine he left Cooperstown, to return only infrequently as a visitor, and that during the four years that followed, the impressionable years between nine and thirteen, he was resident at St. Peter's Rectory at Albany, under the tutelage of the Reverend Thomas Ellison, a High Church Englishman who abominated democracy and who threw about the lad an atmosphere of Old World culture and prejudice and fitted him for college as the sons of English gentlemen are fitted, grounding him thoroughly in Latin and Greek. He found himself with the heirs of many notable men

also tutoring for college. The son of Chief Justice Jay
became his closest friend, and it was solely to be with
him that he later entered Yale.

The lad was not ready for college, save for his classics,
which were brilliant. He was only thirteen. Especially was
he out of place in the blue-law atmosphere of the New
England Sparta. An adolescent of thirteen needs sturdy
parental control, especially an adolescent replica of a
Judge Cooper. Yale was successfully assimilating John C.
Calhoun, but she found the Cooper lad impossible and
after three years expelled him, not for viciousness, but for
boyish pranks. The lad was overjoyed. He wanted to go
to sea, and the old father at Cooperstown sided with the
boy.

No choice of profession could have been more felici-
tous. For an imperious soul like Cooper's in the golden
decade before the War of 1812, the navy offered a sure
road to glory. His apprenticeship was a thorough one. A
year on the Atlantic on a merchant-ship taught him
nautical technique; three years on naval vessels, one of
them on the *Wasp* with Lawrence, fitted him for speedy
promotion in the event of war. The stage for glory was
set. In 1811, the year before the outburst that gave us
our epic roll of naval heroes, Cooper was twenty-one and
as ready for responsibility as his equals in age and experience, Decatur and Somers and Perry.

But the War of 1812 saw nothing of Cooper: he resigned from the navy, had he but known it, at the one
moment in American history when glory for him was
certain. The cause was the conventional one: he had
fallen in love with a maiden as far above him, so it seemed
to him, as a duchess, the exquisite Susan DeLancey of
Heathcote Hall, heiress of one of the most lordly estates
on the Hudson.[1]

[1] "The most feudal of American aristocracies," wrote Parrington,
"fringed the banks of the Hudson from Albany to Manhattan."—*Main
Currents in American Thought* (1927), II, 197.

With true Cooperian impetuousness, he forgot everything else in the world: "I loved her like a man and told
her of it like a sailor."

The marriage came off grandly at Heathcote Hall. At
the wish of the bride, Cooper at once settled down at
"Angevine" on the Hudson and for the next ten years
was a landed proprietor, an American country gentleman
of the English type. His marriage was the pivotal event
in his whole career: all the rest of his life was molded
and colored and fixed by this DeLancey wife. Petite, appealing, winsome, she ruled him by her very helplessness,
chained him fast to her tiny domain while his soul was
winging longingly over the frigate-haunted oceans. "In
general," wrote his daughter Susan, "his thoughts seemed
to have turned upon ships and the sea. . . . His interest
in the navy never ceased. He knew intimately many of the
principal officers and the vessels they commanded." At
his wife's country-seat he would sit for hours at a time
with a naval glass and examine the shipping as it passed
down the river to the sea.

With how much of bitterness he witnessed the rise of
his old companions we shall never know. In the fullness
of his powers he was tied to the shore like an abandoned
hulk. While *Old Ironsides* and the Yankee fleet were
sweeping British shipping from the seas, daily he took
his drive to the market-town, superintended his prosperous acres, and on Sunday drove his growing family to
the Heathcote chapel for worship. A country gentleman
of the ancient type, a ruling spirit at county fairs. Governor Clinton at length added him to his staff with the
rank of colonel. At thirty, in short, Cooper was an American Sir Roger, or, better, he was a Squire Bracebridge of
an American "Bracebridge Hall."

III

Literature as a profession was as far from his thought
as medicine or coal-mining. It came by sheer accident.

His wife, goes the familiar story, was addicted to popular novels. Parcels of them came often to the home from London—"old-fashioned Lord Mortimer romances," Cooper styled them. Evening after evening he read them aloud to her—the son of Judge Cooper of Cooperstown, while his country was at war on the sea, reading "Lord Mortimer" romance to his wife!

But even Cooper's domesticity had its limits. One night there came an overdose; he threw down the book, roaring in disgust that he could write a better himself. A critical moment in the history of American fiction: the first militant revolt against the sentimental novel. What novel could it have been? A family tradition mentions Mrs. Opie, but it could as well have been one of many others: Susan Ferrier's *Marriage* (1818), Lady Caroline Lamb's *A New Canto* (1819), Elizabeth Anne LeNoir's *The Maid of La Vendée* (1810), or Regina Maria Roche's *The Munster Cottage Boy* (1819). It might even have been Jane Austen's *Pride and Prejudice* (1813).

Cooper's rash ejaculation his wife took with all seriousness. Of course he could write a novel! And he must! There was no withstanding her. The family tittered. "The idea," says Susan, "appeared the height of absurdity to his friends." James Cooper write a novel! It would be like the judge, his father, essaying crochet. The ridicule settled the matter: "The first book was written because I was told I could not." Cooper-like indeed.

How much of Mrs. Cooper is in *Precaution* we shall never know. We have evidence, however, that she planned it with her husband, chapter by chapter; that she had him read to her each section as it was completed; and that she discussed it with him at every point. Quickly he wearied of the job, but there was no escape. "After a few chapters were written," records Susan, "he would have thrown it aside, but our dear mother encouraged him to persevere: why not finish it; why not print it?" And

Cooper finished the thing, and he even found a printer. *Precaution* the title.

The book should have had the wife's name on the title-page. From end to end it is colored by the fiction Cooper had read aloud from evening to evening. The hero of it, as in all the "Lord Mortimer" fiction of the time, was Byronic. He was wealthy, he was titled, he lived in a lordly castle; he wore always a "gloom on his expressive features amidst the pageantry that surrounded him." The atmosphere matches the plot. In style it would fit *Godey's Lady's Book:*

The sun had just risen on one of the loveliest vales of Caernarvonshire, as a travelling chaise and six swept to the door of a princely mansion. Everything around this stately edifice bespoke the magnificence of its ancient possessors and the taste of its present master. The lofty turrets of its towers were tipped with the golden light of the sun.

The heroine, beautiful yet poor, "cheerful with a deep conviction of the necessity of piety," is the type so constantly engraved on steel in later years for the annuals. That it was created by main force is everywhere evident, yet it is a novel by no means to be despised. Completely was it in the fashion of its times. Were it republished today as a newly discovered early work by Jane Austen, even the critics might be deceived.

It must be classed as a plot-novel of social portraiture. Its complexity is Dickens-like: there are eighteen characters, and each is a type carefully drawn. A cross-section it is of English gentle society, from Lady Moseley, who entered the church "in a style which showed that while she remembered her Maker she had not forgotten herself," to the vulgar Miss Jarvis, who, at the mention of Thomas Moore, cries ecstatically, "Oh I could live on his beautiful lines," whereupon the heroine in disgust repairs to her room and burns her own copy of the poet

in the grate. The worldly old parson, Dr. Ives, is alive
—we feel him like a veritable presence—and the match-
making old dowagers who play their daughters with all
the strategy of chess are skilfully embroidered after the
Jane Austen patterns.

That the British press reviewed the anonymous work
—pirated by an alert London publisher who had received
the impression that it had been written by an English lady
of rank—uniformly with commendation speaks highly
for Cooper's—or Mrs. Cooper's—powers. As Professor
Cairns has remarked, it is "one of the few American
books that was reviewed exactly like an English book."
Indeed, until its authorship was discovered it received
more contemporary praise than did Jane Austen's work.
The novelist, declared *Colburn's,* is "extremely happy in
his delineations of character. The Jarvis family, the Chat-
tertons, and the Moseleys are all well drawn. The author
displays talent for novel writing which will undoubtedly
secure him the approbation of the public." And the *Gentleman's Magazine* called it a "spirited performance. . . .
Upon the whole, the story is conducted with ease and
consistency through various scenes in domestic life." In
America the book has never been fairly criticized.

The first cause of its ultimate failure was its illiterate
first edition. It was wretchedly printed; it swarmed with
grossest errors of spelling and punctuation and even with
monstrosities of diction. The author, new to the ways of
publishing, had not demanded to read the proofs, and
his manuscript had been carelessly written. When it tran-
spired that the novel had been written by Cooper, the
onus of its illiteracy was heaped upon him alone. Then,
too, the subject of the fiction struck the risibilities of the
critics: James Cooper write an English society novel!
America has never read the book, but America has never
ceased laughing.

To be damned without cause and then to be laughed at

was a thing no Cooper had ever endured. The printed book had failed, but *he* had not failed. He issued promptly a second edition with all errors corrected, but it was too late. Very well, he would produce another novel: "The second volume was written to see if I could not overcome this neglect of the reading world." He would take an American theme with a masculine subject, the story of a spy who had worked in the employ of his neighbor, Governor Jay. He made a tour of the region, gathering materials. Again was his wife the motive power, according to his daughter Susan: "Every chapter of *The Spy* was read to my mother as soon as it was written, and the details of the plot were talked over with her. From the very first months of authorship to the last years of his life my father generally read what he wrote to my mother." And we may add this notation by his biographer, Lounsbury: "The fact forces itself repeatedly upon the attention, that his movements were largely, if not mainly, controlled by his wife." That the book ever was finished at all must be credited to her. He hated the work. He has recorded that even after the first volume was in print, it was months before he could drive himself to begin the second volume.

Cooper accomplished his purpose: this time he won the American public, but from the standpoint of today it is hard to understand why. Doubtless the title gave the book a start—Cooper's whole series of titles was excellent. Then, too, the adventure atmosphere of the book and the background of the Revolution played their part. It came to American readers as Scott's romances had come —as something new and thrilling. From the fictional feebleness of the time it seemed to rise like an oak from among weeping willows. But whatever the cause, Cooper had won his point: he had forced his countrymen to admit that he could write a novel that would sell and would receive approving reviews from leading critics. In 1822 the novel was reviewed at length in the *North American Review* as a new genre in fiction, and the reviewer was William Howard Gardiner of Boston.[2]

There is much in *The Spy* to remind one of *Precaution*. Again the tracks of Mrs. Cooper: it is a novel of the American aristocracy, and, unique phenomenon in its day, all its major characters are Tories—the DeLanceys had been Tories. The intent clearly was to draw the reader's sympathy away from the native "mob" that was fighting the war to the real victims of the Revolution, the loyalists, who are made in every way superior. Even the leading patriotic character is a Virginia aristocrat. The Spy is only an incidental figure, the *deus ex machina:* he exists simply to rescue the aristocracy from danger at critical moments.

The technique of the book is decidedly inferior to that of *Precaution*. The plot is chaotic: the story seems to have grown by accretions, often with forgetfulness of what had preceded. A man of mystery, perhaps Washington, is elaborately introduced, is shown once or twice for no apparent reason, and then abandoned. The style is prolix, the diction at times inflated beyond belief: the Scotch surgeon and Mrs. Flannigan would sink even a classic. Whole pages are "lumber," yet the story holds the reader to the end. There is movement, at times compelling, and there is suspense. It is a running series of fights, captures, escapes, rescues, pursuits, told with convincingness: a formula for nearly all of Cooper's novels.

His literary adventure apparently was over. He had won his point. Even after *The Spy* was on all the bookstands, he had no more thought of becoming a professional novelist than he had of entering the ministry. But the enormous success of the book set him to thinking. His friends everywhere were congratulating him and urging him to further efforts. Boston, always chary of its praise of New Yorkers, in its *North American Review* was

[2] July, 1822, pp. 250–282.

making the novel the text for a discourse on American literature and its future, quoting from it largely and commending it with heartiness. Such praise, rare indeed at any time for an American book, praise that had not then been accorded even to Irving, intoxicated Cooper—and his wife. The review had taken it for granted that other novels were to follow from the same pen. Why not? Why could he not record now the story of his father's settlement, the epic of the Cooper family? The idea grew upon him: he began to write for the first time *con amore*: "The third novel has been written exclusively to please myself. . . . Happier periods, more interesting events, and possibly more beauteous scenes might have been selected to exemplify my subject; but none of either that would be so dear to me."

The Pioneers is not a novel: it is an American *Bracebridge Hall*. Half of it is concerned with the Christmas festivities at "Templeton Hall." The earlier part drags until the author himself apologizes: he is dwelling lovingly upon his father's Cooperstown experiences with little reference to fictional plot. He introduced "characters" known to his own boyhood—the drunken Indian and the picturesque old hunter who lived in a hut across the lake. As far even as Chapter XXVII it is mostly reminiscent sketching; then suddenly at the words, "It was cut with a knife"—this of the thong that had bound the dog—it bursts thrillingly into life. The last seventy pages of the book mark the appearance of new force in the fiction of the world. Hiram Doolittle, by a single stroke of his knife, had set free Natty Bumppo. The mere village "character" becomes at once an epic figure. Melodrama undoubtedly, but alive and compelling. The reader is hurried on to an epic climax. The closing paragraph has in it the soul of American romance:

He drew his hard hand hastily across his eyes again, waved it on high for an adieu, and uttering a forced cry to his dogs, who were crouching at his feet, he entered the forest. This was the last they ever saw of Leather-Stocking. . . . He had gone far toward the setting sun,—the foremost in that band of pioneers who were opening the way for the march of the nation across the continent.

The success of this book turned him definitely to a literary career, and to pursue this profession to the fullest advantage he removed his family to New York City where, by force of personality, he became in a short time the leader of the city literati. He founded the Bread and Cheese Club, which soon had a remarkable membership, and he ruled it as its Dr. Johnson. Four years later, when he went to Europe, the club languished and finally died. Not for a moment must it be overlooked that at every point he touched was Cooper a dominating force. He followed no leader. In later years, when engaged in a running fight with the whole American press, he conducted always his own cases in court, measuring his powers with trained barristers, and invariably he won.

Again sheer accident directed him. Simply to prove that he was right in an argument, he wrote *The Pilot*. A novel, he contended, could be laid on shipboard. And again he won, but this novel also was a *tour de force*. *The Pilot* is one of the poorest of all his fictions, and one of the best. It is brilliant in passages, and it has movement at times irresistible. It was fortunate, too, in its opening paragraphs, which are in the approved atmosphere of romance. Stevenson, two generations later, ruled that a compelling sea-romance should open with a mysterious ship with raking masts dropping into the harbor at sunset and discussed dubiously by the natives. *The Red Rover* has the same opening. It opened, too, with the Cooper man of mystery—an *Ivanhoe* influence, perhaps—a mannerism in many of his novels which always worked to a failure. Elaborate plot machinery at this stage of his art he could not handle, and in *The Pilot* he failed completely. Here the "pilot" is his title character, yet from beginning to end this hero does nothing save by accident. He is taken on board for no explained reason; he forms no part of the *motif* of the story; and he disappears from the tale in a manner wholly unexplained. If he is John Paul Jones, why does he not dominate the action? Even in the sea-fight he is a mere shadow in the background: the central figure for a time is Long Tom Coffin, a minor "character part" which suddenly and seemingly by afterthought comes breezily to life, rolls about for a time in swash-buckling melodrama, and then dies theatrically—and need-lessly—advancing the plot not at all. Half the book is land-romance of the *Precaution* texture: three English maidens of quality in a romantic old abbey by the sea, and three noble lovers on a ship in the offing. The sea part is incidental: a mere display of nautical lingo and sailor technique during a chase, or an escape. The life of it comes from three or four stirring scenes of action: the night run out of the harbor in the teeth of the gale and the efficiency of the unknown seaman who springs to command in the emergency; the naval battle; the wreck of the *Ariel;* and the escape next day through the English fleet. From the artistic standpoint, the thing is a scrap-book, but it is a book nevertheless important in the history of prose fiction. By accident Cooper had blundered again upon a new setting for romance. The nautical adventure it recorded stirred the blood of a nautical race; the tech-nique was realistic and minute and true to salt-water; and the Atlantic seaboard, nursery of the sailors of the world, hailed it with delight. Cooper had opened the magic jar from which, during a century, has poured a veritable cloud of pirates and sea-dogs and men of war and swash-buckling westward-ho adventurers.

There was no question now: Cooper's trade was the novel, and he began to plan not only romances but whole series of romances. He would write *Legends of the Thirteen Republics*—a complete history of the Revolution in thirteen books. He would begin where the war began.

Furiously he fell to work upon *Lionel Lincoln; or the Leaguer of Boston.* Everywhere one finds evidences of his intense seriousness. He would do for America what Scott had done for Scotland: he would embody her legendary history in prose romance. So seriously was he in earnest that for months he actually lived in Boston gathering materials. He laid out his plot more carefully now: his *motif* for his romance is worthy even of a Hawthorne: a shuddery legend of the "Province House" order, an old sin at last emergent after its hidden gangrene had worked itself out. The episode of the wedding in the church at midnight, interrupted seemingly by the supernatural, is effectively told. More, however, may not be said. The book was a failure almost total, and it should have been. The plot straggles at times into hopeless jungles of obscurity; the characters are not alive; the conversations read like a travesty on Scott's wooden dialogues. For instance, General Burgoyne, just entering the church on a Sabbath morning, gets a glimpse of a skulking figure. What he probably said was, "Isn't that the man who escaped over the wall on the day of the battle?" What Cooper makes him say is, "Is not this the shouting philosopher, when feelings were so elevated on the day of Breed's that he could not refrain from flying, but who, more fortunate than Icarus, made his descent on terra firma?" It is too much; no merits could balance such style as this.

And here we touch Cooper's fundamental weakness, a blemish that came from his late start as a writer. Irving and Hawthorne and Poe at thirty had been working in literature for years, and they had learned restraint and artistry and lightness of touch. Cooper, however, totally unpracticed, bore on hard; he told everything in elaborate detail, and he decorated everything with flamboyant embroidery. To him, as to all the unliterary, flowery and inflated circumlocution was beauty of style. His taste was

sophomoric. A simple phrase, "she milked the cow," elevated into polite literature, becomes with him, "she extracted from a favorite animal liberal portions of its
nightly tribute to the dairy." "They got married" must be
heightened to, "The enamoured pair at once made a tri-
umphal march to the temple of Hymen." Peter does not
take off his overcoat, rather he "liberated his body from
thraldom by throwing aside the defence he had taken
against the inclemency of the weather." Hardly a page of
Cooper but contains its ludicrous specimen. He never out-
grew the outrageous mid-eighteenth-century conception
that in polite literature it is a sin to call a spade merely a
spade.

Again an accident rescued him. A chance visit to Lake
George called forth from one of the party the remark
that no better background could be found for an Indian
story than the Glenn's Falls caverns and the lakeland
beyond. Cooper's imagination kindled instantly. Like
Scott, he had a genius for topography : places rather than
people stirred his creative powers. He went over the area
with care, worked out a thread of action, and then selected
his characters. It occurred to him that the old Indian and
the old backwoodsman of *The Pioneers* might be shown
here working out some of those youthful adventures
hinted at in the earlier volume—a thought that was
genius.

The idea of a romance with an Indian *motif* had been
suggested undoubtedly by Gardiner's review of *The Spy*.
No one had yet brought out, he had argued, the romantic
side of the red man of the American wilds. The noble Indian, he maintained,

tracking his foe through the pathless forest with instinctive
sagacity, by the fallen leaf, the crushed moss, or the bent
blade, patiently enduring cold, hunger and watchfulness,
while he crouched in the night-grass like a tiger expecting his
foe and finally springing on the unsuspicious victim with

that war-whoop which struck terror to the heart of the boldest planter of New England in her early day, is no mean instrument of the sublime and terrible of human agency.

Furthermore, it had declared that the best sources of Indian romance were to be found in the "indefatigable
Heckewelder."

Cooper knew little about Indians: he had to get up his
materials precisely as he got up his Revolutionary history
for *Lionel Lincoln*. He read Heckewelder; he went to
Washington and studied a delegation of Indians that had
come in from the West. He visited also the remnants of
the tribes in the lake region of New York. The result we
know: actual landscapes thrown back a century by imagination and peopled with a race of beings of Cooper's
own manufacture. They are Heckewelder's Indians seen
through Cooper's romantic temperament. *The Last of the
Mohicans* is his best story, and it is his best because it is
straight narrative from start to finish, wilderness adventure told with headlong rapidity.

The success of the book was instant in Europe as well
as in America. The world had been prepared for it by the
tales-of-terror romance that had deluged the opening decades of the century, by the *Waverley* novels of Scott,
and by the increasing wonder of Europe as to what really
lay behind the wild frontiers of America. Cooper's own
countrymen for once were unanimous: at last an American classic, a novelist coördinate even with Scott. Cooper
had satisfied even his father's imperious dream: a son of
William Cooper, in one realm at least, ruled America,
had made himself "the first man in it." When the new
novelist set sail for Europe, America looked upon him
as just at the beginning of his career. There was expected
—and Cooper knew it—a series of increasingly powerful
romances, a set of American *Waverley* novels.

Settled in Europe, he threw himself accordingly, with
all the Cooper confidence and abandon, into the work

expected of him. Leather Stocking had been his most successful creation: he would go on with his adventures. The old hunter, left so dramatically at the close of *The Pioneers,* he now followed into the vast West beyond the Mississippi—another flash of genius. It threw wide the doors of American romance. His new creation, *The Prairie,* is an epic of the western march across the continent. Full as it is of grotesqueries and impossibilities, vague as it is in plot and feeble in characterization, it is nevertheless a fundamental book in the history of American fiction.

Suddenly, however, Cooper was awakened by a disconcerting discovery: *The Last of the Mohicans* had made alarming inroads into his materials. The change of locality for the following volume had made possible a new background: the prairies with their buffalo stampedes and sweeping fires and their savage horse-riding tribes, but for most of his material he had had to repeat what he had already written. It was his first discovery of a fundamental law of fiction: the novel is the epic of achieved civilization; it needs the complexity of an old and elaborate social régime. The crude Indian with his narrow round of life, the squalid and thinly-populated frontier, the unhumanized wilderness could furnish a few fascinating situations and types, but to remain long was only to repeat.

He turned, accordingly, to the second field of his discovery, the ocean, and was astonished to find himself confronted by the same difficulty. We can do no better than to use his own words;

The history of this country has very little to aid the writer, whether the scene be laid on the land or on the water. With the exception of the well-known though meagre incidents connected with the career of Kidd, indeed, it would be very difficult to turn to a single nautical occurrence on this part of the continent in the hope of conferring on a work of the imagination any part of that peculiar charm which is derived from facts clouded a little by time. The annals of America are surprisingly poor in such events; a circumstance that is doubtless owing to the staid character of the people, and especially to that portion of them which is most addicted to navigation.

His next experiment, therefore, was pure romance: facts thrown overboard completely. In *The Red Rover* he declared he "had found it necessary to invent his legend without looking for the smallest aid from tradition or facts."

In vain. This book, too, was a failure: it lacks body and soul; it is but a series of nautical chases, with sailor technique in elaborate detail. Its attempt at a supernatural *motif* is grotesque. Moreover, for the first time in Cooper we find shrill melodrama. Everywhere the book is pitched to the key of *Godey's Lady's Book:* the Red Rover and Gertrude and Henry DeLancey—one may find them by the dozen in the steel engravings of the *Token*. *The Water Witch* is even shriller melodrama. Cooper was entering the romantic thirties. He tried another historical romance, *The Wept of Wish-ton-Wish,* locating its action in the Massachusetts of King Philip's War. This, too, was a failure—a failure so complete that it ended the first period of his literary career. It is notable, however, as the first real purpose-novel in the history of American fiction, but otherwise it is a grotesquerie.

IV

Cooper's literary life had three phases, each a decade. His first, the period of accident and experiment, was confined to the 1820's, itself in the history of American literature a decade of accident and experiment. Irving all through the twenties was a literary adventurer; Bryant was a prospector, seeking everywhere for an opening; Prescott was writing fiction. Cooper was a lucky blunderer: without a thought of a literary career, he had found, wholly by accident, one of the richest areas of romance. In half a dozen places he had found virgin gold—but for him it was but placer metal. He had not the equipment or the patience to dig deep, and he was soon prospecting in new fields.

Grenville Mellen's review of *The Red Rover* in the *North American Review* of 1828 unquestionably exerted upon Cooper at this critical moment a strong influence. It confirmed his own diagnosis. The astute reviewer, challenging the then popular principle that "works of imagination should report the character and manners of the country where they are written," declared boldly:

It is a mistaken idea that to constitute an American novel either the scene must be laid in the early wilderness of this country, or that events of so recent a date as those connected with our revolution must occupy a prominent portion of its pages. It is the author, not his theatre or his matter, that nationalizes his work.[3]

He was inclined to doubt if Cooper had ever produced any work worthy of being called a novel: "There is not enough in the character and life of these poor native Indians to furnish the staple of a novel"; and as to the life in the American settlements, certainly it was too new and thin and bare for romance.

Cooper had pledged himself definitely now to literature as a career, and, Cooper-like, he refused to be anything less than "the first man in it." Deliberately, therefore, he turned to what he considered adequate subjects in what, from his new European standpoint, seemed the higher ranges of literature. For a decade, therefore, he abandoned American themes. *The Bravo,* a tale of early Venice, was his first venture, an elaborate romance into which he threw his best powers. He wrote it not, as the popular myth long has had it, with controversial intent, but with the deliberate design of making a masterpiece.

[3] July, 1828, pp. 139-154.

And in many ways he accomplished his object. It is his strongest novel; it is worth recording that to the end it was his own favorite among all his works.

The opening exposition with its impressionistic study of St. Marks and the atmosphere of Venice is beautiful work; the plot with its headlong movement and its unflagging interest culminates in a well-managed catastrophe; the characters, even the "females," are vivacious and alive: the profligate son, Hosea the Jew, and the Carmelite are especially vivid and compelling. It is a novel unsentimentalized: the Byronic hero dies wretchedly at the end; the saintly Antonio is cruelly murdered by the oligarchy; the Bravo's heroic father rots and dies in a dungeon. Wrong everywhere seems to triumph, and it leaves one hot and angry. Strictly speaking, it is not a purpose-novel: it is a tragedy. The English press at first was enthusiastic: the *London Literary Gazette* called it the best thing Cooper had done. Then readers began to discover the preface which Cooper had put in after the romance was completed, and praise ceased. It claimed too much: it damned the book. Few ever read beyond it. It seemed to say: this tale of despotism in medieval Europe reveals what European government even now really is. "The mildest and justest governments in Europe are at this moment theoretically despotisms": look to America and reform. Read simply as fiction, however, the novel is innocent enough. One has to study it to find in it anything provocative of anger of even controversy. It is as mild in its picturings as any of Scott's fictions.

Cooper defended himself at length and without bitterness in the preface of his next volume, *The Heidenmauer*. He had been misunderstood, he said. If his previous volume had contained unwarranted criticisms or exhibitions of national vanity, he implored pardon. He had written with no such intent: he had written as Scott and as all the other romancers had done, with the single end to entertain: "We profess to write only for the amuse-

ment—fortunate shall we be if instruction may be added
—of our own countrymen." In vain. *The Heidenmauer*
and then *The Headsman* were received everywhere not as
novels, but as controversial documents. Could the untact-
ful prefaces and half a dozen passages thrown in by seeming impulse have been omitted and the novels read without political animus, as Scott's were read, they would
have been praised, for they deserved it, and Cooper would
have undoubtedly gone on to stronger and stronger work.

His main difficulty was lack of tact. Reared in the
atmosphere of his father's dominating border individualism, which had ruled and had brooked no opposition, and
indoctrinated by his years among the DeLancey aristocracy, he held himself, especially after his triumphant
entry into world dominion as a novelist, in the attitude
of a leader, a censor, a reformer, a dictator. It was in his
blood.

In all good faith he began now to educate Europe concerning the American Republic. His two volumes, *Notions
of the Americans* and *Democracy,* pointing out weaknesses in the British system and showing the superiority
of American democracy, were honestly made. For the
most part his judgments, even the most wrath-compelling
of them in the days of their newness, seem today singularly sane and singularly searching. So with his volume
A Letter to His Countrymen, written to show America
its weaknesses and crudities as compared with the refinement of Europe.

A storm of criticism now greeted him from *both* sides
of the Atlantic. He was misunderstood, and, in America
at least, he was brutally reviewed. It was not in the
Cooper blood to remain passive under fire. He retorted,
and his literary fame in Europe gave swift wings to his
words. In France he found himself in hot altercation over
the question of the relative expense of republican government as compared with monarchial. He wrote a book to
prove himself right. He *was* right, but he was anything

but tactful. Europe soon classified him as a bumptious American of the most offensive type, and soon fair treatment of anything he might write was impossible. His travel-sketches, *Gleanings in Europe,* volumes containing some of his finest literary work, ten volumes of them, were reviewed only to expose certain anger-producing passages, as, for instance, such remarks as the Lord Chancellor "looked like a miller with his head through his wife's petticoat."

Legitimate romance and honestly given criticism having failed, Cooper tried another line of attack: *The Monikins* is a satire as bitter as *Gulliver's Travels,* a satire not alone upon his enemies and critics, but on the whole human race. It starts as a story, but swiftly the hero finds himself in an empire ruled by monkeys, and the rest of the book is pure satire. America has produced nothing more caustic. In the land of the Monikins, evolution has evidently been reversed in its action:

The monkey is a creature more intellectual and more highly civilized than man. . . . Both belong to the improvable class of animals, and monkeys were once men, with all their passions, weaknesses, inconsistencies, modes of philosophy, unsound ethics, frailties, incongruities, and subserviency to matter; they passed into the monikin state by degrees, and large divisions of them are constantly evaporating into the immaterial world, completely spiritualized and free from the dross of flesh.

The satire is aimed first at the English cry of "property is in danger," but quickly it becomes more general and ends with an arraignment of American civilization. The traveler finds two Monikin governments, one a monarchy, one a republic, and he records the arguments of the monkey-savants upon the two systems. To satirize the New Englanders, he introduces Noah Pole of Stunnin'tun, Connecticut, a specimen of the Yankee Yahoo species just captured by the Monikins and, after due trial, sen-

tenced to decaudilization, their extreme penalty. The
book ends with fifty-two observations—fundamentals of
their philosophy. Even Mark Twain in his latest years was
not more pessimistic. It had been agreed among them:

That every man loves liberty for his own sake;
That of all the 'ocracies (aristocracy and democracy included) hypocrisy is the most flourishing;
That religion is a paradox, in which self-denial and
humility are proposed as tenets, in direct contradiction to
every man's senses;
That phrenology and caudology are sister sciences, one being as demonstrable as the other, and more so.

And so on through the fifty-two canons of the Monikin
creed.

America, especially in its New England area, was inclined to be critical of the new Cooper. American readers
wanted romance, not squabblings with Europe or enlight-
enments as to their own shortcomings. Their criticisms
embittered the man still more. He had been fighting for
America, he believed; he had been showing to Europe,
especially to England, their lack of knowledge of American institutions and their own shortcomings when compared with the democratic régime, and his countrymen
had not supported him in his fight. It seemed like basest
ingratitude. His volume, *A Letter to His Countrymen,*
had failed completely of its purpose: it had been laughed
at. His travel-sketches, ten volumes of them, had made
no impression, while Willis's *Pencillings by the Way*
(1835–1844), which he felt were inferior—as they were
—were greeted everywhere with enthusiasm; his elaborately wrought romances of European life, which he had
hoped to make the crown of his literary career, had called
forth only impatience and caustic advice. He had been
ordered, even by his own America, to check his bumptiousness and confine his literary efforts to those safe
areas where he had won his earlier success. It angered

him. He wrote *Homeward Bound* and followed it with *Home as Found,* the first American "Babbitt" novel. The book struck fire; satire can hardly be more caustic. D. L. Lawrence, in *Classical American Literature,* was inclined to view it as Cooper's supreme achievement. Lawrence was British.

Tact, gentle measures, conciliation, compromise had been no part of the man's endowment. He would maintain his position even against the whole American people. For the rest of his life he was in a running battle. His outbursts against his critics and against the weaknesses of democracy remind one of the latter-day Menckens and Dreisers. Nothing modern has been more caustically critical. And strangely enough, as read today, the judgments seem the cold observations of a philosopher rather than rantings of an angry man. This, for instance, of American democracy:

The tendencies of democracies are, in all things, to mediocrity, since the tastes, knowledge and principles of the majority from the tribunal of appeal. This circumstance, while it certainly serves to elevate the average qualities of the nation, renders the introduction of a high standard difficult. Thus we find in literature, the arts, architecture and all acquired knowledge a tendency in America to gravitate toward the common center in this, as in other things, lending a value and estimation to mediocrity that are not elsewhere given.

Returning from seven years in Europe, he was impressed, as visiting Europeans had been impressed, with the crudeness and vulgarity of the new land, its lack of a long-established aristocracy, social and intellectual. He had found in the America he had so proudly held up to Europe a "vast expansion of mediocrity . . . so over-whelming as nearly to overshadow everything that once stood prominent. . . . I saw towns increased more tawdry than ever," and so on and on.

New York always reminds me of the silk purse and the sow's ear.

We have the sensitiveness of provincials, increased by the consciousness of having our spurs to earn, on all matters of glory and renown, and our jealousy extends even to the reputation of the cats and dogs.

I should say that the English were thin-skinned, and the Americans raw. Both resent fair, frank, and manly comments with the same bad taste, resorting to calumny, black-guardism, and abuse, when wit and pleasantry would both prove more effective and wiser, and perhaps, reformation wisest of all.

The causes of it all he sums up in a single sentence:

A great deal is to be imputed to our provincial habits; much to the circumstance of the disproportion between sur-face and population,—something to the inquisitorial habits of our pious forefathers—; while a good deal is to be conceded to the nature of a popular government whose essential spirit is to create a predominant opinion, before which, right or wrong, all must bow until its cycle shall be completed.

It is one of our literary tragedies that this part of Cooper's work has remained, until recently, unpublished— a whole century and fifteen volumes, Cooper the critic and philosopher, Cooper at his best. No one has pointed more clearly at the fundamental weaknesses of American de-mocracy, and no one has written with more wisdom of the characteristics and institutions in Europe. His obser-vations in France, his philosophizings upon her people, her manners, her institutions are especially valuable.

The chapters entitled "National Characteristics," "Learning and Literature," "Etiquette," "Justice," "Roy-alty on Display," "Social Uses and Scandals," and "Par-liamentary Usage" form a study of France comparable with Emerson's study of the British in *English Traits* or Hawthorne's *Our Old Home*.

Balked in all his literary ventures, Cooper now tried to regain his lost prestige by breaking into a new literary area, one peculiarly within his powers. He wrote the history of the American navy, throwing himself into the task with enthusiasm and seeking with thoroughness all the possible sources of material. Undoubtedly he produced what even now may be recognized as the best of American naval histories, but he received from it no satisfaction and no glory. No sooner was the book off the press than it was assailed with a veritable tempest of criticism. Cooper had measured the naval heroes with his own scale. He had taken from Perry, for instance, the glory of the battle of Lake Erie and transferred it to another. The battle roared on for years. It is useless to fight it again; it need only be recorded that another honest attempt of Cooper to gain literary recognition had failed completely. His wrath, which had been added to by private quarrels at Cooperstown, now burst beyond all bounds. He charged like a baited bull upon everything in sight. His lawsuits for libel quickly mounted into the dozens. Usually he was right, usually he won, but he lost completely the American public. He had become a synonym for bumptiousness, rebuked and turned into litigious wrath. Nothing he might say or write now could secure, at least in America, respectful hearing.

v

The last phase of Cooper, covering the decade of the forties, we may denominate his period of propaganda. In the ten years he wrote eighteen novels, all of them, save possibly four, produced with the avowed purpose of combating and destroying some false belief or iniquitous system, or, as in the case of *The Crater,* describing some new Utopia. The similarity between the Cooper of this period and the later Mark Twain is startling. Both began as border-educated individualists, parochial-minded, intoxicated with the new American idealism; both by travel and by wide contacts with urban pessimism were educated into blasé cosmopolitanism; both ended as embittered fighters against every form of oppression of or cruelty to the weak; and both went out at last in utter misanthropy. It is an American evolution.

He began the period by yielding twice to the universal demand for more Indian stories. He wrote *The Pathfinder* and *The Deerslayer* in the manner of his earlier *Last of the Mohicans*—straight stories of adventure with no moral, no projected reform, and no didacticism. But the Cooper of this period was in no mood for simple narrative. Tales like *The Deerslayer* are for the long quiet evenings by the campfire and for hours of peaceful and romantic retrospect, and Cooper had become a soap-box orator driven by the hot tide of resentment within him to lash abuses and preach furious sermons. The novel for him became now a platform from which he thundered his hard-bitten beliefs, his prejudices, his infallibility, his contempt for American Babbittism—the American "mob." In *Wing and Wing* he preached against fanaticism; in the three "Littlepage" novels he lectured on economic conditions; in *Jack Tier* he excoriated profiteers and denounced the Mexican War; in *Ways of the Hour* he pointed out the weaknesses of the jury system. Could they be stripped of their heavy load of purpose, all of them would be good stories. *Ways of the Hour* has in it the elements of a fascinating detective story, but the interest is lost in a desert of propaganda: *Jack Tier* in sheer story-telling power is one of the best of his fictions.

Cooper stands for arrested development. Had he had his countrymen at his back from 1826 to the end; had he felt sure at all times, as Scott did, of a perfectly sympathetic audience; had he surely known that the best art he could command would not be searched for its political opinions but enjoyed for its literary merit, he perhaps never would have lapsed into the bitterness and propagandism of his final period. For even in the final and discredited period his story-telling power steadily grew. One may find everywhere flashes of real inspiration, but, weighted as the tales are with controversial purpose, they are lost. Everything that he wrote after *The Deerslayer* has long been deservedly forgotten.

VI

It is easy to criticize Cooper, and it is also useless. Mark Twain, in his slashing critique, has done all that ever needs to be done in this peculiar field. One may fill note-books with grotesqueries and faulty technique and even with solecisms, but returning laden with this ignominious spoil one is sure to be confronted by Cooper's simple defense of himself. There is no escape from his argument. For him, fiction-making was governed by only a single law:

To the devil with you and your rules! So long as the reader laughs when I laugh, weeps when I weep, and feels the force of the moral I would inculcate, I care not a straw for either.

Modern realism, could he ever have known of such a thing, Cooper would have rejected with fine scorn. His question was never, "Is it true to life?" He asked only, "Will it *seem* true to the reader? Does it create a world that the reader will accept and live in without a question? If it does this, what more can any novelist do?" Of Scott's art he could say:

I did not condemn the want of historical truth in its picture. I did not consider *Ivanhoe* as intended to be history. It was a work of the imagination, in which all the fidelity that was requisite was enough to be probable and natural. . . . Nothing could *seem* to be more true than Scott's pictures.

It disarms criticism. Beyond the shadow of a doubt, Cooper's best novels commanded completely the *readers of their own day,* and to a large degree they control their readers still after a century has gone.

The novelist must be weighed always in the scales of his own generation, for the art of fiction is to a large degree a fashion man-made, changing from decade to decade. Cooper's feminine characters, for instance, have been disparaged by all later critics. Lowell's dictum that all his women were drawn from one model and that they are "All sappy as maples and flat as a prairie" has been echoed by two generations of critics, but the readers of the twenties made no such complaint. Miss Edgeworth could declare that the Irish washerwoman in *The Spy* was one of the finest characterizations in fiction. Cooper took often as models overfeminized and provincially affected subjects, undoubtedly—his wife and her English-aping friends among the Hudson aristocracy—but his depicting of them is precisely in the manner of the fiction of his day. His women are the *beau-monde* women of the eighteenth century, the fashionable type: unschooled, nerveless, indoctrinated with sensibility and reverence for the conventions, helplessness their leading charm. That he held to this type so consistently came from the influence of his wife, his ever-present critic. That Cooper *could* depict other types of femininity, witness Judith Hutter, the first "vampire" in American fiction, and witness Cora, partly African by her father's sin and loved to desperation by two Indian chiefs.

The most serious charge against Cooper lies deeper than all this: with his unquestioned powers of creation, he did not measure up to what fairly might have been expected of him. He squandered his literary resources; he let his temperament rule his art. He stands as the father of the American novel in half a dozen of its varieties, yet he left behind him no great novel. His creative imagination exceeded always his execution. He wrote forty-eight volumes in thirty and more varieties of literary texture—experiments, most of them. There is but one adjective that can describe his work—*desultory*. No other American writer has tried fields so many and so various. Perhaps it was his temperament; perhaps it was his times which, for literature, unquestionably were out of joint; perhaps it was his wife; perhaps it was all of these combined.

At still another vital point he failed: he dealt with the surfaces of life—rapidly—with picturesque objectivity. He created for the most part by outer inventory. His sea-novels deal with the anatomy of ships, with nautical technique and lingo, with the *modus operandi* during chases, with the surface of the sea, with the multitudinous varieties of the weather as affecting the sailor's art. The mystic soul of the ocean, "the mystery of the ships and the magic of the sea," as one finds it in Conrad, Cooper touches hardly at all. His sea-dogs, even Long Tom, are never so human that we *feel* them. They are part of the machinery of the ship; they are theatric, melodramatic, made up with oakum beards. Even the best of them, Captain Spike in *Jack Tier,* a novel that might have been written by Jack London, reeks of the make-up box. The ship in each novel is the real hero, and the technique of handling it is the *motif* of the tale. There is little of soul. We are kept excited by the stirring action, we are snatched through wild chases in the forest and on the ocean, but the movement and the picturesque settings are all. The moving-pictures—the "movie"—began with James Fenimore Cooper.

He must be dismissed as one whose enormous good fortune it was to be born into literature at the one golden moment when new vast realms of romance were ready for discovery. He was the first to enter and explore, and his influence upon all who have followed him has been enormous. His pupils have all surpassed him in all that makes for fictional art, but still he towers and will tower above them all. Always will he be the father of the American novel of the forest and the ocean, the Columbus who first discovered virgin lands and blazed the forest trails which later have become populous highways and city streets.

CHAPTER XXII

THE DISCOVERY OF THE INDIAN

I

THE NORTH American Indian as a literary theme has had four different phases in four different periods: first, the Indian of the eighteenth-century revolutionists in Europe, especially in France—"the noble savage"; second, the sentimentalized Indian of the new feminine school; third, the romanticized Indian of the Walter Scott era, the Indian with the unique American forest as background; and lastly, the melodramatic Indian of the mid-century dime novel.

The "noble savage" was a symbol, not an actuality, a mythical creature created by idealists and poets and revolutionists, an embodiment of their conception of the perfect freedom of primitive nature untouched by the curse of civilization. Of the actual American Indian, which had so terrified the early settlers, they knew nothing at all, and cared nothing. They had a theory. The French Revolution was precipitated by a romantic philosophy, one area of which was bolstered up by the Indians of America. Rousseau is full of them:

The American savages who go naked, and live entirely on the chase, have always been impossible to subdue. What yoke indeed can be placed on men who stand in need of nothing?

It was iron and corn which first civilized men, and ruined humanity. Thus both are unknown to the savages of America, who for that reason are still savage.

Not only in philosophy, this noble savage, but in poetry and in romance: in such classics as Saint-Pierre's *Paul et Virginie* and Chateaubriand's *Atala, or the Love and Constancy of Two Savages in the Desert* and *Les Natchez*. In England, too, eighteenth-century literature made much of the "Back to Nature" *motif*. The romantic revolt professed to be a return to the primitive. Wordsworth, Southey, Coleridge, Byron, Campbell, Rogers—all at one time or another dreamed of America as a modern forest of Arden where one might find perfect freedom, the freedom of the noble savage.

Crèvecœur's *Letters from an American Farmer*, which reached London in 1782 and Paris in 1784, translated by their author into French, seemed to this revolutionary school a document most convincing. Here was a man who, according to his journal, had actually lived the life of freedom in the útter wilds, who had slept, so he declared, in the wigwams of the savages and had found them all he had dreamed. In France undoubtedly the book had a moment of influence. Issued in Philadelphia, however, in 1783, its influence was small. Americans knew the life of the frontier and they knew the Indian.

The French savant, Chateaubriand, also visited the American Arden for romantic materials. Reaching Philadelphia in 1791, he toured the American wilds for seven months, visited Niagara Falls, and penetrated the more westerly regions over routes impossible to identify from his misty reports. Of Indian life he professed to have seen much, but in the record of his journey and in his three romances there is nothing that can be checked as positive results of actual observation. Everywhere impossibilities and idealizations. The characters in his romances are not Indians at all, save in name. Works of rare literary art undoubtedly, but, read in the light of actuality, the art disappears and they become monstrous perversions. Crèvecœur had traces of realism in his volume, but no trace of genius; Chateaubriand had traces of genius in his volumes, but no trace of realism. *Atala,* translated by Caleb Bingham, was published in America in 1802, but it made no more impression than did Crèvecœur's earlier volume.

II

Americans knew the actual Indian. They had been reared on stories of the early settlers to whom the creatures were demons, not human beings. Nevertheless, even the New England poets could sentimentalize "a fading race," dispossessed by force of their ancestral holdings, forced from their ancient hunting-grounds into the unknown West, exterminated like vermin, rotted out by the white man's rum. Scattered through the poetry of the post-Revolutionary period one finds a considerable body of lyrics dealing with the "fading race" theme. Carey's *American Museum* (1787–1792) was fond of Indians served up in poetry. It published all of Freneau's Indian lyrics and even attributed to him the anonymous "Death Song of a Cherokee Indian." [1]

Freneau was the first in America to admit into poetry the despised savage, but of the actual Indian even he knew little. His series of magazine papers, *Tomo Cheeki, The Creek Indian in Philadelphia,* are satires on American life after eighteenth-century English models, but they tell us nothing at all of Tomo Cheeki, the savage reporter. Two or three times, as in "The Prophecy of King Tammany" (1782), "The Dying Indian" (1784), and "The Indian Burying Ground," he sentimentalizes the race, with criticism of the whites, but in his later lyrics, "The Indian Student, or Force of Nature" (1788) and "The Indian Convert" (1787), he ceases to romanticize and takes a sarcastic fling at the "noble savage" thesis.

Knapp, in his *Lectures* (1829), was inclined to assign the first epic creation with an Indian subject to John

[1] The best study of the authorship of this poem is to be found in Albert Keiser, *The Indian in American Literature* (1933).

Lathrop (1772-1820). Lathrop, a Bostonian who had traveled widely, in 1802 had published in Calcutta after a residence there of ten years an epic with the title *The Speech of Caunonicus, or an Indian Tradition.* Knapp's comment is worthy of reproduction: The poem, he believed, was

the first production of that school of poetry, which has since been so prolifick in lovers of the Aboriginals. The Indians of our country, up to this time, had not met with much sympathy, or had many songs of praise or justice lavished on them. . . . The day of retribution has, however, come; and some of our poets are making these sons of the forest the heroes of epics and the knights of song. It is no small praise to be called the pioneer in this course of magnanimity and justice.

More magnanimity by far has the poem than poetic value. It belongs on the same shelf as Barlow's *Vision of Columbus.* Caunonicus, before making his long "speech," must have been a faithful student of Pope and Goldsmith.

The Bostonian "Philenia," Mrs. Morton, however, would seem to have a better claim to pioneer honors. Her Indian epic, *Ouâbi: or the Virtues of Nature, an Indian Tale in Four Cantos,* came out in 1790. The first, unquestionably, was she to Della-Cruscanize the Indian. Like all the eighteenth-century poets, she professed to have founded her tale on the strictest truth. "Should any be induced to think that I have given too many perfections to a rude and uncultivated savage," she quotes the French writer, M. Mercier, and also General Lincoln, who took pains to acquaint her with "the local rites and customs alluded to."

The poem begins not unpoetically:

> 'Tis not the golden hill, nor flowery dale,
> Which lends my simple muse her artless theme;
> But the black forest and uncultur'd vale,
> The savage warrior and the lonely stream.

But for the most part it is a gush of sentimentalism. This picture, for instance, of the heroine Azakia, the Indian girl:

> Her limbs were straighter than the mountain pine,
> Her hair far blacker than the raven's wing;
> Beauty had lent her from the waving line,
> Her breath gave fragrance to the balmy spring.

Everywhere avoidance of the plain statement, everywhere Della Cruscan inversions, everywhere superlatives. Her Indian discharges his gun, but, as reported by "Philenia," this is what happened:

> Soon as Celarno view'd the murd'rous scene
> Quick from his vest the deathful tube he drew;
> Its leaden vengeance thundered o'er the green.

Tied to stake for execution, her Indian sings his death-song, but no mortal Indian ever sang such a mess. The sources of her inspiration are openly confessed: the volume ends with an address to the Muse of her poem, the divine Della Crusca.

Those who knew the actual Indian were equally superlative, but with a difference. In 1792 H. H. Brackenridge sent from the Pittsburgh border to Alsop's little magazine, the *Echo,* his own opinions:

> I consider men who are unacquainted with the savages like young women who have read romances, and have as improper an idea of the Indian character in the one case, as the female mind has of real life in the other.

To him, "an uncivilized Indian is but a little way removed from a beast,"

> And those brown tribes, who snuff the desert air,
> Are aunts and cousins to the skunk and bear.

Charles Brockden Brown had much the same feeling. The first to introduce Indians into prose fiction, he treated them, he declared, with utmost realism. He would exhibit Indians only as he knew Indians in real life from his own observation. As a result, he depicted automatons, wooden savages of the cigar-store type. The whole tribe is killed one by one by the sleep-walker. They stand like cows while he shoots them down. Only one survives, the Indian witch, a live character which should have been worked to a romantic end, a character indeed with elements like those in Scott's Meg Merrilies of later years.

Mrs. Rowson, in her *Reuben and Rachel; or, Tales of the old Times;* a novel (1798), used Indians simply as material pedagogic and moral:

To awaken in the minds of my young readers a curiosity that might lead them to the attentive perusal of history in general, but more especially the history of their native country. . . . To impart in their innocent minds a love for piety and virtue.

She knew nothing of Indians: they are simply the villains in her tale. They capture children, they kill without mercy women and babies. But her Indian maiden Eumea, a Pocahontas creature, daughter of a Mohawk chief, loves the young white hero, and when she sees him happily married to the heroine, she destroys herself—a plot to be much used by later writers. The first American novel to use Indian characters throughout.

Dennie hooted at the maudlin sentimentality of such stuff. He had no faith in Indians as material for literature. Viewed from the office of the aristocratic *Port Folio,* the Indian was to be classed with the lower orders of creation. This from his pen in 1807:

An Indian is a natural brute beast. He has not so much sensibility as the wolf he kills. He is neither an orator, nor a poet, nor a musician. Between him and the bear that growls through the forest there is a perfect resemblance. Like him, for half the season he is torpid, and like him, he presents every image of dulness, ruggedness, and ferocity.

The whole sentimental school, which persisted well into the nineteenth century, a school that included Phi Beta Kappa speakers, "The-Fate-of-the-Indians" orators, and poets, is forgotten today. Aside from some four lyrics which still are to be found in the more comprehensive anthologies—Freneau's "Indian Burying Ground" and "The Dying Indian," Tyler's "Death Song," and William Dunlap's "Cololoo, an Indian Tale Thrown into English Verse," first issued, so far as I can discover, in the *American Poems* collection in 1793—aside from these, the effusions of the entire group have perished.

Emerson in 1845 disposed of the entire question with a single penful of ink: "We in Massachusetts see the Indians only as a picturesque antiquity—Massachusetts, Shawmut, Samoset, Squantum, Nantasket, Narraganset, Musketaquid." [2]

III

The novels of Scott and the tremendous success of Irving and Cooper set the literary bells ringing all over America. The new literary fashion was romance—the metrical romance of the *Marmion* type and the historical romance patterned upon *Waverley*. But romance records only the past, the forgotten, the unrecorded, and America had no past. Men were alive in 1820 whose great-grandfathers had come over in the *Mayflower*. The beginnings of America, as compared with beginnings in Europe, were mere matters of yesterday. Alexander Meek, in a Phi Beta Kappa address, believed this to be the chief "difficulty which fetters and defies domestic invention":

Genius dare not take liberties with a history so well known, and approaches her task with a cautious apprehensiveness

[2] *Journal,* VII, 23.

which is inconsistent with her noblest executions. The poet
and romancer are only strong where the historian is weak,
and can alone walk boldly and with entire confidence in those
dim and insecure avenues of time which all others tremble
when they penetrate.

The Indian as a literary subject had early proved most
attractive to Phi Beta Kappa orators, especially at Cambridge. Theodore Dehon, in his address "Upon the Importance of Literature to our Country," Cambridge, 1807,
had pleaded for the Indian as the chief hope for an original American literature. The same note was struck by
William Tudor, Jr., in 1815. "This country," he argued,
"does have an original American literature. . . . I now
refer to the oral literature of the aborigines."

But the tide toward romance was wider far than this,
wider than mere academic argument. The magazines had
laid hold upon it. The Boston *Monthly Anthology* in
October, 1805, was reviewing Scott's *Lay of the Last
Minstrel,* and afterwards it was following Scott with reviews of volume after volume of his work. Dennie's *Port
Folio* was doing the same thing. The *North American Review* from its first number (1815) joined in the general
hue and cry for romance—American romance after the
Scott patterns. Campbell's *Gertrude of Wyoming* (1809)
and Cooper's *The Spy* were added elements increasing the
demand for the new literary vogue. Cooper, declared the
North American Review, "had added a new province to
literature."

The key-word now was "legends." Irving had discovered the Hudson and had thrown theatric lightings
upon the barge-laden old river. America, now declared the
critics, is covered with areas equally romantic, and it was
the task of the American romanticist to find them. Where
in all the vast area of the land was a spot without its Indian legend, without at least its Indian lover's leap?

After Eastburn and Sands's romance, *Yamoyden,* the
North American Review purred with satisfaction. The

future of American literature was at last secure. The *Edinburgh* and the *Contemporary* reviewers had been answered. No more dependence upon England for literary models and themes:

There are the Indians, a separate and strongly-marked race of men—with all the bold group lines of nature yet uneffaced upon them—phlegmatic but fierce, inconstant, etc. . . . Picturesque was the land, when a line of thriving villages enclosed a space of Indian hunting ground, and rivers with banks all gay with vegetation, ran down into solitary lakes; when the cultivated farm was bounded with the boundless forests, when the wolf and red-deer found their way among the herds, and the Calvinist in his doublet and beaver crossed the path of the native in his peag and plumes; when the little settlement read the fate of its twenty miles distant neighbor in the reddened sky, and men who had been honored guests in the halls of nobles, slept without a tent to cover them in swamps or nursed the sick Indian in his miserable hut.

He who shall give them their just place in poetry will differ from any delineator of artificial manners almost as much as a landscape of Salvator Rosa differs from an artist's draught of a modern house.

Whoever in this country first attains the rank of a first rate writer of fiction, we predict will lay his scene here. The wide field is ripe for the harvest, and scarce a sickle yet has touched it.

The rising new school of young writers took eagerly to the Scott romance, especially on its poetical side. According to Parke Godwin, Bryant early composed a long poem with an Indian subject. Longfellow, in his graduation oration at Bowdoin College (1825), held up the Indian and his legends as the hope of American literature, and seven years later, in January, 1832, he did the same thing in his defense of poetry in the *North American Review*. Edward Everett, in his Phi Beta Kappa oration, August 27, 1824, was eloquent in his plea for Indian romance. Others were as enthusiastic. Willis, in his tale "The

Cherokee's Threat," had expressed the belief that "the noble aborigines of America" were destined ultimately to "become the poetry of the nation." In 1828 he had edited two volumes of an annual which he entitled the *Legendary,* volumes filled with legendary lore. Sir Walter Scott at one period planned a romance dealing with the Indians and even collected some materials for the work, but finally gave them over to Henry Brevoort. In the Scott meters the young Whittier wrote *Mogg Megone,* which in later years he excluded from his approved canon. As readable is it as Scott, full of action, often melodramatic, resonant with war-whoops, and well equipped with tomahawks and vermilion paint and war-gear. An interesting poem unquestionably, but it is not Whittier. "The Bridal of Pennacook" is more literary and more genuine. In 1832, in the introduction to *The Literary Remains of John G. C. Brainard,* he wrote what would have been equally appropriate as an introduction to Whittier's own earlier volume, *Legends of New England* (1831):

It has been often said that the New World is deficient in the elements of poetry and romance; that its bards must of necessity linger over the classic ruins of other lands; and draw their sketches of character from foreign sources, and paint Nature under the soft beauties of an Eastern sky. On the contrary, New England is full of Romance; and her writers would do well to follow the example of Brainard. The great forest which our fathers penetrated—the red men —their struggle and their disappearance—the Powwow and the War-dance—the savage inroad and the English sally— the tale of superstition and the scenes of Witchcraft—all these are rich materials of poetry.

Hawthorne hated Indians. Thoreau, however, was stirred in his imagination every time he found an arrowhead. His study of his observed Indians in the Maine woods is romanticized science. To him, Indian lore was as valuable as the old classics:

Why make so great ado about the Roman and the Greek, and neglect the Indian. We need not wander off with boys in our imaginations to Juan Fernandez, to wonder at footprints in the sand there. Here is a print still more significant at our doors, the print of a race that has preceded us, and this the little symbol that Nature has transmitted to us. Yes, *this* arrow-headed character is probably more ancient than any other, and to my mind it has not been deciphered. Men should not go to New Zealand to write or think of Greece and Rome, nor more to New England. New earths, new themes expect us. Celebrate not the Garden of Eden, but your own.

This as late as 1857. Longfellow's *Hiawatha* was the supreme classic of the school. After his great success nothing more was possible. Indian romance was a thin soil quickly exhausted. The fact was discovered early. John Bristed, in his *Resources of the United States of America* (1818), pronounced romance an impossible thing in America, especially romance dealing with Indian life:

Of native novels we have no great stock, and none good; our democratic institutions placing all the people on a dead level of political equality; and the pretty even distribution of property throughout the country affords but little room for varieties and contrasts of character; nor is there much scope for fiction, as the country is quite new, and all that has happened from the first settlement to the present hour respecting it is known to every one. There is, to be sure, some traditionary romance about the Indians, but a novel describing these miserable barbarians, their squaws, and papooses, would not be very interesting to the present race of American readers.

Others were equally positive. The *United States Literary Gazette,* reviewing in 1826 *The Last of the Mohicans,* asked this searching question:

It will never do to make up the whole story of our novels of such materials as these. . . . A Yankee once asked a

British officer, who was boasting of the signal success of His Majesty's arms at Bunker Hill, how many such battles he could afford to gain. We put the same question to Mr. Cooper: how many novels can he afford to write? How many changes can he ring upon scalping, shooting, tomahawking, etc.?

Two years later the *North American Review* expressed the same opinion:

There is a barrenness of the novelist's peculiar circumstance in the life of a savage, which cannot easily be got over, when we set about a story of him in his hut and in his wanderings; . . . There is not enough in the character and life of these poor natives to furnish the staple of a novel. . . . Such seems to be the insuperable obstacle in the way of those, who venture into our early wilderness for a plot. They leave the abodes of civilization.[3]

Cooper, always sensitive to criticism, especially if it emanated from Boston, agreed fully in this opinion. In his *Notions of the Americans* (1828) he took this extreme position:

It certainly would be possible for an American to give a description of the manners of his own country in a book that he might choose to call a romance, which should be read because the world is curious on the subject, which would certainly never be read for that nearly indefinable poetical interest which attaches itself to a description of manners less bald or uniform. All the attempts to blend history with romance in America have been comparative failures, since the subjects are too familiar to be treated with the freedom that the imagination absolutely requires. Some of the descriptions of the progress of society on the borders have had a rather better success, since there is a *positive* though not very poetical, novelty in the subject.

It was his valedictory to Indian themes, as he believed. He had published *The Prairie,* recording the final passing

[3] July, 1828. Review of Cooper's *The Red Rover.*

of La Longue Carabine, and he sought to escape from the subject. Despite popular misconceptions, Cooper was a man of culture. European romance, with its rich backgrounds, appealed to him strongly.

His departure to Europe after six attempts at American romance was, like Irving's, an escape into a land that had richer possibilities. He was abroad seven years, and he wrote three romances with European materials—*The Bravo,* excellent work, *The Headsman,* and *The Heidenmauer.* No one reads them, yet fiercely were they condemned and fiercely was their author ordered back to his wigwams and his tomahawks, just as Melville in later years was condemned when his romances no longer contained cannibals and tropic maidens and beach-combing adventure. Both men considered themselves crippled by their times, thwarted creators.

IV

The number of romances and narrative poems with Indian themes written during the 1820's and the 1830's is surprisingly large. Here are thirty-four typical specimens, the best, perhaps, produced during the two decades:

1817   *The Bridal of Vaumond,* Robert C. Sands.
        Captain Smith and Pocahontas, an Indian Tale, John Davis.
1820   *Yamoyden,* James W. Eastburn and Robert C. Sands.
1821   *The Pioneers,* James Fenimore Cooper.
1822   *Logan,* John Neal.
        Traits of the Aborigines, five cantos, Lydia H. Sigourney.
1823   *The Wilderness; or Braddock's Time,* James McHenry.
        The Savage Beauty: a Novel, P. W. Sproat.
        Logan, Joseph Doddridge.
        The Spectre of the Forest, or Annals of Housatonic, James McHenry.
1824   *Hobomok,* Lydia M. Child.

1826   *The Last of the Mohicans,* James Fenimore Cooper.
        Wumissoo, or the Vale of Hoosatunnk, a Poem,
        William Allen.
1827   *Northwood: A Tale of New England,* Sarah Josepha
        Hale.
1828   *Tokeah, or the White Rose,* Charles Sealsfield [Karl
        Postl].
        The Prairie, James Fenimore Cooper.
        The Wept of Wish-ton-Wish, James Fenimore
        Cooper.
1829   *Metamora,* John Augustus Stone.
1830   *The Shoshone Valley: a Romance,* Timothy Flint.
        *Tales of the Northwest, or Sketches of Indian Life
        and Character,* William Joseph Snelling.
1831   *The Dutchman's Fireside,* James K. Paulding.
1832   *Legends of the West,* James Hall.
1833   *Harpe's Head, a Legend of Kentucky,* James Hall.
1835   *Mogg Megone,* John Greenleaf Whittier.
        The Yemassee, W. G. Simms.
1837   *Nick of the Woods,* R. M. Bird.
1838   *Rob of the Bowl,* John P. Kennedy.
1839   *The Last of the Lenape and Other Poems,* S. M.
        Janney.
        Wild Scenes in the Forest and Prairie, C. F. Hoff-
        man.
1840   *Pocahontas and other Poems,* Lydia Sigourney.
        The Pathfinder, James Fenimore Cooper.
1841   *Pocahontas,* W. W. Waldron.
        The Deerslayer, James Fenimore Cooper.
        Powhatan, a Metrical Romance in Seven Cantos,
        Seba Smith (reviewed by Poe).

Feeble stuff it is for the most part, especially the poetry.
Cooper alone has survived his century.

With the coming of the annuals in 1826, the short story
of Indian times or Indian legend became a ruling favorite
with the editors. Not an annual without its Indian tale or
its Indian lyric. Paulding, in quantity at least, was the
leading contributor, and Miss Catherine Sedgwick was
second in popularity. Scarcely a writer of the period from

Bryant down to Ned Buntline but supplied his quota of short tales and sketches.

On the whole, they are of better texture than the long romances. The short story in the annual was strictly limited as to space, and as a result it acquired perforce compression and unity and avoidance of general looseness. But even in this literary area, even with its unique characters and backgrounds, one would have to search long for a specimen of narrative suitable for a modern anthology of the American short story.[4]

[4] The best treatment of the whole subject as yet is to be found in Albert Keiser's dissertation, *The Indian in American Literature* (1933).

CHAPTER XXIII

THE CONSUMPTIVE POETS

I

"AMERICAN critics," complained Dennie's *Port Folio* in 1811, "seem in almost all cases to have entered into a confederacy to exterminate poetry"—a statement illuminating: ever since 1801, the birth-year of the *Port Folio*, American poetry has been under the whip. Criticism in the periodical-essay columns, in the quarterlies, in the book-review articles, in the Phi Beta Kappa orations and poems has been, even to the present, condemnatory, with copious advice as to manner and materials and rhetoric. Even the conservative Charles Brockden Brown, long an editor of literary magazines, could pen in 1806 a judgment like this:

> Good poetry is the most scarce of all literary commodities, though poetry, or matter that, by courtesy, bears the name, is sufficiently abundant. There has not lately been published in America any poetical *volume* of much value.

Bad this early poetry undoubtedly was, and sadly in need of criticism, but its badness is not the first impression it makes on the modern student. One is impressed by the unbelievable quantity of the stuff. The volume of it is amazing. Books of verse, paid for always by the poet or by victimized subscribers secured after infinite toil, were necessarily few. Kettell listed only eighty-seven volumes of native verse issued before 1815; but the newspapers—a rapidly increasing pack—and the monthly magazines were enormously addicted to rhyme. Quality, it would seem, was not a requisite. Winthrop Sargent (1753–1820), in his long Dr. Johnson-like satire, *Boston,* gave this description of the product then current:

> Sonnets and riddles celebrate the trees,
> And ballad-mongers charter every breeze.
> Long odes to monkies, squirrel elegies,
> Lines and acrostics on dead butterflies:
>
> Endless effusions, some with Greek bedight,
> And hymns harmonious, sweet, as infinite,
> So freely flow, that posey ere long
> Must yield to numbers and expire by song.
> Elegiac lays such taste and truth combine
> The lap-dog lives and barks in every line.
> Each rebus-maker takes the poet's name
> And every rhymer is the heir of fame.

And America not only read the stuff but reissued it in endless collections, as if every scrap of it were precious. From the first we have been the land of anthologies, literary safe-deposit boxes for an inpouring tide of poetic iron pyrites that seemed to be gold-dust.

Samuel Kettell in 1829 issued a three-volume *Specimens of American Poetry,* with 452 poems from 189 and more poets and with the first comprehensive bibliography of published books of native poetry, listing 445 "works of American origin which have come under notice in the course of this undertaking"; but even he was inclined to apologize for the quality of his selections:

Authors have been too few to create competition, and the public, to whom they addressed themselves, too much occupied with matters of direct personal interest to bestow any high consideration upon the talents which are exerted only in the embellishment of life. Hence we have never known till the present day such a thing as a professed author. All the talent and industry of the people have been called into the field of active employment, and the most of what has been written among us consists of such productions as were executed in the early days of our authors, before the serious business of life was entered upon; or in such leisure moments as were snatched from constant and laborious occupations. We have obtained therefore only the unripe fruits of their youth, or the imperfect performances of casual moments.[1]

No such collection of poetic trash before in the whole history of the world, but even this was to be surpassed in voluminous worthlessness one generation later by the amazing industry of the Reverend Rufus Wilmot Griswold.

II

Scarcely a stalwart soul in two generations of verse-makers! A feeble folk—conies whimpering in the rocks! Paradox, truly—masculine America with its frontier-breakers, its hewers and builders and wrestlers with the soil, represented in poetry by cooing and whimpering weaklings.

Consumption was the scourge of early America. The hardships of the new land were not always toughening and strengthening. In every family a "runt," a frail one over whom hung the threat of tuberculosis. Too weak for exacting physical toil, often he was sent to college. On the stony acres of rural New England many a feeble lad, after days of grinding toil, has had a call to preach. Griswold records of Carlos Wilcox that when a small boy he was injured by an ax. "It was a cause of suffering for a long period, and lameness during his life; it made him a minister of religion and a poet." Frail adolescents sent to college when they needed the open air, intense souls, oversensitive, overstimulated by religion, often hopelessly in love, introspective, "Thanatopsis"-

---

[1] *Specimens of American Poetry,* introduction, p. xlvii.

minded—fertile soil they were for the bacillus tuberculosis, most destructive of stimulants.

Not only were the poets themselves feeble, but they had in their hands the poetry of English consumptives like Kirke White, who led them to sick-beds and church-yards. White, who had died at the age of twenty-one became the patron saint of the consumptives. His little opera, "The Dance of the Consumptives," and his lyrics, "Consumption" and the like, were everywhere read and imitated. Without him it is doubtful if Bryant would ever have been a poet. Consumption became a poetic theme. "The hectic beauty" of untimely decay was praised in superlatives. This from James G. Percival:

> There is a sweetness in woman's decay,
> When the light of beauty is fading away
> When the bright enchantment of youth is gone. . . .
>
> O! there is a sweetness in beauty's close,
> Like the perfume scenting the wither'd rose.

And so on to the hectic ending.

The death-list of the early American poets is a startling document. Consumptives, almost all of them:

St. John Honeywood ....1765–1798........33 years
William Cliffton ....1772–1799........27 "
John Blair Linn ....1777–1805........29 "
Carlos Wilcox ....1794–1827........32 "
Joseph Rodman Drake ....1795–1820........25 "
J. G. C. Brainard ....1796–1828........32 "
James W. Eastburn ....1797–1819........22 "
John Everett ....1801–1826........25 "
E. C. Pinkney ....1802–1828........26 "
Lucretia Davidson ....1808–1825........17 "
Willis G. Clark ....1810–1841........31 "
Lucy Hooper ....1817–1841........24 "
Margaret Davidson ....1823–1838........15 "

Thirteen poets who died, if we take the average, not far from the age of twenty-five, the age of Keats at his death. And the list could be lengthened.

But not all of the consumptives died. Bryant was a consumptive: the disease colored the whole of his early product. Irving's early life was a running fight with consumption; the fact is written over all his sketches. Whittier, frail and narrow-chested, expected for years to die of the disease. She who might have become his wife— Lucy Hooper—died at twenty-four. Even the out-of-door Thoreau passed away at forty-five, a victim of tuberculosis.

III

William Ellery Channing defined poetry as "that thirst or aspiration, to which no mind is wholly a stranger, for something purer and lovelier, something more powerful, lofty and thrilling, than ordinary or real life affords." The poetry of early America was an attempt, doubtless, to rise above the rough, bare prose of American life, but the young poets were given little help and no encouragement. Bryant in 1818, after naming thirteen poets worthy of being "interrupted in their passage to Oblivion"—all thirteen today known only to searchers in Kettell, Griswold, and Duyckinck—diagnosed the disease affecting the makers of verse as "slavery to a style in too many instances, tinged with a sickly and affected imitation of the peculiar manner of the late popular poets of England": true enough, as all readers of poetry well know. For fifty years, and it may be for twice that figure, scarcely a week has gone by when in some magazine or Phi Beta Kappa poem or literary-club address this judgment has not been reiterated. It has become an American literary *cliché*. Under this constant barrage of the critics, our poets, all of them young, even adolescent, have been rendered self-conscious, model-minded, conventional.

Cramped, too, have they been by home conditions: religious narrowness, exhortations everywhere to avoid in "poesy" all but the "proper and the ethereal, and a pious optimism which was forever sighing "whatever is is right." Bryant, in his *Selections from the American Poets* —seventy-eight poets he samples—excluded from his volume all "amatory poems and drinking songs, notwithstanding the skill or the spirit with which they might be written . . . as not proper for a book designed to be placed in a school or family library." The world is good, was his thesis: no one must doubt it; wickedness is the exception, and it is always punished: *"Alle schuld recht sich auf erde";* goodness is rewarded by happiness. God is in his heaven: to complain is atheism. Thus Bryant and, for decades, it was the leading *motif* of American song.

IV

Only one of my list of consumptives is still represented in modern anthologies—Joseph Rodman Drake, whose *The Culprit Fay,* a metrical romance of fairyland, seemed a pleasing departure from the Scott model. All else of his is forgotten, even the flamboyant "American Flag" lyric which so impressed the twenties and the thirties. His *Culprit Fay* "was the two-days' diversion of a very young man," says William Ellery Leonard, "and published posthumously" (1835).[2] In his lifetime he was known only as the author of certain of the "Croaker" lyrics.

The first statement about Drake concerns the New-Yorkness of the man. He was a native of the city, the son of a physician, and later himself a doctor of medicine. As in the case of Irving and Cooper, no trace of Puritanism, no college education, no demand for literary seriousness, no literary timidity in the fear of a Harvard or Yale literary junto. If he had any model at all, it was

[2] *Cambridge History of American Literature,* I, 281.

Salmagundi, but Professor Leonard deems it wholly original :

> Though in a sense exotic, for it roots in no folklore despite the setting on the Hudson, *The Culprit Fay* reports quite as well as Drayton's *Nimphidia,* its nearest analogue, the antic characteristics of elfland of man's universal fancy.

A youngster of buoyant temper, impetuous, sentimental, full of prankishness, Drake had read the English poets as completely as had Keats, whose life was almost exactly synchronous, but he had had no dreams at all of a literary career. He was a young physician—with time on his hands. Poetry was an exhilarating sport, especially if made in conjunction with his boon companion, Fitz-Greene Halleck. In high glee they set out to *Salmagundi*-ize New York again : "Instruct the young, reform the old, and castigate the age." The result was the "Croaker" papers which ran for some weeks in the New York *Evening Post* (1819). Today the poets would be called columnists, and their poetic miscellany a column. Light stuff unquestionably, entertaining, spicy, winged often with good-natured personalities. Drake's unquestionably was the lightest pen among the early poets. Note a *vers de société* touch in a paragraph like this :

> The serious world will scoff and ban,
>   In clamor loud and hard,
> To hear Meigs called a congressman,
>   And Paulding styled a bard;
> But, come what may, the man's in luck
>   Who turns it all to glee,
> And laughing, cries, with honest Puck
>   "Great Lord! What fools ye be!"

His "The American Flag" was one of the "Croaker" lyrics, the last stanza Halleck's.

Unlike his poetic contemporaries, Drake seemed to work without models or masters. In thirteen stanzas he outlined

the American poet's theme: it should be the glorification
of America:

> Are there no scenes to touch the poet's soul?
> No deeds of arms to wake the lordly strain?
> Shall Hudson's billows unregarded roll?
> Has Warren fought, Montgomery died in vain?
> Shame! that while every mountain stream and plain,
> Hath theme for truth's proud voice or fancy's wand,
> No native bard the patriot harp has ta'en,
> But left to minstrels of a foreign strand,
> To sing the beauteous scenes of nature's loveliest land.

There is a tradition that *The Culprit Fay* was written
to demonstrate to doubting friends that American scenery
and American names could be used in an American epic.
If so, the poet achieved no great success. Aside from
"Cronest" and perhaps two or three other Hudson River
allusions, and the names of a few birds and insects peculiar to America, the poem could as well be laid on the
Thames or the Danube. Only in fairyland could such a
creation find actual footing. A poem of the child world:
the greater part of it is descriptive of fairy equipment
and fairy flora and fauna.

Drake was all but undiscovered by his own generation.
He was merely a "Croaker" who for a few weeks had
amused New York. The resonant lyric, "The American
Flag," one of the "Croaker" series, had reached New
England, but nothing else. But in 1835 was issued *The
Culprit Fay and Other Poems,* to be followed by editions
in 1836, 1844, 1847, 1859, 1860, and nine editions still
later. The poet was a late discovery and was made much
of. Poe reviewed the volume at length, but chiefly to
maintain the thesis that the poem, *The Culprit Fay,* was
an exhibition of fancy rather than of imagination. In
later years Charles F. Richardson, the historian of American literature, discussed Drake under the heading "The
Dawn of Imagination." [3] The dawn was it rather of lyric

---

[3] *American Literature,* II, 24.

lightness, of poetry unweighted with morals or message, of poetry timeless and placeless; and with these characteristics it has survived, while hundreds of better-made and more serious volumes have sunk forever.

v

In New England much was expected of John G. C. Brainard. At Yale even in his student days he had been, according to Whittier, marked as a "genius." Poetry flowed from his pen without effort, poetry unpremeditated, unrevised. The college had created a poet: he would live by poetry. But the family profession was the law, and perforce he studied it and mastered it, and perforce he practiced it in Middletown, Connecticut. But as with Bryant and a dozen other poets, the actual practice of the law proved to be impossible. He abandoned it and found refuge finally, as did Bryant, in journalism. For the rest of his life he edited in Hartford the *Connecticut Mirror*.

His poetry from this time on was contributed to his newspaper, all of it hastily written, all of it unrevised. He wrote by impulse. Indolence ruled him. His friends, realizing his wasting powers, urged him to more ambitious poetic effort, but in vain. As recorded by Goodrich, his best-known lyric, "The Fall of Niagara," was dashed off in slap-dash "takes" for the printer's devil to rush to the workmen in the last moments of a "make-up."

A small volume of his poems he published in 1825, but it brought him not at all the "financial betterment" he had hoped for, and it brought little notice: it had been published in New York. The Boston *Literary Gazette* discovered it, however, pronounced the greater part of it mediocre, but commended the rest as highly above the average of American poetry. Three years later the poet died in literary obscurity.

Then suddenly had come the discovery: the man was a "genius." Accordingly, New England outdid itself. In the first number of *The Token* Mrs. Sigourney embalmed him in sentimental verse as if a demigod had fallen, and in Kettell's *Specimens* a year later came a five-page sketch hailing him as the "American Burns," a sketch later claimed by S. C. Goodrich:

> Yet these productions, so little elaborated, and written under such causes of enervation, are stamped with an originality, boldness, force, and pathos, illustrative of genius, not perhaps inferior to that of Burns, and certainly much resembling it in kind. What could not such a man have done, had he been sustained by fortune equal to his merit, and incited by those impulses which give energy and efficiency to the exertions of other men![4]

Goodrich devoted a chapter to him in his *Recollections;* Griswold, in his *Poets and Poetry of America,* gave him more space than he gave Fitz-Greene Halleck; and Whittier in 1832 edited his poetical "Remains" with an appreciative memoir.

According to Whittier, Brainard was first of all a *New England* poet, as completely so as Burns had been Scottish. He was individualistic and for the most part uninfluenced by models. And he was a nature-poet, singer of his own observations in forest and field, a depicter of New England life and landscape and legend as faithful as Whittier.

Much of his poetry is unreadable today. It is hasty and slipshod and too often conventional, but here and there one stumbles upon fragments that startle and compel— this, for instance, in the lyric "To the Memory of Charles Brockden Brown":

> No whining rhymster with his schoolboy song
>   May wake thee with his muling minstrelsey.
>
> Some western muse, if western muse there be,
>   When the rough wind in clouds has sway'd her form,

[4] *Recollections*, II, 147–149.

Shall boldly wind her wintry horn for thee,
And tune her gusty music to the storm.

Whittier singled out for praise the long poem, "To the Connecticut River," "The Black Fox of Salmon River," and the poet's last effort, "The Invalid on the East Side of Long Island." He himself might have written them. None of the anthologists have omitted "The Sea Bird's Song," and it is well:

> On the deep is the mariner's danger,
>   On the deep is the mariner's death,
> Who, to fear of the tempest a stranger,
>   Sees the last bubble burst of his breath?
> 'Tis the sea-bird, the sea-bird, the sea-bird,
>   Lone looker on despair,
> The sea-bird, the sea-bird, the sea-bird,
>   The only witness there.

In his last poem a lyric despair deep as that in the "Ode to the Nightingale." A lesser Keats. Both young poets eager for life, both obsessed with the dream of beauty and the certainty of quick death.

From the poem "To the Connecticut River" Whittier most certainly got the hint for his "Snow-Bound." Note a fragment like this from "To the Connecticut River":

> In what Arcadian, what Utopian ground
> Are warmer hearts or manlier feelings found,
> More hospitable welcome, or more zeal
> To make the curious "tarrying" stranger feel
> That, next to home, here best may he abide,
> To rest and cheer him by the chimney-side;
> Drink the hale Farmer's cider, as he hears
> From the grey dame the tales of other years.
> Cracking his shagbarks, as the aged crone,
> Mixing the true and doubtful into one,
> Tells how the Indian scalp'd the helpless child
> And bore its shrieking mother to the wild,
> Butcher'd the father hastening to his home,

Seeking his cottage—finding but his tomb.
How drums and flags and troops were seen on high,
Wheeling and charging in the northern sky,
And that she knew what these wild tokens meant,
When to the Old French War her husband went.
How, by the thunder-blasted tree, was hid
The golden spoils of far fam'd Robert Kidd;
And then the chubby grand-child wants to know
About the ghosts and witches long ago,
That haunted the old swamp.
        The clock strikes ten—
The prayer is said, nor unforgotten then
The stranger in their gates. A decent rule
Of Elders in thy puritanic school.

A collection completely in key with the Connecticut of
Brainard's day, redolent everywhere of the life he knew
and the landscape, and containing more of actuality and
of originality than anything else written in Brainard's
day.

VI

Another early-dead poet sincerely mourned was Grenville Mellen, a native of Maine, educated at Harvard,
finishing his legal course in 1820. Poetry, however, was
to be his life-work. Never young student more eager,
more obsessed with poetic ambitions. To the first five
volumes of *The Token* he contributed twelve poems, to
the *United States Literary Gazette* a running series. Short
stories he wrote for the annuals and the magazines,
enough for a volume—*Glad Tales and Sad Tales* (1829)
—dreary stuff, however, for the most part. He was a poet.
His most significant collection, *The Martyr's Triumph*,
appeared in 1833. That it was dedicated to Lydia Huntley
Sigourney is commentary enough.

The poetic honors poured upon him were continuous.
In 1826 he read his poem, "The Rest of Empires," before
the meeting of the Peace Society of Maine; in 1828 his

poem, "The Light of Letters," before the Athenian Society of Bowdoin College; in 1830 his poem, "The Age
of Print," before the Phi Beta Kappa Society at Harvard;
and in 1839 he was Phi Beta Kappa poet at Yale. Never
a region so avid of poetry, seemingly, as the New England of the consumptive epoch. At every commencement
Phi Beta Kappa poems in every college an hour long.
Every learned society graced with a poet, every magazine,
even the early *North American Review,* heavy with rhym-
ings. As one pores over these endless Phi Beta Kappa
effusions, one is filled with wonder that ever there could
have been a generation of men and women who really
enjoyed them.

His most inspired lyric was perhaps "Lines on Seeing
an Eagle Pass near me in Autumn Twilight." John Neal
was superlative in its praise, considering it "as containing a share of the boldest and purest poetry of our age—
ay, or any other age." Kettell described him as "a writer
of fertile imagination, . . . peculiarly happy in the expression of tender and delicate sentiment." And the American *Quarterly Review* of September, 1837, brought out
all its elegant superlatives:

Among the numerous poets who have strung their lyres
on the banks of the Hudson and amidst the vallies of New
England, there is none who, in our estimation, has breathed
sweeter and purer strains than Grenville Mellen.

In other words, Mellen, correct, "elegant," sentimental,
conventional, satisfied his own generation and called forth
criticism equally "elegant," sentimental, conventional.
That both the poetry and the criticism it called out are
dead today beyond all resurrection need not concern us.
We are telling the story of the 1820's and 1830's.

VII

The consumptive school reached its sensational climax
with the Davidson sisters—Lucretia, who died at the age

of seventeen, and Margaret, who died in her fifteenth year. Griswold was inclined to believe that precosity was an American characteristic: "Those who are familiar with our literary history remember that a remarkable precocity of intellect has been frequently exhibited in this country." But nothing, he believed, had been more remarkable than the poetical achievements of these two children. "It is doubtful," he wrote, "whether the annals of literary composition can show anything, produced at the same age, finer than these poems." No other poets of the twenties or the thirties were exploited so sensationally. In 1829 appeared *Amir Khan, and Other Poems: The Remains of Lucretia Maria Davidson, who died at Plattsburgh, N. Y., August 27, 1825, aged sixteen years and eleven months; with a Biographical Sketch by Samuel F. B. Morse.* In 1841 came *Biography and Poetical Remains of the Late Margaret Miller Davidson,* by Washington Irving. (My copy is marked "Third Edition.") And in 1843 a volume entitled *Selections from the Writings of Miss Margaret M. Davidson, with a Preface by Catharine M. Sedgwick.* The volumes were everywhere commented on and reviewed. Even Robert Southey paused to review them in a long article.

Two sensitive, highly wrought children with a neurotic, overreligious, oversentimental mother, they needed not so much a diet of the English poets as a life of exercise in the open air. Two hothouse plants killed by the hothouse régime. Their poetry as we read it today, heavily rhymed, heavily accented in its finger-counted meters, redolent of older poetry—of Moore, Thomson, Bryant, Kirke White—is not remarkable stuff even for children to make. One searches it with growing impatience to find real lyricism, lines or phrases that open magic casements or even for an instant compel the memory.

VIII

And then it dawns on one that the criticism applies with equal force to the nonconsumptive poets of the early century. For two decades and more the leading American poet was selected from this sacred seven—I arrange them alphabetically: William Cullen Bryant, Richard H. Dana, Fitz-Greene Halleck, James G. Percival, John Pierpont, Charles Sprague, Nathaniel P. Willis. Morris in 1828 published an engraving of the American poets with Percival in the center. Poe a little later declared that "Our principal poets are, perhaps, most frequently named in this order: Bryant, Halleck, Dana, Sprague, Longfellow, Willis and so on. . . . For my own part, I should have it thus—Longfellow, Bryant, Halleck, Willis, Sprague, Dana."

To place the wooden, mechanical, endlessly-drawn occasional ponderosities of the elegant Boston banker, Charles Sprague, among the significant American poems is ridiculous. He won his place undoubtedly by his social charm, his stately presence, his wealth, and his oratory. Boston took him at his own valuation but dropped him before the century had reached its middle year. John Pierpont, too, never popular, yet somehow with his *Airs of Palestine* felt to be a rising star, was also quickly lost sight of; Willis went off into prose; and Dana survived for years his early fame. Halleck went to New York, became worldly, Byron-minded, at times trivial, and lasted longer. So closely is his name associated with Drake's that easily—though he lived hale and hearty until sixty-seven—he may be classed with the consumptives. He was born in Guilford, Connecticut, in 1790 and was resident there until he removed to New York City in 1811. His first long poem to attract the attention of New York was *Fanny* (1819), enlarged in 1821, written in the *Don Juan* metrical form and the *Don Juan* spirit. A brilliant poem on the whole, with the sparkle of wickedness and fun so impossible in New England poetry. Even in its palpable imitation of the *Don Juan* stanza and manner it has originality. It is Byronic only in form. It is an early *Rise of Silas Lapham* in Byronic verse: a family suddenly rich, and, attempting to rise in the social circles of New York, just as suddenly falling. This the final catastrophe:

> The sun is loveliest as he sinks to rest;
>   The leaves of autumn smile when fading fast;
> The swan's last song is sweetest—and the best
>   Of Meigs' speeches, doubtless, was his last.
> And thus the happiest scene, in these my rhymes,
> Closed with a crash, and usher'd in—hard times.

> St. Paul's toll'd one—and fifteen minutes after
>   Down came, by accident, a chandelier;
> The mansion totter'd from the floor to rafter!
>   Up rose the cry of agony and fear!
> And there was shrieking, screaming, bustling, fluttering,
> Beyond the power of writing or of uttering.

> The company departed, and neglected
>   To say good-by—the father storm'd and swore—
> The fiddlers grinn'd—the daughter look'd dejected—
>   The flowers had vanish'd from the polish'd floor,
> And both betook them to their sleepless beds,
> With hearts and prospects broken, but no heads.

> The desolate relief of free complaining
>   Came with the morn, and with it came bad weather,
> The wind was east-northeast, and it was raining
>   Throughout that day, which, take it altogether,
> Was one whose memory clings to us through life,
> Just like a suit in Chancery, or a wife.

Halleck's season of productiveness was short, coördinate almost with Drake's ten years. In this brief springtime he wrote "Alnwick Castle" (1827), "Burns" and "Red Jacket" (1828), and, most popular of all, perhaps, "Marco Bozzaris," spouted by two generations of school-boys. In the desert of the century's 'teens and twenties Halleck, especially in worldly New York, seemed like a veritable oasis. His sentiment, his wit, his kettle-drum time-beat, his freedom from moralizing cant pleased his generation. Griswold in 1842 spoke the last word: "Mr. Halleck," he wrote, "is the only one of our poets who possesses a decided local popularity." He pleased New York, undoubtedly, but to please New York one must be the poet of a day, a journalist, as quickly forgotten as the flying leaves upon which he has inscribed his moment's entertainment.

Fragments of his work have survived. "Marco Bozzaris" still is to be found in the anthologies and, best of all, the opening stanza of "On the Death of Drake," the best remembered of all American epitaphs:

> Green be the turf above thee,
>   Friend of my better days;
> None knew thee but to love thee,
>   Nor named thee but to praise.

In 1848, at the death of John Jacob Astor in whose employ he had been for many years, he retired to his native Guilford with an annuity of $200, and, plump and unworried and famous, he spent his declining years in literary sterility. For half a century he survived the young poet who first had kindled him into poetic fire.

Percival, too, I class with the consumptives, though never was he consumptive. A clear case he was, however, of pathological abnormality. Shy, morose, morbidly sensitive, despondent at times even to attempted suicide, an unbalanced temperament was his undoubtedly. At Yale he was regarded as erratic but brilliant even to the bounds of genius. Certainly his later career was erratic. He mastered law, then medicine, then natural science centering in geology. He was professor of chemistry at West Point in 1824; he made geologic surveys of Connecticut and Indiana; he was surgeon in connection with the recruiting service at Boston; he assisted Webster on the 1829 edition of his dictionary; he was Phi Beta Kappa orator at Harvard and commencement poet at Yale; and for three numbers he edited a magazine of his poetry which he christened *Clio*.

Poetry, however, gushed from his pen all the while in a steady stream, poetry ornate, elegant, totally unrevised, and his New England contemporaries seem to have taken it at its author's valuation. Percival himself had no doubt as to his poetic rank. "Perhaps I do not say too much," he wrote in 1822, "when I assert that I have gained more reputation as a poet than any American before me." Kettell in his anthology gave him fourteen pages, to Dana nineteen, to Neal twenty-two, to Bryant nineteen. Griswold in his volume reckoned him as among the leading American poets and praised him for his latest volume "which embraces more than one hundred and fifty varieties of measure."

Such valuations, even when considered from the standpoint of the man's own time, are amazing. The man was an intellect, a scholar, a phenomenal memory rather than a poetic soul. He lacked sympathy, he lacked the wizard touch that transforms prose into the more ethereal world we call poetry. He is to be rated, if rated he must be, far below Brainard and indeed far below all of the consumptive group. Reverend Henry Ware, reviewing him in 1826, came near saying the last word:

There is an excessive diffuseness in the style of Mr. Percival. It is not sufficiently compact. It wants pith and point; it lacks the energy, which conciseness imparts. Every thing is drawn out as far as possible, always flowing and sweet, and therefore sometimes languid and monotonous. His poetry is too much diluted. It consists too much in words, which are music to the ear, but too often send a feeble echo of the sense to the mind. There is also a superabundance of images in proportion to the thoughts.[5]

[5] *North American Review* (April, 1826), p. 327.

And so on through pages of the *North American Review*.

That America did not finally accept him as her leading poet distressed Percival's last years. He died embittered and resentful. The final blow that utterly annihilated him he did not live to feel—he died in 1856—the sharp review in 1867 by James Russell Lowell of Julius H. Ward's biography issued in 1866.

CHAPTER XXIV

THE ANNUALS AND GIFT-BOOKS

"Yearling literature" or "our baby annuals," as John Neal dubbed them, began in America with the publication of the *Atlantic Souvenir and New Year's Offering* in Philadelphia in 1826. In its earliest preface it was announced as "a work, which on a plan by no means novel in other countries, has never yet been introduced among us":

On the Continent of Europe, indeed, such a volume has long been the usual attendant of the season, and the shops of Germany and France abound every winter with those which are suited to every age and every taste. For a few years past, the same design has been adopted in London, and not with less approbation. With what success the present effort will be attended in our own country is yet to be seen.

Not long had they to wait. All unconsciously the publishers Carey and Lea had blundered upon a gold-mine. "The success of this species of publication,", wrote S. C. Goodrich, the Boston publisher, "stimulated new enterprises of the kind, and a rage for them spread over Europe and America." [1] There had opened what he denominated "the Age of Annuals." Soon every publisher in America made haste to pad his book-list thickly with flamboyant imitations of the *Souvenir,* and for a time it paid: "Even in the United States alone," to quote Goodrich again, "four thousand volumes of one of these works

[1] *Recollections,* pp. 259–260.

[souvenirs and gift-books], at the price of twelve dollars
each, have been sold in a single season!" By 1830 no less
than forty-one volumes of annuals and gift-books had
appeared, and dozens were in preparation. They were the
literary sensation of the times. Frederick W. Faxon records in his *Literary Annuals and Gift-Books* that "as
the English 'tokens' gradually disappeared, the American
publishers issued an ever-increasing number, until from
1846 to 1852 an average of sixty appeared each year—
sixty-six have been recorded for 1851, and there were
probably others." All the magazines reviewed them, and
even the universities became aware of their presence.
Grenville Mellen, Phi Beta Kappa poet at Harvard in
1830, discussed them merrily as the latest literary fashion
in "The Age of Print":

> For mark yon Book of Beauty—gentle thing!
> All silk outside, and satin all within—
> Call'd New-Year's Presents—and so sung and sold,
> Though born back, sure, full three months in the old.
> With pictures so ineffable, you feel
> You'd proffer pearls for such returns in steel—
> Each leaf of that last daintiness, it seems
> For fairy fingers made, which stir our hair in dreams.

No literary event in early America is more important
in view of results accomplished than the establishment
of these little periodicals. The publishers builded better
than they realized. The most valuable element came almost as an accident. In the 1826 preface of the *Atlantic
Souvenir* there had been this significant statement:

> Every article is the production of our own citizens, sev-
> eral of them highly distinguished in this and foreign coun-
> tries by their writings, and embracing among others, the
> names of Paulding, Bryant, Barker, Sedgwick, and Waln.
> The embellishments, too, it may not be improper to add, are
> in the most finished style of our native artists, and it is be-
> lieved that some of the designs will not injure the reputation

which an American painter has attained in the academies of Europe.

In the second publication (1827) the statement was reiterated:

Flattered and encouraged by the success which last year attended their efforts to introduce a little work to the American public, of a character previously unknown on this side of the Atlantic, the publishers again present their annual volume. In preparing it no effort has been neglected, no expense has been spared, to make it worthy of the patronage, of which they have already received such flattering promise. They have not deviated from the plan, which they at first adopted, of relying solely on our countrymen, both in the literature and embellishments of the volume.

The periodical was also to be kept at the highest literary levels possible in America. The preface to the 1828 edition was emphatic:

The literary portion of the work embraces nearly twice as many articles as were inserted last year; much greater variety has been introduced in their character; a large portion of the most distinguished writers of the country are included among the contributors; and no expense or effort has been spared to obtain and produce the best specimens of native genius. The embellishments have been attended to with, if possible, still more care.

As a result, there grew a tradition which for a decade or more ruled all the more important annuals: American materials only! "The plan at first adopted," announced the *Atlantic Souvenir* in the preface of its third issue, "of making the work exclusively American, has been strictly observed." The same in Volume III of *The Token:* "From the beginning it has been the design of the proprietors to make *The Token* strictly American, we ought to lead the English because of our peculiar scenery and the rich mines of poetic and legendary materials which lie buried in our general and local history."

To the school of young authors just pointing their new quills this was vastly important. The amazing success of Irving and of Cooper had formed clubs of aspiring young writers in Boston, in Philadelphia, in New York, in Baltimore. "There is a rage of authorship," announced young Grenville Mellen. In every community a potential Irving—if only there were means of publication. And this literary newness, the annual, was a happy solution. The *North American Review* in 1829, reviewing a half-dozen specimens just received, hailed the "little golden specks . . . just glimmering above the dim horizon" as perhaps "the twilight dawn of American literature":

These little works, made up of short articles of poetry and prose seem especially suited to the instant genius of our land. The body of our writers are yet young. Few of them have acquired experience and strength enough to venture alone into the world. Here seems to be a fair and pleasant field for them to exercise together, to prove their powers and to prepare them for future and nobler exertions. Not that we would allow our young men to devote their time or talents exclusively, or even to any considerable degree, to work like these. They are literary toys. They serve as a kind of sampler, on which they may practice those niceties and beauties of expression hereafter to be worked in upon more enduring materials.

For the wisdom of this judgment consider the case of Nathaniel Hawthorne. It was Goodrich, editor of *The Token,* who discovered the young author and gave him the adequate publication which perhaps saved him for literature. In his *Recollections* he writes:

I had seen some anonymous publication which seemed to me to indicate extraordinary powers. I inquired of the publishers as to the writer, and through them a correspondence ensued between me and "N. Hawthorne" . . . At this period he was unsettled as to his views; he had tried his hand in literature, and considered himself to have met with a fatal rebuff from the reading world. . . . I combatted his despondence, and assured him of triumph, if he would persevere in a literary career. He wrote numerous articles, which appeared in *The Token*.

For the first time the discouraged young romancer had a free outlet for all he might write, and at prices that kept his pen in motion. In the issue of 1837 Goodrich used eight of Hawthorne's tales, and in all *The Tokens* twenty-six that are surely from his pen. Always anonymous, his pieces in *The Token* are doubtless in excess of this figure.

I

So multitudinous and so miscellaneous were the different publications issued during what Goodrich denominated this "Age of Annuals" that it is necessary to make definitions. First of all, the annual proper, a literary magazine with one issue each year, a miscellany of sketches, short stories, and poems illustrated with illuminated title-pages and steel-engraved plates. During the first decade of "the craze," as Faxon termed it, 1826–1836, an honest effort was made to keep the publications at the highest standards of literary and artistic excellence possible in America. The great success of the *Atlantic Souvenir* in Philadelphia induced Goodrich, leading publisher in Boston, to issue a similar volume, *The Token,* in 1828. "In 1832," his *Recollections* record, "*The Atlantic Souvenir* ceased, and after that time by arrangement with the publishers, its title was added to that of *The Token*." Undoubtedly the leading literary product of "the Age of Annuals," it persisted until 1842. The story is preserved in Goodrich's *Recollections:*

The Token was continued annually till 1842, when it finally ceased. The day of Annuals had, indeed, passed before this was given up, and the last two or three years, it had only lingered out a poor and faded existence. As a matter of business, it scarcely paid its expenses.

Highest in literary quality during this early period before the gift-book and souvenir dissipation began to undermine the whole annual structure were perhaps the following seven publications, in order of merit:

> *The Token*
> *The Atlantic Souvenir*
> *The Talisman,* edited by Bryant
> *The Gift,* with contributions by Poe
> *The Literary Souvenir*
> *The Boston Book*
> *The Opal*

The general public, however, did not buy books for their literary contents: they wanted elegance and show and the consciousness that the book they were buying was at the height of the literary fashion. As a result, the high-grade annual quickly began to degenerate into the second variety of our classification, the gift-book and the souvenir, sporadic publications never exceeding a single issue and depending for their salability almost wholly upon their exquisite bindings and their attractive illustrations. For titles they drew from all the poetic areas of floriculture: *The Dahlia, The Moss Rose, The Hare-bell, The Hyacinth, The Lily, The Magnolia, The Rose of Sharon, The Lily of the Valley, The Amaranth,* and dozens more. They were keyed in their titles and their illustrations and their outer inventory to an age prevailingly sentimental. Gift-books were wanted, and the fact that they were to be had must be made so clear that even the country youth in search of a gift for his sweetheart could find it though blindfolded. According to Faxon's bibliography,[2] no less than twenty of the souvenirs have

[2] Frederick W. Faxon, *Literary Annuals and Gift-Books* (1912).

titles containing the word "Gift." Primarily the volumes, too, were made for feminine destinations: no less than twenty-seven of them contain the word "Ladies'" or "Lady's."

"The public taste," said Goodrich in 1856, retrospective after a long career as a publisher,

grew by feeding on these luscious gifts, and soon craved even more gorgeous works of the kind, whence came Heath's *Book of Beauty*, Lady Blessington's *Flowers of Loveliness*, Bulwer's *Pilgrims of the Rhine*, Butler's *Leaflets of Memory*, *Christmas among the Poets*, and many others of similar design and execution. Many of the engravings of these works cost five hundred dollars each, and many a piece of poetry, fifty dollars a page. In several of these works the generous public spent fifty thousand dollars a year!

At this precise point was born the subscription-book nuisance, the elaborate publication with its steel engravings, its illuminated pages, its scarlet and gold bindings, its contents keyed skilfully to the taste of the gullible public. The drawing-room tables of a whole generation were covered with them. One need but mention such productions as *The Knickerbocker Gallery* (1853), got up as a benefit for the retiring editor of *Knickerbocker's Magazine*, Lewis Gaylord Clark; *The Republican Court, or American Society in the Days of Washington*, edited by the Reverend Rufus Wilmot Griswold; and the whole incredible list of the Griswold editings.

Bryant, in a review of the *Atlantic Souvenir* in his magazine the *United States Review*, was inclined to view the unmistakable tendencies of the annual and the subscription-book "craze" with a shade of pessimism:

There is also a considerable class of rich men who do not read. These latter, however, are not generally insensible to the pleasures of show—they fill their houses with splendid furniture. A book got up like the one before us, with splendid binding, beautiful type, fine paper, and elegant engravings, filled with tales and poems furnished by the most popular writers of our country solicits their attention as a pretty object for a parlor window or a dressing table.

It was the beginning of the best-seller debauch. Everybody was buying, therefore everybody bought—not, however, in the later period of the annuals, with any idea of reading their purchases. Miss Sedgwick, in a souvenir-book tale entitled "Cacoëthes Scribendi," tells of a lover who, on a visit to Boston in the season of "the periodical inundations of annuals," bought two of the pretty things as a present for his sweetheart, and she, "Poor simple girl! she sat down to read them, as if an annual was meant to be read," and the result was a horrible habit, a moral collapse, and finally madness.

Under the third classification I place anthologies, a variety of gift-book publication that became increasingly numerous until at last it festered into a nuisance and worse. During the earliest period of the annuals, the 1820's, anthologies had been made with editorial skill. Such volumes as *Tales from the English Souvenirs* (1829), *Beauties of the Souvenirs* (1829), and *The Spirit of the Annuals* (1831) contained honestly-made selections of the best current fiction and poetry, foreign and domestic; but during the gift-book decade and beyond, the anthologies, an increasing mass of sentimental twaddlings, became insufferable. Young ladies, it would seem, were in danger every moment of corruption, and the only safeguard was to feed them copious doses of pious and sentimental poetic antiseptics—such volumes as *The Young Ladies' Cabinet of Gems, The Ladies' Wreath, a Selection from the Female Poetic Writers, The Lady's Book of Flowers and Poetry,* and a hundred others culminating in the anthologic debauch of the amazing Reverend Rufus Wilmot Griswold.

The final decade, 1846–1856, I have denominated "the racketeering period" of souvenir publication, the period of literary counterfeiting, the period of old wares refurnished, retitled, and sold for new publications. The extent of such counterfeiting seems incredible. Publishers would buy for a nominal price old plates and old engravings and from them reissue year after year new annuals with new names. According to Faxon,

The case of *The Wreath of Wild Flowers,* a book of miscellanies, by John Milton Stearns, published in New York in 1846, and copyrighted in that year, will serve as a final example of how some publishers met the demand for a new annual each year. With the addition of a preliminary poem, and some extra plates, Mr. Stearns' work was used as *Amaranth* in 1851, Boston; *Garland* in 1852, Boston, edited by Emily Percival; *Keepsake of Friendship,* in 1853, Boston, edited by G. S. Monroe; *Tokens of Friendship,* 1854, Boston, and also New York, and finally as *Magnolia,* with a preface date of 1853.

Some of the annuals went through as many as twelve republications with different names. A doting husband during this racketeering decade might buy for his wife as a wedding-anniversary present in 1849 *The Amaranth;* in 1850, *The Garland;* in 1851, *The Keep-sake of Friendship;* in 1852, *The Magnolia;* in 1853, *The Token of Friendship;* in 1854, *The Casket;* in 1869, *Memory's Gift,* and then discover that all the volumes were but reprintings from the old plates of the 1849 *Amaranth,* with changed titles and changed engravings. It is a commentary upon the literary condition of the times that dozens of these flamboyant counterfeits were sold in profitable editions every year, and that no one seems to have complained.

Faxon, in his invaluable bibliography, *Literary Annuals and Gift-Books* (1912), describes 1,115 individual American annuals and gift-books, and an exhaustive search could probably add to his list several hundred more titles. Every organization, religious or social or political, seems to have had its annual:

The Liberty Bell (anti-slavery), 15 volumes
The Masonic Offering
The Missionary Memorial
The Teacher's New Year's Present
The Mourner's Chaplet
The Wedding Gift
Housekeeper's Annual
The Jackson Wreath
The Know-Nothing Token
National Temperance Offering
The Odd-Fellow Offering, 10 volumes
The Rose of Sharon, a Religious Souvenir, 17 volumes
The Religious Souvenir, 7 volumes

By the mid-forties the editing of such volumes had become a profession.

II

One man stands preëminent—Rufus W. Griswold.
Lowell pelted him merrily in his *Fable for Critics:*

But stay, here comes Tityrus Griswold, and leads on
The flocks whom he first plucks alive, and then feeds on—
A loud-cackling swarm, in whose feathers warm dressed,
He goes for as perfect a — swan as the rest.

The greatest of American anthologists, and no area of
American literature has been more diligently worked; no
other nation has so voluminously anthologized its literary
product, especially its poetry. The pioneer work done by
Mathew Carey and by Elihu Smith we have already noted.
Carey alone can vie with Griswold as a collector. For his
American Museum he resurrected 550 specimens of American verse, and in 1794 he supplemented the mass with
another volume of collections which he published with
the title *The Columbian Muse.*
   The next spasm of miserly gathering came in the
1820's: in 1822, *Specimens of the American Poets,* Lon-

don; in 1826, *The Philadelphia Souvenir, a Collection of Fugitive Pieces from the Philadelphia Press;* and the same year, *Miscellaneous Poems; Selected from the United States Literary Gazette.* With 1828 had come the flood. These the opening volumes: *American Commonplace Book of Prose, a Collection of Eloquent and Interesting Extracts from the Writings of American Authors,* by George B. Cheever, 1828; *Specimens of American Poetry, with Critical and Biographical Notices; In three volumes,* by Samuel Kettell, 1829; *The American Common-place Book of Poetry, with Occasional Notes,* by George B. Cheever, 1831. Then close upon their heels had come the collections of Keese, Morris, Bryant, and the rest, culminating in the incredible accumulations of Griswold. Note his editings, most of them made in a single decade:

> *The Biographical Annual,* 1841
> *Gems from the American Female Poets,* 1842
> *The Poets and Poetry of America,* 1842
> *Readings in American Poetry,* 1843
> *The Cypress Wreath: A Book of Consolation,* 1844
> *Illustrated Book of Christian Ballads,* 1844
> *The Poets and Poetry of England,* 1845
> *Poetry of the Sentiments,* 1846
> *Scenes in the Life of the Savior,* 1846
> *Prose Writers of America,* 1847
> *Female Poets of America,* 1848
> *The Sacred Poets of England and America,* 1848
> *Gift Leaves of American Poetry,* 1849
> *The Poetry of Love,* 1849
> *Poetry of the Flowers,* 1851
> *The Gift of Affection,* 1853
> *The Republican Court,* 1853
> *Gift of Flowers, or Love's Wreath,* 1853
> *Gift of Love,* 1853
> *Gift of Sentiment,* 1853
> *Gift of Love,* 1854
> *Gift of Sentiment,* 1854

Three of these volumes have survived, have secured, indeed, a place on the working-desk of every American critic—his *Poets and Poetry of America,* his *Prose Writers of America,* and his *Female Poets of America.* They preserve not only a vast amount of material which otherwise would be inaccessible, but they are full of biographical documents most valuable. Griswold, in preparing his editions, wrote to every living author he was to include in his work and secured not only the biographical matter to be used, but the poet's choice of his work for the collection. Especially is this true of his volume, *Prose Writers of America.* Many of the letters written to him for use in this volume have been reissued in *Passages from the Correspondence and Other Papers of Rufus W. Griswold.*

Griswold's influence upon the mid-century literature was considerable. He edited for a time *Graham's Magazine,* displacing Poe from the editorship and he published a critical review of *Duyckinck's Cyclopœdia of American Literature* (1856) and circulated it as a pamphlet. His part in the Poe tragedy has been much discussed. His biographical introduction to Poe's works unquestionably was unfair in its estimates and full of errors, but that Griswold deliberately tried to defame Poe is to be doubted. He worked with the materials at hand—not many when compared with what we have today; he took many of Poe's wild statements for fact; and he allowed his Puritanic New Englandism to rule his judgment as to Poe's morals. But to make, as many critics do, the Reverend Rufus Griswold the deliberate villain in the sad tragedy of Poe is to work with prejudice rather than facts.

III

One other growth of the vast three-decade swamp of annuals was destined to be significant. In 1830 Lewis A. Godey, a publisher in Philadelphia, viewing the whole craze from a strictly business standpoint, found that the money-making powers of the gift-books lay in a single element: the pleasing of the ladies. Then why not make money by pleasing them oftener? Why not—to use a Hibernianism—a monthly annual? Why not pitch the work exclusively for ladies? The result was *Godey's Lady's Book,* got up with gift-book covers, illuminated title-page, steel engravings, and all the gift-book "fixings," and, in addition, a monthly fashion-plate in colors. A combination was it of the annual and the popular magazine. At only one point was it weak: it lacked a guiding hand, without which it was destined to follow the road of all the annuals, which ran unchanged until they became conventional and ceased publication in about three years. Godey was no editor. Like the later founder of the Curtis Publishing Company, he was only an inspired publisher. He needed an editor, and, glorious luck! he was able to find the one person in the whole United States perfectly fitted for the job: Sarah Josepha Hale of Boston. Moreover, he brought her to Philadelphia, backed her with financial aid, and, with her genius for the work, *Godey's Lady's Book* soon became a national institution.

From the first, Mrs. Hale put the emphasis of her editing upon the feminine. She organized departments for mothers, for daughters, for housewives; she introduced pages of popular music; she made the fashion-plates a distinctive feature; and she organized newnesses with almost every issue. But her success came chiefly from the fact that she trained a school of feminine writers. The age of what Griswold denominated "the female poets" and "the female prose-writers" began with Mrs. Hale and *Godey's Lady's Book.* Women had with her in her magazine the literary right of way—it was a *lady's* book. At length she was able to boast that every article in her magazine had been written by a feminine pen.

By the mid-forties the gift-books and even the few annuals surviving had come to be edited to a large extent

by women. "Emily Percival," a feminine Griswold, edited
no less than twenty-two gift-book volumes; Miss Sarah
C. Edgarton and, later, Mrs. C. M. Sawyer kept *The Rose
of Sharon* annual alive for eighteen years; Mrs. Sigourney
edited some ten volumes with titles like *Voice of the
Flowers, The Religious Keepsake,* and *Young Lady's Offering;* Sarah Josepha Hale edited eight volumes; and
Lydia M. Child, Eliza Leslie, Frances S. Osgood, Hannah F. Gould, Clara Arnold, Alice and Phœbe Cary, and
a dozen others produced at least one gift-book offering—
some, many more.

And the masculine editors, knowing their clientele, were
as sweetly feminine as the women. There was Henry F.
Anners, with his eleven volumes of *The Hyacinth* and
his nine volumes of *The Gift of Friendship;* and it is not
unkind to add to the list Nathaniel P. Willis, with his
two volumes of the *Legendary,* and his long list of other
editings—such titles as *The Gems of the Season* and
Thought Blossoms: excellent training for work on such
journals as the *Mirror* and the *Broadway Journal.* And
one notes that in the final fifties Willis had learned a
literary trick from the counterfeiters of the annuals: he
republished his own early writings under new titles as if
they were being issued for the first time.

The example of *Godey's* was followed quickly by other
publishers. Nearly all of the mid-century magazines, like
Graham's Magazine, Burton's *Gentleman's Magazine,* and
Peterson's and *Sartain's* magazines, used steel engravings,
illuminated title-pages and even fashion-plates, popular
music, and feminine departments.

IV

The episode of the annuals has been neglected in histories of American literature, but to ignore these multitudinous volumes that so made colorful an epoch is an
error. In their early phases they gave help when help was

needed by writers who later were leaders of their generation. Bryant contributed to at least fourteen annuals,
Poe contributed to ten, Emerson to six, Whittier to eighteen, Holmes to twelve, Longfellow to sixteen, Lowell to
sixteen.

They were an important seed-bed, as we shall see, for
what has grown to be a peculiarly American form of
fiction, the short story, and they gave to woman her first
real chance for literary expression. Then, too, they contributed to the success of American art and engraving.
John Cheney (1801–1885), the foremost engraver of
portraits of his time, and John Sartain (1808–1897),
perhaps the greatest of American steel-engravers, owed
much of their success to the steady demand for their work
by these yearly publications.

A curious episode it was, however, this gift-book debauch, and many of its later phases are almost unbelievable. As one stands today in an alcove filled with these
butterfly volumes with their bindings of purple and gold,
their exquisite specimens of the now lost art of steel engraving, their conventional acres of poetry and prose, not
one sentence of which, as a contemporary once boasted,
contains an improper suggestion or an unchaste word—
not a page that could not be read aloud to the children in
a Methodist parsonage—one gets a vision of what the
pious, conventionalized mid-nineteenth century really was
in America.

No one is fitted—and I say it after handling nearly half
of the whole output of three decades—no one is fitted to
criticize Poe or Hawthorne or Longfellow or Herman
Melville or Walt Whitman until one has felt the atmosphere of this amazing jungle in which they were
compelled to work, this jungle of the annuals, the gift-
books, and the anthologies. In an atmosphere created by
Emily Percival and Mrs. Sigourney and the interminable
tribe of pietists and sentimentalists; in an atmosphere of
literary commonplacenesses issued as classics and bought

with eagerness; in an atmosphere of literary ignorance and contempt for literary "high-browism" involving ninety-nine per cent of the whole population, Poe was forced to spend his entire literary life—an editor catering classic creations to a people who bought gift-books as their only literary concession. Longfellow, fresh from Europe, attempted to educate the vulgar mass; Hawthorne retreated from the crowd into romantic seclusion, and at one time came near to quitting entirely the literary game; Herman Melville refused to feed cannibal stories to vulgar readers, and quit entirely; Whitman alone was able to rise from the compost-heap and dominate it, interpret it, and force it into blossom and fruit.

It is useless to denounce them. It is better to echo Samuel L. Knapp who in 1829, in his *Lectures on American Literature,* called them "periodicals of great taste and beauty of execution . . . which have called forth much of the youthful and vigorous literature of our country. . . . It is delightful to look over these fashionable publications, and find so much fine writing in them. A gem of prose is followed by a floweret of poesy, in which sweet descriptions and chaste fancies, give evidence of the improving taste among our scholars."

CHAPTER XXV

THREE DECADES OF THE SHORT STORY

FICTION in shortened form was, at the start, a forced growth from peculiarly American conditions. In an age of fiction, an age when Scott's novels were dominating the English-speaking world, when three-volume novels by a dozen strong British writers loaded the book-stands, the young fiction adventurer in America had little chance. In the absence of international copyright law it was cheaper and surer for American publishers to issue English best-sellers at the mere cost of reprinting than to pay a percentage to an unknown author whose book would probably not pay expenses.

The enormous success, however, of Irving in England with his *Sketch Book* and his *Bracebridge Hall* set the literary bells ringing all over America. A new literary generation was coming on, the second literary generation of the Republic. They were eager to write and to publish novels *à la* Walter Scott, but publishing novels, unless one could pay for having them published, was out of the question. Irving had won his success with sketches and sketchy tales published in a small magazine issued by himself at irregular intervals and later republished as a volume. As a result, a swarm of American sketches. But how get the things into print? Some, imitating Irving, issued their material in the *Sketch Book* manner, in irregularly issued numbers later to be collected into a volume. Thus in 1818–1819 John P. Kennedy and Peter Hoffman Cruse issued their *Red Book;* thus in 1820 Pres-

cott and a group of young Harvard men issued the *Club
Room;* thus in 1821 Richard H. Dana began his *Idle
Man;* and thus in 1827–1828 Bryant, G. C. Verplanck,
and Robert C. Sands put out the *Talisman,* which ran
for three numbers and later was reissued as an annual.

But this was expensive work; it was cheaper to publish
one's Irvingesque sketches in the weekly newspaper or in
some struggling magazine. Poe and Hawthorne were
obliged to contribute their earliest work to village newspapers. But even this literary vehicle was a limited thing,
and it paid nothing for its fiction. Then had come the
annuals and *Godey's Lady's Book,* and then a deluge of
literary magazines. England might prevent the publication of novels in America by glutting the market with her
superior products, but England was not exporting popular magazine material. American effort, therefore, centered itself perforce upon literary forms usable in magazines.

First of all, it *must* be short. Moreover, to be published
within the limits of an annual the tale must be not only
short, but condensed. The demand by all the magazines
was the same: stories complete in a single number, stories
short, compact, entertaining, unsermonic. The short story,
therefore, is simply fiction forced to conform to magazine
conditions. The "art of the short story," concerning which
so much has been written of late, is but the compulsions
forced upon the early magazine writers when they found
themselves obliged to cramp a two-volume novel into a
compass of some five thousand words.

I

All varieties of the lighter literature, especially fiction,
fared better in New York and even in Philadelphia than
in Boston. "The American Athens," as I find Audubon
terming the New England capital as early as 1825, was
serious, classic-minded, impatient of anything that savored

of rebellion or newness. Fiction for generations it frowned upon as a frivolous thing, a destroyer of morals, especially the frail morals of "females." But it was jealous of New York with its Knickerbocker group, and jealous of Philadelphia with its literary magazines. New England, however, never for long suffered itself to be outdone by other sections. Nowhere else has there been such a complete salvaging of all historical and literary traditions. Irving in his *Sketch Book* had told legends of the Hudson. It was two whole generations before Boston awoke to the fact that she, too, in the Irving era had created a classic legend, one as good as "Rip Van Winkle"—"Peter Rugg the Missing Man," the story of the man who lost Boston—Oh, tragedy!—and spent the rest of his life frantically trying to find it. This weird tale, written by William Austin, a Harvard man, a lawyer of the city, had appeared in its earliest version in Buckingham's *New England Galaxy,* September 10, 1824, but it had never been definitely hailed as a classic until Thomas Wentworth Higginson discovered it and so hailed it in his article in the *Independent* of 1888. Since then critics have made much of the tale and much of its author, though he wrote nothing else of value. Boston now can claim a classic written in their barren period that is equal perhaps to Irving's work and better perhaps than anything of Charles Brockden Brown's. Austin has been given major literary honors: in 1890 was issued *Literary Papers of William Austin* and in 1925 *William Austin, the Creator of Peter Rugg,* a biography.

Sadly defective in all that is now considered as making for good short-story art, the tale must nevertheless be rated as an important step in the history of an evolving literary form. It influenced the art of young Nathaniel Hawthorne, a college student at Bowdoin when it appeared in its first version, and unquestionably it has about it an aura of strangeness, of supernatural machinery made

realistic and believable, which is like Poe's and Hawthorne's work which was soon to follow.

Irving still earlier than this had bewitched a group of
young Bostonians fresh from Harvard. Under the leadership of William Hickling Prescott, they had formed a
club, a "literary phalanx, pledged to take the citadel of
fiction by storm." Their *Sketch Book*-like magazine, however, the *Club Room,* ran for only four numbers and it
is today chiefly notable because of Prescott's review of
it in the *North American Review,* April, 1822, under
the title "Essay Writing"—the first critical recognition
of the short story as a distinct literary form. Of the contributors to the book—Prescott, W. H. Gardner, Edward
Everett, Franklin Dexter—Dexter alone, with his tale,
"Recollection," "The first well-told ghost story written
in America," deserves notice save in an exhaustive treatment of the American short story.

II

The founding of the *Atlantic Souvenir* in 1826 marks
the second stage in the development of the short-story
form. In the seven years of this periodical it gathered
about itself what may be called the first "school" of
American "tale"-writers. Forty-six short stories the seven
volumes offered its readers in its seven years, or seven
in each issue. It was the period of anonymous work; not
more than fifty per cent of all contributions to the *Souvenir* or to any other periodical of the time are traceable
as to authorship. Of the known authors, eleven in all,
Paulding wrote eleven tales, William Penn Smith and
Godfrey Wallace each four, Catharine Maria Sedgwick
and William Leete Stone each three, and Lydia Maria
Child two.

Paulding, after Irving's *Tales of a Traveller finale* in
1824, dominated, in quantity at least, a full decade. No

less than forty-eight tales in various gift-books and magazines are traceable to him between the years 1826 and
1836. "Irving put forth no tales between 1824 and 1832,"
says Amos L. Herold, the latest biographer of Paulding;
"Hawthorne and Poe were yet apprentices; and the interval may be fairly named the Paulding decade of the
short story." During the whole of his literary career, according to Herold, the man produced no less than seventy-
six tales.[1]

To Paulding the tale was a journalistic form, a bid for
cash and for literary popularity. He was the first to apply
to the form journalistic devices: variety, timeliness,
stylistic attractiveness, and "movie"-like headlongness. As
a result, he was popular. His work never was anonymous;
on the contrary, it was usually heralded with much exultant horn-blowing. The annual or the magazine that
had secured one of his tales advertised the fact with
methods that seem modern.

Paulding himself considered this shortened fiction of
subliterary importance. He wrote it hastily, as editors
write newspaper editorials, and he made no effort to republish it. His son William in his biography makes no
mention of the tales. Everywhere, even until after the
Civil War, the tale was regarded by all the American
writers and publishers as an inferior creation. Young
writers dreamed of creating novels, but there must first
be an apprenticeship—the creation of magazine stuff.
Hawthorne's first long literary breath came when he found
a market for his novel, *The Scarlet Letter*. No more
Twice Told Tales! He had dreamed of a novel even while
in college, and had written one, had started publishing
it at his own expense, but, his money failing, he had been
compelled to leave it finally half published, a mere torso—
his *Fanshawe* (1828).

The short story has never in America been rated as a

[1] Amos L. Herold, *James Kirke Paulding, Versatile American*
(1926). A complete bibliography is given of the seventy-six stories.

major art form. John Neal, reviewing in 1828 Grenville
Mellen's *Sad Tales and Glad Tales,* had rebuked the
author for issuing mere fragments of fiction:

Why does he not try a novel? These stories, even when
they are well told, are never cared for, never read a second
time, nor ever remembered. People have no time to get
acquainted with your character before they are done with it.
Believe me, you that are scribbling short stories for Albums
and Souvenirs and the whole tribe of yearling literature, and
teachable books, ye are all running to waste. A good story in
twenty-five pages, ought to contain the very pith and marrow
of a good story in three volumes. If so, how can you afford to
throw it away?

Paulding after leaving the Secretaryship of the Navy
in 1841, had much leisure time, and fiction-writing became to him, during a period of fourteen years, what golf
is to many business men of the present day.

Voluminous he certainly was, but not ignorant of
literary art. In such critical essays as "Americanisms"
in the *Analectic Magazine* (1814); certain chapters in
Letters from the South (1817); "National Literature"
in the second series of *Salmagundi* (1820); in the
Fielding-like interchapters of *Koningsmarke,* where he
thoroughly dissects the novelist's art, he lectures like a college professor, and always with critical insight. The whole
chapter he devotes to the arts of extempore writing; in
"Blood-Pudding Literature," about 1849, and in several
of his introductions and prefaces, he laid down the main
requirements of fictional art. One of the earliest was he
to advocate realism, which he termed "rational fiction";
and one of the earliest to protest against the current type
of romance:

The aid of superstition, the agency of ghosts, fairies,
goblins, and all that antiquated machinery which till lately was
confined to the nursery, is not necessary to excite our won-

der or interest our feelings. . . . Real life is fraught with
adventures, to which the wildest fictions scarcely afford a
parallel; and it has this special advantage over its rival, that
these events, however extraordinary, can always be traced
to motives, actions, and passions, arising out of circumstances
no way unnatural, and partaking of no impossible or supernatural agency.[2]

Moreover, he demanded for fiction a style stripped of its
literary affectations and high-flown vocabulary.

But Paulding knew better than he builded. His own
tales do not illustrate his rules. About fifteen of them—
undoubtedly the best specimens of his short-story art—
deal with the New York Dutch first introduced by Irving.
"Cobus Yerks" and "The White Indian" are best, perhaps; tales founded on thorough knowledge of his subject and written with sympathy, unquestionably, yet not
one of these depictings of his own people and their ancient history and superstitions has about it anything like
Irving's inimitable charm. Violating his own rules, he
wrote often of ghosts and fairies, and at times he even
could use European backgrounds. He knew his readers,
however, and he prospered. Why say more? His works
are summer-apples, perfect for their early season but
utterly without keeping-power. He was in middle life
when he began to write his tales: he wrote without enthusiasm; he wrote too much. Deliberately he invented his
situations and his climaxes. He worked in cold blood,
with no moments of inspiration. Realism, truth, simplicity
of expression, American materials are excellent, but with
them there must be that final spark, that nimbus-glow,
that something which in our pitiful poverty of vocabulary
we still call *genius*.

III

When Bryant in 1823, leaving his "dregs of men" profession in the Berkshires, established himself as a *littera-*

[2] "National Literature," *Salmagundi*, II (August, 1820), 266.

teur in New York, he soon found himself in a new atmosphere. For a decade or more New York seemed to be
the literary capital. There he found Cooper, Halleck,
Robert C. Sands, Verplanck, Drake, and a dozen others
with literary ambitions. For a year or more, however, he
was forced to fight as a literary adventurer. His experiment with a literary magazine failed most dismally. With
a family now to support, with only his pen to bring him
income, he frantically tried every literary device he could
conceive of. A sheaf of poems he sold to the *United States
Literary Gazette* for two dollars apiece. Prose alone could
be spoken of in terms of money, and the best-selling prose
of the moment was the annual. Accordingly, in 1828,
1829, and 1830, with Verplanck and Sands, he edited
The Talisman, a gift-book so prosperous that it went
into a second edition in 1833 with the title *Miscellanies.*
Bryant for his share in the partnership contributed eight
short stories, enough to have convinced him that the short
story was not his literary form, but two years later, when
the contributing group, adding to its number Miss Sedgwick, Paulding, and William Leggett, issued another volume, *Tales of Glauber Spa* (1832), Bryant wrote for it
two more—"Medfield" and "The Skeleton's Cave." Poor
work, all of it. "Medfield," the predecessor of de Maupas-
sant's *"Le Hula,"* Ambrose Bierce's "The Damned
Thing," and Fitz-James O'Brien's "What Was It?"—
the story of embodied forces potent yet invisible—with
better art might have been made a classic, but Bryant had
served no apprenticeship in prose fiction.

All the short stories of the period fail because of errors
which it would seem any writer would have felt—even
the crudest. What may be called the *Edinburgh Review*
opening held sway even in the limited space of tales in
annuals. An anonymous reviewer in the *North American
Review* of 1818, after a rambling dissertation filling four
pages, approached his real subject with this naïve paragraph:

But enough of this; now to our author. He must excuse
us, for even reviewers, like the ladies, must follow the fashion; and a reviewer nowadays, without a dissertation at its
head, would look about as singular as a slender maid of
sixteen in close rapt muslin and simple smoothly plaited
hair, amidst expanded hoops and storied headdresses, on a
St. James Court-day.

For artistry one does not go to the early American short
story:

Bryant in his "The Marriage Blunder" begins with a
lengthy dissertation upon marriage, then tells with detail of
a journey he once made into the Red River country, describes a peculiar man he encountered there, and then, after
twelve pages, or one-third the total number of words, have
been used, proceeds to the tale proper.[3]

IV

It was 1828 before Boston awoke to the publication
opportunities of the literary annuals. S. C. Goodrich,
imitating the *Atlantic Souvenir* in its every feature, started
his *Token* annual with a tremendous fanfare of trumpets.
Boston at that time, says Goodrich in his *Recollections of
a Lifetime* (1856),

was notoriously the literary metropolis of the Union—the
admitted Athens of America. Edward Everett had established
the North American Review, and though he had now just
left the editorial chair, his spirit dwelt in it, and his fame
lingered around it. Rich'd H. Dana, Edw'd T. Channing, Jared
Sparks, George Bancroft, and others, were among the rising
lights of the literary horizon.

If Boston was to have an annual, it must be an annual
up to the Boston standards of seriousness and literary
quality, an annual that should surpass Philadelphia's *Atlantic Souvenir* and New York's *Talisman*. And in the

[3] Fred Lewis Pattee, *Development of the American Short Story*
(1923), Chapter II.

end Goodrich accomplished both purposes. *The Token* is the classic among the annuals.

In every issue the statement that no expense and no pains had been spared in getting from the best authors of America the best literary work they were capable of doing. "The literary contributions were," says Goodrich, "equal, on the whole, to any of the Annuals, American or European. Here were inserted some of the earliest productions of Willis, Hawthorne, Miss Francis, now Mrs. Child, Miss Sedgwick, Mrs. Hale, Pierpont, Greenwood, and Longfellow." [4] And, he continues,

The most prominent writer for it was N. P. Willis; his articles for it were the most read, the most admired, the most abused, and the most advantageous to the work. I published his first book, and his two first editorial engagements were with me. . . . Everybody thought Willis worth criticising. He has been, I suspect, more written about than any other literary man in our history.—Next to Willis, Mrs. Sigourney was my most successful and liberal contributor. . . . To Miss Sedgwick, also, *The Token* owes a large share of its credit with the public.[5]

Miss Sedgwick undoubtedly was to *The Token* what Paulding was to the *Atlantic Souvenir*. Every annual and gift-book forgot its practice of anonymity and published always the full names of each of these two contributors with the contributions when fortunate enough to secure them. The short stories of both writers were always put as leading articles and always gloated over in the preface of the volume. Miss Sedgwick, who had early been inspired by Scott, was primarily a novelist, a weaver of her native New England history and tradition into long sentimental fictions or of wild romances laid in the Pyrenees and the Apennines with heroes and villains, mad monks, revengeful queens, rescuing knights and faint-

[4] *Recollections,* II, 263–274.
[5] *Ibid.*

ing maidens superlative in beauty. Her pietistic philosophy was everywhere evident, her moralized endings, her
prim avoidance of everything not in most proper form
and repute. Her fictions, even her sensational romances,
were therefore allowed to circulate in the most Puritanic
parlors. She must be reckoned with as one of the forces
that educated out of New England its narrow prejudices,
an education that was necessary before there could be a
Hawthorne and a *Scarlet Letter*.

Of fictional art, however, she knew little. She simply
sharpened her quill and wrote on and on until she had
two volumes. But the annuals and the magazines demanded
short stories, and she did for them her best. Always need-
ing unlimited room, always impatient of restraint, always
in doubt from chapter to chapter as to what was coming
next, she began her short stories as if they were to be
novels, worked them leisurely until the assigned limit of
words had been reached, and then, inventing hastily a
quick ending, left the thing a torso. For example, her "Le
Bossu" in *Tales of Glauber Spa*. Despite her abundant
output and despite the great popularity of her short-story
work in her own day, not one of all her fictions survives.

The short stories of the gift-book period, then, may be
summed up in general as lacking in constructive art, as lacking compression, as lacking in simplicity and naturalness and
verisimilitude, as lacking indeed most of those elements which
in later years followed the realization that the short story is
not a novel in miniature, but an independent art form with
laws definite and compelling. Yet, despite all these imper-
fections, even in 1830 Miss Mary Russell Mitford, the English novelist and sketch-writer, could declare that American
"lighter fiction" surpassed anything of the kind in Great
Britain, and could deem it worth while to issue three volumes
of it gathered from the gift-books and the annuals in order,
as she expressed it, to remedy this deficiency in her country's
literature.[6]

Poor stuff, all of it, when judged by the standards of today, but out of the vast swamp of it came Nathaniel Hawthorne and Edgar Allan Poe and the beginnings of short-story *art*.

CHAPTER XXVI

SYDNEY SMITH ANSWERED

By 1829 American editors were crowing exultantly. Sydney Smith had been answered. America had produced authors who had been best-sellers in the English markets; American literature was running at high tide with promise unlimited: *an era of literary good feeling.* As early as 1825 the *United States Literary Gazette,* published in Boston, reviewing the volume of poems reprinted from its own columns, *Miscellaneous Poems Selected from the United States Literary Gazette*—Bryant, Longfellow, Percival, and others—could say that "The last six years have witnessed an entire revolution in American literature. We now read American books, and are proud of our American authors."

All at once a series of exultant exhibitions—anthologies, text-books of American literature. The first of them, Samuel Kettell's *Specimens of American Poetry,* filled three volumes. Declaring there had been no orderly and critical collection of American poetry and no treatise "designating with fulness and accuracy, the character of the various performances in verse of our native authors, nor even a tolerably complete list of their names," he made with infinite labor a book that is encyclopedic in its gatherings of stuff for the most part as extinct now as the passenger-pigeon of the same period. From his own standpoint, however, he was the guardian and exhibitor of the nation's most valuable asset, a collection of jewels, as he saw it, that would make Sydney Smith's question seem foolishness.

We are now becoming a literary people, and are already inquisitive upon all matters connected with our character and prospects in that relation. We begin to show a national spirit in letters, and deem it important not only to exhibit to the world what manner of men we are, but to cast an eye upon those who preceded us in the career of literary improvement, and look seriously into the grounds of the insinuation thrown out some years ago by our neighbors across the ocean, that there was no such thing as an American book worthy of being read. Our countrymen have done sufficient since that period to free us from the apprehension that the charge will be repeated; still it is a matter of interest to inquire whether nothing had been achieved before the days of Irving and Cooper and Pierpont and Percival, or whether, on the contrary, there were brave men living before Agamemnon.[1]

Another symptom that an old period was closing and a new one was at hand was the publication the same year, 1829, of Samuel L. Knapp's *Lectures on American Literature*. He, too, would show Sydney Smith the egregious errors of his now infamous review:

. . . you are aware that it has been said by foreigners, and often repeated, that there was no such thing as American literature; that it would be vain for anyone to seek for proofs of taste, mind, or information, worth possessing, in our early records; and some of our citizens, who have never examined these matters, have rested so quietly after these declarations, or so faintly denied them, that the bold asserters of these libels have gained confidence in tauntingly repeating them.[2]

Knapp would convince such skeptics by displaying to them all the American poetry, even back into the Colonial and the Revolutionary periods. The charges of the English critics, he maintained, came from sheer ignorance. Amer-

---

[1] *Specimens of American Poetry* (1829), Vol. I, Preface.
[2] *Lectures on American Literature* (1829), Preface and p. 186.

ica should be proud of a literary history covering two centuries. Like Kettell, he exalted the American poets, especially the recent poets of the new Republic:

This may be said to be an age of poetry. . . . I have no hesitation in saying, that we abound in good poets, whose writings will remain to make up the literature of a future age.[3]

Only two living poets did he appraise—Freneau and Trumbull—and these doubtless only because the two "patriotick bards are so near, in the course of nature, to the confines of a better world, that I felt no reluctance to speak of them."

A noteworthy volume; the first formal history of American literature; a volume, considering the date of its composition, remarkably subdued in its critical tone. Almost wholly are its estimates free from superlatives.

The second anthologist of the period, George B. Cheever, took sharp issue with both Knapp and Kettell. Issuing in 1831 his *American Common-Place Book of Prose,* he argued in his preface, signed "Boston, 1828," that "there are more good prose writers in our country than there are poets" and that compilations have hitherto embraced only the *"morceaux délicieuses"* of English genius. Boston-like, therefore, he would center his work upon the more solid meats of literature; he would bring "the happier efforts of higher minds within the reach of all classes of society."

Volumes indeed symptomatic! They mark the end of an era—American literature become retrospective, evaluated, gathered into historical settings, exhibited as work completed.

I

"Who looks at an American picture or statue?" Smith had demanded. Knapp in 1829 answered with an entire

[3] Knapp, *op. cit.,* p. 187.

chapter of his *Lectures on American Literature:* America, he admitted had indeed produced little of great art, but why look for art in America?

The fine arts can only flourish in the bosom of refinement. They are the latest offsprings of the muse. Poetry is her first born, and painting and statuary the youngest of her children; and there has generally been a long interval between the births of the sisters. Poetry may live in sylvan scenes, and with a primitive people; but the arts must be cherished by wealth and taste, and grow in the sunshine of patronage.[4]

Forced by the plan of his book to omit all mention of living workers, Knapp could present only a pitiful showing of American artists, such ancients as John S. Copley, Benjamin West, Gilbert Stuart—"The fame of Stuart is secure: no chance can destroy it"—Edward G. Malbone and Colonel John Trumbull. The new and brilliant school of artists—Washington Allston, Horatio Greenough, Hiram Powers, William W. Story, Thomas Crawford and the rest—the group which two decades later was to be written up in a volume by H. T. Tuckerman with the title *Artist Life, or Sketches of American Painters,* was too young in 1829 for much glorification, even had Knapp's plan permitted its treatment.

II

Smith's next question, "Who goes to an American play?" was also an embarrassment in the crowing thirties. There had been William Dunlap, with his adaptations, and there had been James Nelson Barker, whose metrical play, *The Indian Princess, or la Belle Sauvage,* founded on the Pocahontas legend, had had a run in London, the first American play, in all probability, to be produced in

[4] Knapp, *op. cit.,* p. 189.

England. But Barker, even though he wrote in Shake-spearean numbers, was no answer to Sydney Smith.

America was seeking a dramatist, however, who would be an answer, and the demand of the twenties was native American themes à la Irving and Cooper. A writer in the *American Quarterly Review,* June, 1827—Paulding, per-haps—reviewing the published plays of Dunlap, presented the matter with clearness:

By a national drama, we mean, not merely a class of dra-matic productions written by Americans, but one appealing directly to the national feelings; founded upon domestic in-cidents—illustrating or satirizing domestic manners—and, above all, displaying a generous chivalry in the maintenance and vindication of those great and illustrious peculiarities of situation and character, by which we are distinguished from all other nations. . . . It is this which we would call a na-tional literature; and, unless we greatly err, it is these char-acteristics which must, eventually, constitute the principal materials of one. We have no peculiar language to create an identity of our own; and it must, in a great measure, be in its apt and peculiar application to ourselves, our situation, character, government and institutions, that our literature would seem destined to become national.

But no such work was forthcoming. In the province of the drama America has always done her feeblest work—until recent years hardly a play that has maintained its position as a classic. But even before the 1820's America had a dramatist whose plays could "make" the English stage. According to Quinn, John Howard Payne's *Brutus, or the Fall of Tarquin* was produced in the Drury Lane Theater, London, December 3, 1818, when its author was twenty-seven:

It was an immediate success, and was performed during the rest of that season more than fifty times. It is interesting to note that more than a year before Sydney Smith uttered his famous "In the four quarters of the globe who reads an

American book or goes to an American play?" the British
public was thronging Drury Lane to see one of the most successful tragedies written in English in the nineteenth century.[5]

Payne was a racial mixture, his father a New England
Puritan, his mother a Jewess—it accounts for the restlessness of the man, his instability, his breaking away
from the conventional. Artistry and temperament and, in
view of the feminine thirties and forties in which the
man lived, early physical charm came from his mother.
"She was of great personal attractions and varied accomplishments," [6] wrote Payne's biographer.

One of his most intimate friends in writing of him says,
"Nature bestowed upon him a countenance of no common
order, and his eyes glowed with animation and intelligence.
A more extraordinary mixture of softness and intelligence
was never associated in a human countenance, and his face
was an index of his heart. He was a perfect Cupid in his
beauty, and his sweet voice, and self-possessed yet modest
manners made him a most engaging prodigy." [7]

A contemporary document that lights up like a lantern
a feminine age with its lady's books, its golden gift-books,
and its Willises.
New York, where Payne was born in 1791, was his
home until he was five, then Boston until he broke away
at twelve to live his own life first in a New York count-
ing-room, then for a few weeks in college, and finally,
to the horror of his Puritan father, in theatrical work.
At eighteen he had found his profession. In the part of
Young Norval in the tragedy *Douglas,* he captured New

[5] Arthur Hobson Quinn, *A History of the American Drama, from
the Beginning to the Civil War* (1923), p. 170.
[6] Charles H. Brainard, *John Howard Payne, A Biographical Sketch
of the Author of "Home Sweet Home" with a narrative of the removal of his Remains from Tunis to Washington* (1885).
[7] *Ibid.,* p. 14.

York. The ladies "adored him," and that in the 1820's was glory. As Young Norval he captivated Philadelphia, Baltimore, Boston, the South, and then in 1813, when he was twenty-two, Drury Lane Theater, London. Success in England came instantly and overwhelmingly: "The performance from beginning to end excited tumultuous applause, and the house rang with thunders of approbation at the power exhibited by Payne in the death-scene in the last act of the play."

Perfectly was the man in chord with an oversentimental, melodrama-loving, feministic age. Payne, Willis, Morris, Fay, Mrs. Sigourney, Sarah Josepha Hale, Grace Greenwood, Fanny Fern—one must read them all with attention before he undertakes Poe, Hawthorne, Melville, Whitman, Thoreau and the others of the thirties and forties who strove for originality in that bog of sentimentalism and cheap glory.

Payne was in Europe nineteen years. Leaving the stage early, he threw all his powers into the work of supplying the London theaters with plays. Originality was not among his literary canons. He was a dramatic distiller, a revamper, an adapter. His hunting-ground he found richest in France. And all of his skilful revampings were accepted eagerly by the London managers, often to meet with surprising success. For his best play, *Brutus,* he distilled the best elements of some ten previous dramas. He had no ambitions save the success of the moment. In the preface of his adaptation of Ducange's *Thérèse ou l'Orpheline de Genève,* an adaptation done in three days to meet a great success in Drury Lane, February, 1821, Payne confessed that he had abandoned all hope of literary distinction. The play, he explained,

. . . is a work planned for stage effects exclusively, and printed for managers and actors only. It is so necessary in the production of the modern drama to consult the peculiarities of leading performers, and not offend the restive spirit by means of situations almost pantomimic and too impatient to pause for poetical beauty, that it seems almost hopeless to look to the stage of the present day for a permanent literary distinction.[8]

An instinct Payne had that was genius for catering to the tastes of his audiences, but as to the permanence of his plays they are now as dead as the month-old "movie" of today. Payne lives, and undoubtedly will live, however, because of a lyrical fragment in his play *Clari, or the Maid of Milan,* played in Covent Garden in 1823— "Home Sweet Home." Two stanzas only there are, and the music—the plaintive melody that has done so much to put soul into the words—was not his, yet this single tiny fragment has so touched the universal deeps that are in all men and all nations that when the author of them died in Tunis where he was United States Consul, his own Government and that of Great Britain united in the work—thirty years later, to be sure—of removing his remains to his native land and reinterring them with as much reverence and ceremony as if he had been a Washington or a Lincoln.

Washington Irving collaborated with Payne on the melodrama *Charles the Second; or, the Merry Monarch,* his light, humorous touches everywhere recognizable, but the success of the play in London was due to Payne's intuitive knowledge of stagecraft, of his actors, of his audience. Even Irving's literary touch, however, could not give permanence. Payne, despite the brilliance of his London offerings, has become a mere tradition: a single-lyric poet like Samuel Woodworth and George P. Morris and Francis Scott Key. Quinn, however, would add another laurel: his influence. "In dramatic history, his reputation grows as we watch the influence of *Brutus* upon later playwrights,"' and he instances the work of Edmund Kean and of Sheridan Knowles.

At all odds, the man silenced Sydney Smith. During

[8] Quinn, *op. cit.,* p. 175.

two decades at least an answer to his historic question, "Who goes to an American play?" could be given in two words: all London.

III

Still another American product answered Sydney Smith. Beginning in 1828, there was published in England a work which demanded an initial outlay of some two hundred thousand dollars, which was sold by subscription at two guineas for each of twenty-seven parts, or something like two hundred and seventy dollars a set, and which was paid for in full by British subscribers—Audubon's *Birds of America,* a work that can be pronounced unique. That an unknown American, a man who had spent most of his life on the wild frontier, a man without money or social position or fame, could perform so impossible a feat in the England of the 1820's and 1830's is one of the sensational episodes in our picturesque history.

A romantic figure, John James Audubon. Much doubtful legend has grown up about him, but even when this is stripped away, as it has been by a careful biographer,[9] fully as much of romance still remains. His father, a French sailor, adventurer, ship-commander, merchant, in the 1790's had been for six years a factor for a French trading company with headquarters at Les Cayes, Santo Domingo. Here was born out of wedlock, his mother a Creole of Santa Domingo, the future naturalist. Taken as an infant to France, his birth was legitimized in 1794, he was educated in the schools, and, his tastes inclining toward the graphic arts, he was for a time placed under the tutorship of the French artist David.

The mother disappears at once from the story: we

[9] Francis H. Herrick, *Audubon the Naturalist; a History of His Life and Time* (1917).

know only her name—Rabin. Of his father, later prominent in the French navy, we know more. From him
undoubtedly came Audubon's mercurial temperament, his
restless energy, his versatility. From his mother, perhaps,
came the personal characteristics which, in the sentimental, melodramatic age in which he lived, contributed
so much toward his ultimate success—his striking physical beauty, his charm of manners, his wealth of curly hair
which he wore like a French *coureur de bois,* his ability
to dramatize himself with effectiveness, and his dominating tendency toward the romantic.

His adventures in frontier towns of Kentucky, in the
Louisiana bayous and other regions where he sought for
bird life, we need not follow. He had caught a vision
even as a boy in France of what was to be his life-work
—illustrations of bird life. When he was eighteen he had
been sent by his father to America to an estate he had
acquired near Philadelphia, and here the dream of his
boyhood—to become the depicter and biographer of the
birds—became an obsession. The rest of his life is a story
of wanderings in search for birds. Married early, he
dragged his wife and family into areas of privation where
for mere subsistence—once he was in jail for debt—he
was often forced to teach art, music, dancing, any work
possible to get, but never did he forget his real life-work.
By 1824 he was ready for a publisher, but Philadelphia,
the leading publishing city, was aghast at the magnitude
of his demands. America was unprepared for such a task.
Testimonials, however, it could supply in abundance, and
with a sheaf of these and with funds for the voyage from
his wife's savings, he went in 1826 to England to seek a
publisher—a wild-goose chase, it would seem, that made
John Neal's adventure look trivial. The work demanded
double elephant-folio illustrations to the number, as it
later proved, of 435, and, with these, five volumes of text
with the title *Ornithological Biography.* To find adequate

engravers for such drawings, adequate printers, and, greatest of all, to find subscribers for so colossal a work seemed impossible. Says his biographer, Herrick:

The story of this unknown foreigner's struggles and eventual success in the Europe of that period, which in an economic sense still belonged essentially to the eighteenth century, is one of the strangest romances in the history of science and literature of the past hundred years.

The work, completed in May, 1839, invites at once comparison with the earlier ornithological volumes of Alexander Wilson which had had American publication and American subscribers. Wilson, it will be remembered, was primarily a poet. To him, birds were lyrical subjects. He socialized them, put them into Scotch plaids, as Burns did the mouse and the daisy, and sentimentalized them. Audubon was an artist in the woods, lawless, romantic, melodramatic—a Natty Bumppo with a pencil. He dramatized the birds, set them in theatric poses with appropriate background scenery. Neither of the men was a scientist. They recorded no measurements, no "crop contents," no classifications. They were wandering romanticists with a passion for delineation. The frontier with its limitless mystery, the new unexplored spaces where anything might happen and anything might be found, lured them on and on.

Of the two, Audubon was the less literary. Had Sydney Smith, perchance, been confronted with Audubon's elephant folios he might have retorted, "Yes, but who *reads* this American book?" Certainly not its original subscribers —English noblemen and rich bourgeois illiterates. Primarily the book was not made to be read: the bird biographies were of secondary importance. The drawings sold the book. Scattered through the text, however, are descriptions of frontier scenes and characters, and these today, with published parts of his journals, are his only additions to what may be called *literature*. Valuable enough they are to warrant republication a century after their first printing—*Delineations of American Scenery and Character* (1926), by John James Audubon, London. But even these best pages are valuable chiefly as historical documents, contemporary pictures of the vanished frontier, rather than literary masterpieces.

Audubon's influence, however, like Payne's in his own field, has been far-reaching. Everywhere today is he acknowledged to be "the father of American ornithology." Elliott Coues could hail his one classic as "the greatest monument erected by art to nature." And again: "Vivid and ardent was his genius; matchless he was both with pen and pencil in giving life and spirit to the beautiful objects he delineated with passionate love."

CHAPTER XXVII

THE FEUDAL SOUTH

THE ANALOGY between the Southern plantation and the English landed estate came primarily from a reading of Scott's romances and Irving's *Bracebridge Hall*. The first to mold this analogy into literary form and to make of it a tradition affecting in time the whole South was John P. Kennedy, whose gentle characterizations entitled *Swallow Barn* (1832), strung on a thin thread of story novel-like in its movement, was a treatment of early nineteenth-century Virginia as if the state were a detached county of Georgian England. The chapter entitled "Traces of the Feudal System" is not at all of American democratic texture. *Swallow Barn* might be published as Book II of Irving's sketchy *Bracebridge Hall*—traces of feudal England in English America.

"From Charlottesville," wrote Kennedy in his romance, *Horse-Shoe Robinson,* "both north and south from the Potomac to the James river, there extended a chain of posts, occupied by lordly and open-hearted gentlemen,— a kind of civil cordon of bluff free-livers who were but little versed in the mystery of 'bringing the two ends of the year together.'" And in *Swallow Barn:*

The gentlemen of Virginia live apart from each other. They are surrounded by their bondsmen and dependents; and the customary intercourse of society familiarizes their minds to the relations of the high and low degree. They frequently meet in the intercourse of a large and thriftless hospitality.

Everywhere save in mere geography the English tradition:

The laws of primogeniture exercised their due influence on the national habits; and the odious division of property amongst undeserving younger brothers, whom our modern philosophy would fain persuade us have as much merit, and as little capacity to thrive in the world as their elders, had not yet formed part of the household thoughts of these many-acred squires.

So much for the "F. F. V." aristocracy of the pre-Jacksonian era, the era to be illuminated by the romances of Scott. Not at all was it uneducated, nor in a general way was it unliterary. Like Kennedy's typical aristocrat, Ned Hazard, the heirs of the manor were educated at Princeton or even Harvard, where they diluted their inevitable law studies with flavorings of classic literature.[1]

At their best they had a finer humane culture and greater social charm than any other Americans. But as they felt the world more and more against them, this was not enough. Walter Scott provided the escape. As they devoured his novels of feudal life they came to think of themselves as knights with arms at rest against peoples who did not understand the laws of chivalry, as an aristocracy forced to defend themselves against plebeians. . . . Walter Scott provided the romantic setting for a sort of neo-feudalism in social outlook, and it was said that his books were shipped South in car-load lots. From the fourth decade of the century, Southern books, letters and diaries become glutted with talk about cavaliers and knights.[2]

Kennedy saw Virginia through the reminiscent eyes of his Old Dominion mother. He painted it in softened colors, and he left out all elements of vulgarity and dis-

---

[1] The best treatment of Southern feudalism is in William P. Trent's *William Gilmore Simms*, pp. 31–37, or in Thomas Nelson Page's *The Old South: Essays Social and Political* (1892).

[2] James Truslow Adams, *America's Tragedy* (1934), pp. 95, 119.

cord, yet fundamentally the man was a realist. His picturings of early Virginia personalities are flash-light
revelations: flashlights romantically tinted. This of Ned
Hazard:

He came to his estate, upon his arrival at age, a very model
of landed gentleman. Since that time his avocations have
had a certain literary tincture; for having settled himself
down as a married man, and got rid of his superfluous fop-
pery, he rambled with wonderful assiduity through a wilderness of romances, poems, and dissertations, which are now
collected in his library, and, with their battered blue covers,
present a lively type of an army of continentals at the close
of the war, or a hospital of invalids. These have all, at last,
given away to the newspapers—a miscellaneous study very
attractive and engrossing to country gentlemen.

They even discussed literature in their after-breakfast
gatherings in the parlor, the ladies always voluble at the
mention of poetry:

He fell into conversation with Prudence upon literary
topics, and nothing could be more refreshing than to hear
how much she had read, and how passionately she admired.
. . . Prudence proclaimed Cowper to be her favorite bard,
and that was exactly Swansdown's preference. They both
disliked the immorality of Byron, and admired Scott. And
both recited delicious lines from "The Pleasures of Hope."

As to literary creation by a Southern gentleman or
lady, that was another thing. "Of course," replied
Swansdown, "if a man has ever been guilty in his life of
stringing couplets, he becomes a scapegoat ever after."
It was the period of literary anonymity, of authors who,
like Scott, had the grotesque idea that writing was no
occupation for a gentleman. If such an exalted personage
must write, let him write only what the eighteenth century
called "elegant literature," and in all decency let him, like
Scott, attach to it not his own name but a pseudonym. In

dedicating his *Horse-Shoe Robinson* to Washington Irving, Kennedy could write, "You have convinced our wise ones at home that a man may sometimes write a volume without losing his character," but nevertheless to the title-page of his own romance Kennedy affixed not his own name but the pseudonym "Mark Littleton." An eighteenth-century concept that died hard.

I

For literary analysis, the South falls into three areas—the Virginians, the South Carolinians, and the South-westerners—areas which in the efflorescent forties voiced themselves in three gift-book volumes to prove they were as cultured as Boston or Philadelphia: *The Baltimore Book, The Charleston Book,* and *The New Orleans Book.*

In the first area, Baltimore on the northern border was the earliest to capitalize distinctively its literary assets. As early as the close of the second war with England it had acquired a leader of energy and distinction, Dr. Tobias Watkins, later to hold the office of Assistant Surgeon-General of the United States. At this early period he was amusing himself with a little magazine, the *Portico,* kept alive by a group of young professional men, mostly lawyers with literary leanings. The advent of three headlong New England Yankees—John Pierpont and John Neal, the latter hailed at once as "Jehu O'Cataract," the two in Baltimore on a business venture, and Paul Allen, newspaper editor—brought into the old city a new literary vigor. A roaring young literary society, the Delphian Club, was organized, with Watson as president and Pierpont as vice-president. In its Salmagundi-Club-like meetings young Neal awoke to literature, and Pierpont gained inspiration for his volume of poems, *Airs of Palestine,* for a generation rated North and South as a minor classic.[3] Later, two of the group, Watkins and

[3] The fullest account of this club is in Neal's *Wandering Recollections,* p. 44.

Neal, were to write *The History of the American Revolution,* a volume usually attributed to Paul Allen.

Out of this moment of Baltimore renaissance, however, came only one scrap of literature that deserves today more than mere mention, the translation in *Tales of the Tripod* of a German romance which Tobias Watkins rechristened "The Adventures of a Watchman." Elsewhere I have characterized this work:

It is the first bit of American fiction, original or otherwise, that has sprightliness of style, rapidity of movement by means of conversation and sparkling dialogue. Good dialogue came late into our literature.[4]

He who was to become the leading Baltimore author, however, was too young to be a member of the club— John P. Kennedy. This from a letter he wrote to Griswold:

They had a club called "The Delphian," where they let off all their gas which was too sharp for the public. I was very young, at least not of age, and wrote several articles for *The Portico,* but was not a member of "The Delphian" nor was my friend Cruse. He and I soon after this, in 1818, got up our *Red Book* which was rather *anti-Delphian.*

The model of this *Red Book* was undoubtedly Irving's *Salmagundi,* at that early period still a book to be modeled after. Published anonymously for two years, 1818–1819, it did to Baltimore society what the earlier Salmagundians had done to New York. The poetry, often sharp with satire, in a series of odes and epodes entitled "Horace in Baltimore," came from the pen of Peter Hoffman Cruse, a young genius whose early death was mourned, and perhaps with reason, as an irreparable loss to American literature. The prose, sprightly, Irvingesque,

[4] Fred Lewis Pattee, *Development of the American Short Story* (1923), p. 36.

humorous even when read in the light of today, was
Kennedy's.

Born in Baltimore of a Scotch-Irish father and a Virginian mother, educated at Baltimore College, trained for
his profession, the law, in the office of his Uncle Pendleton, a soldier in the Revolutionary War early thrown into
politics, thrice member of Congress, then Secretary of
the Navy—this in brief the biography of John Pendleton
Kennedy. Literature was to him an avocation, an escape,
a recreation after strenuous professional work, as some
today turn to golf. Stimulated by Scott and doubtless by
Cooper, he issued in 1835 his long historical romance,
Horse-Shoe Robinson, a Tale of the Tory Ascendency.
Analogous is it with Cooper's *The Spy,* the story of a
war area of divided allegiance, of brother against brother,
with the border superman, Horse-Shoe Robinson, the
counterpart of the earlier hero, Harvey Birch. More
carefully documented is it than most of Cooper's work.
Kennedy wrote it, he explained, "To amuse the lover of
literature" and at the same time "to illustrate the temper
and character of the War of the Revolution." That he
accomplished both of these aims speaks highly of his
powers as a novelist. Starting with the primary thesis
"that the actions of real life are full as marvellous as the
inventions of romance," he gave always the impression
that his tale was bare realism, based, even in its most
unbelievable areas, upon documented truth. His simple
plot allowed utmost latitude: the hero of the story, an
American officer, is captured by the Tories and brutally
handled for upward of two months. His escapes and re-
capturings during this period, the remarkable adventures
of the spy, Horse-Shoe Robinson, the heroic intervention
of the maiden whom in the end the hero marries, the
whole ending in a tremendous fifth act—the Battle of
King's Mountain—allow episodes in romantic profusion.

In characterization and in humor the romance surpasses
anything in Cooper's category. In stylistic graces, too, in

lightness of touch, in use of dialogue it is an improvement upon Cooper. But Kennedy, it must be remembered, was no pioneer. He wrote with full knowledge of all the flood of criticism that had been poured upon the elder novelist. Moreover, his temperament was more Irving-like, more gentle, more intolerant of literary slap-dashery.

One other romance, *Rob of the Bowl,* completes Kennedy's fictional list, a poor showing as to quantity when one considers the man's literary quality. His best powers he gave to public life. He was in Congress, he held state offices, and he was a member of a president's cabinet. Had he surrendered all his powers to the creation of fiction, it is not too much to hazard the guess that he would have surpassed even Irving and Cooper. Even as it is, the volume *Horse-Shoe Robinson,* twice reprinted of late, must be reckoned, all things considered, as the best historical romance created in America before the Civil War.

Of Kennedy's aid to Poe, the first real aid given the struggling young genius, more anon.

Virginia romance before Kennedy was a matter of some half-dozen volumes:

Tales of an American Landlord; Containing Sketches of Life South of the Potomac, 1824, an anonymous volume of religious atmosphere, dull and heavy.

The Valley of the Shenandoah, George Tucker, 1824, containing the first traces of Southern realism. "It contains, a faithful, though not very readable portrait of a decaying planter family." (Hubbell).

The Kentuckian in New York, by a Virginian, 1834.

The Cavaliers of Virginia, or the Recluse of Jamestown, 1834.

The Knights of the Horse-Shoe; a Traditionary Tale of the Cocked Hat Gentry of the Old Dominion, 1845. This and the two preceding by William Carruthers, the most noteworthy literary figure in Virginia before Kennedy. He wrote with verve and color, but he leaned too heavily upon his English models.

The Partizan Leader, Nathaniel Beverly Tucker, 1836.

A certain floridness and flourish—literary embroidery —one finds in all these romances of the South, even at times in the work of Kennedy and William Gilmore Simms. Mark Twain attributed it to the influence of Scott: "It was Sir Walter that made every gentleman in the South a Major or a Colonel, or a General or a Judge, before the war; and it was he also that made these gentlemen value their bogus decorations."

Handicapped by anonymity, by Northern prejudice and Southern indifference, no fiction of the South got the recognition it deserved. Had the North, especially New England, produced these romances, more, perhaps, would have been made of them.

II

In the South Carolina midland area, the dominating city of which was Charleston, there was also a feudal aristocracy, but one less romantic. In place of the New England "Brahmin caste," there ruled a "law-lord" caste —the sons and grandsons of lawyers. The state was legal-minded, sensitive as to rights, argumentative. They took to government, to affairs, to leadership. The analysis by William P. Trent, himself a Southerner, in his definitive biography of Simms, is illuminating:

Very stately gentlemen they were, those distinguished Charlestonians. Courtesy sat upon them like a well-fitting garment, albeit they preserved an air of coldness and reserve, reminding one of their unsociable houses which rose behind walls shutting in beautiful gardens, which it would have been a sacrilege for the public to enjoy. Among their number there were not a few who would have been distinguished for their classical attainments even in a European capital,—men who, in the words of one of their descendants [Paul Hayne], "looked upon literature as the choice recreation of gentlemen, as something fair and good, to be courted in a dainty, amateur fashion, and illustrated by apropos quotations from Lucretius, Virgil, or Horace." [5]

And again:

While professing to hold culture and literary attainments in high repute, they have consistently snubbed or disregarded all efforts that looked toward the creation of a home literature. While chivalrously careful of the sensibilities of their equals, they have ignored, as a rule, the existence of such sensibilities in their inferiors.[6]

Which leads us to the leading literary personality produced by the whole South—if we exclude, for the moment, Poe—William Gilmore Simms.

Simms, though Charleston-born, was not at all of the Charleston aristocracy. In his own words:

I am a native of Charleston—my father came from Ireland when a boy. My mother's family came from Virginia. . . . My father was a volunteer in the Creek War under Jackson in Coffee's brigade of mounted men.[7]

And again:

My mother died when I was an infant. My father failed as a merchant, and emigrated to the West about the same time, leaving me with an aged grandmother, and a small maternal property which the latter hoarded so religiously as to withhold the appropriations necessary to my education. In consequence of this, the utmost of my attainments were those of a grammar school, irregularly attended, for I was so frequently sick in boyhood that it was almost the conviction with all that I could not be raised. But even sickness had

[5] Trent, *op. cit.,* p. 25.
[6] *Ibid.,* p. 30.
[7] Quoted by Trent, *op. cit.,* p. 79.

its advantages. I got books, devoured them—books of all kinds without order or discrimination.[8]

In everything a youth of intensity, a Southern John Neal. He studied law and abandoned the profession, edited for a year a literary magazine which failed, made two journeys on horseback into the wild Southwest border regions where his father lived a life of adventure, and issued six volumes of verse before he was twenty-six. Then finding that his native city would help him not at all, he made his first trip to the North, visited Bryant and the leading Knickerbockers, and even penetrated into New England where he settled for a period to write what he felt the whole literary world was to hail as a classic, his *Atalantis; A Story of the Sea*. A tale intense with Celtic fervor and mysticism. A sea fairy is persecuted by the love of an ocean demon and is rescued by mortal intervention. But the North was as indifferent to his work, it proved, as had been the South. Though adequately published in New York, it aroused no enthusiasm. All through his life eager for recognition as a poet, he never once won it. Enough. Why disinter the dead?

Recognizing his defeat as a poet, he now turned to prose romance, his first attempt being *Martin Faber* (1833). Then had come the deluge. In the next thirty-seven years he poured out thirty-four volumes of fiction and forty-two other volumes as I count them: poetry, biography, Shakespearean editions, orations, dramas, criticism, and miscellanies. Trent, counting everything, lists in his biography 103 items; Oscar Wegelin, in his Simms bibliography, lists eighty-three.

During much of his early career the novelist resided in the North where were published all of his books. "One is almost tempted," wrote Trent, "to regard him as a Knickerbocker." His friendship with nearly all the North-

[8] *Passages from the Correspondence and Other Papers of Rufus W. Griswold*, 1898, p. 78.

ern literati and publishers had a most salutary effect, since it did much to obliterate the prejudice felt by New York and Philadelphia and Boston for Southern writers. Vastly better was he treated in New York than in Charleston. His novel *Guy Rivers* was for a time more popular than the current romances of Cooper and Bird and Flint and Paulding. In the North he had arrived, but return to the South brought him bitterness. "In Charleston," says Trent, "he still found himself a nobody, and he bitterly contrasted the warmth of the North with the coldness of the South." Never did he overcome this aristocratic coldness, even after he had won literary fame surpassing any other writer below the Virginia line and had founded literary magazines in the city that were to be to the South what *Graham's* and the *Atlantic Monthly* were to the North. Even when, after the death of his first wife, he married into the ranks of the aristocracy, he still was treated with contempt. He was not to the manner born: it explains, perhaps, his failure to achieve a success in literature commensurate with Irving's and Cooper's and Hawthorne's.

The success of *Guy Rivers* intoxicated the young writer. Inspired by Cooper's Leather Stocking romances, he wrote *The Yemassee, a Romance of Carolina,* a tale centered in early Indian life, yet one differing completely from the Cooper model. To Cooper, the Indian was an Uncas, a "noble savage" created and equipped from his imagination; to Simms, the Indian was the drunken brute he had seen in the gutters of frontier towns, or else the dignified chiefs he had glimpsed in his travels in the Southwest. Both types he treated with realism; at times, however, with melodrama.

In 1835 and 1836 come two romances of *The Spy* order—*The Partisan; a Tale of the Revolution,* and *Mellichampe, a Legend of the Santee*—the first of seven historical romances dealing with the great struggle:—*The*

Kinsmen, or the Black Riders of the Congaree; Katharine Walton, or the Rebel of Dorchester; The Sword and the Distaff; The Forayers, or the Raid of the Dog-Days; Eutaw, a Sequel to the Forayers.

Unquestionably these fictions surpass Cooper's in the same field. They have verisimilitude: they win and hold the reader, even the modern reader; they have movement, headlong at times; and they present a picture of the Southern phase of the Revolution more accurate than may be found elsewhere in fiction. There are episodes and even chapters that burn themselves into one's memory and refuse to be erased, like the massacre by Cornwallis of the prisoners taken in the Battle of Camden. There are other episodes that stir the blood, as, for instance, the rescue of Walton by the "Swamp Fox." Always, however, the movement gallops, or seems to gallop, along the brink of melodrama; in such creations as *Richard Hurdis, Border Beagles,* and *Beauchampe* it topples over. But is it melodrama? Approaching the volumes after a session with Longstreet's *Georgia Scenes,* one is inclined to rate it as realism. Simms knew his South Carolina, especially the two-thirds of it that lay outside the areas of the aristocratic tradition. The Revolution had been a civil war, and the frontier Tories had been murdering devils. And Simms painted them in their true colors, shrinking from nothing, however physically disgusting. And right at this point he broke with his parent South. Poe, usually superlative in his praise of Simms, put his finger unerringly upon this fatal blemish: he had forgotten the gentle readers of Scott in the Charleston manor-houses:

The "bad taste" of the *Border Beagles* was more particularly apparent in *The Partisan, The Yemassee,* and one or two other of the author's earlier works, and displayed itself most offensively in a certain fondness for the purely disgusting or repulsive, where the intention was or should have been merely the horrible. The writer evinced a strange pro-

pensity for minute details of human and brute suffering, and
even indulged at times in more unequivocal obscenities.[9]

It is the verdict of a literary aristocrat condemning a
born literary commoner. The same charge could not
be brought against Cooper, for Cooper was a romanticist
and an aristocrat. Vast areas of the life of the times
that he dealt with he avoided as if it were outside the
realm of literature. So in limited degree with Kennedy,
who worked in the same materials as did Simms.

The failure of Simms came at this very point: suffering from literary astigmatism, a realist of the modern
type, a born democrat, striving to be a romanticist, striving to enter the holy areas of a "Hotspur" aristocracy.
Realizing the truth of Poe's criticism, he tried, like
Cooper, to work with wholly refined materials, foreign
backgrounds: *Pelayo; a story of the Goth, The Damsel
of Darien, Vasconselos.* In vain; to depict aristocracy was
beyond his powers.

That he had to look to the North for publication, for
praise, for support—the North that despised literary
Southerners; that he had to find his congenial friends in
Northern offices and Northern homes, hurt him far more
than his contemporaries knew. All that a man could do
for his native city and his homeland South he did. He
was nurse of her literary bantlings. *The Charleston Book,
a Miscellany in Prose and Verse* (1845), which he edited,
in it no scrap of his own writing, was an exhibition of
worthlessness, but he made it in good faith for the glory
of his city. So with his magazines, his constant help to
Hayne and Timrod and the rest. Finally his impetuous
heart was broken by the failure of the war, the loss of his
home burned by Sherman's raiders, and the decreasing
demand for the writings into which he had put his life.

A man of driving force most unusual, of picturing
power not often surpassed, of courage that dared present

[9] Poe's *Works,* 1836 edition, III, 272.

in modern fashion even utter realism, Simms was hamstrung by his times and his environment. The upholders of "the great tradition" in the North, the Transcendentalists, the Harvard literary aristocracy, were aware of his self-education, his crudeness, his Southern patriotism. And South Carolina, to its shame, gave him small aid in his literary battlings. The tiny niche he now occupies in our literary Hall of Fame marks simply one of the tragedies of the South.

III

Henry Timrod (1829–1867) and Paul Hamilton Hayne (1830–1886), aristocrats later ruined financially by the war, worked under no such handicap as Simms. From the best families of Charleston, they had every advantage of which the elder writer had been deprived. Both attended Charleston College, though Timrod did not graduate. Ill health was his handicap. Physically frail, consumptive, sensitive, he found in poetry the only profession his soul could endure. Eagerly he wrote for the magazines, especially the Charleston publication edited by Hayne—*Russell's Magazine* (1857–1860)—and in 1860 he was able to issue from a Boston house a thin volume of lyrics. Then like a tropic storm burst upon him the Civil War. Army life was too strenuous for his feeble physique, and during the years of the struggle he was a newspaper worker, sending forth from time to time stirring lyrics which were to the South what Whittier's were to the North. The march of Sherman's army for a moment silenced him: it swept away his home and all he had, leaving him to die two years later in utter poverty.

No truer poet ever produced by the South. Touched unconsciously, perhaps, by Keats-Tennyson models, and overflowing at times into mere prettiness, overornament, and sentimentality, he nevertheless was able to picture in lyric music his native South and at times to reach the heights of lyric expression. When the war broke out, stirred to the depths of his life, he cried out in major key, but his dainty instrument was not a trumpet: no soul was ever more unfitted for the harshness of war. A few stirring notes he blew—"Spring," "The Cotton Boll," "A Cry to Arms"—but not for long. At thirty-eight he was dead, as much a victim of the war as the soldiers who fell in battle.

Almost identical the biography of Hayne. Nephew of the orator Robert Y. Hayne, whose fame is coupled with Webster's, born in one of the oldest and most famous of the South Carolina families, Paul Hayne had been given every advantage that Charleston could furnish. The boy's father, a lieutenant in the American navy, had died early, leaving the rearing and education of the son in the hands of his mother, a remarkable woman, a daughter of the old régime of the South. Educated in the college of his native city, he was early attracted to literature, especially to lyric poetry, which he determined to make his profession—the first in America, perhaps, to make lyric creation his sole life-work. No poet with dreams more glorious. With Simms and Timrod and others, he set out to establish in Charleston a magazine—*Russell's Magazine*—which was to be for the South what the *Atlantic Monthly* was to the North. He, too, had begun with a volume of lyrics, issued by no less a house than Ticknor and Company of Boston.

But when his hopes were highest, there burst upon him the storm of the Civil War. Like Timrod, too frail to enter the Southern army, he became an aide on the staff of Governor Pickens. Then, as with Simms and Timrod, had come the supreme tragedy. During the bombardment of Charleston his house and his magnificent library were burned, and all his property was swept away. He, too, was hastened into consumption, dying a lingering death in the pines of Georgia as late as 1886. In 1872 he issued a collection entitled *Legends and Lyrics,* in 1873 he prepared an edition of Timrod's lyrics, and in 1875 he published his volume, *The Mountain of the Lovers*. A complete edition of his poems appeared in 1875 and again in 1882.

Unlike Timrod, Hayne has been a diminishing figure since the early superlatives following his pathetic end. He was in every way a Victorian, adding nothing original to his poetry save now and then a newness of subject matter. He was over decorative, florid often, superlative. And like all of his American contemporaries, he was sentimental. One may read long in his carefully polished lyrics now and receive not a single lyric thrill. A touch of real pathos there is in a stanza or two of "Forgotten," but, viewing the lyric in its entirety, one can only say, "Too much!"

IV

As one descends lower into the South and out into the Southwest, one finds oneself in a literary desert. Even in *The New-Orleans Book* (1851), selections from all the New Orleans writers, one finds nothing save the single lyric by Richard Henry Wilde, "My Life is Like the Summer Rose." "We are not a literary people," confesses the editor in his preface. "In the all-important matter of education, until recently we have been sadly deficient. . . ."

In a city like New-Orleans, where the great mass of the people are absorbed in business—some with the desire of becoming rich, and many by the stern necessity of earning their bread—it is not astonishing, though it is much to be regretted, that the cultivation of letters should have been so much neglected.

Everywhere in this Louisiana anthology a tropic profusion of ornament and an oratorical flourish even in the otherwise excellent history sketches of Charles Gayarré.

Only one volume do I find made before 1870 in the whole area of the lower South that would be worthy of republication in any series of the American classics, and that volume is *Georgia Scenes* (1835), by Augustus Baldwin Longstreet (1790–1870). A native of Georgia, he was a member of the class of 1813 at Yale. At Litchfield, Connecticut, he began the study of law, but after the death of his father he finished his legal studies in Augusta, Georgia.

Returning to his native sod after his New England residence, he saw for the first time the picturesqueness and the uniqueness of the Georgia "crackerdom," the frontier uniquenesses that he had known in his youth, and in high spirits he recorded his recollections.

Certainly is the book unique among American publications—a humorous inversion of the *Bracebridge Hall* type of romancing, with highly individualized border types, coarse and uncontrolled, in the place of Irving's civilized aristocrats. A landmark, the book, in the history of American realism; a document in the history of the American frontier as well as in the history of autochthonic American humor.

The history of the volume has been peculiar. Its author in later years became a man of dignity and aristocratic influence: lawyer, judge, Methodist minister, and president successively of three important colleges—Emory, the University of Mississippi, and the University of South Carolina. The book he considered a youthful indiscretion that haunted him, and he fain would suppress the thing. As a Southern gentleman, he had committed an unpardonable literary sin: he had told the "low-down" truth about his native state. To the second edition (1840) he gave no help. Gladly would he have suppressed it. But the demands from the reading public were insatiable. The democratic mass roared over the book and read and re-

read it. Editions were demanded in 1842, 1846, 1850, 1854, 1857, 1858, 1860, 1884, 1897, and perhaps at later dates. Unquestionably the book must be rated as an American classic.

PERIOD III

THE MID-CENTURY RENAISSANCE

1835–1870

CHAPTER XXVIII

THE MID-CENTURY RENAISSANCE

I

WITH the 1830's began the work of the third literary generation since the Revolution. The first generation had centered in the midlands about Philip Freneau and Brockden Brown and in New England about Timothy Dwight; the second generation had produced Irving and Cooper and Bryant; the third generation, now gathering, was to be led on its intellectual side by Emerson, by Harvard scholars and Boston preachers, and on its subliterary side by the Robert Bonner press, by the Street and Smith periodical romances, and the feminine best-seller novels. Realism, subdued at first and hardly recognizable in its skilful disguises, was peering over the horizon.

Both in America and in Europe social unrest, enormous changes, unprecedented breakings-away from what had seemed to be fundamental conventions. In America the triumph of unlimited democracy. The early presidents had been aristocrats, but in 1828 the imperious Westerner, Andrew Jackson, had driven to defeat the one-time Harvard professor of rhetoric and oratory, John Quincy Adams, and during the early thirties he had ruled from Washington with border conceptions of government. It was jazz following a symphony. Harvard yielded per force, even in 1833 decorating the grim warrior with an LL.D., but the New England Brahmins breathed hard.

And still harder they breathed during the Harrison and Tyler debauches, with their wild cries of "log cabin and hard cider" and "Tippecanoe and Tyler too." The mob, so feared by John Adams and the Federalists, was completely in the saddle and riding hard. The individualism of the border seemed to be destined to become the national religion.

Stirring indeed was the whole period. Between 1830 and 1870 there was enacting in America an epic drama unprecedented, headlong, colossal, a continent its stage. In thirty years, a single generation, America was totally changed. Never such a kaleidoscope picture of color, of action, of picturesque adventure. Consider the hodgepodge of its elements: the settlement of the Mississippi Basin, the California gold-rush, the buffaloes and their destruction, the plains Indians, the Nicaragua route to the Pacific, the Mexican War, the Alamo, the Book of Mormon (1827) and the Mormon trek to Utah (1847), Transcendentalism in Boston, anti-slavery, Whittier, John Brown's Raid in Kansas and Harper's Ferry, William Lloyd Garrison, Brook Farm, Bronson Alcott, Poe, Emerson, Thoreau, P. T. Barnum, Henry Ward Beecher, Walt Whitman, Melville and *Moby Dick, Godey's Lady's Book,* Bonner's New York *Ledger,* McGuffy's *Readers, Uncle Tom's Cabin, The Wide Wide World,* the Fugitive Slave Law, the secession of the South, Lee, Lincoln, Grant, Stonewall Jackson, the settlement of the "Great Desert," the transcontinental railroad—and all in one generation—epic, amazing, bound as the centuries gather and go to be a reservoir of romance and epic song.

Given a period like this, with elements so rich and varied, there should have been an outburst of original native literature—the voices of the new democracy, literature democratic, the ancient canons thrown to the democratic winds. Nothing of the sort occurred. Instead, a parlor generation of writers, a school of writers too timid and feeble for the western march across the continent, content to contemplate Europe through "My Study Windows," echoing in its songs decadent German romance, translating Dante and Lope de Vega—ancient classicism viewed through the Indian-summer haze of dying Scott romance. According to Harvard critics, America had produced no literature at all. This in 1830 from William Ellery Channing:

> Do we possess, indeed, what may be called a national literature? Have we produced eminent writers in the various departments of intellectual effort? Are our chief resources of instruction and literary enjoyment furnished from ourselves? We regret that the reply to these questions is so obvious. The few standard works which we have produced, and which promise to live, can hardly, by any courtesy, be denominated a national literature.

Pessimism, however, was not confined to Harvard. Timothy Flint, long resident in the West and then the South, in a series of papers on American literature published in the *London Athenæum* in 1835, declared that literature in America was in a condition almost hopeless, that American people were too absorbed in business to read or to appreciate art if they did read, that they demanded the whipped syllabubs of fiction rather than any solid food. Moreover, he declared, the few writers America had produced were, to the last man of them, slaves to the English models and powerless "to bid defiance to the pride and conceit of the English world of letters."

As late as 1845 Joseph Rocchietti published in New York a volume entitled *Why a National Literature Cannot Flourish in the United States of America.* Its present literature, he declared, is unworthy of the great nation that has produced it. It is too much mixed with religion.

Thus literary America in the mid-nineteenth century.

During the decade of the thirties occurred eleven major literary events:

1830   Channing's critique "On National Literature" in the *Christian Examiner,* Boston.

1831 Garrison's *Liberator,* Boston.
1832 Hall's *Legends of the West,* Cincinnati.
1833 *Knickerbocker's Magazine,* New York City.
1833 *The Southern Literary Messenger,* Richmond.
1835 The New York *Herald.*
1836 Verplanck's Phi Beta Kappa oration, "The Advantages and the Dangers of the American Scholar," at Union College, New York.
1836 Emerson's *Nature,* Boston.
1837 Mrs. Hale made editor of *Godey's Lady's Book,* Philadelphia.
1837 Emerson's Phi Beta Kappa oration, "The American Scholar," at Harvard.
1839 Longfellow's *Voices of the Night,* Boston.

To call the period that started thus in the thirties the New England period is open to criticism. The permanent literary forces of the period, as we estimate values today, were many of them extra-New-England phenomena like Poe and Whitman, or else forces New England-born and transplanted where they grew into new and luxuriant variations from the old stock, as, for example, Willis, Melville, Sarah Josepha Hale, Mrs. Stowe and the Beechers, Horace Greeley, and James Freeman Clarke. The literary magazines, soon to be the dominating forces, were nearly all of them outside the New England area, and so were all the lighter forms of literature enjoyed by the average reader.

One uniting force there had been that touched the whole nation. Following the death of Scott in 1832, there had arisen the new democratic humorist and satirist and story-teller extraordinary—the Londoner, Charles Dickens. Mourning for the great Scottish romancer had hardly been put aside when there appeared his successor, who was destined to affect America more than had he. *Pickwick Papers* appeared in 1836–1837, *Oliver Twist* in book form in 1838, *Nicholas Nickleby* the year following. And America bought whole editions. Dickens, unlike Scott, could be read by the democratic mass, by stable-boys even who had never read before. America was teaching the people—the "mass," "the mob"—to read, and here was something they could read. Dickens had humor and sentimentality; he had melodrama and sensation and caricature and trueness to life—at least so all his early readers fixedly believed. Scott had dealt with the past, with European royalty and nobility and aristocracy; Dickens was democratic: he could make as his title character a miserable street-waif. So completely did he capture the American reading public that when in 1842 he visited the United States as a self-appointed committee to place the "Boz" novels on a to-be-enacted international copyright basis, he was welcomed like a prince of the blood. His mission, as explained by Goodrich in his *Recollections,* (1856), "proved abortive, and he took his revenge upon us by his Notes on America, in which he plucked out the feathers of the American Eagle, and then called it a very unclean bird." [1] Nothing in our literary history, perhaps, since the famous question of Sydney Smith so aroused literary America to ire as did this volume of Dickens's and its mate which soon followed, *Martin Chuzzlewit.*

Nevertheless, the reading of Dickens seemed not at all diminished. Doubtless to him more than to any other source may be traced the sickly-sweet sentimentality that so flooded the prose and the poetry of America during the forties and fifties and beyond.

II

The breaking of New England into literary efflorescence in these thirties and forties is a phenomenon to be explained by itself. Glacial drift!—in two hundred years it had yielded nothing literary save a stone-crop of sermons. Young Emerson, fresh from Harvard, could be even more superlative:

[1] Vol. II, p. 358.

From 1790 to 1820, there was not a book, a speech, a conversation, or a thought in the State of Massachusetts. About 1820 the Channing, Webster, and Everett era began, and we have been bookish and poetical and cogitative ever since.

What was this new era? What brought it? What fertilizer to bring Emersons and Alcotts and Channings out of the polypod-hardhack acres of New England? A century of perspective has answered the questions—in part.

First of all, there had come to the old Puritan stronghold an apprehension that the foundations, once believed to be eternal, were shaking. Back of New England lay the great tradition of the theocracy, possession unique. The little province was still a religious area. Said George E. Woodberry, "Spirituality was the essence of New England from its birth, and underlies its historic democracy as the things of eternity underlie the things of time." From the first it had been a group of states independent, self-contained, apart. It had joined the Union with mental reservations—Rhode Island not at all for years. Unlike the other democratic areas, its population was homogeneous, almost wholly native-born, and to a large extent church-going by habit. With changing times and conditions it had modified much its ancient beliefs and severities and in places had lapsed into formalism and lifeless ritualism, but not in the least had it moved from its fundamental conception of a deity ruling the universe, an Imminent God who manifested Himself in spiritual lives.

The old régime was passing, but in its dying moments it burst into hectic beauty. Religions, governments, institutions often yield their ripest fruitage in the season of their final decay. The New England renaissance was the Indian summer of the old régime, and greatest and most fruitful was it the moment of its passing away. And in this day of its beauty it seemed not like an end, but like a beginning. Emerson, who was soon to be a leading part of it, believed it to be a new era.

It had begun with Channing, who had brought from Europe a gentle liberalism. He would head no revolt: he would simply put foot-stoves in the "ice box of Unitarianism." Everett had brought back German-university ideals for Harvard, but his reforms soon evaporated into oratory. But "nerve and dagger" were at hand. England was near to revolution, as were Germany and France, and all three countries were full of young Americans who had been sent over to "finish" their education. After the glorifications by Irving and Cooper and Willis and Longfellow, everyone dreamed of a Continental tour. Oliver Wendell Holmes, sailing in 1833, wrote home: "I do believe that half Boston is going out in the packet." No American writer of the period, save Simms and Whittier and Thoreau and Whitman, who did not finish his education abroad. Edward Everett was away five years in all, his brother Alexander twenty years, Holmes three years, Cooper and Hawthorne seven years, Longfellow five years, Sumner three years. Even Emerson had not found himself until after a year in England and on the Continent.

And wild "bootleg" literature they brought back, these young *wanderjahr* adventurers—strange books in their handbags, strange tracts even in the clerical sermon-bags. A flutter there was in the Boston parsonages when young George Ripley set out to publish a series of them with the running title *Specimens of Foreign Literature*. These, for instance:

Philosophical Miscellanies, from the French of Cousin, Jouffroy, and Benjamin Constant, 1838.

Select Minor Poems from the German of Goethe and Schiller, 1839.

Conversations with Goethe in the Last Years of His Life, Translated from the German of Eckermann by S. Margaret Fuller, 1839.

Introduction to Ethics, from the French of Jouffroy, 1840.
German Literature from the German of Wolfgang Menzel,
1840.

Wild exotics, surely, to be read in homogeneous old New
England. Intoxicants indeed. Emerson, in his "New England Reformers," has described the incredible orgy that
seemed to result:

What a fertility of projects for the salvation of the world!
One apostle thought all men should go to farming, and another that no man should buy or sell, that the use of money
was the cardinal evil; another that the mischief was in our diet.
. . . Others attacked the system of agriculture, the use of
animal manures in farming, and the tyranny of man over
brute nature; these abuses polluted his food. . . . Others
assailed particular vocations, as that of the lawyer, that of
the merchant, of the manufacturer, of the clergyman, of the
scholar. Others attacked the institution of marriage as the
fountain of social evils.[2]

Everywhere soon a gnat-swarm of "isms"—mesmer-
ism, Mormonism, hydropathy, "homeopathy and kindred
delusions," phrenology, Milleriteism, and, as added by
Emerson, "Dunkers, Muggletonians, Come-outers, Groan-
ers, Agrarians, Seventh-day Baptists, Quakers, Abolition-
ists." The torrid Gulf Stream of modernism had reached
the Arctic current of the old Calvinism, and there was
fog. In New England strange new charts for the darkness. There was "Transcendentalism"—a groping for the
beyond, for anchorages in the unseen.

It began in the Boston ministerium. According to
Frederick Hedge, he and George Ripley and Ralph Waldo
Emerson met on a Boston street one day in 1836 and immediately began "on the state of current opinion in
theology and philosophy, which we agreed in thinking
very unsatisfactory. Could anything be done in the way

[2] *Essays,* 2nd series (1844), III, 252.

of protest and introduction of deeper and broader views?"
The result was a committee, for they were Americans,
and soon a discussion club, the Transcendentalists, with
these as members: Emerson, Alcott, Thoreau, Margaret
Fuller, F. H. Hedge, J. F. Clarke, A. A. Bartol, Elizabeth
P. Peabody, Theodore Parker, W. H. Channing,
J. S. Dwight, Jones Very, Orestes Brownson, George
Bancroft, C. P. Cranch. As a mouthpiece for the move-
ment there was started a magazine, the now famous *Dial*
(1840–1844), edited first by Margaret Fuller, then by
Emerson assisted by Thoreau.

Of the Transcendentalism discussed by these Boston
intellectuals, it is enough now simply to define it, and
what definition better than Emerson's own in his essay,
"The Transcendentalist"?

What is popularly called Transcendentalism among us, is
Idealism: Idealism as it appears in 1842. As thinkers, mankind have ever [been] divided into two sects, Materialists
and Idealists; the first class founding on experience, the
second on consciousness; the first class beginning to think
from the data of the senses, the second class perceive that
the senses are not final, and say, The senses give us representations of things, but what are the things themselves, they
cannot tell. The materialist insists on facts, on history, on
the force of circumstances and the animal wants of man; the
idealist on the power of Thought and of Will, on inspiration,
on miracle, on individual culture.[3]

To go farther, one needs but study the life of the central
figure in the movement, Ralph Waldo Emerson, just as
to understand the Civil War one needs but to concentrate
upon the single life of Abraham Lincoln.

[3] Emerson's *Works*, Centenary Edition, I, 325.

CHAPTER XXIX

EMERSON

I

To COMPREHEND Emerson, one must begin, perforce, with ancestry. No family in all New England more completely illustrative of Holmes's theory of "the Brahmin caste," outlined in the first chapter of *Elsie Venner*. According to G. W. Cooke, biographer of Emerson,

Eight generations of cultured, conscientious, and practical ministers preceded him. In each generation they held the most advanced positions in religious thought. . . . More than fifty of the family have graduated at New England colleges, and twenty have been ministers.

From the first a clan rebellious, individualistic, sayers of "no" rather than sayers of "yes." The grandfather of the poet, first occupant of the Old Manse at Concord, had preached on the Sunday before the battle at the Concord Bridge a sermon with the title "Resistance to Tyrants in Obedience to God." His son William became from 1799 until his death in 1811 pastor of the Second Church of Boston. "His pulpit talents were considered extraordinary." He was a scholar and a writer, a leader of the group of preachers "who gave a new character to the religious life of Boston, who aroused a taste for classical learning, and who inaugurated the first literary period in New England history."

His early death from consumption left a family of five children, a widow, and no estate. William, the oldest

child, was ten, and Ralph Waldo, the next, was eight. The
result was not poverty, but conditions not far removed.
The church helped as it could; the children were forced
to do their part; the mother took in boarders. The family
cow was pastured on Boston Common, and the boys took
turns in driving it. *Res angusta domi* with a vengeance,
and, according to their fundamentalist Aunt Mary Moody
Emerson, the problem was added to by the fact that all
Emersons were "born to be educated." And the mother
accomplished it. William and Waldo went to the Latin
School wearing the overcoat on alternate days. No time
was there for play; every moment, under the watchful
eye of Aunt Mary Moody Emerson, must be rich in
accomplishment. Entered at fourteen, Waldo at Harvard
became the president's errand-boy and waiter in the college commons. At eighteen he had his degree. Then for
four years, sorely against his will, he was school-teacher
for mere support. He attended lectures in the Harvard
Divinity School, as he could, and in 1826, at the age of
twenty-three, he was "approbated to preach" by the Mid-
dlesex Association of Ministers.

But the action brought him little satisfaction. "Health,
action, happiness—how they ebb from me," he wrote in
his journal. He was unsatisfied with his Harvard career.
Only one man of the teaching force had really moved
him—the young Everett, fresh from Europe. Moreover,
the dread disease that had destroyed his father had
fastened itself upon him. For years he lived, as did the
youthful Bryant, in the shadow of anticipated early death.
As a forlorn hope, he was sent to the South, to Charleston, South Carolina, then to St. Augustine, Florida, and
he came back with the disease seemingly under control.

To understand the later Emerson, one must consider at
least three early elements that bit into his life. First, those
boyhood years of poverty. They emphasized his natural
New England frugality until there was a pinched narrowness at times in his living and his philosophy. "Self Re-

liance" has a basis of practical getting-on in the world
that is Franklinian. He hitched his wagon to a star, but
the contents of the wagon were not entirely ethereal.
Never a time but he knew the substantial facts about his
income. Read his letters to Carlyle. Yankee thrift to
parsimony. Standing on the glacial drift amid the bowl-
ders of an Ice Age not long past, with five hard-won acres
about him and a dollar in his pocket, the Yankee Puritan
dreamed of streets of gold. He would be thrifty, even
Godward. Thrifty even with his sermon-paper, sentences
trimmed of all adjectives—"let the verb do the work"—
wisdom in small parcels, compact. Style Puritanic.

Then the influence of his Aunt Mary Moody Emerson,
a woman intellectual, a Calvinist to the limits of fanaticism, but withal an influence always toward the life of the
spirit, the realm of idealism as opposed to materialism, the
fundamentalism of faith in the life religious. The voluminous correspondence between this strong soul and the
struggling young student one must read to understand
Emerson.

But another and perhaps stronger force in his molding
has been neglected by his later critics—his frail health.
He is to be listed with the consumptive poets. His physical
frailness barred him from the life of action, as later
Whittier was to be barred. It directed his life into country
living without professional burdens; it robbed him to a
degree of "nerve and dagger."

Returning from Florida, he attempted the conventional
profession of the Emersons. In 1829, aged twenty-six, he
was ordained as colleague of the Reverend Henry Ware
of the Second or Old North Church of Boston. In reality
it was as pastor of the church that he was inaugurated,
for Reverend Ware, on leave for his health, was not to
return. Two years and nine months was this pastorate.
Opening happily—he was married in September following his ordination in March—it ended in tragedy. His
young wife died of consumption in two years, and his

own health became again precarious. Moreover, he had
found himself not in sympathy with his work. Religious
rites which through long usage had become mere ceremony disgusted him. He was opposed to public prayer as
a set part of a religious service and to the "Lord's Sup-
per" ceremony observed as an enjoined "sacrament." And
with a courage hard today to realize, since we cannot
enter the atmosphere of a century ago, he preached a
sermon outlining his criticism and, at his own request,
was removed from the pastorate.

His health was broken, also to a degree his spirit.
"Waldo is sick," wrote his brother Charles in November,
1832. "I never saw him so disheartened. When a man
would be a reformer, he wants to be strong. When a
man has stepped out of the entrenchments of influence
and station, he would fain feel his powers unimpaired and
his hope firm." And again in December: "Waldo is meditating a departure for Italy." To his brothers it seemed
like running away from battle. "Foreign skies cannot
change him; yet it almost always breaks up the life of
quiet progress, and transforms one's ways of thinking
and behaving. I felt like you; I wished him well; that he
might work out his way up-hill and triumph in the end
by his own force of character."

On December 25, 1832, he sailed from Boston in the
brig *Jasper* bound for the Mediterranean. It seemed indeed like failure complete. He had failed in his professional life, his home had been broken, and now his health.
But to quote his biographer: "A winter voyage in a little
trading-brig, in close quarters and living on pork and
beans, seems to have been just what he needed in this
'solstice of health and spirits.'"

The nine months on the ocean and in foreign lands
brought him again to health. Otherwise the months were
disappointing. He could thank God, as he did in his
journal, that he had seen the men he had "wished to see—
Landor, Coleridge, Carlyle, Wordsworth; he has thereby

comforted and confirmed me in my convictions." But he had found in none of them "a mind of the very first class." And all of them he had found "deficient, all these four—in different degrees, but all deficient—in insight into religious truth. They have no idea of that species of moral truth which I call the first philosophy."

Totally unsettled, he went back with his mother to what, more than any other place, was the ancestral home of the family, the Old Manse in Concord. "It is better for a man of letters," he wrote to his friend Alexander Ireland, "to nurse himself in seclusion than to be filed down to the common level by the compliances and imitations of city society." A John the Baptist complex it was: a retreat to the wilderness after a view of the world. And in the solitude of the Old Manse he voiced himself in a tiny volume, his first book, *Nature* (1836), prose that at times is near to poetry. Almost alone among his multitudinous prose works it was written with no thought of an audience; it was a spontaneous outburst well-knit in texture, with no patchwork of note-book jottings. Like Bryant, he had discovered Nature as the ultimate healing and restoring power, spiritual as well as physical.

In it the doctrine of the Over-Soul, as he termed the God of his own creation. For the nature of this divinity that was to rule him, read his enraptured finale; "Every soul is of the divine essence, and may have communication with all that is divine in the universe; and since all things and all actions are manifestations of the divine, it may read a spiritual lesson in every work of nature or of art."

II

Fundamentally the man was a preacher, not a pastor—a preacher without surplice. Sermons ran in his blood as they had run in the blood of his father who had fought against entering the ministry but who had been compelled into it by forces within. Sermons he wrote in his note-book, and sermons he wrote and preached nearly every Sunday for years. Impossible was it for him to avoid it. To say "New England" at any time during three hundred years was to say "Sermons." The clergyman—and there was one in every hamlet—was "the preacher," and always he preached from prepared manuscript. Twice every Sunday and often once during the week the minister preached—sermons logical: firstly, secondly, thirdly; sermons theological, expository, exegetical. Never a people so besermonized in the history of the world. Increase Mather preached for sixty-six years, and of every day save the seventh he spent hours in his study writing sermons. His son Cotton was even more voluminous. "No less than ten of the Mathers," declared John Henderson, "are serving the Lord and his People in the ministry," and all of them writing sermons. And this but a single family. What barrels and barrels of the stuff accumulated during the three New England centuries! And some of it was printed:

It is calculated that hardly a clergyman has lived in Connecticut within the last seventy years who has not printed at least one sermon. . . . The proportion is not small who passed forty of fifty years in the ministry and never suffered their pens to lie fallow for a day.

And oh, the mass of the unprinted! In the Yale Library, for instance, 1,200 manuscript sermons preached by Jonathan Edwards. And the audiences followed them. Sermon-tasters rarely critical were all New England church-goers. After the sermon they might even argue with the preacher as to the soundness of his doctrines.

And Emerson preached: there was no avoiding the pulpit. Churches were seeking candidates, supplies, preachers for special occasions. For a year or more he served a church in Salem and for more than a year a church in Lexington. Often he preached in Boston. And now a curious evolution: Boston asked for a week-day sermon.

In January, 1834, he addressed the Mechanics Institute, his "first attempt," as he later expressed it, "at a public discourse after leaving the pulpit." As a result, a course of lectures the following winter—lay-sermons. "Preaching is the expression of the moral sentiment in application to the duties of life," he said in his Divinity School address. In 1839 he could note in his journal, "For the five last years I have read each winter a new course of lectures in Boston, and each was my creed and confession of faith. Each told all I thought of the past, the present, and the future." In other words, rejecting the sacred desk of the Boston church, he had accepted a secular call and had become lay-preacher for all Boston. And soon his parish was to widen until it included the entire nation.

A year in the Old Manse, and he bought a house in the little town, was married, and, aside from visits to Europe in 1847 and in 1872, lived there in a seclusion broken only by his winter lecture tours. In a letter to Carlyle in 1838 this idyllic picture:

I occupy, or improve, as we Yankees say, two acres only of God's earth; on which is my house, my kitchen garden, my orchard of thirty young trees, my empty barn. My house is now a very good one for comfort and abounding in room. Besides my house I have, I believe, $22,000, whose income in ordinary years is six per cent. I have no other tithe or glebe except the income of my winter lectures which was last winter $800. Well, with this income, here at home I am a rich man. I stay at home, and go abroad, at my own instance. I have food, warmth, leisure, books, friends. Go away from home, I am rich no longer. I never have a dollar to spend on a fancy. As no wise man, I suppose, ever was rich in the sense of freedom to spend, because of the inundations of claims, so neither am I, who am not wise. But at home I am rich, —rich enough for ten brothers.

My wife Lidian is an incarnation of Christianity—I call her Asia—and keeps my philosophy from Antinomianism; my mother—whitest, mildest, most conservative of ladies, whose only exception to her universal preference for old things is her son; my boy a piece of love and sunshine, well worth my watching from morning to night; these and three domestic women who cook and sew and run for us, make all our household. Here I sit and read and write, with very little system, and as far as regards composition, with the most fragmentary result: paragraphs incompressible, each sentence an infinitely repellent particle.

In summer, with the aid of a neighbor, I manage my garden; and a week ago I set out, on the west side of my house, forty young pine trees to protect me, or my son, from the wind of January. The ornament of the place is the occasional presence of some ten or twelve persons, good and wise, who visit us in the course of the year.

His profession had chosen him. He was to be, like all the Emersons, a preacher—"lecturer," he called it—presenting spiritual matters to his people. "I religiously read lectures," he wrote in 1837, "every winter, and at other times whenever summoned." In a limited way he was a settled preacher. "He lectured," says Higginson, "in forty successive seasons before a single 'lyceum'—that of Salem," and he lectured in Boston, in New England cities, and over the entire West east of the Mississippi.

III

After the mid-thirties his lectures began to strike fire. "Irving, Bryant, Greenough," he wrote in his journal, "Everett, Channing, even Webster in his recorded eloquence, all lack nerve and dagger." In 1837 it seemed as if the dagger had arrived. Emerson was chosen the Phi Beta Kappa orator at Harvard, and he entitled his oration "The American Scholar." Nothing new was it, in a way. Verplanck, at Union College, speaking with the same subject had touched upon every key that Emerson was to sound, and so had William Ellery Channing in a paper much earlier. But here was a new spirit. Here was a John the Baptist preacher, crying not "ye generation of

vipers," but nevertheless laying axes at the foot of trees.
The long night of American scholarship dependent upon
Europe was past, he declared. A new type of scholarship
was at hand. "Study nature" was now the gospel. The
scholar is inspired not by old books but by the divine
soul of the present truth. "Books are for the scholar's
idle times. When he can read God directly, the hour is too
precious to be wasted in other men's transcripts of their
readings." The scholar is to be not a monk in a cloister
but a man of action. Without action "he is not yet a
man." Never is he "to defer to the popular cry. Let him
not quit his belief that a popgun is a popgun, though the
ancient and honorable affirm it to be the crack of doom."
"I ask not for the great, the remote, the romantic; what is
doing in Italy or Arabia; what is Greek art, or Provençal
minstrelsy; I embrace the common, I explore and sit at
the feet of the familiar, the low. Give me insight into
today, and you may have the antique and future worlds."

Old doctrines, but doctrines with a new key. A Yankee
Amos was in the pulpit. Consternation!—A man arrived
with nerve and dagger. A year later, 1838, when Emerson
delivered the address at the Divinity School graduation,
consternation turned to wrath. The man was dangerous, a
heretic, an infidel. And yet he had merely pled for the
spiritual as a living force in life and had condemned the
traditional, the formal, the religion merely inherited. His
sentences rang like hammer-blows:

Jesus Christ belonged to the true race of prophets. . . .
He said, in this jubilee of sublime emotion, "I am divine.
Through me, God acts; through me, speaks. Would you see
God, see me; or see thee, when thou also thinkest as I now
think."

Historical Christianity . . . has dwelt, it dwells, with
noxious exaggeration about the *person* of Jesus.

Men have come to speak of the revelation as somewhat long
also given and done, as if God were dead. The injury to faith

throttles the preacher; and the goodliest of institutions becomes an uncertain and inarticulate voice.

The prayers and even the dogmas of our church are like the zodiac of Denderah and the astronomical monuments of the Hindoos, wholly insulated from anything now extant in the life and business of the people.

In how many churches, by how many prophets, tell me, is man made sensible that he is an infinite Soul; that the earth and heavens are passing into his mind; that he is drinking forever the soul of God?

It was Jonathan Edwards without Jehovah and Hell. Until 1840 his journal rings with battle. It has the ring of the scholar as man of action, the scholar in the street before the barricades:

This filthy enactment [the Fugitive Slave Law] was made in the nineteenth century, by people who could read and write. I will not obey it, by God.

Lord Eldon said in his old age that if he were to begin life again, he would be damned but he would begin as an agitator.

The cant and snuffle of our dead christianity. . . .

I find him [Dante] full of the *nobil volgare eloquenza;* that he knows "God damn," and can be rowdy if he please, and he does please.

Whoso would be a man must be a nonconformist.

What a pity that we cannot curse and swear in good society! Cannot the stinging dialect of the sailors be domesticated? It is the best rhetoric, and for a hundred occasions those forbidden words are the only good ones. My page about "Consistency" would be better written thus: Damn Consistency!

I confess to some pleasure from the stinging rhetoric of a rattling oath in the mouth of truckmen and teamsters. How laconic and brisk it is by the side of a page of the *North American Review*.

A minister nowadays is plainest prose, the prose of prose. He is a warming-pan, a night-chair at sickbeds and rheumatic souls; and the fire of the minstrel's eye and the vivacity of his word is exchanged for intense, grumbling enunciation of the Cambridge sort, and for Scripture phraseology.

Look at our silly religious papers. Let a minister wear a cane, or a white hat, go to a theater, or avoid Sunday School, let a schoolbook with a Calvinistic sentence or a Sunday School book without one be heard of, and instantly all the old grannies squeak and gibber and do what they call "sounding an alarm" from Bangor to Mobile. Alike nice and squeamish is its ear. You must on no account say "stink" or "Damn."

Few even in Boston were able wholly to understand the lecturer or to follow him as serenely he strode from peak to peak of his argument. Sentences, epigrams, condensations of wisdom came in steady stream, and one or two of these might remain in the memory and be taken home, but not the whole lecture. Attempting to follow him, his audiences, even the fit and the few, listened eagerly for a time, then lapsed from mental effort as one listens to music simply to enjoy it. There was an air of authority about the man, of mysticism—otherworldliness—that held his hearers they knew not why. Heat-lightning flashes illumined him, noiseless, cold, yet tremendously stirring. Here was a prophet,

> All day thy wings have fanned
> At that far height the cold thin atmosphere.

Why attempt to follow. After such a lecture Lowell wrote this to Norton:

Emerson's oration was more disjointed than usual, even with *him*. It began nowhere and ended everywhere, and yet, as always with that divine man, it left you feeling that something beautiful had passed that way—something more beautiful than anything else, like the rising and setting of stars.

IV

The scholar should be enamoured of action—but with Emerson, action did not necessarily mean physical leadership, or the gathering of disciples, or the heading of a system of philosophy. He could class Wordsworth as a man of action, though his forces were exerted through his poetry. His own leadership came through the spoken and the written word. His profession—a minister of the Gospel. This his definition:

'Tis his to show the beauty of the moral laws of the universe; to explain the theory of a perfect life; to watch the Divinity in his world; to detect his footstep; to discern him in the history of the race of his children.

No man ever more serious—read his early journals; no man ever more spiritually-minded. Seemingly he played no active part in the tragedy of his day. He sat rather with the chorus and philosophized. But he accomplished results. Wishing not at all for disciples, he found them. Whitman took him at his word, mingled with the people who said "stink" and "damn," put into practice what Emerson preached but dared not practice, and became the classic we know. Thoreau took him at his word and went to Nature as Emerson preached it and became himself a classic. Bronson Alcott and George Ripley found action in the founding of communities where men were to live as brothers. Margaret Fuller joined the insurgents in Rome. John Brown went to Harper's Ferry. Emerson simply preached, dreamed, and lectured about supermen—"Representative Men," dominating individualists—and gradually dropped the "nerve and dagger" from his sermons. A serene influence he became, not an executive. He listened while the Transcendentalist Club argued; he paid the fine when Thoreau was jailed for refusing to pay taxes to a

state that sided with the slave-holding South; he helped
clear up the wreckage of Alcott's Fruitlands; and he
listened to the plans for the Brook Farm Community, and
even visited it, but he joined it not at all. Hawthorne he
touched, and Melville, with his serene gospel, and some in
the vigorous West.

The period of his seeding was short. Bliss Perry, editing *The Heart of Emerson's Journals,* selected not much
after the late forties. Gradually in his Concord home, with
Boston not far away, his journal became less stormy. His
soul may have longed to ride with the horse-car drivers
as Whitman did in New York, but in Boston it would
not do. *Leaves of Grass* he hailed with joy, but soon he
was pleading with Whitman to omit "The Children of
Adam." Before the forties were over he was wishing for
a professorship in a college. His strongest books all are
of this single decade. In 1844, his second volume of essays; in 1849, *Nature; Addresses and Lectures;* and in
1850, *Representative Men.*

Action undoubtedly he got every winter on the lecture
circuit. His name was on every lyceum list. Moreover, a
roll-call of his orations on special occasions shows at times
activities often tropic in their intensity. He wrote to
President Van Buren protesting against the removal of
the Cherokee Indians from the State of Georgia. He
aroused the citizens of Concord again and again on antislavery topics, and once he became fiery in a meeting
called to protest the attack upon Sumner in the Senate
Chamber. Then, too, he was a champion of John Brown,
defending him in a mass meeting, Sept. 1856, which he
called in the home town-hall. And at the death of Lincoln
in 1865 he delivered in Concord an address that is a
classic.

v

The publication of his lectures in 1841, in a volume
entitled *Essays,* rounded the evolution of his sermonic

prose into literature. In the process usually three steps: first, the making of note-book jottings, then these gathered and expanded into sermon or lecture, then the lecture —sometimes two lectures—recast, revised, rewritten sometimes into the final essay.

The method left its marks. The note-book fragmentariness often was not obliterated. It left a style perfect in its sentences, but often unconnected. He thought not in ordered systems, not in Q.E.D. culminations, but in flashes. Everywhere epigrammatic sentences. One may open him at random and find a sentence that will stand alone. No writer more quotable. Made for oral delivery primarily, the essays, when read aloud, yield their message more quickly than when read with the eye. Clearest of all were they when the preacher-lecturer-orator added his living presence and the marvelous influences of his voice and his eye. That the sentences lacked often cartilage and logical sequence one noticed then not at all. One gets, when reading aloud, the organ-roll of his style that so held and charmed his original hearers. Wrote Lowell in one of his letters:

That he had a sense of the higher harmonies of language no one that ever heard him lecture can doubt. The structure of his prose, as one listened to it, was as nobly metrical as the King James version of the Old Testament, and this made it all the more puzzling that he should have been absolutely insensitive to the harmony of verse.

Essays ethical and didactic, the greater part of his prose editions. The general content of his work up to 1840 he has himself defined: "In all my lectures I have taught one doctrine, namely, the infinitude of the private man." The last and perhaps the greatest champion he was of frontier individualism, the individualism that had planted New England and made it a power during two centuries and a half. At the moment when the first symptoms of decline might have been felt by sensitive souls arose this master

individualist with his message of self-reliance, his doctrines of the divinity of every man, his rejection of tradition, and his demand for independence in the vital today.
"I am my own man more than most men"; "Trust thyself: every heart vibrates to that iron string"; "Let a
man know his worth, and keep things under his feet."
And standing today at the end of the first third of the
twentieth century in the era of advancing socialism, we
realize that it was a call to the crumbling dikes, a call for
sand-bags for the widening crevasses, a call to arouse a
sleeping people—for the soul of America was in danger,
he felt; the old freedom, the independence that had created
the Republic, was weakening.

No other of the New England group was so completely
American. He had felt the greatness of the West, a greatness that had come from the highly individualized personages born on its frontiers. As early as the days of the
Dial magazine he had contributed an editorial that could
declare that England at last was to be mastered by this
Western power:

The powerful star [Europe] it is thought, will soon culminate and descend, and the impending reduction of the Transatlantic excess of influence . . . is already a matter of easy
and frequent computation. Our eyes will be turned westward
and a new and stronger tone of literature will result. The
Kentucky stump-oratory, the exploits of Boone and David
Crockett, the journals of the western pioneers, agricultural-
ists, and socialists, and the letters of Jack Downing, are
genuine growths which are sought with avidity in Europe,
where our European books are of no value.

His lecture tours through the West had a double effect:
they brought to the frontier areas a vision of the Eastern
culture, and they brought back from the West a vision of
the new democracy and individualism which, after the
Civil War, was to flower in such personalities as Mark

Twain, Bret Harte, William Dean Howells and John Hay.

All New England used him as a synonym for Transcendentalism. Emerson? Oh, Emerson is a Transcendentalist, but just what the term meant no one was quite sure. Always has he been discussed in terms of Transcendentalism. Forget it. With Emerson, Transcendentalism meant simply that he adhered to the old foundations of Puritanism, that he believed in a spiritual world that transcended, went beyond, the merely physical world. The Jehovah of the Old Testament and the Triune God of the New he could reject as tradition now lifeless, but it was only a changing in outward form. Transcending all materialism was the world of the Over-Soul described in his magnificent prose-poem essay, "The Over-Soul."

He was at heart, however, a realist: he demanded foundations. Romanticism, as explained by Coleridge and practiced by Poe, he could not endure, though romanticism as defined in terms of revolt interested him. Carlyle, a blast from the North, exhilarated him. The French Revolution volume of the Germanized Scotchman stirred his blood:

It might be more simple, less Gothically efflorescent. You might say no rules for the illumination of windows can apply to Aurora Borealis. . . . The young men say it is the only history they have ever read. The middle-aged and the old shake their heads, and cannot make anything of it. In short it is the success of a book which, as people have not fashioned, has to fashion the people.

For a time it looked as if Carlyle might be induced to settle in America. Emerson worked hard to find lectureships for him:

Boston contains some genuine taste for literature, and a good deal of traditional reverence for it. . . . If the lectures succeed in Boston, their success is assured at Salem, a town thirteen miles off, with a population of 15,000. They might, perhaps, be repeated at Cambridge, three miles from Boston, and probably at Philadelphia thirty-six hours distant. At New York anything literary has hitherto had no favor.

The project, however, came to nothing. It was Emerson who first introduced the man to America, editing and even marketing one edition at least of his writings. And the correspondence that passed between the two during years, now published as a volume in Emerson's works, is indispensable to the student of either of the two writers.

For Emerson, a writer, to be worth the printing, must possess originality, truth, and inward light for his reader. Tennyson for him was "a beautiful half of a poet." Everett was a "pure triumph of Rhetoric. This man had neither intellectual nor molar principles to teach. He had no thoughts. It was asked what truths he had thrown into circulation and how he had enriched the general mind." Of Webster, though he was a near relative, he could say: "There is not a single general remark, not an observation on life and manners, and not an aphorism that can pass into literature from his writings." And in June, 1838, he could record: "Elizabeth Peabody brought me yesterday Hawthorne's *Footprints on the Seashore* to read. I complained that there was no inside to it. Alcott and he together would make a man." "In every so great mass of books," he wrote in 1824, "doubtless every appetite must be suited, and so we find a portion which seems especially intended for coxcombs and deficient persons. To this department belong the greatest part of novels and romances."

Thus Ralph Waldo Emerson. In his judgments of others he revealed himself. Nothing better in his voluminous writings than his journal, where he jotted down *himself* with no thought of readers, no thought of literary polish, no thought of reservations or the conventionalities. Here the real Emerson.

VI

But among his works a volume of poetry. What poetry could come from Ralph Waldo Emerson? No feeble stuff, surely; no jingle-man tinklings. Poetry profound, corybantic, mystical, at times beautiful. Wordsworthian it will be surely, not Coleridgian. From his journal:

> I said to Bryant and to these young people, that the high poetry of the world from the beginning has been ethical, and it is the tendency of the ripe modern mind to produce it. Wordsworth's merit is that he saw the truly great across the perverting influences of society and of English literature.

Individualistic it will be, impatient of tradition, unfettered by laws laid down. And so we find it. Poems like "Hamatreya" might have suggested to Whitman the loose-fingered chords of his *Leaves of Grass:*

> Bulkeley, Hunt, Willard, Hosmer, Meriam, Flint,
> Possessed the land which rendered to their toil
> Hay, corn, roots, hemp, flax, apples, wool, and wood.
> Each of these landlords walked amidst his farm,
> Saying, " 'Tis mine, my children's, and my name's."

Loose-fingered in the rhyming, too. Holmes in great glee pointed out this monstrous discord:

> Where feeds the moose, and walks the surly bear,
> And up the tall mast runs the woodpecker.

Emerson had a dull ear, declare his critics. Nothing of the kind. Read his lyrical prose, read a score of his lyrics like "The Rhodora," "The Humble-Bee," "The Snow-Storm." His faulty rhymes came from the fact that he was more intent on the content of his poem than on the mechanics of the versification. It is the small poet who is faultless always in technique. Emerson himself could say of Tennyson's *In Memoriam,* "The consummate skill of the versification is the sole merit." The subject matter was conventional.

His improvisations mark undoubtedly the highest reaches of his thinking. They are full of quotable lines like his prose, some of the lines universally current. A half-dozen of his lyrics are in all the anthologies. "Threnody" is tense with feeling, and so is "Terminus."

More one cannot say. His appeal, almost without exception, is to the intellect, not to the imagination. One reads him in cold blood, never with a quickening heartbeat. To speak in Emerson's own words, there is a lack of that final, unanalyzable something "that makes the merit of an ode of Collins, or Gray, or Wordsworth, or Herbert, or Byron—and which is felt in the pervading tone rather than in brilliant parts or lines." This from Gamaliel Bradford: "All the wit and all the epigrams would be just as good in prose. This is the cardinal defect of Emerson's poetry: the best part of it is not poetry at all. He was a man of wide and far-reaching intellectual power. He was not a poet."

VII

Around the clear light of Emerson fluttered a swarm of night-moths wth luminous eyes. The Transcendentalist Club buzzed against the windows and accomplished nothing—save talk. Most spectral-like was the apparition of Bronson Alcott, a man born in the wrong century, a reincarnation, it would seem, of old Plotinus or Diogenes. His flutterings and flashings seemed to exert a peculiar fascination upon Emerson. He could not keep away from him. His conversations seemed brilliant beyond expression, yet "when the conversation is ended all is over." "A tedious archangel." But nevertheless he filled his note-books with observations upon the man. He was kindled at times by his enthusiasm, his transcendental point of view. How could one rebuke a man who could counter you with the remark, "If Plato should come to Concord, who would he inquire for?"

As listed by P. K. Foley, Alcott issued twelve volumes, but no one even in Boston read them or could read them. Perhaps the twenty-first century may discover and read them. Light there seemed to be, but no slightest illumination.

For two or three decades much was expected of Margaret Fuller. Profoundly educated, loaded with philosophy, flashing with seeming brilliance, she ruled the Transcendentalists for a time as a veritable *femina dux facti*. Her "Conversations" held in Boston parlors were the joy of the esoteric. She was at once the champion of her sex, the leading feminist of her generation, author of the volume *Woman in the Nineteenth Century*. For the first two years of the *Dial* she was editor, then Horace Greeley called her to New York to be literary editor of the *Tribune*. A strange choice, good advertising perhaps, but to light Broadway with this firefly in a phial was certainly a fantastic experiment. Little she found of appreciation. Lowell, in *A Fable for Critics,* lampooned her as "Miranda," and though Hawthorne himself denied it, he made her the model for his Zenobia in *The Blithedale Romance*. Not until she had journeyed to Europe and had found herself in actual revolution in Italy did she leave the world of her idealization and get her feet upon the substantial earth. Returning to America with husband and child, her ship was wrecked off Fire Island and all were lost. The Margaret Fuller that would have been had this tragedy not occurred it is useless to speculate upon. A literary force, perhaps. Following her death, Emerson, W. H. Channing, and James Freeman Clarke issued her works in six volumes with appreciative memoirs, but they were powerless to save her from the fate that has overtaken her.

Intense personalities everywhere in the feverish decades before the Civil War. By his own generation Henry D.

Thoreau was considered as "cranky" even as Alcott. After his graduation at Harvard he had attracted the attention of Emerson, who at first considered him a mere echoer of his style and philosophy. But in 1863 he could note in his journal, "In reading him, I find the same thought, the same spirit that is in me, but he takes a step beyond." He had been much with Emerson, had lived in his family as man of all work, had helped edit the journal, had talked and argued hours at a time, and in long walks through the woods had given Emerson a vision of nature that otherwise he never would have acquired. The older man never quite understood the young individualist. He summed up his life in a paragraph of negatives. After the early death of Thoreau he sought to bring out his writings and acquaint the world with the unique product that he had produced, but in vain. To his own generation he was simply a freak, a hermit with a wild theory, a sayer of "no" always on the "left-wing." Lowell, in a review of Emerson's editions, voiced the times. He characterized Thoreau as a fantastic theorist. His nature studies did not impress him. "I look upon a great deal of the modern sentimentalism about Nature as a mark of disease. It is "one more symptom of the general liver-complaint." It seemingly finished the man.

Then with the early nineties had come the discovery of Thoreau's journal. New publication began. Then the publication of the entire journal, a classic, coördinate, it was found, even with Emerson's. This later Thoreau I have treated in another volume.[1]

[1] Fred Lewis Pattee, *A History of American Literature since 1870* (1915), pp. 137–144.

CHAPTER XXX

SEBA SMITH AND THE NEW HUMOR
I

THE "YANKEE DOODLE" theme received in 1830 a new impetus. Seba Smith, a Maine Yankee, a graduate of Bowdoin in 1818, was editor and proprietor of a political newspaper, the Portland *Courier*. Politics, not literature, possessed the young editor. The new state, not long before admitted to the Union, was in a ferocious turmoil; the two parties arrayed against each other in the legislature assaulted each other with reckless oratory. Smith lashed the enemy with editorials and then in the heat of battle invented a new weapon. Sheer accident, no thought of literary creation, yet with a single sitting with his pen he made himself not only a force in the political fight of his day but the creator of a new school of native American humorists. In his own words, his device was this:

Bring a green, unsophisticated lad from the country with a load of ax-handles, hoop-poles, and other notions for sale, and while waiting the movements of a dull market, let him blunder into the halls of the legislature, and after witnessing for some days their strange doings, sit down and write an account of them to his friends at home in his own plain language.

A new variety of legislative reporting, a device, as its author declared, until then totally "out of the common track of newspaper writing." But it worked. All unaware of what he was doing, the young editor was releasing a bottle-imp that was to dominate American humorous writings for all time apparently. The first "Jack Downing" letter in the *Courier* of January 18, 1830, was a national event.[1] As explained by Smith at a later day:

The plan was successful almost beyond parallel. The first letter made so strong a mark that others had to follow as a matter of course. The whole town read them and laughed; the politicians themselves read them, and their wrathful, fire-eating visages relaxed to a broad grin. The Boston papers copied them, and all Boston tittered over them. The series was inaugurated and must go on. The letters continued from time to time, and spread over the whole country, and were universally read.

The first intent of Smith unquestionably had been to create political propaganda, but his "doodle," Jack Downing, came to life under his pen as did his invented village, Downingville—"jest about in the middle of Down East." The Downing clan—Grandfather, the veteran, who fought daily "the fatigue of Burgwine"; Uncle Joshua, who would continue interminably to talk politics even when a shower was gathering and he had out six loads of hay; Cousin Nabby, who had entrusted to Jack her bundle of "footings" [knit woolen stockings] to be sold in Portland; the Downingville *hoi polloi,* later to be recruited to put down the Maine border insurrection, and later the South Carolina nullification uprising—real Maine Yankees, all of them. Nothing before in American literature to compare with them. First of all, Jack himself:

I've been here now a whole fortnight, and if I could tell ye one half I've seen, I guess you'd stare worse than if you'd seen a catamount.

And Cousin Nabby, worried about her "footings," answered him in kind:

[1] Only recently has justice been rendered to Smith. See Mary Alice Wyman, *Two American Pioneers, Seba Smith and Elizabeth Oakes Smith* (1927).

Dear Cousin: If you were only here I would break the handle of our old birch broom over your back for serving me such a caper. Here I have been waiting three weeks for that cotton cloth that you got for the footings. . . . You had better let them legislaters alone; and if you can't sell your ax-handles, take 'em and come home and mind your business. There is Jemime Parsons [Jack's sweetheart] romping about with the school-master, fair weather and foul.

Spurred on by Jack's letters, Uncle Joshua becomes himself a Yankee "doodle" and visits Boston Town with "a load of turkeys and some apple-sass," intent on seeing the General Court there in action. True to type, he is pounced upon by a city sharper, but, again true to type, he is enough for the fellow:

I was down in the bar-room, and thought it well enough to look pretty considerable smart, and now and then compared my watch with the clock in the bar, and found it as near right as ever it was, when a feller stept up to me and ask'd how I'd trade? and says I, for what? and says he, for your watch, and says I, any way that will be a fair shake; upon that, says he, I'll give you *my* watch and five dollars; says I, it's done! He gave me the five dollars, and I gave him my watch. Now, says I, give me *your* watch; and, says he, with a loud laugh, I han't got none, and that kind a turned the laugh on me. Thinks I, let them laugh that lose. Soon as the laugh was well over the feller thought that he would try the watch to his ear; why, says he, it don't go; no, says I, not without it's carried; then I began to laugh. He tried to open it and couldn't start it a hair, and broke his thumb nail into the bargain. Won't she open, says he? Not's I know on, says I, and then the laugh seemed to take another turn.

It is the attitude of the frontier, of the Western settlements with their talk of "the effete East," of David Crockett in the halls of Congress, and later of Lowell's Hosea Biglow who represented not the frontier, but the country as opposed to the "smartness" of the town:

The sarjunt, he thout Hosea hed n't gut his i teeth cut cos he looked a kindo 's though he 'd jest com down, so he cal'lated to hook him in, but Hosy wood n't take none o' his sarse for all he hed much as 20 Rooster's tales stuck onto his hat and eenamost enuf brass a bobbin up and down on his shoulders and figureed onto his coat and trousis, let alone wut nater hed sot in his featers, to make a 6 pounder out on.

Before long Jack had become a leading man in the Maine legislature, giving advice right and left, always making a tremendous impression, and finally he was able to go back to Downingville as a veritable candidate for governor of the state. Defeated, though Downingville gave him every vote she had, 117 strong, he began hunting for larger game, departed for Washington, and soon was right-hand man to President Jackson and even spoken of himself as presidential timber. The titles to his letters home suggest his adventures:

Mr. Downing tells how he stript up his sleeves and defended Mr. Ingham on his front door-steps, during the after-clap that followed the blow-up of Gineral Jackson's first cabinet.

Mr. Downing receives a captain's commission in the United States army, with orders to go and protect the inhabitants of Madawaska.

Captain Downing's first military report to the President.

Captain Downing receives a Major's commission, and is appointed to march against the nullifiers.

Finally Jack is able to announce to his Uncle Joshua, "We are coming on full chisel"! The President was on his "grand tour East," and Harvard was preparing to bestow on the great man her greatest honor:

When we were at Boston they sent word to us to come out to Cambridge, for they wanted to make the President a doctor of laws. What upon airth a doctor of laws was, or why they wanted to make the President one I couldn't think. So when we come to go up to bed I asked the General about it. And says I, "Gineral, what is it they want to do to you out to Cambridge?" Says he, "They want to make a doctor of laws of me." "Well," says I, "but what good will that do?" "Why," says he, "you know, Major Downing, there's a pesky many of them air laws passed by Congress, that are rickerty things. . . . You know I've had to doctor the laws consider-able ever since I've been in Washington, although I wasn't a regular bred doctor. And I made out so well about it, that these Cambridge folks think I'd better be made into a regu-lar doctor at once."

Excellent satire. Excellent humor. To give Andrew Jackson a Harvard degree certainly was incongruous. The West awoke with a roar. Democratic America had evolved a court jester, a Yankee "doodle" who rebuked and in-structed and entertained the President and his officials and who philosophized and interpreted and made light of their doings. Never since the first "Downing" letter has America been without this official: Artemus Ward, show-man, who drove away the locust-swarm of office-seekers about Abe Lincoln; Petroleum V. Nasby and "Bill Arp, So-Called," who interpreted Civil War politics; Mr. Doo-ley, who gave the philosophy of the war with Spain; Will Rogers in our own day.

The letters have another value, one that is unique when one considers their origin. Smith in writing them had no thought that he was creating literature. His *literary* am-bitions were embodied later in such volumes as *Pow-hatan; a Metrical Historical Romance* and many essays and stories in the magazines and annuals. He published the letters both in the newspapers and in book form with-out his signature. The critics and anthologists of his generation and later considered them simply as newspaper stuff and neglected them. Thereupon imitators arose, claiming the letters as their own, writing newspaper articles signed Jack Downing, and publishing volumes until the Downing bibliography is in a state of muddle. None of the imitators, however, has equaled the original. Most of them—for instance, Charles Augustus Davis—have vulgarized the character, overdone the dialect, and cheapened the general effect. Smith's Yankee was a spontaneous creation: Smith himself was Jack Downing. The earlier Royal Tyler, in his drama *The Contrast,* had manufactured a theatric Yankee; James Russell Lowell, who worked from both Tyler and Smith as models, created in his *Biglow Papers* a literary Yankee: both Hosea Biglow and Parson Wilbur are elaborately manufactured characters speaking a literary argot. Jack Downing is our first real Yankee character.

Following the "Jack Downing" pattern came the first school of American professional humorists, the Yankee "doodle" turned political philosopher and airing his views in the newspapers. With the 1830's began what was to become a dominating literary product, newspaper humor gathered into volumes in the "Jack Downing" manner. These at the start:

1833   *The Life and Writings of Major Jack Downing of Downingville, Away down East in the State of Maine, Written by Himself.*

1833   *Letters Written during the President's Tour "Down East"; by Myself, Major Jack Downing of Downingville* [pirated from the *Letters* of both Smith and Davis].

1836   *Letters of J. Downing, Major Downingville Militia, Second Brigade, to His Old Friend Mr. Dwight of the N. Y. Daily Advertiser* [written by Charles Augustus Davis.]

Then had followed James Russell Lowell with his "Hosea Biglow," David R. Locke with his "Petroleum V. Nasby," Charles Henry Smith with his "Bill Arp, so-Called," C. G. Halpine with his "Private Miles O'Reilly,"

R. H. Newell with his "Orpheus C. Kerr," F. P. Dunn with his "Martin Dooley," and many others—a colorful element in American life.

II

It was the "Downing" letters, unquestionably, that started the popular flood of "David Crocket" literature, most of it spurious. In Congress a wild man from Tennessee, a professional bear-hunter who had killed a hundred and five bears in twelve months, coarse, bragging, ignorant of books, mighty on the stump—an actual Yankee "doodle" in Congress. Downing had glorified his hero Jackson; Crockett's first volume came as an antidote, for Major David Crockett was no Jackson man:

I let the people know as early as then, that I wouldn't take a collar around my neck with the letters engraved on it, MY DOG. ANDREW JACKSON. . . . No driver at my heels, with his whip in hand, commanding me to ge-wo-haw, just at his pleasure. Look at my arms, you will find no party hand-cuff on them! Look at my neck, you will not find there any collar, with the engraving MY DOG. ANDREW JACKSON.

As a stump campaigner, he always won his audience. Once in the storm-center of a campaign for Congress his opponent, while speaking, was much disturbed by the shrill trumpeting of a flock of guinea-hens near-by. When it came Crockett's turn to address the audience, he began his speech with: "No wonder he couldn't answer 'em. They were all yelling Crockett! Crockett! Crockett!"

In 1834 was published *A Narrative of the Life of David Crockett of the State of Tennessee,* on the face of it, an autobiography full of Indian warfare and bear-hunts told with Southwestern brag, but in reality a political document. It is not to be classified as humor; the humor is simply incidental. That Crockett wrote the book in its present form is inconceivable. This he wrote, or professed to write, in the preface to the volume:

> But I don't know of any thing in my book to be criticised on by honourable men. Is it on my spelling?—that's not my trade. Is it on my grammar?—I hadn't time to learn it, and make no pretensions to it. Is it on the order and arrangement of my book?—I never wrote one before, and never read very many; and, of course, know mighty little about that. Will it be on the authorship of the book?—this I claim, and I'll hang on to it, like a wax plaster. The whole book is my own, and every sentiment and sentence in it. I would not be such a fool, or knave either, as to deny that I have had it hastily run over by a friend or so. . . . In some places, I wouldn't suffer either the spelling, or grammar, or anything else to be touch'd; and therefore it will be found in my own way.

For one who had had the training outlined in the book —only a few weeks of rude schooling, then the raw frontier life of the Tennessee cane-brakes—the biography in its present form seems impossible. Undoubtedly Crockett wrote it, and would that we had the original version, but the literary style of most of the volume reveals the fact that his friends in reality put their stamp, not his, upon much of it. The Crockett element, however, is prominent:

> At any rate, I was determined to stand up to my lick-log, salt or no salt.

> I might as well have sung *salms* over a dead horse, as to try to make the people believe otherwise.

> [Starting two bucks at once] I took a blizzard at one of them, and up he tumbled. Tne other ran off a few jumps and stop'd, and stood there till I loaded again, and fired at him. I knock'd his trotters from under him, and then I hung them both up.

Well salted with such bits of genuineness, the book is a minor classic. Concerning the volume that followed the autobiography, *An Account of Colonel Crockett's Tour to the North and Down East,* there is more doubt. Completely is it a political document. It quotes Jack Downing and counters his doings generally, as, for instance,

When I returned, there was some gentlemen that invited me to go to Cambridge, where the big college or university is; where they keep ready-made titles or knicknames to give people. I would not go, for I did not know but they might stick an LL.D. on me before they let me go; and I had no idea of changing "Member of the House of Representatives of the United States," for what stands for "lazy lounging dunce."

Interminable were his stump speeches, and all of it was at the democratic level that had swept Jackson into the presidency. At once he became an American myth, a "Lochinvar of the Cane-brake" even before his tragic death in the Alamo. Other books followed, like *Colonel Crockett's Exploits and Adventures in Texas* (1836), clearly a forgery, written by one who knew his Southwest only as he had learned of it through Longstreet's *Georgia Scenes,* from which he plagiarizes whole episodes. Speaking as Crockett, the author of the volume launches out with:

it is a huckelberry above my persimmon to cipher out how it is with six month's schooling only, I, David Crockett, find myself the most popular bookmaker of the day; and such is the demand for my works that I cannot write them half fast enough, no how I can fix it.[2]

Doubtless in condemning this book I am placing myself with the critics whom Crockett so despised:

[2] *Colonel Crockett's Exploits and Adventures in Texas,* 6th edition (1837).

They are a sort of vermin that I shan't so much as stop to brush off. If they want to work on my book, just let them go ahead; and after they are done, they had better blot all their criticisms than to know what opinion I would express of them and by what sort of a curious name I would call them, if I were standing near them and looking over their shoulder.

A voice from the grave, one that should be potent.

III

The decade of the thirties was to produce other autochthonic volumes, two others of them classics in their field:

1835 *Georgia Scenes; Characters, Incidents, &c., in the First Half Century of the Republic; By a Native Georgian* [Augustus Baldwin Longstreet].

1836 *The Clockmaker; or the sayings and doings of Samuel Slick of Slickville* [Judge Thomas Chandler Haliburton].

Haliburton, a Nova Scotia judge, posed as recorder of the sayings and doings of a Yankee peddler, Sam Slick, a modern Poor Richard full of wise saws and sharp Down East philosophy. Wiser and cuter than Jack Downing, this is concentrated essence of New Englandism, undoubtedly, but never is he alive. A Yankee Solomon, but never a living Yankee. We hear his sayings and doings reported, but never do we *see* him or *feel* him.

With Longstreet's volume came a new element, the exhibition of highly individualized frontier personalities. The South and the Southwest following the Revolution, especially in the mountains and along the great rivers, abounded in wild types—"crackers," lowland "pikes," "poor whites," "hillbillies," "river rats," "ring-tailed snorters—half horse and half alligator." Like Lincoln in his lawyer days, young Longstreet, compelled to travel a wild circuit, saw much and heard much, and, with youthful abandonment, he wrote it into picturings and narratives for the Augusta, Georgia, *States Rights Sentinel,* issuing them later, as we have seen, in a collected edition as *Georgia Scenes.* The result was a landslide of frontier humor. With the 1840's began the boisterous era of American exaggeration. Nothing new was this crude variety of humor in America. Baron Munchausen's classic volume was known and widely quoted even in Colonial New England. And all along the frontiers of the West are tales equally as wide of all truth as were his. Even before Longstreet's volume there had been smatterings of exaggeration in print. In 1829 Morgan Neville had printed in Judge's Hall's *Western Souvenir* a sketch entitled "The Last of the Boatmen," the first recorded chapter of the "Mike Fink" legend. No brag, surely, in all American recorded localism more colorful and more emphatic:

This is *me,* and no mistake! Billy Earthquake, Esquire, commonly called Little Billy, all the way from North Fork of Muddy Run! I'm a small specimen, as you see—a remote circumstance, a mere yearling; but cuss me, if I ain't of the true 'imported breed,' and can whip any man in this section of the country! Whoop! Won't *nobody* come out and fight me? . . . I'm the very infant that refused its milk before its eyes were open, and called out for a bottle of old Rye! W-h-o-o-p! I'm that little cupid![3]

Twelve typical volumes of this new humor are the following:

1840 William Tappan ·Thompson ("Major Joseph Jones"), *Major Jones's Courtship.*
1843 John S. Robb ("Solitaire"), *Streaks of Squatter Life.*

[3] See Walter Blair and Franklin J. Meine, *Mike Fink, King of the Mississippi Keelboatmen* (1933).

L. H. C. of Mississippi ("Madison Tanzas, M. D."),
The Louisiana Swamp Doctor.

Stahl, *New Orleans Sketch Book.*

1845   William Trotter Porter, *The Big Bear of Arkansas
and Other Tales Illustrative of Characters and Incidents in the South and Southwest.* A collection
of twenty-four tales by different writers.

1846   Johnson Jones Hooper, *Some Adventures of Captain
Simon Suggs, Late of the Tallapoosa Volunteers.*

1846   William Trotter Porter, *A Quarter Race in Kentucky.* Reissued as *Colonel Thorpe's Scenes in
Arkansas.* A collection of thirty-three sketches by
various writers.

1846   Thomas Bangs Thorpe, *The Mysteries of the Back-
woods, etc.,* and *Tom Owen, the Bee Hunter.*

1848   Emerson Bennett, *Mike Fink, a Legend of the Ohio.*

1851   T. A. Burke, *Polly Peaseblossom's Wedding; and
Other Tales.* See also thirty-three tales by *various*
authors.

1930   Franklin J. Meine, *Tall Tales of the Southwest,
1830–60.*

IV

During this stage in the evolution of American humor,
the effort of the recorders was primarily historical. They
were putting before their readers actual characters, real
personalities, even though they seemed gross impossibilities—for example, Mike Fink "the last of the boatmen."

One phase of American history has never been sufficiently emphasized: America from the first was settled
in a series of "booms." The history of the West especially
must be rewritten in the key of Joseph Glover Baldwin's
The Flush Times of Alabama and Mississippi (1853).
The life-blood of all booms is exaggeration, tall talk, inflation.

Nothing at all new was the exaggeration device. One
may find it in the earliest newspapers, even in Puritan
New England. Buckingham has reproduced from the

Portsmouth, New Hampshire, *Oracle* (1822) this extreme specimen, purporting to be a specimen of Yankee advertising, the subject, Dr. Dunderthump's Metalic Boot-Jack:

A member of Congress, while rehearsing in his room a speech in favor of the Missouri Bill, at a fine turned period opened his mouth to such an immeasurable width, that a young deaf and dumb negro, mistaking the passage for the cellar stair-case, ran down the whole length of the orator's throat before he discovered the error. He remained (to the no small inconvenience of both) in this region of darkness, twenty-four hours, in spite of all the usual medical prescriptions and applications. The Metalic Jack was at length produced, and the black-faced gentleman popped his head out of one of the orator's boots, singing

> Nought but gin to live upon, sir,
> And compelled to drink it raw,
> All my hopes were almost gone, sir,
> Ere I left the monstrous jaw.[4]

That before 1822. In early America every man became quickly a Munchausen. America itself, in the imagination of Europe and the early settlers, even before they had made their eventful journey and arrived in the New World, was an exaggeration. The eager, bracing climate, the profuseness of Nature totally untouched by civilization, the amazing flora and fauna, the wild life in all the unexplored hinterlands, the pigeon-flights that darkened the skies for hours, mosquito-swarms that exceeded belief, the Indians always at first a terror-compelling menace —all this, even in its plainest telling, seemed to Europe highly colored with exaggerations. Then later, when the westward march began, when the settlers in the trans-Allegheny world began to realize the vastness of their possessions—the Mississippi River, the Great Lakes, the

---

[4] Joseph T. Buckingham, *Miscellanies Selected from the Public Journals* (1822).

interminable plains, the buffalo herds to be estimated in square miles, the plains Indians, the Rocky Mountains, California—in the face of this colossal panorama the mere truth seemed paltry and unsatisfying. Life everywhere on the frontier was a series of unbelievable adventures, and, as told about camp-fires and country-store fireplaces, it easily grew into tall stories and exaggerated braggings. Always superlatives.

Witness as typical the tall stories of Uncle David Lane, told in 1820 or shortly afterwards. He is chased by a "horn-snake" which had a sharp spear on its tail six inches long, and, notwithstanding the fact that he made forty feet at each jump, he had no chance at all:

. . . I jumped forty foot down the mounting, and dashed behind a big white oak five foot in diamatur. The snake he cotched the eend uv his tail in his mouth, he did, and come rollin' down the mounting arter me jist like a hoop, and jist as I landed behind the tree he struck t'other side with his stinger, and stuv it up, clean to his tail, smack in the tree. He were fast.

Of all the hissin' and blowin' that uver you hearn sense you seen daylight, it tuck the lead. Ef there'd a bin forty-nine forges all ablowin' at once, it couldn't a beat it. He rared and charged, lapped round the tree, spread his mouf and grinned at me orful, puked and spit quarts an' quarts of green pisen at me, . . . I kep' my distunce tell he wore hisself out, then I put a ball right between his eyes, and he gin up the ghost.

Soon as he were dead I happened to look up inter the tree, and what do you think? Why, sir, it were dead as a herrin'; all the leaves was wilted like a fire had gone through its branches.[5]

By a miraculous shot he at last brought down a monstrous buck that had long eluded him: "He dashed round the mounting faster nur a shootin' star ur lightnin'."

[5] *Fisher's River (North Carolina) Scenes and Characters; by "Skitt"* [H. E. Taliaferro] *"who was raised thar"* (1859).

I throwed down old Bucksmasher [his rifle], out with my butcher-knife, jerked off my shot-bag and hung it on the horn uv one uv the purtiest things you uver seen. I thort I'd look at it better when I'd stuck my buck. I knifed him monstrous quick, and turned round to look at the curious thing I'd hung my shot-bag on, and it were gone most out'n sight. I soon seen it were the moon passin' along, and I'd hung my shot-bag on the corner uv it. . . . I went next day, to look fur the moon, and to git my shot-bag. . . . Sure 'nuff, it come moseyin' along, jist at the same time o' day, with my shot-bag on its horn. I snatched it off, and told it to mosey on 'bout its business.

Again at a famous wild-pigeon roost, where the pigeons by the millions had bent the trees fairly to the ground, he hitched his horse to an oak branch and killed hundreds at every shot:

"Arter I'd picked up as many on 'um as my wallets would hold, I looked fur old Nip right smack whar I'd hitched him. . . . I looked a consid'able spell next to the yeth, but, bless you, honey! I mount as well a sarched fur a needle in a haystack. At last I looked up inter a tree 'bout forty foot high, and thar he were swingin' to a limb, danglin' 'bout 'tween the heavens and the yeth like a rabbit on a snare-pole." . . .
"How come him up thar, Uncle Davy?" . . .
"Why, I hitched him to the limb uv a big tree bent to the yeth with pigeons, you num-skull, and when they riz the tree went up, and old Nip with it, fur sure."
"But how did you get him down?" . . .
"That's nuther here nor thar; I got him down, and that's 'nuff fur sich pukes as you ter know."

Baron Munchansen with American Variations.

V

With the 1850's the making of humor based for the most part on the inevitable "doodle" complex had become a national industry. More and more it crowded into the newspapers. The professional funny man had arrived, and the funny newspaper, and the funny magazine. American humor indeed must be defined always in terms of the newspaper or the popular magazine. The new school was born in printing offices. From Franklin and Fessenden to Artemus Ward and Mark Twain and Bret Harte, the majority of the American humorists learned to write with the composing-stick over a newspaper font of type.

To illustrate the flood which during the fifties covered the whole land with a shallow tide, consider six earliest volumes issued in three years:

1854   Benjamin Penhallow Shillaber ("Mrs. Partington"), *Life and Sayings of Mrs. Partington*.

1855   George Horatio Derby ("John Phoenix"), *Phoenixiana; or Sketches and Burlesques; By John Phoenix*.

1855   Mortimer Thompson ("Q. K. Philander Doesticks, P.B."), *Doesticks, What he Says*.

1855   Mrs. Frances Miriam Berry Whitcher ("The Widow Bedott"), *The Widow Bedott Papers, with an Introduction by Alice B. Neal*.

1855   Henry Agustus Wise, *Tales for the Marines*.

1856   Frederick Swartwout Cozzens, *The Sparrowgrass Papers; or, Living in the Country*.

The publication of a single poem by Longfellow could bring out at least six parodies, each one a bound volume:

1856   *Plu-ri-bus-tah. A Song That's-by-no-Author. "A Deed without a Name." Perpetrated by Q. K. Philander Doesticks, P. B.* [Mortimer Thompson].

1856   *The Song of Milgenwater: Translated from the Original Feejee, by Marc Antony Henderson* (Cincinnati).

1856   *The Song of Milkanwatha*, second edition.

1856   *The Song of Drop o' Wather, by Harry Wandsworth
        Shortfellow* [Mrs. Mary Victoria Cowden-Clark]
        (London).
1859   *Wa-wa-wanda. A Legend of Old Orange* (New
        York).
1868   *The Song of Higher-Water,* James W. Ward (New
        York).

Ephemeral stuff, these parodies, and ephemeral stuff
most of the humor laughed at by our grandfathers. Nothing in literature so volatile. In the 1850's "Doesticks"
seemed as sure of literary immortality as Dickens.
N. P. Willis, literary autocrat in his day, could say in his
Home Journal:

Things so copied, so talked of, so pulled out of every pocket
to be lent to you, so quoted and so relished, and laughed
over as Doesticks' writings never before were launched into
print.

And yet "Doesticks" is still in his first editions, and so
are all the rest of the "Yorricks" who so split the sides
of the fifties, save perhaps "John Phoenix." More stable
by far has been the humor of the following decade, the
realistic humor of the "sagebrush" school, strong in
understatement and whimsicality: Artemus Ward, Bret
Harte, Mark Twain, Josh Billings—American jokers
whose fame is not only national but international. At last
in America a native humor with classics that promise to
be permanent.[6]

RECENT WORKS ON AMERICAN HUMOR

The Cambridge History of American Literature, Vol. II,
    Chap. XIX. The bibliography is excellent.
Sixty Years of American Humor, a Prose Anthology, edited
    by Joseph L. French (1924).

[6] See Fred Lewis Pattee, *A History of American Literature since
1870* (1915), Chapter IV.

Crackerbox Philosophers in American Humor and Satire,
Jennette Tandy (1925).
The Frontier in American History, Lucy Lockwood Hazard
(1927).
American Humor, a Study of the National Character, Con-
stance Rourke (1931).

CHAPTER XXXI

THE "MAGAZINISTS"

I

WITH *Godey's Lady's Book* (1830) begins the era of the magazines. By 1840 they had become a dominating literary force. Edgar Allan Poe, himself a "magazinist"—he had applied the term to Willis—was the first to realize what revolution lay in this new tide. "The whole tendency of the age is Magazineward," he wrote. The magazine "in the end will be the most influential of all departments of letters. . . . In a few years its importance will be found to have increased in geometrical ratio." The age of the quarterly review of the *Edinburgh* type, he believed, was ending. It was a literary organ too far away from the great mass of readers; it was overponderous, "out of keeping with the rush of the age":

We now demand the light artillery of the intellect; we need the curt, the condensed, the pointed, the readily diffused —in place of the verbose, the detailed, the voluminous, the inaccessible. On the other hand, the lightness of the artillery should not degenerate into pop-gunnery—by which term we may designate the character of the greater portion of the newspaper press—their sole legitimate object being the discussion of ephemeral matters in an ephemeral way.[1]

Brilliant criticism, but in its last statement misleading. The newspaper in its evolution was not a thing apart from the literary magazine and it was not "pop-gunnery." It was

---

[1] *Marginalia*, No. XXV.

a kindred force; it sprang from the same conditions. The new type of magazine, beginning with the thirties, was matched by the new type of newspaper, beginning at the same time. In 1833, alongside of *Godey's* in Philadelphia, there was begun in New York City the first significant attempt at a penny daily paper, a paper readable by the common people—the New York *Sun.* A year later, 1834, it was followed by the *Evening Transcript,* and a year later still, 1835, by the *Morning Herald,* James Gordon Bennett the editor. The era of dominating journalism had opened. Bennett was a revolutionist, a man with a vision, a dictator with a dream of universal domain. In the world as he visioned it books were to disappear:

I am determined to make the *Herald* the greatest paper that ever appeared in the world. The highest order of mind has never yet been found operating through the daily press. Let it be tried. What is to prevent a daily newspaper from being made the greatest organ of social life? Books have had their day—the theaters have had their day—the temple of religion has had its day. A newspaper can be made to take the lead of all these in the great movements of human thought and of human civilization.[2]

Horace Greeley's New York *Tribune* (1841) was even more revolutionary and comprehensive. The *Tribune* was a newspaper and magazine combined. Greeley had been reared in Vermont, and he imported for his New York sheet a "brain trust" group of New England helpers: George Ripley and Charles A. Dana of the Brook Farm community and Margaret Fuller of the Transcendentalist group, the first woman of note to be given a desk by a major American newspaper. Others in his employ were as noteworthy:

No other American newspaper during Greeley's lifetime could boast of a better staff than that of the *Tribune.* The *Tribune* not only was in truth "a great moral organ" as it was

[2] New York *Herald,* August 19, 1836.

dubbed by its rivals, but it maintained a literary character
unusual in a daily newspaper.[3]

In its weekly edition the *Tribune* penetrated the West
and was a strong influence culturally and educationally.

From this period dates the intellectual domination of
the newspaper, the epic of democracy. News sheets, many
of them with literary departments, sprang up in every
city and even in every country village. Even before the
1830's were over it could be said that America was leading Europe in the number of its journals:

The proportion to which the number of journals in each
quarter of the globe bears to the population is as follows:
. . . in Europe, one for every 106,000; in America one for
every 40,000; and precisely in the same ratio is the comparative progress of civilization in these different divisions
of the earth.[4]

Unquestionably the history of American literature is
interlinked everywhere with the history of periodicals—
magazines and newspapers. The machine had entered the
domain of literature, and it was creating a revolution.
More and more now mere quantity, rapid-production, vast
totals.

The Phi Beta Kappa orators were, as usual, the first
to sound a general alarm. Orville Dewey, for instance, at
Harvard in 1830:

The next effect of the change which has taken place in the
intellectual and social condition of the world, is the prodigious
multiplication of books of entertainment for the people. We

[3] Willard Grosvenor Bleyer, *Main Currents in the History of
American Journalism* (1927), p. 238.
[4] *The American Almanac* gave this quotation under "III: Periodical
Literature throughout the World," with the notation, "From the London New Monthly Magazine, December, 1832: The following table is
sent us by a gentleman as translated from the *Annales des Travaux*
of the Paris Statistical Society, made up from information derived by
M. Balbi, the well-known geographer."

are deluged with works of this class; and the passing tide bears us, every day, not only new productions, but new forms of literary production. It would be a serious task to master even the literature of the Annuals. Meanwhile periodical publications crowd upon us, keeping pace with every division of time but hours and minutes, (for even the newspapers grow learned) filling all the spaces now occupied by larger trifles, and covering, with grievous and pertinacious disorder and disarray, the tables that, fifty years ago, were pressed only by goodly quartos, or reverend folios. Seriously it is impossible to keep up with the literature of the day, without losing sight of things more important.

II

From the first, the two magazine cities were New York and Philadelphia. New York was unpuritanic, worldly, unawed by literary traditions. It dared to give the people what the people enjoyed: mere entertainment, sentimentality, subliterary fiction. In 1823 George P. Morris had started the *New York Mirror and Ladies' Literary Gazette,* a journal for family reading with an abundance of light fiction, sentimental songs with latest music, and expensive illustrations. And it had flourished. In 1831 it welcomed as a brother soul Nathaniel P. Willis, whose gay little magazine had been frozen out of Boston, and with his help it became the prototype of the later New York *Smart Set.* From 1823 to 1842, and then later under different titles and editors—Morris, however, always the leader—it amused and thrilled a wide audience of culture-seeking ladies and gave first aid to many young beginners in literature later to be well known.

But there was another and more serious literary audience in New York. The mellow Irving influence still ruled a gentle little group of writers. As late as 1833 there was founded *Knickerbocker's Magazine* to catch and hold the elusive charm of the genial Washington Irving summer of New York letters now fading into its ultimate autumn. The opening paragraph of the new magazine, indeed, contained the record that its earliest editor—Hoffman, who entitled the thing *Knickerbocker*—had received his inspiration for the work "during one of those delicious 'Indian Summer' days, the peculiar boast of our climate."

Charles Fenno Hoffman, poet, critic, novelist, "magazinist," conceived the magazine and edited the first three numbers, but it was its second editor, Lewis Gaylord Clark, who gave it its winsome character and made it for more than a quarter of a century the most loved of all American magazines. Hoffman, however, deserves more than passing mention. For twenty years, 1829–1849, he was prominent in literary New York, serving as editor at various times of at least six magazines and journals. With Irving, Paulding, Willis, Morris, Leggett, Verplanck, Cooper, Bryant, Sands, John Keese, Henry T. Tuckerman, Poe, Halleck, Hoffman, the twin brothers Lewis Gaylord Clark and Willis Gaylord Clark, New York in the 1830's and 1840's could claim to be the literary capital of the nation. In 1850 the *Church Review* very gravely weighed the Gotham group against the growing Boston group and found the Easterners decidedly wanting. The New York "school," it maintained, has "been industrious without parade of effort, scholarly without ostentation, active without bustle, and efficient without self-conceit; and, altogether, there is about them a unity of manner, thought and moral principle, and even a negative quality of style, which constitute them, with others, a literary school," [5] The last sunset glow it was of the dying eighteenth century in America.

Hoffman's novel, *Greyslaer* (1840), his *A Winter in the Far West* (1835)—he got as far west as St. Louis—and his volumes of poems were all of them extravagantly praised, even by European reviewers. His Western journey was believed to be better written than Irving's *Tour*

[5] Quoted by Homer F. Barnes in his *Charles Fenno Hoffman* (1930).

of the Prairies of the same period—and it was; and his
poetry was to be compared even with Moore's. Griswold,
indeed, in his *Poets and Poetry of America,* gave him
nearly twice as much space as he gave any other poet—
some forty-five poems in his first edition.

Hoffman, however, was but a brief phenomenon in
American letters. In 1849 he broke under the strain of
the work he was attempting, and during the last twenty
years of his life he was hopelessly insane. Reading his
volumes today, one can only wonder at his contemporary
fame. So also with the poetry and prose of the two Clarks
as preserved in *Knickerbocker's.*

Lewis Gaylord Clark remained with the magazine to
the end of its life—some twenty years. Indeed, he *was*
the magazine. As with Hoffman, his contemporary fame
was largely the result of his genial presence, his personal
charm. Clark's ability to attract notable contributors
amounted to genius. His "Editor's Table" department
from month to month, read by its first readers as if it
were the equal of Charles Lamb at his best, is sorry stuff
today. His last years, like Hoffman's, were pathetic. *The
Knickerbocker Gallery,* a volume got up as a benefit for
Clark, is a marker at the end of an era. From the major
list of authors of the period hardly a name is absent from
this golden book, the final monument to the Knickerbockers of New York.

III

Philadelphia, however, was the magazine city. Philadelphians were skeptical whenever was mentioned any new
northern magazine. At late as 1850 this entry in
George W. Child's *Recollections:*

I can recall, as though it were yesterday, a solemn conversation in the office of the Harpers, then on Cliff Street. The
four founders of the great firm were present. I was one of

a group of Philadelphians, and we were discussing the first number of Harper's *New Monthly Magazine.* It seemed so certain to us that the publication would be a failure. "It can't," said one Philadelphian, emphatically—"it *can't* last very long." The only successful magazines then published in the United States were those issued in Philadelphia—*Graham's, Godey's, Sartain's* and *Peterson's.*

First of all there was *Godey's Lady's Book,* established in 1830 by Louis A. Godey and after 1837 edited by Sarah Josepha Hale: "By the middle of the century she had built *Godey's* to a subscription list of 150,000, the largest circulation attained by any monthly up to the day she relinquished her editorship" [6]—in 1877. Godey was a business man, a publisher. His magazine was a growth from the gift-books which by 1830 had become sensationally profitable. Why not increase the profits by issuing a monthly gift-book? The idea was a flash of genius, as was the title *Lady's Book.* He acted instantly: he made a *monthly annual*—illuminated title-pages, steel engravings, sentimental fiction (borrowed at first from England), poetry for the ladies *à la mode,* fashion-plates in gorgeous colors, and departments elegant and domestic for "females." But Godey was no editor. The magazine, despite its title and its aspirations, lacked feminine appeal: it lacked an editor. Again a flash of genius: in Boston was flourishing the first "female" monthly ever established in America, with "the first woman editor in this country"—Sarah Josepha Hale. Godey purchased the monthly, united it with his own, and transported its editor to Philadelphia. That was in 1837, the year, be it remembered, that saw the coronation of Queen Victoria. *Godey's Lady's Book*—Sarah Josepha Hale—forty years —the American Victorian period. To be unconscious of this national institution, *Godey's,* is like studying Victorianism with no mention of Victoria. During the forty years the rise and growing dominance of feminism in

[6] Ruth E. Finley, *The Lady of Godey's, Sarah Josepha Hale* (1931).

America: Lucretia Mott, Susan B. Anthony, Emma Willard, Mary Lyon, Margaret Fuller, Lucy Stone, Lucy Larcom, the Lowell Mill girls, the Carey sisters, the Warner sisters, Harriet Beecher Stowe—and behind every one of them Sarah Josepha Hale and her potent engine, *Godey's Lady's Book.* Her leadership affected every department of her magazine. She made war upon the verbal and sensational extravagance that made ridiculous so much of the feminine writings of the time. Under her leadership, fiction began to leave the Apennines and the Pyrenees and the Rhine castles and come to America where there were no dukes and grand-duchesses. In 1837 no college in America was open to women. Mrs. Hale's editorials and campaigns against such a condition were emphatic. In 1837 women wrote fiction, when they wrote at all, under masculine pseudonyms. Mrs. Hale preferred feminine contributors, paid them well, urged them to drop their masculine pen-names, gave them literary advice, gathered about her as the decades grew a veritable feminine "school." It was Mrs. Hale who first launched Harriet Beecher Stowe.

The nineteenth century, says Ruth Finley, the latest biographer of Mrs. Hale, falls into three periods or "acts":

Sarah Hale was of the first act. She was a product of the eighteenth century, the abandon of which she knew at first hand and hated. She was of the second act, sympathetic with the revolt from Georgian coarseness and hardness, eager for reform, ambitious for the success of popular rule and all it implied for the common man and woman in better standards of living and wider opportunities for culture. She saw only the first scenes of the third act; the far swing of the Victorian pendulum, the full triumph of form over substance she did not live to see.

That *Godey's* and Mrs. Hale were responsible for some of the sentimentalism, the prudery, the moralistic—the

"Victorian"—atmosphere of the feminine fifties before
the explosion of the Civil War is undoubtedly true, but,
balanced against all this, a huge amount stands to her
credit. Her magazine went into all the reading homes of
the nation, and noiselessly it worked revolutions.

IV

In 1841 came the second Philadelphia monthly of national importance, *Graham's Magazine,* a combination of
the *Casket* and the *Gentleman's Magazine,* its proprietor
George Rex Graham. "It was a meteor across the sky
of the forties," at its brightest during the fifteen months
of 1841–1842 when its editor was Edgar Allan Poe, but
during its whole career—it died in 1858, the year after
the founding of the *Atlantic*—it was a major force. For
five years especially, 1841–1845, it "displayed a brilliance
which has seldom been matched in American magazine
history." [7] Graham had all the business ability of a Godey,
and with it editorial imagination. He employed Poe and
after him Griswold, not as editors, but as directors of the
literary work. He himself was editor and proprietor. Like
Godey, he appealed first of all to the reading "mass" with
"gift-book" devices, all those cheapening elements that so
filled Poe with disgust. At the end Poe wrote his friend
F. W. Thomas, "My reason for resigning was disgust at
the namby-pamby character of the magazine. . . . I allude to the contemptible pictures, fashion-plates, music,
and love-tales." [8] Always before Poe's eyes flitted the
will-o'-the-wisp magazine of his dreams, the *Penn Magazine*—perfect, always on the heights of literature as Poe
conceived of the heights. What he might have done with
this perfect magazine of his dream we can only conjecture.
We know what he did for Graham: "At the time of our

[7] Frank Luther Mott, *A History of American Magazines* (1930),
p. 344.
[8] Poe's *Works,* Harrison Edition, XVII, iii.

bargain (a verbal one) he had 6,000 subscribers—when I left him he had more than 40,000."

But Graham sought to combine both literary elements, the popular and the ultra-refined, to "carry water on both shoulders." He began to pay unheard-of prices to his authors and soon was able to advertise the most distinctive list of contributors ever possessed by any American magazine, among them Bryant, Cooper, Lowell, Poe, George P. Morris, Nathaniel Parker Willis, Longfellow, who contributed "The Spanish Student," R. H. Dana, C. F. Hoffman, Holmes, Paulding, T. B. Read, John Neal, Tuckerman, Mrs. Seba Smith, Mrs. Sigourney, and Frances Osgood.

The steel engravings to be found in almost every issue were by Sartain and other masters of the art then at the moment of its perfection. To protect from other journals his expensive purchases which filled their columns with his materials as soon as issued, Graham copyrighted each issue of his magazine, the first in America to do this. Godey quickly followed. For a time, intense rivalry between the two magazines, with *Graham's* in the lead. Poe's critical papers, notably his famous review of Hawthorne, and his short stories, among them "The Murders in the Rue Morgue"; Willis's brilliant essays; the short stories by the increasing clan of feminine writers, Mrs. Smith, Mrs. Osgood, Mrs. Kirkland and the rest; and the abundance of poetry sentimental and feminine— all of this had enormous drawing power. Graham waxed wealthy.[9] But Godey in the end surpassed him; he had two assets at least that no money could duplicate: he had the title *Lady's Book* and he had Sarah Josepha Hale. With random editors, often changed, Graham lost headway, while Godey steadily advanced. As a result, the magazine must be rated merely as a meteor, one that illuminated, however, while it lasted.

[9] "It was said that for some years the magazine yielded its owner $50,000 a year."—Mott, *op. cit.* See the *Critic,* July 21, 1894.

V

In an "Easy Chair" paper in 1884 on the death of Hoffman, George William Curtis remarked of Willis that "His gayety and his graceful fluency made him the first of our proper 'magazinists,' " and in explanation he added, "He had the lightness and ease of touch which are traditionally characteristic of the distinctive writer for the magazines." The statement even today, fifty years later, still stands, as does Curtis's final estimate: "Willis's ease became at last a mannerism, and a certain tone of affectation and apparent insincerity crept over his page."

In all the Jacksonian age, that amazing welter of spread-eagleism and barbarity, of sentimentalism, of feminism, of nascent Victorianism with its annuals and souvenirs and lady's books; the age of the elegant magazines—velvet on the frontier—*couleur de rose* in denim and calico, adolescent dreamings over Byron and Martin Farquhar Tupper and Dickens; the age of Websterian eloquence, of the lyceum lecturers—of Bayard Taylor, the traveler, Edward Everett, Emerson, Wendell Phillips; in all the yearning, turbulent, dreaming, toiling democracy of the three decades before the Civil War no single man was more completely at home in it all than Nathaniel Parker Willis. He was of it; he *was* it as completely as was Barnum or Horace Greeley or Sarah Josepha Hale. Poe fought the age and perished; Willis blended with it, loved it, fed it with sentimentality, gossip, literary stimulants, and amazingly he prospered. Right and left for years he threw his "hurrygraphs," his "dashes at life," "inklings of adventure," "pencillings," "fun jottings," "ephemera"—and amazingly was he paid for it.

Three generations of "magazinists" and publishers went to the making of N. P. Willis. His father, editor in Boston of the *Youth's Companion,* had taken the boy for a year into his printing office but with no thought of compelling him into the ancestral profession. He had college ambitions for the lad and had him thoroughly fitted, not, however, for Harvard, for, says his biographer, Henry A. Beers, "Deacon Willis would almost as soon have sent his boys into the jaws of hell as into such a hot-bed of Unitarianism as Cambridge college." He sent him to Yale where he was to room for four years with Horace Bushnell, later enrolled among the New England Saints. Never college career more sensational. Poetry from his freshman year—scriptural resettings in blank verse, published in all American newspapers; poetry that won handsome prizes—at least three of them—in popular magazines. Before his senior year he was hailed as one of the leading poets of the nation, his scripture paraphrases like "Absalom" and "The Sacrifice of Abraham" crowding even into the school-readers. At his graduation in 1827 Yale made him the commencement poet.

Returning to Boston, he edited for Goodrich the new annual, the *Legendary*, through two volumes in a single year and *The Token* for 1829; then without a penny he launched out for himself as a magazine proprietor and editor. The *American Monthly* was the name of the bantling, an ambitious name but one not at all too ambitious, for the young poet was already hailed as America's leading genius. It was to be limited not at all to Boston or to New England. "The difficulties of transmission over such an immense country," he wrote, "and the comparatively small proportion of literary readers limit our circulation to a thousand or two, at the farthest."

Alas for his dreams, however. The little magazine never got far beyond Boston, and only scatteringly did it cover Boston. Not Willis's fault, however. Never young editor more eager, more hard-working, more desirous to please. Practically the whole magazine month by month he created with his own pen. He aimed at all readers, especially the subliterary mass that demanded lightness and entertainment. In the two years and a half of the magazine's Boston life he wrote some of his best prose work, tales and sketches that he was to use again and again in his later magazines and his collections. Light stuff it was, mere "coxcomberies" as weighed in the Boston balances, and soon he was suffering persecution. Buckingham's newspaper was ferocious—such lightness was an insult to Boston. Joseph Snelling, in a smashing satire upon all the American writers, attacked the editor personally:

> Why, as in a band-box trim he walks the streets,
> Turns up his nose at every man he meets,
> As if at scented carrion? Why of late
> Do all the critics claw his shallow pate?
> True, he's a fool;—if that's a hanging thing,
> Let Prentice, Whittier, Mellen also swing.

The subscription list shrank to nothing; clearly the dapper little magazine was not for Boston, and Willis abandoned it with its $3,000 indebtedness and struck out for New York where lightness was appreciated and paid for. Here Morris and Woodworth and Fay hailed him at once as a fellow workman, added both him and his perished magazine to the flourishing New York *Mirror,* and began a friendship that lasted the rest of their lives.

That the *Mirror* group in scarcely a month was willing to entrust $500 to the young literary adventurer, send him to Europe as a special correspondent—totally unprecedented in 1831, promise him ten dollars for each of his letters written for the *Mirror,* tells much about the winsomeness and the eager personality of Willis. And the young adventurer "made good"; no magazine ever made a better investment.

·VI

In 1835 appeared in London in three volumes Willis's letters collected from the *Mirror* with the title *Pencillings by the Way.* According to the preface of the volume, publication had been forced upon him:

I had resided on the Continent for several years, and had been a year in England, without being suspected, I believe, in the societies in which I lived, of any habit of authorship. No production of mine had ever crossed the water, and my Letters to the New-York *Mirror* were (for this long period, and I presumed would be for ever), as far as European readers were concerned, an unimportant and easy secret. Within a few months of returning to this country, the *Quarterly Review* came out with a severe criticism on the *Pencillings by the Way,* published in the New-York *Mirror.* A London publisher immediately procured a broken set of this paper from an American resident there, and called on me with an offer of £300 for an immediate edition of what he had. . . . The book was printed in three volumes, at about $7 per copy, and in this expensive shape three editions were sold by the original publisher.

As a result, Willis, like Irving, "awoke to find himself famous." Orders for literary work poured in upon him, to be paid for at prices that turned his head. For a year and a half in London he created with fury an avalanche of magazine material, short stories for the most part, over the signature "Philip Slingsby," and all of this a year later, 1836, he issued in a three-volume sumptuous edition entitled *Inklings of Adventure.* By all means was it his best work, better by far than his much-praised book *A L'Abri, or The Tent Pitch'd,* issued three years later.

During the rest of his life he was a "magazinist." His biographer, Henry A. Beers, quoting from Charles T. Congdon, records that "Mr. Willis was the first magazine writer who was tolerably well paid." At one time, about 1842, he was writing four articles monthly for four magazines and receiving $100 each. These he gathered from time to time with such titles as *Dashes at Life with a Free Pencil* and *Ephemera.* And to the *Mirror* he constantly contributed newspaper-column-like serials with such fanciful titles as *Slipshoddities, Just You and I,* and *While We Hold You by the Button.*

No one of his generation, and certainly no American

before him, equaled Willis in the field that he made his own—light literature, charming tittle-tattle seemingly as spontaneous as a bird-song, and sparkling tales with all the earmarks of O. Henry's art two generations later. As a poet he is forgotten completely; as a recorder of travel he is all but unreadable even in his best passages; but his *Fun-Jottings, or Laughs I Have Taken a Pen to* (1835), still are funny, and such short-story nothings with trick endings as "Count Pott's Strategy," "Nora Mehidy; or, the Strange Road to the Heart of Hypolet Leathers," "The Spirit-Love of 'Ione S—,'" and "Mrs. Passable Trott" can be enjoyed today even by sophomores.[10]

VII

The "magazinist" of the 1830's and the 1840's most known today, however, was Edgar Allan Poe. He was a poet, a short-story writer, a critic—he was all three of these —but fundamentally was he an editor. First, in his editorial career, he touched the South—he was editor of the *Southern Literary Messenger;* next he moved to the Philadelphia area to take charge of *Burton's Gentleman's Magazine* and later *Graham's;* and finally he went to New York to work on the *Broadway Journal.* He was a "magazinist" following his market. From no other viewpoint can one understand the man. All of his writings, save his adolescent lyrics, were created with magazine intent. He sought always for timeliness, variety, compelling interest, finesse.

Poe without question has been the most discussed and the most widely exploited of all American writers. The critics have battened on him for a century. He seems un-American, an unexplained exotic in the great American democracy, out of place, out of time. A genius undoubt-

---

[10] For a more complete study of Willis's short-story work, see Fred Lewis Pattee, *Development of the American Short Story* (1923), pp. 77–88.

edly, and who explains genius? One can dwell long on his handicaps. The Fates that dropped him into the vulgarian chaos of the mid-nineteenth century in America were either blind or else cynical beyond human measure. By every standard of criticism he was out of place: race and family, environment, epoch—in not one of them was there harmony. In race broken: his father an Irishman outside of Ireland, an outcast from his family because of refusal to keep step with family tradition; becoming a third-rate actor rather than lord of the Maryland manor of the American Poes; married at last to an English variety actress of the barn-storming line. But all the genius Poe possessed came from this elfin mother who had been born on the Atlantic—in no-man's land. All her life was she a tiny thing, fundamentally a romp, vivacious, a child her life long. The father, on the contrary, was heavy of personality, slow, unresilient. For three years the two were members of a stock company stationed in Boston, and from contemporary newspaper reviews [11] we can reconstruct the two. Everywhere such touches as these: "Mrs. Poe's Priscilla Tomboy was an excellent performance." . . . "Mr. Poe did not attain much celebrity in Frank Rochdale. We hope he may yet learn more dignity in elevated scenes." . . . "Mrs. Poe received her father with great effect." . . . "Mr. Poe was Count Bassett and acted, as usual, quite tamely." . . . "Miss Jenny in Mrs. Poe had an able representative. The hoyden is remarkably adapted to her powers." And so on for three years. Life she knew only as a stage thing. From her earliest years she had been an actress, tripping fairy parts and impersonating cupids in her very babyhood. She knew little besides.

Poe remembered her only as a marvelous being with large eyes hovering over him. A miniature of her, an elfin thing, is said to have been his most treasured possession.

[11] Notably Joseph T. Buckingham's *Polyanthos,* from which I have made my quotations.

Both father and mother were dead before he was old enough to realize them, and he had been adopted by a Scotch tobacco factor of Richmond, John Allan. When five years old he had been taken by his foster-parents to England, and there he attended English schools until he was eleven. Another wrench and he was back in Richmond in the local schools to prepare for college. At seventeen he was sent to the University of Virginia, supplied by the thrifty old Scotchman, his foster-father, with an allowance that paid not over half of his legitimate expenses. Wounded in his pride, pressed for money, he resorted to gambling and lost heavily, and then for an overcoat and other necessary clothing he contracted a considerable debt. This the Scotch father refused to pay. In a rage he took the boy home, brutalized him, even turned him out of his house. The letters recently released by the Poe Shrine of Richmond tell a tragic story. Mr. Allan is revealed in a sinister light, and Poe, alternately abject and then demoniacal in rage, presents no admirable figure.

His letters during the next two or three years are pitiful. For some reason he went to Boston and with no means at all persuaded a small publisher there to issue a tiny volume of poems, *Tamerlane and other Poems,* by a Bostonian. Then for months he disappeared. In the United States army, it has been proved. His record on the army books is faultless. He was promoted, and perhaps because of this he was discovered by Mr. Allan and through his aid was enabled to enter West Point. As a student he was above the average, and in languages he was brilliant. Then had come news of the death of Mrs. Allan and the certainty that he was not to be the heir of the Allan estate. Why continue at West Point? Without money, he believed, no man could rise as an officer in the army. Deliberately he broke away from the Academy and finally settled with his father's sister, Mrs. Clemm, at Baltimore. Thus the first chapter in the pitiful tragedy.

All his dreams and hopes now centered in literature.

Like the young Longfellow, he would devote his life to poetry. At Baltimore he had published a second volume of lyrics. And now at twenty-two he issued his third book containing such lyrics as "To Helen," "The Sleeper," "Lenore," "The Valley of Unrest," "The City in the Sea," "Israfel," barren of everything save a strange weird music—no range of thought, no genuine emotion, no experience, no "criticism of life." A few haunting phrases, a sense of melody, but the only precipitate left the reader is an aura somehow of awfulness, of irreparable ill, of hopeless despair. And their author not twenty-two.

Living at the home of his aunt, Mrs. Clemm, in Baltimore, Poe now, with all his powers, sought to win recognition and support as a writer. In vain. Like his contemporary Hawthorne, he could find publication for his tales only in obscure newspapers. In 1833 when starvation seemed imminent, he was awarded the hundred-dollar prize offered by the Baltimore *Saturday Visiter*. It was a turning-point in his literary career. John P. Kennedy, a judge in the prize contest, became interested in the high quality of his work and in his forlorn condition and sought to place him as an editor. The *Southern Literary Messenger*, Richmond, he knew, was seeking literary help. The letter which he at once wrote to T. W. White, the proprietor, is illuminating:

Poe did right in referring to me. He is very clever with his pen—classical and scholarlike. He wants experience and direction, but I have no doubt he can be made very useful to you; and, poor fellow, he is *very* poor. I told him to write something for every number of your magazine and that you might find it to your advantage to give him some permanent employ. He has a volume of very *bizarre* tales in the hands of Carey & Lea, in Philadelphia, who for a year past has been promising to publish them. The young fellow is highly imaginative, and a little given to the *terrific*. He is at work upon a tragedy, but I have turned him to drudging upon whatever may make money, and I have no doubt you and he will find your account in each other.

At this point begins Poe's life as an editor. For the rest of his life he was an editor of magazines, with intervals of unemployment.

VIII

An inferiority complex accounts for Poe. His adolescent life had been a tragedy, blow after blow upon his pride. First the complex of the adopted child, then the humiliation of the college experience, the brutality of the Scotch foster-father, the awakening from the dream of inheriting the Allan estate. Trained he had been like a second son in all the instincts and habits of life of a feudal Southern gentleman, then brutally dropped into the democratic mass where he had originated. Again, one must approach the man by way of his health. George E. Woodberry alone has emphasized this defect:

He was then penniless; he was solitary, proud and despairing. Hereditary weakness was in his constitution; there was a blight in the family—father and mother had died early in life, his brother developed youthful dissipation and was already dead, his sister at the end of her childhood without any apparent cause had failed inwardly, and, though she lived long, remained mentally in a state of arrested development. A constitution such as this family history indicates, however reinforced by a well nurtured boyhood and hardy outdoor life, must have been tried by bodily privation and mental strain, even if Poe had led a less intellectual and less nervously exhausting, to say nothing of such influences as his youthful use of liquor may have had. He had reached the years when, in such a nature after such a career, a nervous crisis was due.[12]

At the very start of his editorial assistance to White on the *Messenger,* September, 1835, this pathetic statement to Kennedy:

[12] *The Life of Edgar Allan Poe* (1909), I, 122.

Alas! it appears to me that nothing can now give me pleasure—or the slightest gratification. Excuse me, my dear Sir, if in this letter you find much incoherency. My feelings at this moment are pitiable indeed. I am suffering under a depression of spirits such as I have never felt before. I have struggled in vain against the influence of this melancholy—I am wretched, and I know not why.

It is time for a pathological life of Poe.

The inferiority complex explains his earliest prose, his *Tales of the Folio Club* collection, fated never to be issued under that title. Sixteen tales there seem to have been in the collection, all the prose he is known to have written before the period of the *Messenger*. Kennedy characterized them as for the most part "bizarreries." To Poe he wrote: "Your fault is love of the extravagant," and Poe, defending himself, explained that

Most of them were intended for half banter, half satire—although I might not have fully acknowledged this to be their aim even to myself. "Lionizing" and "Loss of Breath" were satires properly speaking—at least so meant—the one of the rage for Lions, and the facility for becoming one—the other the extravagances of Blackwood.

Satire is the breath of inferiority and slighted worth. These tales are inferiority complexes, sneers at successful mediocrity: "Silence" and "Shadow," are travesties upon Boston "high-hattedness"—Transcendentalism; "Lionizing," a facetious view of Willis; "King Pest," a representation of Bulwer; and so through the list. It is the work of a rejected young genius who sees the magazines full of work inferior to his own condemned stuff. Everywhere this complex: his slashing attacks upon Theodore S. Fay and Thomas Dunn English, his attempts in his tales and reviews to display profound erudition, his snubbing of New England culture by reading to his Boston audience mere juvenile verses. Through his whole

later life he was like a dispossessed second son, forced in
utter poverty to be patronized or pitied.

IX

After his arrival in Richmond to conduct the literary
work of the *Messenger* (1831–1835), Poe was a "magazinist"—he himself made the classification. To Charles
Anthon he wrote:

I have written no books and have been so far essentially
a magazinist, bearing not only willingly but cheerfully sad
poverty and the consequent contumelies and other ills which
the condition of the mere magazinist entails upon him in
America.

And yet over and over in his letters and "Marginalia"
he defends the magazine. It was the coming literary vehicle of power, he believed. In his essay, "Magazine Writing," he could call it "A branch which is daily growing in
importance—and which, in the end (not far distant) will
be the most influential of all the departments of letters." [13]
With this starting point the rest is easy. His rules for
the short story, in the review of Hawthorne's *Twice-Told
Tales*—a review of his own work rather than Hawthorne's—are simply the requirements of a magazine
editor. For the magazine must have shortness in its fiction, and in order to accomplish this there must be the
constant thought of compression, condensed and striking
openings and endings, "a certain unique or single effect,"
"totality," "unity of effect or impression." Poe's demand
for originality, for novel effects, was also a magazine demand. In his critique of Elizabeth Oakes Smith, for example, this expression of belief:

"*Ceteris paribus,* every class of fiction is the better for
originality; every writer is false to his own interest if he

[13] Poe's *Works*, Redfield's Edition, IV, 397–398.

fails to avail himself at the outset, of the effect which is certainly and invariably derivable from the great element, *novelty.*" [14] Monotony in a magazine's contents repels readers. Hence Poe's enormous variety—tales of horror, detective stories, stories impressionistic, scientific, poetic, humorous, hoaxes and pseudo-scientific excursions, melodrama, and sentimentalism.

Again, for magazine use there must be timeliness. In all ways must the reader be caught and held. No better bait than horror, than the melodramatic, the swift-moving of sensation. A letter from Burton, owner of the *Gentleman's Magazine* when Poe was editor, illumines the man's editorial standards:

We shall agree very well, though I cannot permit the magazine to be made a vehicle for that sort of severity which you think "so successful with the mob." I am truly much less anxious about making a monthly "sensation" than I am on the point of fairness. . . . You say the people love havoc, etc.

Studiously Poe kept himself in the current of his times. As an editor, he had access to the foreign magazines and reviews. He knew intimately the work of Bulwer-Lytton, Byron, Moore, Disraeli, the *Blackwood's* writers, the later German romancers, the French symbolists and decadents. His debt chiefly was to Bulwer. From him he learned the secrets of vaults and dungeons. "The Assignation," for instance, draws not from Hoffman's "Doge and Dogaressa." There is scarcely a point of similarity. It is colored throughout by "Pelham" and "The Pilgrims of the Rhine." Note the passages that he edited out of the first edition of the tale as it appeared in *Godey's Lady's Book,* January, 1834. Poe's dependence upon *Blackwood's,* too, is a theme for a doctor's thesis. Enough. My complete

[14] Poe's *Works,* Edition of 1856, III, 132.

analysis of Poe's prose fiction stands in my volume on the history of the American short story.[15]

There remain his criticism and his later poetry. Like all other magazine editors, he was studious as to manner. He knew the rules of the game. Literature was to him a thing to be weighed in the editorial balances, to be analyzed and assessed. He knew Coleridge's *Biographia Literaria,* and he appropriated from it his literary philosophy. This, for instance, concerning poetry:

Beyond the limits of Beauty its province does not extend. Its sole arbiter is Taste. With the intellect or with the conscience it has only collateral relations. It has no dependence, unless incidentally, upon either Duty or Truth.

And again:

If Longfellow would claim the sacred title of poet, he should limit his endeavors to the creation of novel moods of beauty, in form, in color, in sound, in sentiment; for wide range has the poetry of words domain.

According to Harrison, the influence of the German critics August Wilhelm von Schlegel and his brother was "profound," and his tendencies to morbid inquiry and metaphysical speculation placed him, against his will, perhaps, in the camp of Jung Stilling, Lavater, Spurzheim, and La Motte Fouque.[16]

Then, too, Poe was analytical, even to the limit of explaining his methods of poetical creation. A critic in *Blackwood's* found this his leading "complex":

No passion in these tales, neither is there any attempt at dramatic dialogue. The bent of Mr. Poe's mind seems rather to have been towards reasoning than sentiment. . . . But the tales rivet the attention. There is a marvellous skill in putting together the close array of facts and of details which make

[15] Fred Lewis Pattee, *Development of the American Short Story* (1923), Chapter VI.
[16] Poe's *Works,* Harrison's Edition, X, viii.

up the narrative, or the picture; for the effect of his description, as of his story, depends never upon any bold display of imagination, but on the agglomeration of incidents, enumerated in the most veracious manner.[17]

His criticism for the most part dealt with manner, with plot analysis, with technique generally. For one who could at times reach such heights of excellence in his critiques, it is amazing that at times he could fall so low. He criticized contemporary writings always with the creating author primarily his text. He punished his enemies and patted his friends regardless of the literary merit of their work.

X

What of Poe's ten volumes at the present day, eighty years and more after the pitiful tragedy that ended his life at Baltimore? His criticism, overloaded as it is with pedantic affectations, had little influence even upon his own generation and, aside from the single review of Hawthorne, is unread today save in colleges where it is required. His tales, too, are old-fashioned in their style, often ludicrous in their Della Cruscan affectation. Realism was no part of his literary equipment, and all his attempts at humor were pathetic. His dialogue is invariably melodramatic, his characterization is theatric make-up—witness the Negro in "The Gold Bug." In everything touching artistry, however—manner, technique, architectonics —the man was brilliant. He had, moreover, the devilish power to create an atmosphere that dominates, even today, his reader like a poison-gas. It is impossible to read a tale of his, even the Della Cruscan and monstrously impossible "The Fall of the House of Usher" or "The Black Cat," without a sensation that is hard to explain.

Emerson's characterization of Poe the poet as "the

[17] *Blackwood's Magazine,* November, 1847.

jingle-man" is unfair and extreme, but it touches the
heart of the matter. Poems like "The Bells" are mere
rhetoric, mere tinklings of colored glass, and "The
Raven" barely escapes the same classification. If Poe's
own words can be believed, it was made in cold blood as
one cuts a jig-saw puzzle. No light save a glow-worm
glimmer of decay, no original voicings. Melody, weird
music, a few memorable lines in "To Helen," "Israfel,"
"The City in the Sea," "The Raven," "The Haunted
Palace," *"To One in Paradise,"* "Ulalume," "Annabel
Lee," "The Conqueror Worm"—what poet has ever risen
to Poe's fame with so tiny a portfolio?

The growth of his fame has been gradual. New England under the leadership of Lowell sought to obliterate
him as a cancer that must be cured by surgery. For a time
they succeeded, but the clumsy, possibly unkind, editings
of Griswold, and the spirited battle that followed, the un-
covered romance of Mrs. Whitman, and the pathetic ending at Baltimore have made the man a myth. Everywhere
mystery. A multitude of specialists at work on the problem, and no two agreed. And the end is not yet.

His influence has been considerable, not in America
especially, but in Europe. In France he became the patron
saint of a cult. Baudelaire made of him a superman, and
the decadent school of which he was the leader modeled
themselves upon his work doubtlessly because of its uncolored clearness, its artistry, its Gallic spirit, its complete
freedom from the puritanic and the didactic. Most vividly
did it illustrate their theories of "art for art's sake," and
the very fact that it was concealed in a foreign language
whose nuances they had to translate into their own imag-
inings made it for them veritable perfection. In England
the poetry made no real impression. It was nothing new.
But the tales were read, and in one case at least they became a notable influence. Conan Doyle made no secret of
the fact that he found his model for the Sherlock Holmes
fictions in Poe's "The Murders in the Rue Morgue."

XI

I end as I began: Poe was a genius thrown into the muck-heap of an unliterary generation, the feminine thirties and forties of democratic America. Powerless was his genius to lead or to control. He lacked the physical power; he was devoid of all spiritual forces; he grasped at a few colored straws and went down in miserable defeat. He was a "magazinist," a caterer for the mere moment. Nothing had he to say, nothing new to add to the world's store, nothing even suggesting a criticism of life. He amused with his tricks, his hoaxes, his sensational variety a crude and sentimental generation. One reads him today for the curious quality of his atmospheres, reads him in spite of the archaic style, the monstrous artificiality, and the studied climaxes that violate every law of the natural world. To read him with fullest effect, however, one must be conscious at every moment of Edgar Allan Poe. He has been kept alive these two generations or three not because of his work but because of himself. And the mystery has become a myth, the shadow of which lengthens with the years.

Walt Whitman's summation has never been improved upon:

For a long while, and until lately, I had a distaste for Poe's writings. I wanted, and still want, for poetry, the clear sun shining, and fresh air blowing—the strength and power of health, not of delirium, even amid the stormiest passions— with always the background of the eternal moralities.[18]

[18] *American Literature,* January, 1935, p. 435.

CHAPTER XXXII

LONGFELLOW

I

THE PIONEER settlers came to America to avoid Europe. Romance for them was in the West, but the second generation of the Republic, especially the college-bred of the 1820's and the 1830's, began to look back with reverence to "Our Old Home." Scott's romances in prose and verse bathed in sunset colors the whole East, and then had come Washington Irving with his *Sketch Book* and *Bracebridge Hall*. The return to Boston of Washington Allston, and to Harvard of the pioneer matriculants in German universities—Ticknor, Everett, Felton, Bancroft—had emphasized the actual Europe tremendously in the imaginations of those long fed on mere books. It was not, however, until Willis worked out the route of "the grand tour," Byronized it, romanticized it, fitted it with guidebook descriptions, that Europe began to be thought of in terms of actual visitation. After Willis's letters in the *New York Mirror* between February 13, 1832, and January 14, 1836—a part of them, nearly one-half, republished in London in 1835 as *Pencillings by the Way*—and after Longfellow's *Outre Mer* (1831–1835),[1] there had come a deluge of travel-books, most of them in the key of *Alice in Wonderland*. T. S. Fay of the *Mirror* board of editors went abroad in 1833, and his letters, later published with the title *The Minute Book*, appeared in the

[1] Most of *Outre Mer* had been published as a series of sketches in the *Atlantic Monthly*, July, 1831, to February, 1833. It was published as a volume by *Harper's* in 1835.

Mirror side by side with Willis's. William Cox, author of *Crayon Sketches by an Amateur,* was also at the same time pouring travel-letters into the *New York Mirror.* Elsewhere there were appearing Cooper's *Gleanings in Europe,* ten volumes in all, David Porter's *Constantinople* (1835), and Henry T. Tuckerman's *Italian Sketch Book* (1835). All of these in four years.

For the atmosphere of all these romanticizings of travel one has but to leaf through the volumes of Willis's *Pencillings.* Everywhere superlatives, glorification, wonder. His first day on the Continent all but overcame him with emotion:

I certainly have seen more that is novel and amusing since morning than I ever saw before in any seven days of my life. Not a face, not a building, not a dress, not a child even, not a stone in the street, nor shop, nor woman, nor beast of burden, looks in any comparable degree like its namesake on the other side of the water.[2]

In Venice language failed him completely. Venice by moonlight:

Abroad in a summer's moonlight in Venice, is a line that might never be written but as the scene of a play. You can not miss pleasure. If it were only the tracking silently and swiftly the bosom of the broader canals, lying asleep like streets of molten silver between the marble palaces, or shooting into the dark shadows of the narrower, with the black spirit-like gondolas gliding past, or lying in the shadow of a low and not unoccupied balcony; or did you but loiter on in search of music, lying unperceived beneath the windows of a palace, and listening, half asleep, to the sound of the guitar and the song of the invisible player within; this, with the strange beauty of every building about you, and the loveliness of the magic lights and shadows were enough to make a night of pleasure, even were no charm of personal adventure to be added to this enumeration.[3]

[2] Letter (1844 edition), p. 4.
[3] Letter XXXII, p. 51.

With Byron in his hands, he swept through the Cyclades:

Passed an hour in the mizzen-chains with "the Corsair" in my hand, and "Coran's Bay" opening on the lee. With what exquisite pleasure one reads, when he can look off from the page, and study the scene of the poet's fiction:

> In Coran's Bay floats many a galley light
> Through Coran's lattices the lamps burn bright
> For Seyd, the pacha, makes a feast to-night.[4]

So through three volumes. A romanticized reporter who knew his readers. It is like the journal of a Prince of Wales. He meets everybody, he is dined by everybody of importance, he hobnobs with all the authors of a kingdom, and he characterizes and romanticizes with a touch that is genius. And provincial America read it like Scott's novels, or Bulwer-Lytton's.

The result was inevitable: the first wave of European travel. First, the students who brought back Europe in their baggage. The flame that we call the New England renaissance of the mid-nineteenth century was a backfire kindled from Germany and France and England. Consider the education of Henry Wadsworth Longfellow.

II

The *poet* Longfellow was born in Europe in 1836; the physical Longfellow had had birthplace in Portland, Maine, February 27, 1807. His father, a Harvard man, a lawyer, a member of Congress, had sent the boy to Bowdoin well prepared in languages. An active lad he had been, yet enamoured of books and inclined to live in a sentimentalized world constructed from his voluminous reading. More he got from the college than did his class-mate Hawthorne. The Greek and Latin came easily. Time there was for reading—and for writing. Like Hawthorne, he had awakened to literature. Perhaps it was Professor

[4] Letter LXIX, p. 121.

Samuel P. Newman who awakened him to the broader meanings of literature—Newman, brilliant scholar, whose treatise on rhetoric had gone through sixty editions in the United States and had found publication in England. Longfellow's own testimony laid his awakening to the *Sketch Book*. He records that he

read each succeeding number with ever increasing wonder and delight, spellbound by its pleasant humor, its melancholy tenderness, its atmosphere of reverie—nay, even by its gray-brown covers, the shaded letters of its titles, and the fair clear type, which seemed an outward symbol of its style.

Authorship had become a concrete idea in his mind even before his graduation. He was writing poetry for the papers and dreaming, in the Irving way, of Europe. As a junior, he was filling his letters with tones like this:

If I were in England now (and I have been wishing myself there all the day long so warmly that, if my wishes could but turn to realities, I should have been there) I should become a bacchanalian for a while. I do not believe any person can read the fifth number of the Sketch Book without feeling, at least, if not expressing, a wish similar to my own.

But Europe and literature as a profession were out of the question. The father was a Yankee lawyer in Congress. "A literary life," he wrote the dreaming senior at Bowdoin, "to one who has the means of support, must be very pleasant. But there is not wealth enough in this country to afford encouragement and patronage to merely literary men." And, unlike his classmate Hawthorne, he abandoned his dream and, home with his diploma, began the study of his father's profession. And but for an accident there would have been no poet Longfellow.

Where else can record be found of a struggling little country college sending a boy of nineteen to Europe to fit him for a chair in a new subject, one that only Harvard has recognized? Benjamin Orr, a trustee of Bowdoin, had been impressed by the young senior's translation from Horace and had made the nomination. And the youth was off for Europe, the enchanted land of Irving's *Sketch Book*.

For three years he studied and read and absorbed languages in France, Spain, Italy, Germany, England, and he came back to take the new college chair an enthusiast, an interpreter of European culture. For the next five and a half years he moved amid an atmosphere of perpetual wonder and mild excitement. To talk to him, to listen to his glowing lectures, was to get a whiff from that Old World which to the provincial little college community was so far off and wonderful. He began his work as one opens a mission station in a foreign land. There were in all America then no adequate text-books for the learning of foreign languages: he would make them himself. There were few copies of European classics: he would edit work for his classes. Grammars, readers, editions he made—ten of them. He gave courses of lectures. Bowdoin was too small for his mission work: he wrote studies and introductions and appreciations of the Romance languages and published them in the *North American Review*.

And he would be an Irving, too: the dream over the *Sketch Book* was still with him. Even before he had left Europe he had outlined a volume of Irving-like sketches. "I am writing a book," he had written to his father from Göttingen, May, 1829, "a kind of a Sketch-Book of France, Spain, Germany, and Italy." The book became *Outre Mer; A Pilgrimage Beyond the Sea* (1835). Irving in every chapter—a shadowy, emaciated Irving, to be sure, stripped of his pleasant humor, his melancholy tenderness, his atmospheres of revery, yet nevertheless Irving. Bombastic it was, and inflated in diction—every book is a "tome" and every clock a "horologue"; one of the swarm of fluttering moths that whirled for a time about the *Sketch Book* candle.

This, then, the young Professor Longfellow who in April, 1835, in his twenty-ninth year, sailed with his young wife for his second tour among the universities of Europe. He was joyous: the world was good. He had been called to Harvard, second occupant of the new chair of modern languages. George Ticknor had been the first. The world was good. It was quite another Longfellow who, late the next year, came back alone. On November 29 his wife had died in childbirth at Rotterdam.

We know little of this crisis in the man's life. His brother Samuel passed over it briefly. T. W. Higginson and a few later students have added letters. What it meant in a foreign land, immeasurably more foreign in that early period, among utter strangers, we can only imagine. Four days after her death, with her last words still in his ears, "O, Henry, do not forget me. I will be with you and watch over you," he had pushed on to Heidelberg as he had originally planned and had tried to drown his memory in work.

Then had come the second blow—news of the death of his dearest friend, his brother-in-law. Loneliness now unutterable. "Oh, my dear George," he wrote his friend Greene, "what have I not suffered . . . and I have no friend with me to cheer and console me." His solitude, his brooding, his sentimentality, his introspective soul brought abnormal visions. The image of his lost one was ever before him. "Hardly a day passes," he wrote a year later, "that some face, or familiar object, or some passage in the book I am reading, does not call up the image of my beloved wife so vividly that I pause and burst into tears—and some times cannot rally again for hours."

Everything was turning him to romanticism: his subjective, sentimental temperament; his mystic soul, heritage from his Puritan ancestry; his wrought-up and receptive condition; his solitude; his loneliness; the old medieval town with its castle ruin; the romantic nooks and groves and legends; the opening springtime with all its German softness and beauty; and, above all, the atmosphere of romantic poetry that was shimmering all about him. Almost incessantly he read. During the long winter evenings and the dim, foggy days he read, interminably he read. And his authors were all of them from that earlier school which even then was still dominating German literature. His literary contacts nourished his growing romanticism. While on a visit to Bonn he called upon and conversed with the venerable August Wilhelm Schlegel. We know that he read much of Goethe, Tieck, Hoffman, Jean Paul Richter:

Many hours were spent in solitary rambles in the neighboring woods . . . in sketching among the castle ruins, or enjoying the magnificent views from its terraces. Under the garden trees he read Herder. Sitting on the benches of the road that climbs to the Wolfsbrunnen, Richter's Kampaner-Thal is his companion.[5]

"Hyperion" reveals fully the nature of his reading. He was familiar with Tiedge's "Urania," Bettina Arnim's "Goethe's Correspondence with a Child," Arnim and Brentano's "Boy's Wonder-Horn," Novalis's "Heinrich von Ofterdingen," Hoffmann's "Tales," Fichte's "Destiny of Man," Schubert's "History of the Soul," Goethe's "Faust," Müller's "Songs of a Wandering Horn Player," Jean Paul's "Titan," Uhland's "Poems," Werner's "Dramas," Tieck's "Poems," Carove's "Story Without an End," Salis and Matthisson's "Lyrics." These save some few casual allusions, are all the writers mentioned and criticized in "Hyperion," and it is notable that with the single exception of Goethe they belong all of them to that weird choir which sang the decadence of the German *Sturm und Drang.*

[5] Samuel Longfellow, *Life of Henry Wadsworth Longfellow* (1886), I, 229.

III

The parallel between the Longfellow of this experience and the German mystic, Novalis, is striking. Both, through intensity of bereavement, became poets of the night. The earlier mystic, in the third number of his *Hymns to the Night,* records that once while he was weeping on the grave that had swallowed his very life, "alone as no other mortal had ever been alone," suddenly there had descended upon him a shuddery twilight, a new atmosphere, that swept from him forever all desire for day. He had entered a new world, the transfigured world of night. Then through the mist there had appeared to him the glorified figure of his lost beloved, and henceforth she became for him an abiding presence, and from that moment he had had "an eternal, unchanging faith in the heaven of Night."

So with the Longfellow of the Heidelburg winter; the utter bereavement, the loneliness, the brooding, the vision of the angel wife, the ministry of Night, the mysticism— a German romantic, an American Novalis, a poet of the Night. Though living a long lifetime amid the headlong materialism of a new world, though all about him were the din and shoutings of a lusty nation in its adolescence, building a new commonwealth with revolution in its soul, he remained in his library with its eastern windows and looked into the shimmering past, for, says Novalis, "He who has once stood on Earth's borderland and perceived that new country—the dwelling of Night—returns no more to the tumult of life, to the land where light reigns amid ceaseless unrest."

IV

After the winter at Heidelburg and the summer journey through Switzerland, where he had met Frances Appleton, he had settled down in the old Cragie House at Cambridge for three years of loneliness, years of teaching languages to Harvard students, years in which he continued to brood and dream over his Goethe, Jean Paul, Tieck, Hoffman. And from out these German years emerged the strange romance, *Hyperion*. Not yet had poetry expressed his soul, though much of this prose tale hovers perilously near it. Like Hawthorne, he was living in his own individual world, self-contained, introspective, abnormal. "Most of the time I am alone," he wrote to Greene two years after his return from Europe. "I want to travel. Am too excited, too tumultuous inwardly. And my health suffers. . . . This dragooning of schoolboys in lessons is like going backward."

To get to the full meaning of this period, we must read the romance *Hyperion* (1839). The events of the romance may be "mostly fictitious," even as the author declared to Greene; but the events are the smallest part of *Hyperion*. "It contains my cherished thoughts for three years." He might have said: "It contains my naked soul." The shadowland of the romantic poets, the heart-hunger, the ministry of Night, the presence of the lost one, and now a new element, the new love incredible, impossible, and the struggle of this love with the specter of the past—it is all here.

The Longfellow of *Outre Mer* had been another personality. *Hyperion* is a German book, like a translation of one of those thousand shoots that sprang up around the trunk of *Wilhelm Meister*. It is a rambling, chaotic creation, full of Jean Paul interludes and digressions, with the slenderest thread of plot and without climax or dramatic force. Everywhere romance; atmosphere above all; the "mingling of daylight and starlight"; "a dreamy, yearning, ideal indistinctness." We can visualize nothing. The heroine, even after two pages of description, is simply voice and eyes. It is a book written in the night, to be read "the evening having come and the tall candles being lighted"—a book without predecessors on this side of the ocean, an exotic, a pale and marvelous night-moth that has fluttered over from the ruins of the Old World. Everywhere twilight. The plot moves, when it does move at all, from moonlight to moonlight. To get its atmosphere, read of Emma of Ilmenau who shunned "the glare of daylight and society, and wished to be alone. Like the evening primrose, her heart opened only after sunset; but bloomed through the dark night with sweet fragrance."

It was a book written with a purpose, however. "It is a sincere book," its author wrote Greene, to whom more than anyone else he confided his inner life, "showing the passage of a morbid mind into a purer and healthier state." For the problem, the struggle, the heart of the book, read the chapter entitled "The Fountain of Oblivion." The student Hieronymus has been dazzled by the beautiful Hermione until, like one who has looked at the sun, he can see nothing else, and he seeks to drown his new love in the Fountain of Oblivion. And looking deep into its waters he beheld the great City of the Past, with silent marble streets, and moss-grown walls, and spires uprising with a wave-like flickering motion. And amid the crowds that thronged those streets he beheld faces once familiar and dear to him, and heard sorrowful, sweet voices singing, "O forget us not! forget us not!" and then the distant mournful sound of funeral bells that were tolling below in the City of the Past. A struggle between the quick and the dead, and at the close nothing settled.

Moodiness, aimlessness, idle dreaming, vain regrets were unmanning him, and his Puritan conscience was in protest. His lyric, "A Psalm of Life," written with the same quill that had produced that penultimate chapter of *Hyperion*, was a call to the manhood within him. The poem had first been made public in a lecture to his Harvard class on Goethe—doubtless to illustrate the spirit of *Wilhelm Meister*. Goethe, too, had had his period of dreaming, of melancholy, of irresolution. "That the life of man is but a dream," he had written in his *Sorrows of*

Werther, "has come into many a head; and with me, too, some feeling of that sort is ever at work." But the Goethe of the *Wilhelm Meister* period is another man. Life is no longer a dream, but a place for work. Be self-reliant, self-forgetful, he cries; away with introspection and morbid dreams:

> Life's no resting, but a moving;
> Let thy life be deed on deed.

He could say now to the Werther of his youthful creation:

> Once more then, much-wept shadow, dost thou dare
>   Boldly to face the day's clear light,
> To meet me on fresh blooming meadows fair,
>   And dost not tremble at my sight?

His trembling soul he lashes to action: "art is long, life is short, judgment difficult, opportunity transient—therefore, be doing."

> Keep not standing fixed and rooted;
>   Briskly venture, briskly roam!
> Head and hand, where'er thou foot it,
>   And stout heart are still at home.

The message came to Longfellow, as indeed it had come to all Europe, like a breath from the living North. Frederick Schlegel expressed his belief that the nineteenth century was molded by three great tendencies: Fichte's *Wissenschafslehre,* Goethe's *Wilhelm Meister,* and the French Revolution.

It was this ringing message of action, this challenge to aimlessness and dreaming and sentimentality, that Longfellow put into verse for his own soul-discipline. His first intent was that it should be for no eyes but his own. Read with this in mind, "A Psalm of Life" becomes a living thing, a landmark in a life. There is no haziness even in the much-criticized first stanza. Stripped of its verse form, this is the heart of the poem:

Life's no time for dreaming. The soul that simply slumbers and dreams is not living at all. The world, it is true, seems to be a mere shadow, but it is not. Things are not what they seem. Life is real. Art is long, life is short—act. Look the moment in the face. It is not for me to muse idly on the future, building castles, nor to be looking back and living in the past. It is for me to be up and doing to-day.

Months after the issue of *Hyperion* he was in a tumult of uncertainty, doubtful of his literary future, perplexed as to the direction of his literary powers. "Meditating what I shall do next. Shall it be two volumes more of Hyperion, or a drama on Cotton Mather?" His poems—"psalms," he called them—were for the expression of his own innermost soul. No eye but his should see them. Thus the Novalisque lyric which in later versions he printed as "Footsteps of Angels," written during the lonely period in the old Cragie House. To know Longfellow one must know this revealing lyric. "Evening Shadows" was his first title. I quote the poem in its first form:

> When the hours of day are numbered,
>   And the soul-like voice of night
> Wakes the better soul that slumbered
>   To a holy calm delight;
>
> Ere the evening lamps are lighted,
>   And, like spectres grim and tall,
> Shadows from the fitful firelight
>   Dance upon the parlor wall,—
>
> Then the forms of the departed
>   Enter at the open door;
> The beloved ones, the true-hearted,
>   Come to sit with me once more.

And with them the being beauteous
  Who unto my youth was given,
More than all things else to love me,
  And is now a saint in heaven.

With a slow and noiseless footstep
  Comes she, like a shape divine,
Takes the vacant chair beside me,
  Lays her gentle hand in mine.

And she sits and gazes at me,
  With her deep and tender eyes,
Like the stars so still and saint-like,
  Looking downward from the skies.

Here we have the soul of Novalis. The life of the night
has become the real life. Day is the unreality. The "better
soul" sleeps until the coming of twilight. Again and again
this note:

Have I dreamed? or was it real,
  What I saw as in a vision,
When to marches hymeneal
In the land of the Ideal
  Moved my thought o'er Fields Elysian?

The worlds of waking and dreaming lie close together
in Longfellow. Read "Haunted Houses," "Song of the
Silent Land," "The Two Angels," "The Haunted Chamber," "*Auf Wiedersehen.*" Years later, when his early romanticism had become less mystical, he still was saying
that it is the Night that rules the Day, and without this
reality, Day would be unendurable:

Into the darkness and the hush of night
  Slowly the landscape sinks, and fades away,
  And with it fade the phantoms of the day,
The ghosts of men and things, that haunt the light.
The crowd, the clamor, the pursuit, the flight,
  The unprofitable splendor and display,
  The agitations and the cares that prey
Upon our hearts, all vanish out of sight.

> The better life begins; the world no more
>   Molests us: all its records we erase
> From the dull commonplace book of our lives,
> That like a palimpsest is written o'er
>   With trivial incidents of time and place,
>   And, lo! the ideal, hidden beneath, revives.

The success of "A Psalm of Life" and the few lyrics that had followed it, together with the importunities of his friends, induced Longfellow, late in the year 1839, to issue a collection of his lyrics and translations. The title he chose is significant—*Voices of the Night*. The nine original poems, the soul of the book, are shot through and through with the softness and sentiment of mid-century German romanticism. The "Prelude," which opens the collection with a bit of Tieck's *"Waldeinsamkeit,"* finds the poet amid the shadows of a solemn and silent wood, dreaming under a patriarchal tree. He determines that hereafter his songs must not be of the external and the objective things of the daylight, but of the world within him, of the solemn voices of the night. In the next poem we are in the full tide of romanticism: "manifold, soft chimes, That fill the haunted chambers of the Night"; "From the cool cisterns of the midnight air, My spirit drank repose"; and

> O holy night! from thee I learn to bear
>   What man has borne before!
> Thou layest thy finger on the lips of Care
>   And they complain no more.

In precisely the same key had sang Novalis: "But sacred Night, with her unspoken mysteries draws me to her. . . . Dost thou not feel pity for us, O holy Night? . . . My whole being awakes. . . . Night has aroused me to life and manhood." Over and over this dominating note in Longfellow's "psalms": "The Light of Stars," "The Beleaguered City," "The Bridge," "The Day Is

Done," "The Rainy Day," "Daylight and Moonlight," "Afternoon in February," "Curfew," "The Wind over the Chimney."

V

The classic spirit—"perfection of form imposed upon strength of feelings"—was by these lyrics brought to the American bourgeoisie. Genuine they were, the poet's own inner experience, and they inferred a richness of life that most had never known. Their mysticism was in key with the religious emotions they had felt in the church services. Moreover, there was over them the drawing-room atmosphere and the softened German romance they had felt as they had read Scott and later Irving. America, awaking to its frontier rawness and violence and crudeness of soul, welcomed the lyrics. Longfellow in a moment became the people's poet. A half-century after his death he still holds his place.

Singing with the *Spätromantiker*—late romantic lyrists, Uhland, Freiligrath, etc.,—it was inevitable that sooner or later he should have essayed the ballad. He had read Arnim and Brentano. " 'The Boy Wonder-Horn!' " he had exclaimed in *Hyperion,*

I know the book almost by heart. Of all your German books, it is the one which produces upon my imagination the most wild and magic influence. I have a passion for ballads! . . . They are the gypsy-children of song, born under green hedgerows, in the leafy lanes and by-paths of literature,—in the genial Summer-time.

"The Wreck of the Hesperus" was the fifth poem of his new poetic period. But even before the *Voices of the Night* he dreamed of ballads. "I have been looking at the old northern sagas," he wrote in his journal in 1838, "and thinking of a series of ballads or a romantic poem on the deeds of the first bold Viking who crossed to this western world, with storm spirits and devil machinery under water." He proposed to Hawthorne that they collaborate in Arnim-Brentano style for the production of a collection of marvelous fairy-tales and ballads for boys, but Hawthorne was congenitally a soloist.

Longfellow's Wonder-Horn rang at intervals during his whole life: "The Skeleton in Armor," "The Norman Baron," "Walter von der Vogelweid," "The Phantom Ship," "Tales of a Wayside Inn," "A Ballad of the French Fleet," and many more. Many read like translations from Uhland. True ballads: their charm lies in their simplicity, their haunting melody, their human interest, their mystic indistinctness. American, many of them, in theme, they are not in reality American. "The Wreck of the Hesperus" might have happened in the North Sea, and "Paul Revere's Ride," with but a change of names, might have been an episode of the German wars.

VI

What Longfellow was after the publication of his second volume of poems he remained. His residence in Germany in 1842 deepened his romanticism but did not modify it. He had discovered his profession. The sudden and widespread popularity of his poetry had at first astonished him and then it had sobered him. The voice of the people was like a call from on high. He would give them the best within him. Poetry now was his study. "I have been giving as much time as possible to the young poets," he wrote from Mariensberg. Freiligrath he visited in his romantic home on the Rhine and lingered for days.

He came home to write "The Belfry of Bruges," and "Nuremberg," poems breathing romanticism from every line. Nearly half of his poetical work is medieval in background, the medievalism of Uhland. In work like "The Golden Legend," an adaptation of *"Der Arme Heinrich,"* he surpasses the original. To G. P. R. James, the poem resembled "an old ruin with the ivy and the rich blue mold upon it. It is rather the dream of a monk over his rubrics."

Like all his school, he drew for his imagery from the ceremonials and traditions of the Romish church. The old clock on the stairs is "a monk, who crosses himself and sighs, Alas."

> And the hooded clouds, like friars,
>   Tell their beads in drops of rain,
> And patter their doleful prayers
>   But their prayers are all in vain,
>   All in vain.

To read the poet, indeed, is like entering a Gothic cathedral, with its subdued light, its crumbling monuments of Crusaders, its murmuring organ, its shuddery vaults with their bones, its processions of chanting monks. One feels it in the sonnets of the Dante translation, beyond which, in poetic power, his art never reached:

> I enter and I see thee in the gloom
>   Of the long aisles, O poet Saturnine!
>   And strive to make my steps keep pace with thine.
> The air is filled with some unknown perfume,
> The congregation of the dead make room
>   For thee to pass; the votive tapers shine;
>   Like rooks that haunt Ravenna's groves of pine
> The hovering echoes fly from tomb to tomb.
> From the confessionals I hear arise
>   Rehearsals of forgotten tragedies
>   And lamentations from the crypts below;
> And then a voice celestial that begins
> With the pathetic words, "Although your sins
>   As scarlet be," and ends with "as the snow."

Again, "the romantic school," as Professor Beers once wrote, "sought to reinforce its native stock of materials by *motifs* drawn from foreign literatures, and particularly from Norse mythology and from Spanish romance." Long-

fellow all his poetic life had a passion for both. His translations and adaptations, and above all, his *Hiawatha* in
the meter and spirit of the Finnish "Kalevala," attest this
fully. So indeed the early drama, "The Spanish Student."

Romanticism may be defined as the spirit of youth.
With the middle years of life, disillusion begins, the colors
fade, and the vague melancholy, peculiar to adolescence,
is forgotten. Life more and more takes on restraint and
incredulity. Uhland ceased to sing long before middle life;
Heine was a romanticist only during his early years.
Longfellow's distinctively romantic period was over before 1849. It was then that he began to think of the larger
art and to plan a "tower of song with lofty parapet."

But it is not the work of his later period, tinged as it
is with romanticism, that stands today in the popular mind
as Longfellow. It is the little handful of lyrics written
before 1840 that is associated universally with his name.
The dramas, the later lyrics, the "Christus," even the
"Tales of a Wayside Inn," are unknown to the man in
the street, but he knows "A Psalm of Life" and "The
Bridge." A college class of two hundred men, asked to
write without preparation each a list of the poems of
Longfellow, handed in altogether thirty titles, and of these
only *The Song of Hiawatha,* "The Courtship of Miles
Standish," and "Paul Revere's Ride" were written after
1849. This is Longfellow as the people know him, but it
is also the Longfellow of the Heidelberg vision.

Though half of his poetry is in dramatic form, he was
distinctively a lyrist. No more was he a dramatist than
Uhland, who also wrote dramas. The drama requires action, plot, distinctness first of all. There must be evolution
of character, cause and effect, and a steady and irresistible
march of events toward a final culmination. It must deal,
too, with intensely individualized characters who stand out
objectively against a background that does not dominate
or distract. But Longfellow was first of all subjective; he

saw through the lens of his own soul—shadowy ethereal
beings; he could tell of his own emotions and aspirations
and longings, but he was powerless, like all other romantic
poets, to view life objectively, to paint with sharp outlines, to work with plain colors.

His *Spanish Student* is essentially lyric, not dramatic.
A young man's dream over a volume of Spanish romance,
gorgeous, effects without cause, characters vague, charming situations in place of development. To quote a criticism once made on Tieck,

. . . all its author's care is lavished upon what he calls the
climate of events, their atmosphere and fragrance, tone and
color, the mood they inspired, the shadow they cast, the light
in which they are seen, which is invariably that of the moon.

Nine volumes it takes for Longfellow's poetry, yet if
his lyrics alone were published, they would scarce fill one,
a fact indeed remarkable when we consider that he was
as preëminently a lyrist as was Salis or Pierre de Ronsard.

VII

In reading-courses and school-anthologies much has
been made of the two long poems, *Evangeline* and
Hiawatha. Hawthorne considered for a time the *Evangeline* theme and abandoned it as too vague and dis-
persive. To Longfellow it was simply pathos; he could feel
it; why ask more? He had never visited the Grand Pré
region, or Louisiana, or the Mississippi, or the Falls of
Minnehaha; there was no need of it. Johann Hölderlin
had never visited Greece before he wrote his *Hyperion*.
To have made the visit might have spoiled the picture.
Realism, truth to actual externals, even to historical facts,
were secondary things compared with atmosphere and
feeling. Poetry for him was a thing of the *märchenwelt*.
For him only the golden light and the pathetic human

figure dimly seen—Evangeline, mere abstraction, a "beautiful shadow, embodied moonshine." "French romanticism," says Georg Brandes, produces clearly defined figures; the ideal of German romanticism is not a figure but a melody, not definite form but indefinite aspiration." Evangeline is a feminine Heinrich von Ofterdingen, seeking the world over for the blue flower and losing it in the end just as it was in her grasp.

So with *Hiawatha*. Atmosphere and melody are everything: moonlight, starlight, romantic love, days that are forgotten, sentiment, pathos. The Indians are monks, medieval knights, first cousins to the gods of Northern mythology:

> Downward through the evening twilight,
> In the days that are forgotten,
> In the unremembered ages,
> From the full moon fell Nokomis,
> Fell the beautiful Nokomis,
> She a wife, but not a mother.
>
> Downward through the evening twilight,
> On the Muskoday, the meadow,
> On the prairie full of blossoms.
> "See! a star falls!" said the people;
> "From the sky a star is falling!"
>
> There among the ferns and mosses,
> There among the prairie lilies,
> On the Muskoday, the meadow,
> In the moonlight and the starlight,
> Fair Nokomis bore a daughter.
> And she called her name Wenonah,
> As the first-born of her daughters.
> And the daughter of Nokomis
> Grew up like the prairie lilies,
> Grew a tall and slender maiden,
> With the beauty of the moonlight,
> With the beauty of the starlight.

A dream of fairyland, monsters and marvels, the
fancies of a childlike people, and its main charm is "the
moonlight and the starlight" atmosphere. But as Ibsen
said of Schiller's "Jungfrau," "there is no experience in
it. It is not the result of powerful personal impressions,
but is a composition." The poet had become a professional
man of letters, increasingly popular, and he had resigned
his college chair to devote himself to poetry. Deliberately
had he sought out this poetic theme and day by day had
worked it through.

One final area of his work remains, his sonnets, sixty-
five of them, a small volume. Distinctive work : the best
sonnets yet written in America. Here are his deepest emotions, his tenderest experiences. This from Charles F.
Richardson: "The numerous sonnets produced in the last
twenty years of his life not only equalled anything he had
previously written, but very easily put him at the head of
all American sonneteers." Most distinctive of them all,
the six Dante sonnets, "Victor and Vanquished," "My
Books," the "Three Friends of Mine" sequence, and "The
Cross of Snow," found among his private papers after his
death.

VIII

Walt Whitman, reared on Longfellow's poetry, summed
him up at last as "poet of the mellow twilight of the past
in Italy, Spain, and in Northern Europe." But America
in the forties and fifties and sixties needed the finished
art and atmosphere of Europe. Emerson's dictum was that
"He induces a serene mood." But the America of the mid-
nineteenth century sorely needed serenity. The younger
critics berate him often for sentimentality, but sentimentality was not Longfellow's failing. To accuse him of this
is to confess that one has not yet known the deeps of
human life, its tragedy, and its heartache. In all Longfellow, genuine emotion never overdone. And as to his

use of foreign art and atmosphere instead of creating for himself an American art, listen to Howells's dictum: "He accepted the sole conditions on which poetry at the time could embody itself."

Thus Henry W. Longfellow: for good or for evil, his impress is on one whole generation of American poets. He educated America when America was in utter crudeness artistically. For years he was a kind of literary pastor leading his flocks, for the most part women, beside the still waters of Old World culture. But his influence was wider far than his own land. In 1866 Moses Coit Tyler wrote this from England, and with it I close my survey:

The supreme literary reputation in England is that of Longfellow. His renown has diffused itself into every household; his poems are in every drawing-room; he has more readers in England than any living English poet. His is the one only American literary name that may be mentioned in all companies with as much certainty of recognition as the name of Shakespeare, though even with Shakespeare's name it would not be safe to go below a certain tide-mark of English Society.[6]

[6] *Glimpses of England* (1898), p. 303.

CHAPTER XXXIII

HAWTHORNE

I

THE SPORADIC nature of the New England literary
"renaissance" is shown by the emergence of the strange
unrelated figure of Nathaniel Hawthorne. One would
hardly look for a literary master among the shipmasters
of old Salem, who were his ancestors. No Brahmin caste
there, no sermons in the blood, no scholarship. Stern,
practical men, the whole intolerant line. His father, a ship-
captain, had died in the Caribbean when the son was four
years old. The molding influence of this death cannot be
overstressed. The mother, on receiving the news, became
for the rest of her life a psychopathic case and went into
complete seclusion, even to the extreme of having her
meals served in her locked room. Individualism became a
mania. No household more "queer," no childhood more
abnormal. It left upon all the three children marks indelible. The son-in-law, George P. Lathrop, has left this
weird picture of the family habits even in the period following Hawthorne's graduation at Bowdoin:

He had little communion with even the members of his
family. Frequently his meals were brought and left at his
locked door, and it was not often that the four inmates of
the old Herbert Street mansion met in family circle. . . .
It was a custom of this household for the members to remain
very much by themselves: the three ladies were perhaps as
rigorous recluses as himself.

When the boy was nine had come the second molding
force, lameness caused by an accident. It confined him to

crutches and to the house for months and even years. Unable to attend school, he was taught at home by a tutor—Joseph Worcester, later of dictionary fame. The result was solitude and an orgy of reading. Before he was eleven he had read a small library of books like Shakespeare and Bunyan and Spenser's *Faerie Queene*. Poetry and romance were his favorite books. According to a letter written his sister when he was fifteen, he had read within a period of a few weeks *Waverley, The Mysteries of Udolpho, The Adventures of Ferdinand Count Fathom, Roderick Random,* and *The Arabian Nights*. A year later he could announce that he had read, with the exception of *The Abbott,* all of Scott including the metrical romances. In Godwin's *Caleb Williams* he had found huge delight, and also in *St. Leon,* and *Mandeville.*

Then had come a third influence equally formative: he was sent to live with his uncle near Sebago Lake. "I lived in Maine," he later declared, "like a bird of the air, so perfect was the freedom I enjoyed. But it was there I got my cursed habits of solitude." Individualism to extremes, imagination become a ruling force.

Then had come the four years at Bowdoin College. The lexicographer Joseph Worcester, his tutor, had prepared him thoroughly so far as requirements were concerned, but in all other respects he was as totally unfitted for college life as a plains Indian. Shyness had become with him wellnigh a disease. He avoided his fellows; he was diffident in the class-rooms; he refused to appear for the required public speaking; he clung closely to his room or else took long walks in the woods. Sometimes he drank and caroused with local roughs. In his room he either whittled at his desk or read library books of his choice.

Then in his senior year he began to write. Like his classmate Longfellow, he had been impressed by Irving's work, especially the *Sketch Book*. The romances of the great Unknown Scotchman, too, author of *Waverley,* had laid strong hold upon his imagination. That he himself began to write in similar key we have the evidence of a letter written his sister, in which he informed her that he was writing a novel and also a collection to be entitled *Seven Tales of My Native Land,* a title most suggestive: "Tales"—the Irving influence undoubtedly; "My Native Land"—the Scott influence, legends of New England as his were legends of Scotland. The books found no publishers. Finally in a rage he tore up the manuscript of the *Tales* and burned it in the stove.

Another shaping force—home from college with his degree, it was necessary to choose a profession. This was New England: for a young man to refuse work and calling was to invite criticism and even suspicion. His uncle, who had helped him through college, was insistent. But what profession? Law, medicine, the ministry, business, teaching—impossible! His solitary, brooding, indolent youth had fitted him for nothing, and his shyness, which had become pathological, made active contact with the world seem impossible. And he settled down in his mother's abnormal home and waited. And knowing what the neighbors and the town thought of such a life, he kept out of sight as if he had committed a crime:

It was my fortune, or misfortune, just as you please, to have some slender means of supporting myself, and so, on leaving college in 1825, instead of immediately studying a profession, I sat down to consider what pursuit in life I was best fit for. My mother had now returned [to Salem] and taken up her abode in her deceased father's house, a tall, ugly, old, grayish building . . . in which I had a room; and year after year I kept on considering what I was fit for, and time and my destiny decided that I was to be the writer that I am. I had always a natural tendency . . . towards seclusion, and this I now indulged to the uttermost, so that for months together I scarcely held human intercourse outside of my own family, seldom going out except at twilight, or only to take the nearest way to the most convenient solitude, which was oftenest the sea-shore. . . . I had very few acquaintances in Salem, and during the nine or ten years that I spent there in this solitary way, I doubt whether so much as twenty people in the town were aware of my existence.

Self-imposed solitary confinement beween the ages of twenty-one and thirty-three, confinement almost dungeon-like in its solitude. Self-consciousness became a dominating force; adolescent urgings suppressed, believed to be of the devil, for this was in New England; youthful broodings on the unpardonable sin and damnation, for Calvinism ruled the community, and he was in the atmosphere of it even in his solitary chamber. He read the Salem library straight through, and every day he wrote. He would make fiction his profession, but how market his creations? Publishers who could have Scott and Bulwer for the mere printing would not pay for the work of an unknown American beginner. In desperation he published his novel at his own expense, anonymously, with the title *Fanshawe, a Tale*. Brief enough for a tale it was, yet its ground plan was Scott-like: two groups of characters—high, low; two lines of action in alternate chapters; movement leisurely as if space were unlimited; characters in numbers. The hero and all the rest are abstractions. It is of books bookish, the creation of one who has dreamed over volumes of romance, who knows little of life in its actuality. Was there ever a time when a college student, seeing a trout in a pool, would say to the girl with whom he was walking that he wished he had a "piscatorial instrument of death"? A truncated romance: evidently chopped off when the money failed, a three-decker novel reduced to one. Enormously important, however, as a revealing document.

No novel again for years. Irving's influence again: legends, native stuff, sketches. At many points the two were alike: impatient of continued effort, romance-ridden, temperamental. The prose tale was as broad a literary stride as either was able to measure. Even *The Scarlet Letter* of later days is a short story. The type of work he was doing appears from the titles of his abandoned collections: *Seven Tales of My Native Land, Provincial Tales, Old Time Legends*—the Irving complex, American legends. The Indian as a romantic theme, however, disgusted him; in *Sketches from Memory* (1835) he wrote:

It has often been a matter of regret to me that I was shut off from the most peculiar field of American fiction by an inability to see any romance, or poetry, or grandeur, or beauty in the Indian character, at least till such traits were pointed out by others. I do abhor an Indian story.

Seeking the legendary, what else could this descendant from Puritans, this native of old Salem, this solitary youth who had heard shuddery tales of the curse hurled at his clan by the victim of the inflexible old Judge Hathorne, this solitary romance-haunted soul, who as a lad had crept out to Gallows Hill where the witches had been hanged and had shuddered in Poe-like horror when he discovered it covered with a ghastly moss unlike anything else in the region—what else could he find for a subject in ancient New England history and tradition but tragedies of Puritanism?

Just what he wrote at first and destroyed we do not know. We must be content with the pitiful fragments left us by time from this formative period in his life and art. Denied publication elsewhere, he printed in the local paper, the *Salem Gazette,* five of his sketches: "The Hollow of the Three Hills," "Sir William Phipps," "Mrs. Hutchinson," "An Old Woman's Tale," "Dr. Bullivant." First fruits, so far as we can know, of his short-story art.

But solitude was working upon the youth. He was becoming, like his temperamental mother, a neurotic case. Documents there once were that would have helped our diagnosis, revealing letters to his friend Horatio Bridge, but they were burned by strict orders from their author. Bridge's replies, however, we possess, and they disclose much. The man was near to suicide. A monomania possessed him, mainly religious. Had he committed the unpardonable sin, like Ethan Brand? In later years Emerson diagnosed the disease that finally destroyed him: "The solitude of the man became at last intolerable, and he died of it." So intolerable it became that even in the days of his self-immurement he would spend several nights each week with a hard-drinking, card-playing set at the village hotel, a set in every way below him. His classmate Bridge expostulated in vain. "The stubborn Hawthorne pride," cold, hard, rebellious; the neurotic mother-complex, selfish, jealous, "set"; the abnormal sisters—how escape from such a hell as that? This in a letter to Longfellow, 1837:

By some witchcraft or other—for I really cannot assign any reasonable why and wherefore—I have been carried apart from the main current of life, and find it impossible to get back again. Since we last met . . . I have secluded myself from society; and yet I never meant any such thing, nor dreamed what sort of life I was going to lead. I have made a captive of myself and put me into a dungeon; and now I cannot find the key to let myself out . . . and if the door were open, I should be almost afraid to come out . . . there is no fate in this world so horrible as to have no share in either its joys or sorrows. For the last ten years, I have not lived, but only dreamed about living.

The one ambition of his life, publication of his fiction, had been denied him; what else to live for? Bridge saw but a single avenue of escape: unknown to Hawthorne, he financed—$250—an edition of his short work, nineteen of his pieces with the title *Twice-Told Tales* (1837).

S. C. Goodrich had also been a saving power. Hawthorne's sixth tale, "Sights from a Steeple," had appeared in *The Token* of 1831, and it had been paid for. Following it had appeared a succession of paid-for tales in *The Token,* some twenty-nine in all. Indeed, in the single issue of 1837 had appeared eight of his tales, one-half of the whole volume.

Twice-told tales—a miscellany: Gothic romance tempered by New Englandism, characters created in the author's own image in a world of unreality. In all his volumes key-hole peepings at life by a shrinking personality who himself must not be seen: "Sights from a Steeple," "Night Sketches from under an Umbrella," "Footprints on the Seashore," "Little Annie's Ramble," and the like. But New Englandism in the blood must voice itself in the sermonic. Note his secondary titles—the italics are mine: "The Minister's Black Veil, *A Parable*"; "Fancy's Show-Box, *A Morality*"; "The Toll-Gatherer's Day, *A Sketch of Transitory Life*." Even in his *Legends of the Province House,* sermonic legends. "Lady Eleanor's Mantle" would not be out of place if substituted for the sermon in any Protestant service. At the end of his strange parables and allegories often the formulated moral. At the close of "The Village Uncle"—"And now for a moral to my reverie. . . ." This the summary of "Wakefield," which is a flashlight upon Hawthorne's own soul:

Amid the seeming confusion of our mysterious world individuals are so nicely adjusted to a system, and systems to one another and to a whole, that by stepping aside for a moment a man exposes himself to a fearful risk of losing his place forever. Like Wakefield, he may become, as it were, the outcast of the universe.

And this from "The Prophetic Pictures":

Is there not a deep moral in the tale? Could the result of one or all our deeds be shadowed forth and set before us, some would call it fate and hurry onward, others be swept along by their passionate desires, and none be turned aside by the prophetic pictures.

In his note-books, jottings again and again for these moral endings. The note-book of a Puritan preacher. What sermons could be written from topics like these!

The device of a sun-dial for a monument over a grave—with some suitable motto.

A man to swallow a small snake—and it to be the symbol of a cherished sin.

To trace out the influence of a frightful and disgraceful crime, in debasing and destroying a character naturally high and noble—the guilty person being alone conscious of the crime.

An auction of second hands—then moralizing how the fashion of this world passeth away.

With this volume reviewed in superlatives by Longfellow in the *North American Review,* new hope came to the suicide-haunted man. With an effort he aroused himself and tried pathetically to face the reality of life. In a kind of desperation he accepted S. C. Goodrich's offer to do editorial work in Boston. Then in January, 1839, he was appointed "measurer of salt, coal," etc., at the Boston custom-house. Reality enough in that. Two years, however, despite his salary of $1,500, was all that he could endure. Again he was in Salem, but not for long now. A second adventure in reality: a thousand dollars paid down for a working membership in the romantic communistic stock-company that was to prove it was possible for all men to dwell together as brothers with plain living and high thinking. A year and a half he lived at Brook Farm, but not in the spirit of the community. He had gone to live in Arcady, he complained, and "had found himself up to the chin in a barn-yard." Impossible to endure, for it was work: after a few weeks he rebelled and became a boarder. Then his third venture in reality—a venture now indeed—his marriage with Sophia Peabody and *dolce far niente* for months in the Old Manse. A single sketch was the literary result, "The Old Manse," most spontaneous of his papers.

Poe's famous review of the 1842 *Twice-Told Tales* helped him not at all. New England abominated Poe. I can find no evidence that anyone read it—until it was discovered in later years. And after all, it explained not Hawthorne but the art of Poe.

Then in 1846 another collection, *Mosses from an Old Manse,* old material mostly from the periodicals. Hawthorne himself has characterized it:

They have the pale tint of flowers that blossomed in too retired a shade—the coolness of a meditative habit which diffuses itself through the feeling and observation of every sketch. Instead of passion there is sentiment; and even in what purports to be pictures of actual life, we have allegory, not always so warmly dressed in its habiliments of flesh and blood as to be taken into the reader's mind without a shiver. . . . The book, if you would see anything in it, requires to be read in the clear, brown, twilight atmosphere in which it was written.

Read outside of this twilight in the realistic atmosphere of the present, these highly wrought tales seem as artificial as wax flowers. Not alive, surely, these formal characters with their impossible dialogue. The sketches—"pure essays," Poe called them—are more to be commended. Models, some of them, in formal English. Nature sketches realistic. In much of this work the style can be described as poetic. The culminating scene, for example, of "The Hollow of Three Hills" has a time-beat in unison with the theme, a monotonous rhythm like the death-march at an execution:

> Then came a measured tread
> Passing slowly, slowly on,
> As with mourners with a coffin
> Their garments trailing on.
> The ground. . . .
> Before them went the priest
> Reading the burial service

While the leaves of his book
Were rustling in the breeze.
And though no voice but his
Was heard to speak aloud
Still there were revilings
And anathemas
Whispered but distinct
From women and from men,
Breathed against the daughter
Who had rung the aged hearts
Of her parents, and the wife
Who had betrayed the trusting
Fondness of her husband,
The mother who had sinned
Against natural affection
And left her child to die.

II

When *The Scarlet Letter* appeared in 1850, Hawthorne
was forty-six years of age. His literary product had been
fragments—sketches, note-book jottings, moral tales.
Only short stories and sketches—a hundred of them by
1850—and the short story an inferior literary form,
practice-ground for adolescents. Four years of brooding
idleness he had passed on the shippingless wharves of old
Salem, collector of revenue in the revenueless old custom-
house. His job, a political one, suddenly lost, he was in
consternation. He could only write; no money elsewhere;
but how avoid starvation while he was creating a thing
to sell? His thrifty wife, however, had faced the danger
months before and had saved from the salary. Thus compelled, Hawthorne wrote *The Scarlet Letter*. And by accident he published it. James T. Fields discovered him at
work, pried loose the manuscript, and issued it with a
salvo of advertising. At last the "great American novel."
And it became from the first a best-seller. A loud outcry
there was that the thing was a sex novel, that it would ruin
the morals of youth, and this enormously helped to in-

crease the sales. The critics, even in Boston, found it a masterpiece, a classic even. Hawthorne had arrived, even though his book was ruled from many libraries.

In method, the romance was a new thing. Adultery? Yes, but of the actual sin we are told nothing at all. It is inferred: we have indeed to study the text to find what the letter "A" on the woman's breast really stood for. It is a study of results, of the corroding power of a sin concealed and lived with for years. The few characters, really four in number; the concentration upon the single *motif;* the compression; the single dominating atmosphere; the "totality" of effect, to use Poe's term—all this makes it of short-story texture. It accomplishes its end, but it does it by artificial means. The characters are symbols; the dialogue is unnatural; the character Pearl unreal, impossible, despite the claim of the family that she was a careful study of the eldest Hawthorne daughter, Una; the scaffold scene, made to be climactic in the plot, is ludicrous. Tragedy was the intent, unrelieved by humor, but emotion is lacking, gripping power, realism. It can be read in cold blood with thoughts only of the method, the literary artifices, the highly finished style.

Better in parts, the next novel, *The House of the Seven Gables.* Again a moral made constantly evident: "The wrong-doing of one generation lives into the successive ones, and, divesting itself of every temporary advantage becomes a pure and uncontrollable mischief." After the strong opening chapters, the story wanders—Clifford becomes Hawthorne's self. Unconsciously to the author the tale becomes autobiographic. The breaking in of reality in the person of the modern young photographer and the reaction upon the shadows who so long had been immured in the moldy old dwelling are drawn from the history of his own soul.

From a modern standpoint, the strongest work of Hawthorne is his *Blithedale Romance,* which was based upon his own experiences at Brook Farm. Here he leaves the dim world of his early creations and comes out into the light of day with characters studied from life. He has actuality to work with now. He has seen the body of a drowned girl taken from the stream at midnight by the light of lanterns; he has attended the woodland carnival he describes; and he has known the vibrant feminist Margaret Fuller and the visionary George Ripley, from whom he draws the strong-minded Zenobia and the dominating reformer Hollingsworth. Uncertain the book is in purpose, however, compared with the compact and emphatic *Scarlet Letter,* but it is not a ghostly thing like a plant struggling toward the reality of the sun in a cellar; it is a transcript from the actual.

III

Of Hawthorne's seven years·abroad little need be said. *Our Old Home* has excellent papers, and the romance *The Marble Faun* is strong in parts. It is fatally diffuse, however; a short-story plot lengthened into a romance. Again a problem in sin, but a strange solution: the marble faun come to life, exuberant, joyous, unknowing of tomorrow or of trouble; he would have gone on forever in his happy ways but for the sin he committed, which turned him into a human being with a soul to worry about.

Home at last, in the Concord residence that he had finally acquired, Hawthorne entered that final period of mystery which culminated with his death in 1864. A blight, physical and mental, seemed to be upon him. Romance after romance he began but could not finish. One cause, undoubtedly, was the fact that he chose short-story themes to be made novels. Crippled had he been while writing his four major romances by the fact that his entire early life had been devoted to shortened fiction. Like Poe, he had been mastered by his own art. But the heart of the man's mystery lies deeper, and it is allied without doubt to the mystery of his solitary youth. Every critic has offered a solution. Mystery has grown into legend; it has helped to keep his name vivid during the years.

The Scarlet Letter, defective though it be, has won its place as an American classic. One can echo Newton Arvin, that "Nothing could be clearer than the dramatic purpose of *The Scarlet Letter,* or better regulated than its progress. Almost literally nothing is told that does not need to be told; nothing essential, as in *Blithedale,* is left out. In its singleness of direction, in its integrity of effect, *The Scarlet Letter* has the perfection of the best of Hawthorne's short tales." And then one can add, as Arvin added, "but elevation is not the prime virtue of great fiction, and *The Scarlet Letter* has too much the quality of a pageant—or of an opera—to be a novel of the very first order."

So with the *House of the Seven Gables* with its sluggish movement; so with *The Marble Faun* with its excrescences; so even with the more modern *Blithedale Romance* with its flashes of actuality.

One other masterpiece remains, the "Hawthorne Microcosm" which first appeared in the *Dollar Magazine* (1851) with the title "The Unpardonable Sin." More than a mere short story is it: in its final version it was given the title "Ethan Brand, A Chapter from an Abortive Romance"—a fragment, but a fragment which many critics have placed at the head of all his writings. C. F. Richardson perhaps was the first. Most have considered it a self-diagnosis, a study of the neurosis that was consuming him. Of all his tales it has the most grip, the most compelling power. Bliss Perry, in *The Amateur Spirit,* has, for me, said the last word:

Hawthorne found Ethan Brand—or a potential Ethan Brand—in his own heart. He believed in an Unpardonable Sin; and it is by this faith in the reality of the moral life, after all is said, that he takes his rank as an artist. He chose moral problems, the truths of the human heart, and made them plastic; he created, not abstract types, but men and women, charging them with spiritual force; and the result is that Ethan Brand, with his homely garments and heavy shoes, bending over the fiery lime-kiln on the slope of Hoosac, is a figure with all the moral passion, the tragic dignity, of Empedocles of old casting himself despairingly into the crater of Mount Etna.[1]

[1] P. 138.

CHAPTER XXXIV

WHITTIER

I

THE SPRINGING up in mid-century New England of a sporadic scattering of writers, each a unique phenomenon, seems at first thought unexplainable, like the wild new growths after a forest fire. And in a way, New England had been fire-swept, even ancient landmarks destroyed, but the primitive soil remained. George Rice Carpenter could even say that the new crop had been caused by the firing:

In the early nineteenth century, New England, that part of the land in which intellectual and spiritual life among the common people had been most continuous and vigorous, was thoroughly fertilized, as it were, by generations of mental activity, and was ready to bear the natural fruit of the vitilized soil—the man of letters, the man of fashions, in visible speech and in the mysterious forms of the imagination, the latent ideals and aspirations of his dumb fellows. And men of letters sprang up in abundance, great and small, in all the territory of these ancient colonies.

Strange "sports," many of the new growths—Alcott, Thoreau, Hawthorne, Longfellow—some of them paradoxical, the most war-like a Quaker.

John Greenleaf Whittier, born in a Haverhill, Massachusetts, farm-house that had been occupied by the Whittier family continuously since 1688, was undoubtedly the most provincial of all the American writers. His life, like Thoreau's, must be written in negatives: except for a few short absences, he never left the neighborhood in which he was born; he never was strong physcially, often being so feeble that his life was despaired of; he never married, never traveled abroad, never received school training save for a few red-school-house terms and a winter or two at the Haverhill Academy where he supported himself by shoemaking; and never was he in doubt religiously. Most "holy" was he of all the American poets, last survivor, perhaps, of the New England "theocracy"—and he a Quaker whose ancestors had been persecuted by the theocracy.

II

The important chapter detailing his impressionable years is quickly finished. The Whittier farm was secluded, first by its natural position and second by the unorthodox nature of the family. A rocky, hilly farming land they lived in, like Scotland. For days and weeks they might not see other than their own circle save on First and Fourth Days, when they rode eight miles to the Friend's meeting-house. Scotland, indeed, with its background of near hills and its tall hinterland of the White Mountains and its lakes and wild ravines. And instead of traditions of Southrons and Scots, wild traditions of Indian raids, for the father had been a border ranger in pioneer days.

A boyhood of hardest labor was his from the days of his earliest memories. To wring a living from a New England farm requires work. The native winters were ferocious, and the father believed in the primitive doctrine that children should be "hardened in," should wear in winter the same clothing as in summer. It all but destroyed the boy, laid the foundation indeed of his later ills. Very little there was to stimulate intellectual life. Whittier's own account is specific:

We had only about twenty volumes of books, most of them the journals of pioneer ministers in our society. Our only annual was an almanac. I was early fond of reading, and now and then heard of a book of biography or travel, and walked miles to borrow it.

When I was fourteen years old my first school-master, Joshua Coffin, the able, eccentric historian of Newbury, brought with him to our house a volume of Burns's poems, from which he read, greatly to my delight. I begged him to leave the book with me, and set myself at once to the task of mastering the glossary of the Scottish dialect at its close. This was about the first poetry I had ever read (with the exception of that of the Bible, of which I had been a close student), and it had a lasting influence on me. I began to make rhymes myself, and to imagine stories and adventures.

Rhyming became early an obsession with the lad. To his sister, totally without knowledge of literature, the thing seemed miraculous. Her brother must be "a genius," and without consulting him she sent one of his poetical experiments, "The Exile's Departure," to young William Lloyd Garrison's newspaper, the *Free Press,* of Newburyport. Mere "Poet's Corner" trash, but its publication was a turning-point in Whittier's life. That was in 1824; he was seventeen, and from that moment until his death at eighty-five he supplied newspapers with verse. Never such a meteoric shower of worthlessness as came from his early pen—little of it is in his final edition. There have been located over a hundred and seventy poems printed in newspapers between 1829 and 1835 and none of them reprinted.[1] But country readers and country editors, like Whittier's sister, were amazed at the boy's "genius." A local lad writing poetry in that far day was a phenomenon worthy even of a newspaper editorial. The Haverhill *Gazette,* which alone first and last was to print over a hundred of his verses, ended a review of his "effusions" with this climacteric:

If nature or the "sacred nine" inspire him to write such poetry under his present disadvantages, we surely have

[1] Frances Mary Pray, *A Study of Whittier's Apprenticeship as a Poet* (1930).

reason to expect much of him, should his genius be assisted by a classical education.

And again two months later:

His effusions . . . indicate we should say, considering his disadvantages, a genius unparalleled among American poets. Such richness and sublimity of language and brilliancy of imagery and delicacy of sentiment have not, we believe, distinguished any of the early productions of the most celebrated modern poets.

Country criticism at which we may smile, yet enormously important: it kept the poet's candle alight during a critical period. The *Gazette* even advertised an edition of the "effusions" to be entitled *The Poems of Adrian,* the profit from the edition to be used for the author's education. There were not enough subscribers, and the volume, luckily for Whittier, never appeared. More and more a formal education became for him an impossibility. In a letter in 1828, his twenty-first year, he could write:

I have renounced college for the good reason that I have no disposition to humble myself to meanness for an education —crowding myself through college upon the charities of others, and leaving it with a debt or an obligation to weigh down my spirit like an incubus, and paralyze every exertion. The professions are already crowded full to overflowing— and I, forsooth, because I have a miserable knack of rhyming, must swell the enormous number, struggling awhile with debt and difficulties, and then weary of life, go down to my original insignificance, where the tinsel of classical honors will but aggravate my misfortune.

But the poetry had another effect: it brought him contacts with the world outside his father's farm. The most important was William Lloyd Garrison, who had accepted his first venture. Contact with the headlong enthusiast led the young farmer, seemingly, into a profession. He became the editor of a weekly journal, the *American Manufac-turer,* "devoted to the interests of manufactures, mechan-ics, agriculture, internal improvements, literature, educa-tion, and general intelligence." Editorials he wrote, and even book reviews. A veritable education it was, but after a year and a half he was forced by his father's illness and death to leave editorial work and take full charge of the farm work at home. Soon, however, without leaving his home base, he became editor of the Haverhill *Gazette,* then after six months of editorship he removed to Hartford to serve as editor of the *New England Review,* a "Clay paper" which, during the editorship of the fiery George D. Prentice, had been hot in its politics. Whittier was in charge of the paper from July, 1830, until near the end of the next year, when ill health forced him to resign. The end of his editorial career. The three years in Boston and Hartford had been a college course. They had taught him literature, but they had also taught him politics. Politics, he believed, was to be his life-work: but as a sick man he could only write verses.

It was the "legend" period of American poetry and prose. Willis had issued his two volumes of *The Legend-ary;* the *North American Review* had published its influ-ential critique of Cooper, calling for native legends. Indians now, and legends. In 1831 was issued the young poet's first book, *Legends of New England,* seven sketches in prose and verse, none of them republished in the later *Prose Works.* "New England is rich in traditionary lore," he wrote in the preface. "A thousand associations of superstition and manly daring and romantic adventure are connected with her green hills and her pleasant rivers."

Then had come his posthumous collection of the poems of John G. C. Brainard (1832), with thirty pages of introduction:

New England is full of Romance; and her writers would do well to follow the example of Brainard. The great forest which our fathers penetrated—the red men—their struggle

and their disappearance—the pow-wow and the war-dance—
the savage inroad and the English sally—the tale of superstition, and the scenes of witchcraft—all these are rich materials of poetry.

As a result, his next book was a metrical romance of
the Revolution, *Moll Pitcher* (1832), and following it,
in 1834, *Mogg Megone,* an attempt to treat New England
legends as Scott had treated those of Scotland. Inferior
work, condemned by the later Whittier to appear only in
the appendix of his *Works,* though perhaps not on account
of its literary crudeness. "I send thee a copy of Mogg
Megone," he wrote to Lucy Hooper. "I was unable to
finish it as I could have wished. It is, in my mind, liable
to one grave objection. It is not, I fear, calculated to do
good."

III

Despite his illness, ambition was ruling him. He
dreamed of politics. His friends were prepared even to
run him for Congress. And eager he was to give to them
his entire powers. A letter to Mrs. Sigourney, February 2,
1832, seems like a farewell to the Muse:

I love poetry, with a love as warm, as fervent, as sincere,
as any of the more gifted worshipers at the temple of the
Muses. I consider its gift as something holy and above the
fashion of the world. . . . Politics is the only field now open
for me.

And a few months later, January, 1833:

I have been compelled again to plunge into the political
whirlpool; for I have found that my political reputation is
more influential than my poetical: so I try to make myself
a man of the world—and the public are deceived, but *I* am
not. They do not see that I have thrown the rough armor of
rude and turbulent controversy over a keenly sensitive bosom,
—a heart of softer and gentler emotions than I dare expose.

A letter from Garrison was the kindling spark: one single sentence—"My brother, there are upwards of two million of our countrymen who are doomed to the most horrible servitude which ever cursed our race and blackened the page of history. . . ." Enough. Nothing mild or uncertain about William Lloyd Garrison. He followed his letter to Haverhill, and Whittier was ready to follow him to any extreme. Immediately came his war-cry salutatory: "Justice and Expediency: or, Slavery Considered with a View to its Rightful and Effectual Remedy, Abolition" (June, 1833). From this moment he was first of all an abolitionist, even to the addressing of mass-meetings, most of them hostile. In Concord, New Hampshire, he was mobbed.

What he might have become with vigorous health we can only conjecture. But at every step he was halted imperatively. One cannot understand the man without a study of this dominating fact. On August 8, 1867, he wrote Celia Thaxter that daily and even hourly there were borne in upon him admonitions of his frail hold upon life. Ill health had turned him from his newspaper career, from political life, and now it barred him from effectiveness in the career that had won his heart. It kept him from going to London as an abolitionist delegate, and twice from going to Halifax, Nova Scotia. Almost completely it incapacitated him: at times he would work with his pen but an hour or two daily. It anchored him to his secluded home, kept him provincial and deeply religious.

A "moral warfare" he could keep up with his pen, however. The rhetoric and the imitation now died from his poems. War songs were needed. "Poetry that won't speak and ring," he wrote in 1841, "is worse than none. The poetry is the match, the torch to our little field-piece, and if it is not fiery, if there is no ignition in it, no explosion, we might as well put an icicle to our priming."

Poetry was now a weapon in a battle. His whole fiery soul he poured into it:

> A hate of tyranny intense
> And hearty in its vehemence.

Nowhere in American poetry can one find lyrics more completely individual, more autochthonous, more single in aim, more intense. Almost a century old they are; the crisis that called them forth is all but forgotten; many of the allusions we do not know; and yet the poems are still alive. Touch them anywhere and they cry out.

> What, ho! our countrymen in chains!
>   The whip on woman's shrinking flesh!
> Our soil yet reddening with the stains
>   Caught from her scourging, warm and fresh!
> What! mothers from their children riven!
>   What! God's own image bought and sold!
> Americans to market driven,
>   And bartered as the brute for gold!

Day by day the newspapers furnished him with themes. The statement in a Southern paper that at a pro-slavery meeting "the clergy of all denominations attended in a body" received a blast beginning:

> Just God! and these are they
> Who minister at thine altar, God of Right!
> Men who their hands with prayer and blessing lay
>   On Israel's Ark of light!
>
> What! preach, and kidnap men?
> Give thanks, and rob thy own afflicted poor?
> Talk of thy glorious liberty, and then
>   Bolt hard the captive's door?
>
>   .   .   .   .   .
>
> Woe to the priesthood! woe
> To those whose hire is with the price of blood;
> Perverting, darkening, changing, as they go,
>   The searching truths of God!

In the sentimental forties and fifties lines like these could arouse like trumpet-notes:

Gone, gone—sold and gone,
To the rice-swamp dank and lone,
From Virginia's hills and waters;
Woe is me, my stolen daughters!

His savage lash spared not even his own kin. His cousin,
Daniel Webster, after the Fourth of March speech he
branded as Ichabod:

Of all we loved and honored, naught
Save power remains;
A fallen angel's pride of thought,
Still strong in chains.

All else is gone; from those great eyes
The soul has fled:
When faith is lost, when honor dies,
The man is dead!

And when the war was over and the amendment abolish-
ing slavery signed, this Hebraic burst of ecstasy:

It is done!
Clang of bell and roar of gun
Send the tidings up and down.
How the belfries rock and reel!
How the great guns, peal on peal,
Fling the joy from town to town.

.   .   .   .

Loud and long
Lift the old exulting song;
Sing with Miriam by the sea,
He has cast the mighty down;
Horse and rider sink and drown;
"He hath triumphed gloriously!"

.   .   .   .

Ring and swing,
Bells of joy! On morning's wing
Send the song of praise abroad!
With a sound of broken chains
Tell the nations that He reigns,
Who alone is Lord and God!

But ill health bound him down. Not his pen, however. In the quiet of his home he wrote not alone abolitionist lyrics, but even during the stormy decade before the war some of the very best of his nonpolitical verse. In 1850 he published his *Songs of Labor,* the best poems proletarian yet produced in America, poems written from the life he knew—really the *only* life he knew, since slavery was for him a mere abstraction. To this early period, too, belong his best-known ballads—"Cassandra Southwick," "The Bridal of Pennacook," "Barclay of Uri," "The Angels of Buena Vista," "Maud Muller," "Mary Garvin," "The Garrison of Cape Ann," "Skipper Ireson's Ride," "The Swan Song of Parson Avery," "Mabel Martin," "The Prophecy of Samuel Sewell." What he wrote of Brainard applies to his own work:

There is one important merit in his poetry which would redeem a thousand faults. It is wholly American. If he "babbles o' green fields" and trees they are such as of right belong to us. He does not talk of palms and cypress where he should describe the rough oak and sombre hemlock. He prefers the lowliest blossom of Yankee-land to the gorgeous magnolia and the orange bower of another clime. It is this which has made his poetry popular and his name dear in New-England.

After the war came the volumes *Snow-Bound, A Winter Idyl* (1866), *The Tent on the Beach and Other Poems* (1867), *Among the Hills and Other Poems,* (1869), and *Ballads of New England* (1870). Always New England. Recently John Macy has remarked that "No American poet has sung of his neighborhood with naïve passion, as if it were all the world to him." Whittier has done so. He knew nothing else; he loved nothing else. Like a farmer he loved it, like a peasant he knew it and described it, omitting nothing. All his life mountains on the horizon, and beyond them he cared not at all. To Emerson he wrote in 1853:

> What folly to run abroad over the Old World, when all that is beautiful may be seen from our own door-stone! Munich, the Louvre, and the Vatican are doubtless well worth seeing, but I fancy I see all and much more in my own painted woodlands. At any rate I am satisfied. Oh, that I could put into words the hymn of gratitude and unspeakable love which at such a season as this is sung in my heart. I wish thee could have been with us the other day on the Merrimac. We wanted an interpreter of the mystery of the glory about us.

Snow-Bound is as redolent of the old New England as *Cotter's Saturday Night* is of the Scotland of Burns's day. It is primitive in its feelings, simple, intensely human. Every character was drawn with Dutch-painter minuteness from life—no types, no grotesqueries. The snowstorm actually happened. *Snow-Bound,* the *Tent on the Beach* collection, and the *Mountain Pictures* lyrics stand high in the American gallery of nature-studies in verse.

One other side there was to his art. From the standpoint at least of quantity in all the hymn-books, Whittier is the leading American hymn-writer. None of our poets has been so fundamentally religious. Everywhere in his biography letters like this to Harriet Minot, 1837:

> Thee would not judge perhaps from the tone of this letter that my mind has been a good deal exercised of late on the subject of religious obligation. Yet such is the fact. The prayer of Cowper is sometimes in my mind, "Oh for a closer walk with God." I feel that there are too many things of the world between me and the realization of a quiet communion with the pure and Holy Spirit.

And in this Cowper-like attitude he wrote with no thought of musical setting a dozen poems easily adaptable for hymn-book use. And not one that is not a genuine thing, the voice of his own passionate soul. Everywhere, however, confidence and perfect trust:

> I know not where His islands lift
> Their fronded palms in air;
> I only know I cannot drift
> Beyond His love and care.
>
> And so beside the Silent Sea
> I wait the muffled oar;
> No harm from Him can come to me
> On ocean or on shore.

V

For a poet reared in the seclusion of a farm, unschooled, self-educated, crudeness is to be expected. One notices first the abundance of faulty rhymes. Open at random: *Dawn, corn, fawn, morn, borne, scorn. Sword* he rhymes with *blood* and *God,* but *blood* he can rhyme with *wood.* Seemingly he rhymed with the eye: *brow, throw; root, foot.* Many, however, are simply pure Yankee argot: *upon, gun; help, scalp; stone, gun; again, been.* As originally published in the *National Era,* one stanza of the poem "The Drovers" ran like this:

> From many a northern lake and hill
> To ocean's far-off water
> Shall fancy play the Drover still
> And make the long night shorter.

When the poem was to be published in *The Songs of Labor,* Fields criticized on the proof-sheet the faulty rhyme, and Whittier rewrote the stanza:

> By many a Northern lake and hill,
> From many a mountain pasture,
> Shall Fancy play the Drover still,
> And speed the long night faster.

Expostulated with again, the poet refused to make further change, remarking naïvely: "Pasture, faster, water, shorter, both are good Yankee rhymes." Right. Beyond the Yankee borders his imagination did not extend. Of what the Germans call the "Fatherland spirit" he had little. Before the Civil War, America had not anywhere awakened to the sense of a *whole* fatherland. Provincialism, despite the Constitution, was dominant. To Whittier, New England was not only fatherland, but it was the whole world.

His ballads lack compactness. They straggle often; they end with haziness at times; they lack in stanza after stanza the magic touch. Not often was he on the poetic heights which he was capable of reaching. Like all other poets, he is best in a few select pieces. Even his most fiery war lyrics are not in all their stanzas fiery. Ballads, however, he wrote, ballads genuine by any definition. They are the native stuff; they are homely and crude; they are genuine in their emotion; they are unliterary in their atmosphere and diction. America has produced none better.

No equal body of poetry more serious than Whittier's. Not a line is there of humor, or even of lightness. Poetry to him was a holy thing. To write it, he wrote to Lucy Hooper, unless it were "consecrated to the sacred interests of religion and humanity, it would be a criminal waste of life, and abuse of the powers which God has given for his own glory and the welfare of the world. Mere intellectual renown is valueless." His standards were rigid. After examining Thoreau's *Walden,* he could report that it was "capital reading, but very wicked and heathenish."

His ill health had much to do with his state of mind, and undoubtedly his celibacy played its part. As with Irving's work, there is everywhere the breath of an atmosphere of tender regret, of something precious forever lost. But to pursue the subject beyond this point is ridiculous. To write sensational feminism into his biography is to confess total ignorance of the real Whittier.

VI

A final word about his prose—a surprising amount, if one think of the man simply as a poet. His volumes *The Stranger in Lowell* (1845), *The Supernaturalism of New England* (1847), *Leaves from Margaret Smith's Journal* (1849), *Old Portraits and Modern Sketches* (1850), and *Literary Recreations and Miscellanies* (1854), would have given him a place in our literary history even had he written no poetry. Almost without exception they are interpretations of New England, and always with knowledge not only of facts but of deeper meanings. The *Leaves from Margaret Smith's Journal,* a fictitious narrative dealing with the early days of the settlement, is a classic. Work, even as G. R. Carpenter has ruled, that does "not show genius," but work nevertheless that deserves far more attention than it has hitherto received.

CHAPTER XXXV

THE FEMININE FIFTIES

I

THE 1850's published the leading books of what has been called the New England school. It was a culminating decade: everything tense, emotional, explosive, but it issued ten books that may be claimed as classics:

1850   *Representative Men,* Ralph Waldo Emerson.
         The Scarlet Letter, Nathaniel Hawthorne.
1851   *Moby Dick,* Herman Melville.
         The Conspiracy of Pontiac, Francis Parkman.
1852   *Uncle Tom's Cabin,* Harriet Beecher Stowe.
1854   *Walden,* Henry David Thoreau.
1855   *Hiawatha,* Henry Wadsworth Longfellow.
1855   *Leaves of Grass,* Walt Whitman.
1858   *The Autocrat of the Breakfast Table,* Oliver Wendell Holmes.
1860   *Poems,* John Greenleaf Whittier.[1]

Five of these at least were revolutionary documents—stones from slings: *Moby Dick, Walden,* Whittier's *Poems, Leaves of Grass,* and *Uncle Tom's Cabin.* An arsenal of weapons in the intense decade before the war, emotional, alive with criticism, too full of earnestness to be anything else than original.

In every way the decade was climacteric. The year 1850 marks the full ending of the Knickerbocker influence. Irving was to linger on for eight more years, busy with his

---

[1] Thoreau I have treated in my *History of American Literature since 1870,* Chapter VII; Whitman, Chapter IX; Melville in *The New American Literature,* Chapter XXI.

polished and brilliant life of Washington, but Irving the creator had died with Scott in 1832. Bryant the *poet* had perished three decades before in the editorial office of the *Evening Post.* Poe had died in 1849, Cooper in 1851, John Howard Payne in 1852. Paulding had closed his literary work in 1849 with his historical romance *The Puritan and His Daughter.* Halleck had gathered his poems into final edition in 1847. The *Knickerbocker Magazine* was in the late shimmering afternoon of its Indian summer, its popular editor, Lewis Gaylord Clark, striving by sheer personality to keep it from perishing. In 1854 his loyal contributors had financed for him a benefit volume, *The Knickerbocker Gallery,* and mercifully allowed the magazine to die. The roll of contributors to this beautifully bound volume, each of which contributed free an original piece—worthless stuff—is like the hero-names on the monument commemorating a bygone age.

In the place of it, new magazines—*Harper's New Monthly Magazine* (1850), opening with a serialization of the latest novel by Dickens. "The design," it declared in its "Word at the Start," "is to place within the reach of the great mass of the American people the unbounded treasures of the periodical literature of the present day. . . . The publishers intend to place everything of permanent value and interest in this literature in the hands of the people." Literature now for "the great mass of the American people."

As a result, *"Harper's* reached a fabulous circulation. Probably no periodical in the world was ever so popular or so profitable." To rebuke its Briticism and its popularity, *Putnam's Monthly Magazine* was started in 1853 with George William Curtis as editor. Original American work was to be used exclusively in the magazine, work of highest literary quality. For a time it sailed high. E. C. Stedman and Richard Henry Stoddard covered "Literature at Home," Bayard Taylor "Foreign Literature," and Curtis published as serials several of his own books.

So much for classic literature in America during the fifties. But the great mass of the American people were not reading classics. Nine out of ten had never read a word of Emerson, had never even heard of the man. Many of them, however, had read Dickens, and all of them, especially the women, were reading Sylvanus Cobb in Bonner's New York *Ledger*. Starting his paper in 1851, Robert Bonner had appealed to the mass of readers that had been prepared for him by *Godey's Lady Book*. Fiction was his chief dependence, fiction that could be advertised for arresting qualities. Sylvanus Cobb was his star attraction. In serials like *The Gunmaker of Moscow, The Painter of Parma, Alaric, or the Tyrant's Vault,* and *The Scourge of Damascus* he was able with uncanny skill to blend the elements most effective at the time—sentimentality, sensation, mystery, romance with foreign background, plot, story-telling power that held the reader to the end of the tale.

The first man, was Bonner, to make of literature a "big business." Says Algernon Tassin in his *The Magazine in America:*

It was Robert Bonner who first made the newspapers and the public appreciate what could be done with advertising. He would take a whole page of a paper, and say in it over and over again "Fanny Fern writes only for the *Ledger*." My success, he cried aloud frankly and reverberatingly from every housetop, is owing to my liberality in advertising. "I get all the money I can lay my hands on and throw it out to the newspapers," he said, "and before I can get back to my office, there it all is again, and a lot more with it."

It made him a millionaire, the first man in the history of the world to make millions from mere fiction.

But Bonner was not alone in his discovery of the non-literary reading masses. The fifties and the sixties saw the sudden springing up of a crop most amazing of rankest literary weeds. "Dime novels" has become the generic name. Who sowed the first seeds is a subject for debate. Perhaps Cooper. Around the main trunks of his Indian tales sprang up, we know, a veritable forest of sap-shoots, some of them noteworthy. Robert Montgomery Bird, for instance, wrote as early as 1835 *The Hawks of Hawk Hollow* and, two years later, *Nick of the Woods; or, The Jibbenainosay, A Tale of Kentucky.* In 1845 "Ned Buntline"—E. Z. C. Judson—began his sensational series, to be followed by Emerson Bennett, E. S. Ellis, and dozens of others. During the fifties the making of "yellow-backed shockers" became a business of surprising proportions. The soldiers at the front demanded car-loads of the stuff, as they did tobacco and rum. The pulpit thundered against the "yellow peril" that was corrupting the youth; parents and maiden aunts were vigilant in their watchfulness. All in vain: not a boy in a whole generation who had not in fearful secrecy and with nerves on edge enjoyed at least a dozen of them.[2]

That they were a moral menace is doubtful. Never did they condone wickedness. On the contrary, they were melodramatic in their contention that crime and villainy always are punished. Through nine-tenths of the novel the powers of evil may be in complete control, but the hero's "Hah, I have you now" is sure in the last chapter to relieve all suspense. "Redskins" "bit the dust" in these fictions, but always were they bad Indians who richly deserved their fate. Had the novels been condemned for their lack of truth, their melodramatic exaggerations, their imbecility in the interpretation of fundamental human characteristics, and their ignorance of Indians and villains generally, there would have been more of reason in the condemnation.

II

Another element not "classical" was becoming a dominating force. The feminine writers created and nourished

[2] See Edmund Pearson, *Dime Novels* (1929).

by *Godey's Lady's Book* and Sarah Josepha Hale during two decades were, in fiction at least, becoming the best-sellers in all the literary markets. Four years after the publication of his *House of the Seven Gables,* Hawthorne wrote to his publisher:

America is now wholly given over to a d——d mob of scribbling women. I should have no chance of success while the public taste is occupied with their trash—and should be ashamed of myself if I did succeed. What is the mystery of these innumerable editions of *The Lamplighter* and other books neither better nor worse?—worse they could not be and better they need not be, when they sell by the hundred thousand.

And again a month later:

Generally women write like emasculated men and are only to be distinguished from male authors by greater feebleness and folly; but when they throw off the restraints of decency, and come before the public stark naked, as it were—then their books are sure to possess character and value.

What troubled him was the fact that his own books were running with comparative sluggishness in a market that was booming with a dozen best-sellers. Consider the leaders during the decade:

Susan Warner's *The Wide Wide World,* 1850, and *Queechy,* 1852, sold 104,000 copies in three years; *Fern Leaves from Fanny's Portfolio,* 1853, by "Fanny Fern" (Sarah Willis Parton), sold 80,000 the first year; the novels of Caroline Lee Hentz in three years sold 93,000; *Alderbrook* by "Fanny Forrester" (later the wife of the missionary Adoniram P. Judson) sold 33,000 in a few months; and figures equally large might be quoted for the novels of Emma D. E. N. Southworth, the first of which, *Retribution,* appeared in 1849, of *Dollars and Cents,* 1852, by "Amy Lothrop" (Anna B. Warner), of *The Lamplighter,* 1854, by Maria S. Cummins, and of many others besides.[3]

[3] Fred Lewis Pattee, *Development of the American Short Story* (1923), p. 149.

III

Identical in texture was the work of Harriet Beecher
Stowe, whose *Uncle Tom's Cabin* (1852) became the best-
seller in the whole history of American fiction. Always
domestic home-life, always predominating femininity, always appeal to women readers, always sentiment Dickens-
ized into sentimentality, and always the humanitarian
motif. But Mrs. Stowe all unconsciously touched a universal chord. The country—the whole world indeed—was
ready for the kindling spark. England especially, which
had wept over Little Nell and Paul Dombey and had been
through the fever of Mrs. Gaskell's *Mary Barton* (1848)
and Kingsley's *Alton Locke* (1849) and *Yeast* (1848).

Mrs. Stowe, born Harriet Beecher, had been reared in
a home as rigidly Puritanic as that she describes in her
Oldtown Folks. Her father, Lyman Beecher, pastor at
Litchfield, Connecticut, and later at Boston, was one of
the leading religious forces of his generation. In 1832
Dr. Beecher became President of Lane Theological Seminary in Cincinnati, and his two daughters, Caroline, aged
twenty-two, and Harriet, two years younger, went with
him to found in the city a school for girls, a "Female
Institute" to afford girls to some degree the education
denied them by all the colleges. Four years as a teacher
and Harriet was married to Calvin E. Stowe, a professor
in the theological seminary.

Cincinnati in the 1830's was in the "far West." It had
taken the Beecher family eight days to cross the mountains to Wheeling, West Virginia. They had found a
growing, prosperous city largely composed of transplanted
New Englanders who had hailed them joyously as bring-
ers of Eastern "culture." The whole new West, they
found, was eager for the planting in the rich new soil of
the prairies of the finer things of achieved civilization.
In 1828 Judge James Hall of Vandalia, Illinois, had
issued *The Western Souvenir* for 1829, an annual "writ-

ten and published in the Western Country by Western
men." In 1832 he had published his *Sketch-Book* volume,
Legends of the West, to be followed by a series of romances and sketches made with Western materials, and in
1833 he had become editor of the *Western Monthly Magazine* in Cincinnati. His prize of fifty dollars offered for
the best short story in 1834 was awarded to the tale
entitled "Uncle Lot" by Harriet Beecher. Other work
followed later, in 1843 to be published in a volume entitled
*The Mayflower, or, Sketches of Scenes and Characters
among the Descendants of the Pilgrims.* The Semi-Colon
Club of the city, a literary group of readers and writers,
kept alive her pen, greatly in danger during that period of
growing family cares and lessening income of becoming
lost altogether.

In 1850 Professor Stowe secured a professorship in the
theological department of his *alma mater,* Bowdoin College. The salary for a man with wife and six small children
was near the starvation point, but it was return from
exile—it was in New England, home. The wife would do
all the housework—and, in addition, help to increase the
family income with her pen.

During her residence in Cincinnati, the city had been a
frontier battle-ground between anti-slavery and pro-
slavery forces. Mobs time and again had destroyed property. In 1836 James G. Burney had started an abolitionist
paper, the *Philanthropist,* later edited by Dr. Gamaliel
Bailey, whose office was three times raided by a mob. In
1847, in Washington, he started with his wife a new
abolitionist paper, the *National Era,* a paper remembered
now because of three contributions: Hawthorne's "The
Great Stone Face," Whittier's *Margaret Smith's Journal,*
and *Uncle Tom's Cabin.* Friends in Cincinnati, the
Baileys, had asked Mrs. Stowe for a contribution to the
new journal, and she had commenced a narrative that was
announced to run for about three months. But the story,
once begun, could not, according to the later reports of

Mrs. Stowe, be stopped. "The Lord himself wrote it," she would declare in her later years, "and I was but the humblest of instruments in his hand." The story ran from June 5, 1851, until April 1, 1852. It was issued as a book in March. Its instant popularity almost exceeds belief. Within a year there had been issued and sold one hundred and twenty editions, 300,000 copies. Four months after publication her copyright check was $10,000. Publication in England was almost on the same scale. Immediately the book was translated into dozens of languages. It became the most famous book of the century. No book so much translated save the Bible and perhaps Thomas a Kempis's *De Imitationi Christi* and *Don Quixote*. And neither of the two latter reached so thoroughly the ignorant classes.

We can do now what seemed impossible eighty years ago—we can examine the book in cold blood. We can realize that it was a war document, propaganda at a time when the nation, North and South, was boiling with passion. It was written, we realize, with emotion and with no other purpose than to arouse emotion in the reader. Its central *motif* was the tragedy caused by the selling of slaves. No element of pathos omitted: the selling of children from the arms of their mothers, the horrors of the auction-block, the brutalities of professional slave dealers, the religious Negro auctioned at a higher price because of his religion. Everything heightened to melodrama and tremulous with sentimentality. No other book so drenched with tears. After killing Little Eva, Mrs. Stowe herself was sick abed for a week.

Dickens perhaps said the last word about one phase of the book. Asked by Mrs. Stowe for an opinion of her novel, he wrote:

You go too far and seek to prove too much. The wrongs and atrocities of slavery are, God knows! case enough. I doubt if there be any warrant for making out the African race to be a great race, or for supposing the future destinies of the world to lie in that direction.

Unquestionably Mrs. Stowe, a Northerner, did not know the Negro. The prototypes of George Harris and Eliza, mulattoes, she professed to have seen, and as a result they are more real than Uncle Tom, who is fairly canonized into sainthood, or the vaudeville Topsy, who never could have lived and yet who never will die. Her second phase of Uncle Tom, the Uncle Tom of the New Orleans aristocracy, is of *Godey's Lady's Book* texture. She knew no more of fashionable life in the creole city than the "females" of the thirties did of the Apennines where they found the villains for their romances. And the final Simon Legree climax is pure melodrama. Uncle Tom's religion now becomes fairly nauseating.

That Mrs. Stowe wrote the novel to placate the South, that she made of Simon Legree a Northern Yankee to forestall their anger, that she had no thought of any purpose save that of bringing North and South into harmony on the question that was bringing them to the brink of war, is disproved by the novel itself. To put forth such a claim is to confess to not having read the story straight through. The book was a stone from a sling; it was written with singleness of purpose; abolition is written on every page of it. And it accomplished its purpose. One need say no more. To analyze it for defects—and its defects are sophomoric—is totally useless. In the light of its amazing world-wide popularity, all criticism fades into nothingness. It came in the one moment of history when such success could have been possible. But come it did, and there is no escaping the fact that it will stand for long among the greatest masterpieces of fiction.

Mrs. Stowe neglected to protect her dramatic rights when the book was published, and as a result scores of companies were soon on the road with dramatic versions. Far more people know *Uncle Tom's Cabin* from having seen these sensational barn-storming productions than from having read the book. An injustice to Mrs. Stowe, for the versions have omitted the greater part of what she

most would wish emphasized and have retained only the
vaudeville sections and the humor.

Following a storm of criticism, Mrs. Stowe published
The Key to Uncle Tom's Cabin, answering with attempts
at documentation the hundreds of criticisms that had
poured in upon her; and, visualizing herself as God's
amanuensis in a holy war, she wrote her second abolitionist novel, *Dred or Nina Gordon.* In vain. Completely was
it lost in the fierce flame of *Uncle Tom's Cabin.*

Her abolitionist work was done. But at the earnest call
of her publishers she continued to write. Changing her
field completely, she began to write stories of her native
New England: *The Minister's Wooing* (1859), *Pearl of
Orr's Island* (1862), then in 1869, when spending the
winter in Florida, *Oldtown Folks,* a book semi-
autobiographical, made up of her own recollections of
Litchfield and her husband's memories of his boyhood in
Natick. A book with the golden light of memories of childhood upon it, her best work, perhaps. In her preface she
wrote:

My object is to interpret to the world the New England
life and character in that particular time of its history which
may be called the seminal period. I would endeavor to show
you New England in its seed-bed, before the hot onus of
modern progress had developed its sprouting germs into the
great trees of to-day.

New England has been to these United States what the
Dorian hive was to Greece. It has always been a capital country to emigrate from, and North, South, East, and West have
been populated largely from New England, so that the seed-
bed of New England was the seed-bed of this great American
Republic, and of all that is likely to come of it.

As fiction, these works fall short, but for art she cared
little. They present material, interpretation, characters.
Humor enough she had to float even her theology, a deadly
mass, necessary, doubtless, if one is really to interpret

Puritan Connecticut. Her Sam Lawson, a wise old Yankee "doodle" full of stories, overflows into a volume of
tales entitled *Sam Lawson's Fireside Stories*. Excellent,
these New England studies. But more and more it is evident that Mrs. Stowe was the author of but a single book
—her *Uncle Tom*.

Praise even from conservative critics has been in superlatives. The secret of Mrs. Stowe's power Lowell found
to be "in that same genius by which the great successes in
creative literature have always been achieved—the genius
that instinctively goes right to the organic elements of
human nature, whether under a white skin or black, and
which disregards as trivial the conventional and factitious
notions which make so large a part both of our thinking
and feeling." And Howells could call *Uncle Tom's Cabin,*
with all its crudities, "the first great American novel and
the only one produced in this country before the Civil
War." And this final word from The New York *Evening
Post:*

The millions who have wept over the deaths of Uncle Tom
and Eva, as portrayed by every kind of dramatic company,
and thrilled at the escape of Eliza, have doubtless not been
severe critics, nor proof against mawkish sentiment. But
their emotion is explicable on no other ground than at bottom
Mrs. Stowe touched with rare dramatic power the underly-
ing human emotions not only of her generation, but of many
another, and thus proved anew that an appeal in behalf of
human rights, made with justice and passion and self-
obliterating earnestness, can never fail to bear fruit.

IV

Outside the best-seller list, these feminine offerings,
some of them the initial volumes of writers soon to be
better known:

1849   *Poems,* Alice and Phœbe Cary.
1850   *Greenwood Leaves,* Grace Greenwood (Sarah J. C.
         Lippincott).

576 EARLY AMERICAN LITERATURE

A pleasing episode, the Cary sisters. Born on a farm near Cincinnati, they were reared much as was Whittier in Massachusetts. His poems they early knew by heart: by the light of a burning string hung in a saucer of lard, night after night they wrote poetry themselves. And at last with their meager savings of years they were able to visit what to them was a veritable Holy Land—New England where lived the poets. They called on Whittier, who was only twelve or fifteen years their senior, embarrassing him beyond measure, and they found others of the Boston poets.

Home once more, Alice settled down to the making of poems and prose with a determination that brooked no opposition. Her *Clovernook,* with its sketches of Western life, was a promising volume; but to the eager young Westerners, literature meant poetry, and they wrote it. Rufus W. Griswold, making his *Female Poets of America,* they deluged with it, and Griswold, turning over the lyric mass, gave this judgment: "In the West, song gushes and flows, like the springs and the rivers, more imperially than elsewhere."

The amazing Griswold! One can never understand the feminine fifties until one has considered his editings, until at least one has read—a feat requiring physical vigor and unconquerable perseverance—*The Female Poets of America.* And to think of the masculine Melville and Hawthorne and Thoreau condemned to work through their literary lives in an atmosphere like that.

But poetry brought the Cary sisters no money, and perforce Alice turned to prose. Twenty volumes mixed

and miscellaneous, and there was money enough to pur-
chase a modest house in New York City. Gradually the
home became a national institution. The sisters gave
weekly receptions to authors and artists. Every author of
note in America, and many in England, sooner or later
passed a never-to-be-forgotten evening with the Cary sisters. Alice, most motherly and charming, was the Martha
of the combination, but to keep up the hospitality of her
Victorian parlor, she had to work interminably. This from
a contemporary: It "is a sad story despite the upholstering.
Alice Cary, 'as a ballad writer never equalled by any
American man or woman,' did hack work for twenty years
so that Horace Greeley and Sam Bowles and T. B. Aldrich
and John Greenleaf Whittier might lounge around that
parlor Sunday nights, burning out the gas and consuming
ice-cream."

No literary biography of the period without an allusion
to those ambrosial evenings but time has been unkind to
the two poets. But a single fragment of their writings remains, and that by the Mary of the combination—Phœbe's
"One Sweetly Solemn Thought," now found in all church
hymn-books.

CHAPTER XXXVI

THE ATLANTIC MONTHLY

THE ELEGANT volume by Edward Waldo Emerson, *The Early Years of the Saturday Club* (1918), opens with this elegant sentence:

> In the middle of the last century a constellation, which—as separate stars of differing magnitude, but all bright—had for twenty years been visible, at first dimly, in the New England heavens, ascending, was seen as a group, gave increasing light and cheer here and to the westward-journeying sons and daughters; reached our zenith; even began to be reported by star-gazers beyond the ocean.

Which was Bostonese for the statement that the "New England Renaissance," as Barrett Wendell termed it, was a scattered affair without cohesion until 1855, when was organized the Saturday Club, out of which two years later came the *Atlantic Monthly*. Earlier attempts had been made to concentrate literary forces. There had been clubs in Boston, notably the Transcendental Club and the Anthology Club, and there had been the *Dial* magazine, pitched too high even for Boston, and there had been the *North American Review*. But the *Edinburgh* reign was over: the Jeffrey–Sydney Smith review was out of date. It had done a needed work. As T. W. Higginson expressed it, its "traditions of rather tame correctness were what enabled us to live through the Carlyle epoch with safety," but the epoch was now over and the danger past.

But an adequate magazine for Boston and New England had its financial difficulties. Advertising in such a

578

journal was out of the question—an unthinkable vulgarity.
Moses D. Phillips, the leading publisher of Boston,
doubted if enough subscribers could be found even to start
such a magazine.

The Saturday Club, which finally converted him, was
primarily a Harvard affair, made up of Harvard pro-
fessors like Agassiz, Holmes, Longfellow, Lowell, Norton, Felton, Pearce, or alumni like Dana, Emerson, Motley, Prescott. Few outsiders there were before 1860, the
most noteworthy being Whittier, Hawthorne, Whipple.
Brilliant affairs, the frequent dinners of the club. The
noctes ambrosianae when Lowell and Holmes were at
their best have never been recorded, can never be recap-
tured. The club produced no Boswell, unless it were
Holmes, who recorded only himself.

In one respect, however, it accomplished in the end its
desire—an adequate magazine, one that at the same time
could be as profound as Emerson and yet as sparkling as
Holmes, "The vehicle came," records Barrett Wendell,
"only when the strength of the New England Renaissance
was beginning to fail," but it came not too late nevertheless. It received during the next two decades the best that
was produced by the waning renaissance group and with it
much of the strongest work of the gathering new literary
generation nation-wide which followed the Civil War.

I

Lowell had accepted the editorship of the magazine on
the condition that the others, especially Holmes, were to
furnish materials. Why he singled out an oldish physician
is not at first apparent. Holmes, whose life had been given
to medicine, was nearing fifty. "At thirty," he was soon
to say with Boswellian positiveness, "we are all trying to
cut our names in big letters upon this tenement of life.
Twenty years later we have carved it or shut up our jack-
knives." At forty-nine Holmes himself had produced in

literature only two distinctive lyrics, "Old Ironsides" and "The Last Leaf," and to these he had added half a dozen humorous poems and *vers de société* fragments. His "first folio," as he looked it through for something to satisfy the new editor, contained no riches. It

had boyhood written on every page. A single passionate out-cry when the old war-ship I had read about in the broadsides that were a part of our kitchen literature, and in the *Naval Monument,* was threatened with demolition; a few verses, suggested at the sight of old Major Melville in his cocked hat and breeches, were the best scraps that came out of that first Portfolio, which was soon closed that it should not inter-fere with the duties of a profession authorized to claim all the time and thought which would have been otherwise ex-pended in filling it. During a quarter of a century the first Portfolio remained closed for the greater part of the time. Only now and then it would be taken up and opened, and something drawn from it for a special occasion, more particu-larly for the annual reunions of a certain class of which I was a member.[1]

One could write the entire biography of Holmes with similar quotations: old Cambridge his birthplace, and the story of his childhood there—*The Poet at the Breakfast Table,* pages 10–32, and *A Mortal Antipathy,* pages 22–32; his school days, 1819–1825—*Pages from an Old Volume of Life* (1825), page 239; the class of 1829, Harvard—*Over the Teacups,* pages 28–30; his student days in the Harvard Medical School, 1830–1833—*Medical Essays,* pages 420–440; his first visit to Europe, 1833–1835—*Our Hundred Days in Europe;* the "Autocrat" series—*The Autocrat of the Breakfast Table* and *Over the Teacups;* memoirs of Motley and of Emerson—*A Mortal Antipathy,* pages 13–20; and to these add *Our One Hundred Days in Europe* and *My Hunt after the Captain.* But the *whole* of his "Autocrat" series is autobiographical, its subtitle "Every Man his own Boswell."

[1] Oliver Wendell Holmes, *A Mortal Antipathy,* Introduction.

Lowell knew his man. Of the whole Saturday Club group, Holmes was the most brilliant conversationalist. Always the company returned home from club banquet or social gathering or Harvard dinner reporting that Holmes had popped the best pun, told the best story, and let fly the most original epigram of the evening. Long before the days of the Saturday Club and the *Atlantic Monthly* this had been Lowell's estimate of the man:

> There's Holmes, who is matchless among you for wit;
> A Leyden-jar always full-charged, from which flit
> The electrical tingles of hit after hit.

Holmes was as urban as Whittier was rural, and as social as Hawthorne was solitary. His whole life had been spent in the most cultured circles of Cambridge and Boston. As practicing physician in the city and as lecturer for years in the Harvard Medical School, he had a peculiarly wide knowledge of life and its ills. He was of "the Brahmin caste" [2]: he had been born in a manse on the Harvard campus; he was an aristocrat in his point of view:

> I go for the man who inherits family traditions and the cumulative humanities of at least four or five generations. Above all things, as a child he should have tumbled about in a library. All men are afraid of books who have not handled them from infancy.

He was of Puritan stock, but not true to type; he was a "sport," a new variety. Fundamentally, was he a humorist. In college he had produced some of the best light verse written during his period, such lyrics as "The Ballad of the Oysterman," "The Spectre Pig," and "The Height of the Ridiculous." He had read much and retained much. He was a leader, too, in his profession of medicine, a scientist who in paper after paper had enlarged the area of the known in the wilderness of disease.

[2] See *Elsie Venner,* Chapter II.

Lowell knew his man and he was not disappointed. In the first number of the *Atlantic* Holmes began his "Autocrat" series, a series that was to run for years in the columns of the magazine. Table-talk at a breakfast-table—where but in Boston may one look for a brilliant torrent of wisdom and wit at breakfast time? Monologue it is, and being table-talk, it could wander over the entire universe and beyond, and change the subject instantly at the whim of the talker. And wonder of wonders, everywhere the torrent seems inevitable, unforced, spontaneous. This, one feels, especially in the earlier papers, was Holmes himself. "The first of my series," he wrote in his *Over the Teacups,* "came from my mind almost with an explosion, like the champagne cork; it startled me a little to see what I had written, and to hear what people said about it. After that first explosion the flow was more sober, and I looked upon the product of my wine-press more coolly."

Following the first series came the second, *The Professor at the Breakfast Table,* and in 1873, when the author was sixty-four, *The Poet at the Breakfast Table,* a series more essay-like and somber. Then in the white winter of the "Autocrat's" eightieth year came *Over the Teacups,* the final volume, a volume largely reminiscent. In four volumes the best prose of Oliver Wendell Holmes. "In these books," he wrote, "I have unburdened myself of what I was born to say."

Columnist material, we would call the work today, a mélange both in prose and verse, for a whole volume of poems lies embedded in the series—at the end of each paper a poem. What better columnist fun than the drinking song as revised by the temperance editor, "Latter-Day Warnings," "Album Verses," and "This is It"? Everywhere vivacity, everywhere wisdom in witty pellets, cocksureness, perfect unction in a torrent. Sometimes there is a thread of story, sometimes even a bit of romance. Chapters and books and final series ripple on and on without restraint or definite aim, now broad and serene, now danc-

ing over the pebbles. Nothing ever at all deep, nothing
that would not be perfectly at home in the Victorian parlors of the brown-front mansions on Beacon Street.

But the series is still alive, at least in selections. The
papers on old age have not been surpassed in America.
But Holmes at least three times attempted to write a novel,
three novels with medical *motifs. Elsie Venner,* a pathological case: rattlesnake characteristics caused by a fright
received by her mother; *A Mortal Antipathy* and *The
Guardian Angel,* "medicated novels" dealing, as Holmes
expressed it, with the "mysterious borderland which lies
between physiology and psychology," all of them really
not novels at all. *Elsie Venner* is another "Autocrat" volume.

We read four chapters before we learn even the heroine's
name. A novel can reasonably be expected to center about
its title character: Elsie Venner speaks seventeen times during the story, and eleven of these utterances are delivered
from her death bed. . . . Digressions are as frequent as
even in the Autocrat papers. A widow is introduced for no
apparent reason, studied for a chapter, and then dropped
from the narrative. . . . We feel like one who is being
personally conducted through New England by a skilful
guide. Note this partial prospectus: Newburyport, Portsmouth, Portland, caste in New England, rural schools, North-
ampton and Mt. Holyoke, mountain vegetation, rattlesnakes
in Massachusetts, the New England mansion-house, school
compositions, the old type of meeting-house, varieties of
school-girls, the old-time India merchant, oysters in New
England, hired help, colonial chimneys, young ladies' semina-
ries, the hemlock tree.[3]

All are treated at length, some to the length, indeed, of
an entire chapter.

Poetry with Holmes flowed easily. Forty-seven per cent
of his poems were written *invita Minerva* at the command

[3] Fred Lewis Pattee, *A History of American Literature since 1870*
(1915), p. 63.

of some occasion. Forty-four of them were made for reunions of his class, the famous class of '29. Phi Beta
Kappa occasions, gatherings for the greeting or the speed-
ing of traveling friends, banquets, birthdays, all levied
upon the genius of Holmes. "Verses made to pop with the
corks," *vers de société* extempore, and church hymns
flowed with equal ease. At banquets he was always lifted
to the table-top, and, standing amid the ruins of the banquet, he would read his lyric in perfect key with the
occasion, precisely as if the performance were spontaneous
and extempore.

The new *Atlantic Monthly* seemed to revive the adolescent in Holmes. In the "Autocrat" series appeared now his
most distinctive poems, "The Chambered Nautilus," "The
Living Temple." A spice of the satiric at times, as in "The
Deacon's Masterpiece"; a dash of hilarity often, as in
"How the Old Horse Won the Bet"; pathos in dozens of
lyrics from "The Last Leaf" to the final class-of-1829
lyric. But in them all nothing too much. Severely was he a
classicist, a true son of the eighteenth century come almost
to the end of the nineteenth. The most prejudiced of all
the New England school, he was perhaps the most liberal
of them all, veering to the left even to deism. Yet two of
his hymns are in all the hymn-books. Never was he a
Transcendentalist, never a reformer, never a romanticist.
Not far did he ever travel beyond the comfortable bounds
of his eighteenth century and the "sunny street that holds
the sifted few."

II

The youngest member of the group was James Russell
Lowell, born in 1819. Fourteen years was he younger than
Emerson, thirteen years younger than Hawthorne. Peculiarly was he a man caught between two periods, too young
to chord perfectly with the older group and too old to be
in full sympathy with the young rebels who succeeded

them. Youth, however, gave to him what the older group, with waning creative powers and lessening driving forces, were beginning to lack. Young as he was as compared with the others, he became their Dr. Johnson, and as editor of the *Atlantic* he even dared to suggest changes in the poems submitted by Emerson and by Whittier and to revise the manuscript of Thoreau until that individual genius refused longer to contribute to the magazine.

Like Holmes, he was born and reared under the shadow of Harvard, a "towny" who even as a small boy knew more about the college than the wisest seniors. He was a minister's son and therefore, so "everybody" professed to believe, destined to go bad. A lively lad undoubtedly, and, knowing the college "ropes" completely, he was "rusticated" in his senior year for a prank and sent to Concord to finish his course under the tutelage of a safe old divine. Lowell was graduated *in absentia,* and his class poem was read by deputy. Then came the question of profession. A hard one to answer, for was he not a poet?

Singularly fortunate had he been in his choice of ancestors and of birthplace. He had grown up in a scholarly and literary atmosphere; books had been daily companions since childhood; his mother, refined and sensitive, had filled him with a love for the old English songs and ballads. His essay, "Cambridge Thirty Years Ago," tells us of this early environment. Early he became a reader of the old poets, and during his college course he haunted the library alcoves and read far more in the poets than in the prescribed courses. Scarce twenty was he when he was graduated. Then for two years he had dreamed and dallied over law books and in the end actually had gained his degree from the law school, but without enthusiasm. Poetry was his only thought, poetry with love its theme, for he had been engaged, even before completing his law course, to Miss Maria White, herself a writer of verse. Marriage, however, had to be postponed. Financial disaster had come suddenly upon his father, and the young dreamers were

soon face to face with actuality. He, perforce, must fall
back upon his profession. A desk he secured in the law
office of C. G. Loring of Boston, but a year of legal practice produced for him nothing but a volume of verse entitled *A Year's Life* (1841).

Then had come a short period of magazine editorship.
He became the silent partner of Nathan Hale, Jr., in his
venture with the *Boston Miscellany of Literature and
Fashion* (1842), his first literary vehicle of many that
were to follow. To it he contributed, in addition to a group
of poems, his first series of critical papers, *The Old English Dramatists*. Then in 1843, in connection with Robert
Carter, he began a magazine of his own, the *Pioneer, a
Literary and Critical Magazine,* to be what the *Atlantic
Monthly* was designed to be fourteen years later. No magazine, surely, ever started with a stronger list of contributors: Poe, Parsons, Story, Hawthorne, Whittier, Lowell,
Jones Very, John Neal, John S. Dwight. Positive was it in
its designs, cock-sure, radical: "The object of the Subscribers in establishing *The Pioneer,*" declared the prospectus, "is to furnish the intelligent and reflecting portion
of the Reading Public with a rational substitute for the
enormous quantity of thrice-diluted trash, in the shape of
namby-pamby love tales and sketches, which is monthly
poured out to them by many of our popular magazines."
A magazine for the literary aristocracy, a magazine totally opposed to the popular delusion that to be an American classic a volume must present American uniqueness,
even though it be a Mike-Fink-like mess of coarseness and
vulgarity.

In his salutatory, Lowell presented the first chapter of
his literary creed:

We are the farthest from wishing to see what many so
ardently pray for, namely, a *National* literature: for the same
mighty lyre of the human heart answers the touch of the
master in all ages and in every clime, and any literature, as

far as it is national, is diseased, inasmuch as it appeals to
some climatic peculiarity, rather than to the universal nature.
Moreover, everything that tends to encourage the sentiment
of caste, to widen the boundary between races, and so to
put farther off the hope of one great brotherhood, should
be steadily resisted by all good men. But we do long for a
natural literature.

The magazine lasted for three numbers. Doubtless, like
the *Dial,* it was keyed too high for its times. The *un*intelligent and *un*reflecting portion of the reading public was
despicable, perhaps, but it did, by mere vulgar payment of
cash, make magazine publication profitable. Then, too, the
anti-slavery slant of the magazine may have repelled some
would-be subscribers. More probable, however, was the
sudden illness of the editor with a disease of the eyes
which for a time threatened blindness. Poetry, however,
he still could write. A volume he published in 1843, to be
followed in 1845 by a volume of prose, *Conversations on
Some of the Old Poets.* Not criticism, however, this
ecstatic outpouring. Coördinate is it with Longfellow's
Hyperion, the voice of a young poet of twenty-six who has
read all of the poets—a youth's first intoxication with life
and love and romantic song. And in a few weeks he was
to be married to a dainty soul as poetical even as himself.
A defense it is of poetry, a pronouncement also of his
own definitions. "It is time," he declared, "to return to
the poetic ideals of the old days when freedom and spontaneous utterance, sincerity and true earnestness prevailed; when poets cared not a rush for fashions and
models, but sang from their hearts." Despite a discursive-
ness at random as in an "Autocrat" paper by Holmes, the
reader is not suffered long to forget the dominant message: "Poetry is something to make us wiser and better,
by continually revealing those types of beauty and truth
which God has set in all men's souls. . . . Nature should
lead the true poet by the hand."
Greatly in 1845 was America in need of this stirring

message. The breath of that spring morning which had awakened Burns and Wordsworth had been long in crossing the Atlantic. America had been too busy to make or read poetry. "It has become a mercantile world," complained the young enthusiast, "and if some murmur of the poet's song creep into the counting room, it thinks of the insane asylum, and runs up another column of figures." Unlike Holmes, he would throw into the discard all the works of Pope as unspontaneous and artificial. The book is a landmark in the history of American poetry. The first protest, was it, against the coming industrial age, the faint rumbling of whose wheels was so soon to be a roar.

The decade ending in 1853 with the death of Mrs. Lowell was the poet's creative period. After she died he sang no more for years: "My moon is set; my vision set with her." But during this wonder-period, poetry was his meat and drink. Eighteen forty-eight was the culminating year: four volumes—*Poems, Second Series; Melibœus Hipponax, The Biglow Papers, Edited, with an Introduction, Notes, Glossary, and Copious Index, by Homer Wilbur, M.A.; The Vision of Sir Launfal; A Fable for Critics*—all this in addition to column-work for the New York *Standard* and a wide variety of occasional poems and criticisms. Exuberance, excitement, poetic rapture. *A Fable for Critics* he wrote "at full speed."

Three Lowells in full voice: Sir Launfal, poet of beauty, visionary, humanitarian, searcher for the Grail; then Hosea Biglow, Yankee "doodle," vaudeville rustic, impetuous, humorous; and finally Parson Wilbur, homiletic, ponderous, Puritanic, Cotton-Matherish in scholarship, vocabulary, and allusions. In all of Lowell's work these three, often all of them in a mixture.

His "Sir Launfal" poetry, found in his earlier collections, conventional in theme and form, uncolored by locality, often beautiful in passages, has disappeared even from the school anthologies, save for *The Vision of Sir Launfal,* still considered beautiful.

It is the Hosea Biglow in the poet that still keeps him in the anthologies. Youth was partly responsible for the poetic antics to be found in *A Fable for Critics* and in *The Biglow Papers*. Never such an overdose of puns and rhymed unrhymables and poetic acrobatics. Hosea is not a genuine Yankee "doodle," like Major Jack Downing: he is Lowell in a character make-up, a rural Franklin. He voices in crude dialect, abominably overdone in its misspelling, the rebel element in Lowell. Deeply ingrained was the come-outer spirit in the man—the swing to the left. It made him an abolitionist, a mugwump, a protester against the Mexican War. It was Hosea who wrote *A Fable for Critics,* a plum-pudding of sophomoricisms:

> I called this a "Fable for Critics"; you think it 's
> More like a display of my rhythmical trinkets;
> My plot, like an icicle, 's slender and slippery,
> Every moment more slender, and likely to slip awry.

New York writers—Cornelius Matthews, E. A. Duyckinck, R. W. Griswold, Willis, Bryant, Cooper, Briggs— he lashes without mercy. Emerson he canonizes in eighty-four lines; Whittier, his fellow abolitionist, in sixty-two. Passages of brilliant criticism one may cull, but the book as a whole, with its fantastically rhymed title-page printed in red and black, its long introduction in heroic meter printed as prose, and its labyrinth of digressions, is to be classed with the curiosities of American literature.

Parson Wilbur dominated his prose. Only a veritable Parson Wilbur could publish a volume with the title *Melibœus-Hipponax.* After reading Lowell's critical volumes straight through, one is convinced that the character of the old pundit is not overdrawn. His formal reviews—like the musing organist, "Beginning doubtfully and far away"—build always a long "bridge from Dreamland" before they even mention their subject: the method of the old quarterlies. Written, it is, for the few. Only a scholar profound, omnivorous in his reading, and Macaulay-like in his memory can recognize his allusions, and he never explains. A sentence like this, caught at random, is typical: "There is Whittier, the fiery Koerner of this spiritual warfare, who, Scaevola-like, has sacrificed on the altar of duty that right hand which might have made him acknowledged as the most passionate lyrist of his time." Truth it may be, but truth dressed in Sunday clothes, with comparisons unusual, with atmosphere of smartness, cock-sureness—at last the last word spoken. Quotable sentences at times, even paragraphs of potent import, but his critical work today is for the most part unread and, as readers average, unreadable. The Reverend Homer Wilbur, even when supplemented by Hosea Biglow and Sir Launfal, is to be classed now with Cotton Mather.

Lowell and his family spent the year 1851 in Europe; in 1854 he was appointed Longfellow's successor at Harvard; he edited the *Atlantic* for four years and the *North American Review* for eight years, 1864–1872. From 1877 to 1885 he was in the American diplomatic service, first in Spain and then in England, where he was showered with honors.

III

Few of the major writers of the American mid-century have been so deflated by the younger critics as Lowell. One whole volume written to denounce his criticism.[4] His major odes are "Under the Old Elm" and "Ode Recited at the Harvard Commemoration July, 1865," the latter characterized by Stedman as "the high-water mark of American poetry."

Passages unquestionably in these odes have in them poetic quality rare in our American literature; this fragment characterizing Washington, for instance, from "Under the Old Elm":

⁴ J. J. Reilly, *James Russell Lowell as a Critic* (1915).

Virginia gave us this imperial man.
Cast in the massive mould
Of those high-statured ages old
   Which into grander forms our mortal metal ran.

.   .   .   .

Mother of States and undiminished men,
Thou gavest us a country giving him.

And this fragment characterizing Lincoln, from the com-
memorization ode:

   Great captains with their guns and drums,
 Disturb our judgment for the hour,
But at last silence comes;
   These all are gone, and standing like a tower,
   Our children shall behold his fame,
 The kindly-earnest, brave, foreseeing man,
   Sagacious, patient, dreading praise, not blame,
   New birth of our new soil, the first American.

Yet critics have swept aside even these as "mere rhetoric."
   One thing, however, of Lowell's still stands and will
continue to stand: his editorship of the *Atlantic Monthly*
and the *North American Review*. During critical years in
the history of American literature Lowell unquestionably
was an uplifting force. Standing on the border between
two periods, heavily weighted with old prejudices gained
from his early education, he leaned in many ways toward
the newnesses which after the Civil War began to come with
force. Parson Wilbur though he was, he could print in the
Atlantic a story by Rose Terry Cooke beginning,
"Mrs. Griswold was paring apples and Lizzy straining
squash." Thackeray had been an influence, Thackeray
with his "I have no brain above the eyes; I describe what
I see." Not a realist was he in the Zola sense, but an in-
sister that the truth be told, and only the truth. A letter he
wrote Mrs. Stowe makes clear his ideals:

My advice is to follow your own instincts—stick to Nature and avoid what people commonly call the ideal; for that, and beauty, and pathos, and success, all lie in the simply natural. There are ten thousand people who can write ideal things for one who can see, and feel, and reproduce Nature and character.

Breath of life was it in the feminine fifties and the sensational sixties. Lowell, during the decade of his editorship of two magazines, did more than any other man or group of men to bring sanity and realism and truth to nature into American literature.

CHAPTER XXXVII

THE CENTURY FROM THE PERSPECTIVE OF TODAY

I

OUR SURVEY of our first literary century ends with the year 1870. In our study we have examined movements and personalities and products by decades; now for a moment change the perspective and view the whole hundred years from the upper air as it were, from the viewpoint of today, the 1930's.

The century was opened by a long and transforming war, and it was closed by an equally long and transforming war. Reckoning from 1770, it produced three generations, or, translating into historical terms, it was a sequence of three periods: the revolutionary, the first national, and the second national. But a period is only another name for a generation: note the generations of a single family, the Adamses of Massachusetts:

1. John Adams, 1735–1826, of the revolutionary period.
2. John Quincy Adams, 1767–1848, of the first national period.
3. Charles Francis Adams, 1807–1886, of the second national period.
4. Henry Adams, 1838–1918, of the period since 1870.

The first generation, the one that fought to a finish the Revolutionary War, was completely an eighteenth-century phenomenon, and naturally so, since its outer limit was the year 1789. The books it read were almost without exception English books, the works of the Dr. Johnson epoch just new from the press. Fundamentally these men were English, and when they wrote, as a few of them did write, they produced nothing vitally new. Only one writer of major proportions in this whole period—Benjamin Franklin. Thomas Paine some would add. Philip Freneau will never disappear from the histories, since he was in many fields a pioneer, but such writers as the once much-lauded "Connecticut Wits" are read today only by special students of literature.

The second generation, the men of the first three decades of the new Republic, were for the most part concerned with affairs rather than with literature. Remarkable scholars this generation contained, men, for instance, like Noah Webster who single-handed made a dictionary (first edition, 1828) that has been a standard authority for more than a century; but makers of "elegant" literature, as it was called, were few. In England a new period was opening—the romantic period led by Wordsworth, Coleridge, and Scott—and America tremendously was influenced by it, but of major writers we produced next to none. In thirty years only two appeared concerning whom now there is no question—Irving and Cooper. Brockden Brown was a pioneer but not a major creator. Some would add Bryant.

The third generation, the one that ran parallel with the early Victorian generation in England, was for the most part a New England matter, a late flowering of a cold springtime. In its own day it was believed that this later "renaissance" produced at least eight major creators: Emerson, Hawthorne, Longfellow, Whittier, Holmes, Mrs. Stowe, Thoreau, and Lowell. Critics of two generations later, however, have made sad havoc with these valuations. Three non-New Englanders they have placed above the classic eight—Whitman, Melville, Poe—and they have reduced the eight perhaps to three—Emerson, Hawthorne, Thoreau.

The third generation of writers lived on, the greater

number of them, far beyond our closing period of the sixties. Three passed on early: Poe in 1849, Thoreau in 1862, and Hawthorne in 1864. Longfellow and Emerson died in 1882; Lowell and Melville in 1891; Whittier and Whitman in 1892, Holmes in 1894; and Mrs. Stowe in 1896. Much they wrote in the mellow afternoon of their lives, in the period following the storm of the sixties, but nothing at all in the new major key. Their day was over. Whitman alone of them all caught and voiced the new spirit. On his rustic bugle, fashioned with his own hands, he blew the marching airs of the new period:

> O you youths, Western youths,
> So impatient, full of action, full of manly pride and friendship,
> Plain I see you Western youths, see you tramping with the foremost
> Pioneers! O pioneers!
>
> .   .   .   .
>
> All the past we leave behind,
> We debouch upon a newer, mightier world, varied world,
> Fresh and strong the world we seize, world of labor and the march,
> Pioneers! O pioneers!

This after-the-war generation, for whom Whitman blew his bugle, had emerged from the conflict, as such veterans always emerge, disillusioned, depressed in body and soul, unsettled, out of step. *The Education of Henry Adams* is its classic production. But the depression was not a long one. Between this war generation and the one that emerged from the great World War of later years there is this tremendous difference: the Government in the sixties and the seventies had at its disposal unlimited public lands, perhaps the richest in the world, and it disposed of them with unprecedented prodigality. As a result, a veritable army joined in a westward march. The generation that had fought in the armies and had supplied the armies from behind the lines became the most remarkable generation that America has ever produced. In thirty years it spanned the continent with railroads, turned the great buffalo plains into corn-fields, built along the wild Santa Fé Trail great cities of the plains, and started industries that changed completely the tempo of American life.

II

Viewed with the perspective of today, certain forces now dominant in our literature may be traced to their sources like rivers followed to their fountain-heads. Perhaps the most influential of these, as we view them today, has been the literary magazine. A tiny thing during the years of our first literary period, the magazine has developed into what today is perhaps our most powerful literary agent. A history of its development indeed is a history also of American literature. A chronological list of our magazines, beginning with Carey's *American Museum,* mostly eclectic, and continuing with the *Port Folio,* the *North American Review, Godey's Lady's Book, Graham's Magazine,* the *New-York Mirror, Harper's Magazine, Knickerbocker's, Putnam's,* the *Atlantic Monthly*—singling from hundreds these alone—from such a list one may trace the entire literary development of a century. One might do the same thing for the period after 1815 had one only a file of the *North American Review.* Most important was it indeed of all the critical forces that shaped our literature in half a century. It reviewed every significant American book from the standpoint of literary dictator; it made and unmade poets and novelists; and it laid down literary laws for the nation. It brought fame to dozens of writers, the list beginning perhaps with Mrs. Child, Cooper, and Hawthorne.

The century as we now see it also developed another significant literary force, the newspaper. The author of an anonymous volume of 1868, *Asmodeus in New York,* made this noteworthy statement:

It may be affirmed that newspapers are the true literature of the United States. They constitute, in fact, the most important branch of literature with democratic societies. . . . To deprive an American of his newspaper would be equivalent to shutting him from the light of day.[1]

Then, too, literary advertising, a tiny trickle in the earlier days, broadened its tide with every decade. After the 1820's literature began to be exploited as a commercial product. The story of the pirating of the popular British authors, especially of Scott, is a sordid one. By 1840 the commercial spirit in the handling and issuing of books had become a ruling motive. The annuals and the gift-books of that decade were produced and marketed by methods actually criminal. With the 1850's came the era of best-sellers, with fortunes hoped for with every issue of a new volume. Then had come Robert Bonner and the New York *Ledger*.

With our new perspective it will be seen that the curious tide of literary anonymity ran with lessening current throughout the whole century. Eighteenth-century snobbery in England was its source. It was deemed vulgar for a gentleman to print, and doubly vulgar for him to attach his name to printed work. Note the case of Sir Walter Scott. In America the first of the annuals, *The Atlantic Souvenir*, first issued in 1826, printed the names of all its authors. *The Token* of Boston after its first issue did the same thing, but the greater number of the magazines, even to the 1860's, gave no hint as to the authors of their articles. "The reviews," says Frank L. Mott in his *History of American Magazines*, "seldom broke over into what they deemed vulgar signing of articles. . . . But more and more the signing custom grew, fostered by the women's magazines and the literary weeklies in particular."

Other literary rills that through the century grew into torrents are now evident. One is the entry of women into

---

[1] [Ferdinand Longchamp(?)] *Asmodeus in New York* (1868), p. 157.

the literary field and the increase in their numbers and their influence until in the 1850's they had, especially in the province of fiction, become a dominating force. Another is the growth of fiction from literally nothing at the beginning of our second period to the amazing best-seller climax of *Uncle Tom's Cabin* in the 1850's.

In every way the century was a vital one; the seed-bed for everything that we find today in our modern literary world.

That the Civil War marks the boundary of a new period in American history and American literature was first noted by the British critic Alexander Smith. In his introductory essay to the volume *Golden Leaves from the American Poets* (London, 1866), he wrote:

Up to the last few years, it may be said that America, from the lack of a distinct and individual national history, and from the fact that its literary models were identical with our own, has not been in a favorable position to produce an original poetical literature. Contemporary American verse might be finer than contemporary English verse—but it was only as the American apple is of finer flavour than the English one—the same fruit all the while, although for the moment grown under more favorable conditions. But the gigantic war which waged for four years over the entire continent has changed all that. During these years the American nation entered on an earnest and passionate manhood. . . . The war has closed, happily or unhappily as may be the opinion of men; but there is one thing certain, that these mighty contests make nations, and that where the soldier's blood flows reddest, there in after years the song-flowers blow the sweetest and the fairest. It is to be expected that American poetry will be less imitative than it has been hitherto, and that the American poets will concern themselves more with the Potomac and the James than with the Thames and the Seine.

III

The period that followed the Civil War we have already treated in *A History of American Literature since 1870*, and the period that followed that, the period beginning in 1890, we have treated in *The New American Literature*. As to what lies beyond us, beyond our present 1930's (and a new period is soon to begin if already it has not started), I can only reiterate Walt Whitman's conception in his Dartmouth College poem of 1872:

Brain of the New World, what a task is thine,
To formulate the Modern—out of the peerless grandeur of
    the modern,
Out of thyself, comprising science, to recast poems, churches,
    art,
(Recast, may-be discard them, end them—may-be their work
    is done, who knows?)
By vision, hand, conception, on the background of the mighty
    past, the dead,
To limn with absolute faith the mighty living present.

INDEX

(1)